Excel Formulas and Functions

FOR DUMMIES®

by Ken Bluttman and Peter G. Aitken

WILEY

Wiley Publishing, Inc.

Excel Formulas and Functions For Dummies®

Published by
Wiley Publishing, Inc.
111 River Street
Hoboken, NJ 07030-5774

Copyright © 2005 by Wiley Publishing, Inc., Indianapolis, Indiana

Published by Wiley Publishing, Inc., Indianapolis, Indiana

Published simultaneously in Canada

For general information on our other products and services, please contact our Customer Care Department within the U.S. at 800-762-2974, outside the U.S. at 317-572-3993, or fax 317-572-4002.

For technical support, please visit www.wiley.com/techsupport.

Wiley also publishes its books in a variety of electronic formats. Some content that appears in print may not be available in electronic books.

Library of Congress Control Number: 2004107915

ISBN: 0-7645-7556-2

Manufactured in the United States of America

10   9   8   7   6   5   4   3

1O/QU/QR/QV/IN

WILEY

Excel Formulas and Functions For Dummies®

Cheat Sheet

Commonly Used Functions

Some functions apply to specific subject areas, but others are general and apply to all needs. This list is of those used by one and all. Check here for a quickie reference to their purpose.

Function	Description
SUM	Calculates the sum of a group of values
AVERAGE	Calculates the mean of a group of values
COUNT	Counts the number of cells in a range that contain numbers
INT	Removes the decimal portion of a number, leaving just the integer portion
ROUND	Rounds a number to a specified number of decimal places or digit positions
IF	Tests for a true or false condition and then returns one value or another
NOW	Returns the system date and time
TODAY	Returns the system date, without the time
SUMIF	Calculates a sum from a group of values, but just of values that are included because a condition is met
COUNTIF	Counts the number of cells in a range that matched a criteria

Logic And Comparison Operators

Operator Syntax	Comment
=	Equals
>	Greater than
<	Less than
<>	Not equal to
>=	Greater than or equal to
<=	Less than or equal to
AND	If all conditions are true, then true is returned, else false is returned
OR	If at least one condition is true, then true is returned, else false is returned

Excel Text Functions

Text functions are very helpful when working with names, addresses, customer lists; or any other data that is text based. Here is list of selected text functions and what they do:

Function	What it does
LEFT	Extract one or more characters from the left side of a text string
RIGHT	Extract one or more characters from the right side of a text string
MID	Extract characters from the middle of a text string. You specify which character position to start from, and how many characters to include
CONCATENATE	Assemble two or more text strings into one
REPLACE	Replace part of a text string with other text
LOWER	Convert a text string to all lower case
UPPER	Convert a text string to all upper case
PROPER	Convert a text string to proper case
LEN	Returns the length (number of characters) of a text string

Order of Operations

Mathematics dictates a protocol of how formulas are interpreted. The following is the order of how mathematical operators and syntax are applied. You can remember this order by memorizing the mnemonic "Please excuse my dear aunt Sally":

1. Parentheses
2. Exponents
3. Multiplication and Division
4. Addition and Subtraction

For Dummies: Bestselling Book Series for Beginners

Excel Formulas and Functions For Dummies®

Cheat Sheet

Understanding References

You can address cells relatively or absolutely. Preceding the row and or column designators with a dollar sign ($) specifies how the addressing is applied:

Example	Comment
=A1	Complete relative reference
=$A1	The column is absolute, the row is relative
=A$1	The column is relative, the row is absolute
=$A$1	Complete absolute reference

Helpful Keyboard Shortcuts

Press this . . .	To do this . . .
Ctrl+X	Cut the active cell or range to the clipboard
Ctrl+C	Copy the active cell or range to the clipboard
Ctrl+V	Paste from the clipboard
Ctrl+B	Apply bolding to or remove bolding from the active cell or range
Ctrl+U	Apply underlining to or remove underlining from the active cell or range
Ctrl+I	Applying italics to or remove italics from the active cell or range
Ctrl+Y	Redo the last action
Ctrl+Z	Undo the last action
Ctrl+1	Display the Format Cells dialog box
F1	Display Help
F2	Edit a cell's contents
Esc	End editing a cell's contents
F4	Toggles relative, absolute, and mixed addressing for a cell reference while editing a formula
Ctrl+Shift+ Enter	Turns a formula or function into an array formula or function

Error Messages

A handful of errors can appear in a cell when a formula or function cannot be resolved. Here is what they mean. Knowing their meaning helps correct the problem:

Error	Meaning
#DIV/0!	Trying to divide by 0
#N/A!	A formula or a function inside of a formula cannot find the referenced data.
#NAME?	Text in the formula is not recognized.
#NULL!	A space was used instead of a comma in formulas that reference multiple ranges. A comma is necessary to separate range references.
#NUM!	A formula has numeric data that is not valid for the type of operation.
#REF!	A reference is not valid.
#VALUE!	The wrong type of operand or function argument is used.

Array Functions

Array functions return an array of values. Some of these functions are FREQUENCY, TREND, and TRANSPOSE. When using them remember these tips:

- A range must first be selected. The size of the range is usually dependent on the size of one of the ranges used as an argument.
- Enter the function once.
- Complete the entry with the Ctrl + Shift + Enter.

For Dummies: Bestselling Book Series for Beginners

Excel Formulas and Functions

FOR

DUMMIES®

About the Authors

Ken Bluttman has been working as a software developer for 15 years. Ken specializes in VB/VBA based applications, often with an emphasis on Microsoft Office. Ken has written several articles on various computer topics including Office/VBA development, XML, SQL Server, and InfoPath. His most recent book is *Developing Microsoft Office Solutions*. Ken lives in New York with his wife, son, and dog.

Peter Aitken has been writing about computers and programming for over 10 years, with over 35 books well as hundreds of magazine and trade publication articles to his credit. His recent book titles include *Powering Office 2003 With XML*, *Excel Programming Weekend Crash Course*, *.NET Graphics and Printing*, *Visual Basic .NET Programming With Peter Aitken*, *Office XP Development With VBA*, *XML the Microsoft Way*, *Windows Script Host*, and *Teach Yourself Visual Basic .NET Internet Programming in 21 Days*.

Authors' Acknowledgments

Much activity goes on behind the scenes in bringing a book from idea to reality. Many people are involved. We wish to thank the great Wiley staff — Jade Williams, Tom Heine, Elizabeth Kuball, Kerwin McKenzie, and everyone on the Production team — for all their hard work!

— Peter G. Aitken and Ken Bluttman

Thanks to co-author Peter Aitken for his contributions, insights, and suggestions. Special thanks to my family for understanding that at times sitting in front of a computer is a priority, even when it means I have to miss something special.

— Ken Bluttman

Dedication

Dedicated to all the ones I love. A special appreciation for Matthew. You keep the shine in my eyes. Gayla, I am very happy we made it through a rough summer.

— Ken Bluttman

Publisher's Acknowledgments

We're proud of this book; please send us your comments through our online registration form located at www.dummies.com/register/.

Some of the people who helped bring this book to market include the following:

Acquisitions, Editorial, and Media Development

Project Editor: Jade L. Williams

Acquisitions Editor: Tom Heine

Copy Editor: Elizabeth Kuball

Technical Editor: Kerwin McKenzie

Editorial Manager: Robyn Siesky

Media Development Supervisor: Richard Graves

Editorial Assistant: Adrienne Porter

Cartoons: Rich Tennant (www.the5thwave.com)

Composition

Project Coordinator: Nancee Reeves

Layout and Graphics: Carl Byers, Andrea Dahl, Lauren Goddard, Barry Offringa, Julie Trippetti

Proofreaders: Laura Albert, Leeann Harney, Jessica Kramer, Carl Pierce, TECHBOOKS Production Services

Indexer: TECHBOOKS Production Services

Special Help: Microsoft Corporation

Publishing and Editorial for Technology Publishing

Richard Swadley, Vice President and Executive Group Publisher

Barry Pruett, Vice President and Publisher, Visual/Web Graphics

Andy Cummings, Vice President and Publisher, Technology Dummies

Mary Bednarek, Executive Acquisitions Director, Technology Dummies

Mary C. Corder, Editorial Director, Technology Dummies

Publishing for Consumer Dummies

Diane Graves Steele, Vice President and Publisher

Joyce Pepple, Acquisitions Director

Composition Services

Gerry Fahey, Vice President of Production Services

Debbie Stailey, Director of Composition Services

Contents at a Glance

Table of Contents

Introduction

· ·

Spreadsheets are such a mainstay in today's world that the term spread-sheet is just about a household word. Certainly in our homes it is. And we don't just mean because we write books on Excel. Spouses use Excel to track household expenditures and insurance claims. A neighbor analyzes his eBay transactions in Excel. The local merchant keeps tabs on his store's inventory on a worksheet.

In the workplace, Excel is one of the most commonly used analysis and reporting tools. Financial statements, sales reports, inventory, project scheduling, customer activity — so much of this stuff is kept in Excel, and it's the ability of Excel to manipulate and give feedback about the data that makes it so attractive.

About This Book

This book is about the number crunching side of Excel. Formulas are the keystone to analyzing data, that is, digging out nuggets of important information. What is the average sale? How many times did we do better than average? How many days are left on the project, and how much progress have we made? That sort of thing.

Formulas calculate answers, straight and to the point. But that's not all. Excel has dozens of built-in functions that calculate everything from a simple average to a useful analysis of your investments to complex inferential statistics. But you don't have to know it all or use it all — just the parts that are relevant to your work.

This book discusses more than 150 of these functions. But rather than just show their syntax and list them alphabetically like a dictionary, we have assembled them by category and provided real examples of how to use them along with step-by-step instructions.

How to Use This Book

You do not have to read the book sequentially from start to finish — although you certainly can. Each chapter deals with a specific category of functions — financial in one chapter, statistical in another, and so on. Some categories are split over two or more chapters. We suggest two ways for you to use this book:

- Use the Table of Contents to find the chapter or chapters that are of interest to you.
- If you are interested in a specific function, look it up in the Index.

What You Can Safely Ignore

If you already know of the function you want to use and need to get a bit of guidance on it, you can find it in the index and ignore any other discussion that is in the same chapter (although it makes us sad to think of that).

Just kidding!

You can ignore any info in the Technical Stuff icons. You can also ignore Chapter 1 if you are already a fairly competent Excel user, especially if you previously used formulas and functions.

Foolish Assumptions

Well, we assume you have a PC with Excel loaded on it. That's a no-brainer! We also assume you know how to navigate around with a keyboard and mouse.

Lastly, we assume you have used Excel before, even just once. We do discuss basics in Chapter 1 but not *all* the basics. If you really need to start from scratch, we suggest you read the excellent *Excel 2003 For Dummies* by Greg Harvey (Wiley).

Other than that, this book is written for Excel 2003 but just between you and us — it works just fine with older versions of Excel. There could be a function or two that isn't in an older version or work slightly differently. But Microsoft has done an excellent job of maintaining compatibility between versions of Excel, so when it comes to formulas and functions, you can be confident that what works in one version works in another.

How This Book Is Organized

This book is organized in five parts. The book explains how to use 150 or so functions, but these are not listed alphabetically anywhere. Instead, the subject matter of each part indicates what type of functions are covered. Use the index to find the page numbers for particular functions. But do read chapters that pertain to your interest. For all you know, there are other functions that are even better suited. With that said, dig into what is inside each part of the book.

Part I: Getting Started with Excel Formulas and Functions

Part I is introductory of course, but not all of it is so basic. Chapter 1 is the de facto intro chapter. That's where you can brush up on how Excel works, or even read a few elements about it for the first time.

Chapters 2, 3, and 4 cover what is likely to be new ground to many readers. Specifically using the Insert Function dialog box, using array formulas and functions, and correcting formulas are covered. Looking through these chapters can help you down the road.

Part II: Evaluating Loans and Investments

As the name implies, Part II is all about money. Several functions in Excel work with loan factors, interest rates, and returns on investments. This is the place to go to create worksheets that track costs, revenue, and the like. Part of the discussion in Part II is about currency formatting.

Part III: Working with Numbers

A rather sizeable Part that covers a rather sizeable topic. Chapters 7 shows you how to use the basic math functions. This is where you read about the SUM, ROUND, and INT functions that are so often used in Excel. Chapter 8 takes this up a notch to cover advanced math functions. This is where you find some real gems, such as SUMPRODUCT and MOD.

Chapters 9, 10, and 11 show you how to work with statistical functions. Each of these chapters focuses on a specific discipline. Chapter 9 covers the functions used in descriptive statistics, such as the ever-popular AVERAGE function, along with many related functions that tell you details about your data.

Chapter 10 is focused on significance tests. Chapter 11 rounds out the statistical functions with a focus on those used in predicting factors. This last chapter is where you read about forecasting and looking for trends.

Part IV: Working with Data

This Part is a biggie. Here is where you read about working with dates and times; how to work with strings of text; and how to pluck out pieces of data from a database (an area of rows and columns that is).

Chapter 12 and 13 are the date and time chapters. Chapter 14 covers a number of cool functions, such as the amazing IF and the workhorses HLookup and VLookup. Chapter 15 explains functions that tell you information about your data and computer; and working with errors.

Chapter 16 is all about strings. No, I don't mean the kind to fly kites. A string is a text value, and there is so much you can do to manipulate them. Lastly, Chapter 17 explains all the database functions.

Part V: The Part of Tens

And then there's the Part of Tens — a *For Dummies* tradition if ever there was one. In this Part, we have included three chapters: Ten tips for working with formulas; the ten top functions (and the winner is . . .); and ten cool functions to do with the Analysis ToolPak. Don't know what that is? Read the chapter!

Icons Used in This Book

A tip gives you a little extra piece of info on the subject at hand. It might be to offer an alternate method. It might be to lead you to a conclusion. It might be to well, give you a tip (just no stock tips, sorry).

The Remember icon is used when there is some basic concept that is good to keep tucked somewhere in your brain.

As it implies, a Warning is serious stuff. These icons tell you to be careful, usually because you can accidentally erase your data or some such horrible event.

Once in a while, some tidbit is interesting to the tech-head types, but not to anyone else. You can read these or ignore them as you see fit.

Where to Go from Here

Roll up your sleeves, take a deep breath, and then forget all that preparing-for-a-hard-task stuff. Using Excel is easy. You can hardly make a mistake without Excel catching it.

If you need to brush up on the basics, go to Chapter 1. This is also the best place to get your first taste of formulas and functions. After that, it's up to you and what you want to do. The book is organized more by area of focus than anything else. So if finance is what you do, go to the finance part. If math is what you do, go to the numbers part. Seek and you will find.

Part I

Getting Started with Excel Formulas and Functions

The 5th Wave   By Rich Tennant

We're looking for applications that work well on a particularly open and distributed network.

In this part . . .

We cover the basics with a quick study in workbooks, worksheets, formulas, and functions. Everything you need to get going! If you are a beginner or need to brush up on Excel, Chapter 1 is the place to start. But that's not all, folks. Chapter 2 tells you about a key dialog box that makes your working with functions much easier, enabling you to concentrate on more important details, such as where you are going to go on your lunch break. Part I finishes with a one-two punch of using arrays and correcting formulas.

Chapter 1

Understanding Fundamentals, Formulas, and Functions

*E*xcel is to computer programs what a Porsche or a Ferrari is to the automotive industry. Sleek on the outside and a lot of power under the hood. Excel is also like a truck — it can handle all your data, lots of it. In fact, a single worksheet has 16,777,216 places to hold data. And that's on just *one* worksheet!

Excel is used in all types of businesses. And you know how that's possible? By being able to store and work with any kind of data. It does not matter if you are in finance, sales, run a video store, organize wilderness trips, or just want to track the scores of your favorite sports teams — Excel can handle all of it. The number crunching ability of Excel is just awesome! And so easy to use!

Just putting a bunch of information on worksheets does not crunch the data or give you sums, results, or any type of analysis. If you want to just store your data somewhere, sure you can use Excel, or you can get a database program instead. In this book, we show you how to build formulas and how to use the dozens of built-in functions that Excel provides. That's where the real power of Excel is — making sense of your data.

Don't fret that this is a challenge and that you may make mistakes. We did when we were learning. Besides, Excel is very forgiving. It won't crash on you. Excel usually tells you when you made a mistake, and sometimes it even helps you to correct it. How many programs do that!?

But first the basics. This first chapter gives you the springboard you need to use the rest of the book. We wish books like this were around when we were learning about computers. We had to stumble through a lot of this.

Working with Excel Fundamentals

Before you can write any formulas or crunch any numbers, you have to know where the data goes. And how to find it again. We wouldn't want your data to get lost! Knowing how worksheets store your data and present it is critical to your analysis efforts.

Understanding workbooks and worksheets

A *workbook* is the same as a file. Excel opens and closes workbooks, just as a word processor program opens and closes documents. Use the File ⇨ Open, File ⇨ Save, and File ⇨ Close menu commands for opening and closing the workbooks. One detail you should know about Excel files is that the file extension is .xls.

Excel files have the .xls extension.

When Excel starts up, it displays a blank workbook ready for use. If at anytime you need another new workbook, choose File ⇨ New from the menu and select a Blank workbook. When you have more than one workbook open, you pick the one you want to work on by selecting it in the list of workbooks under the Window menu.

A worksheet is where your data actually goes. A workbook contains at least one worksheet. If you didn't have at least one, where would you put the data? Figure 1-1 shows an open workbook that has three sheets — Sheet1, Sheet2, and Sheet3. You can see these on the worksheet tabs near the bottom left of the screen.

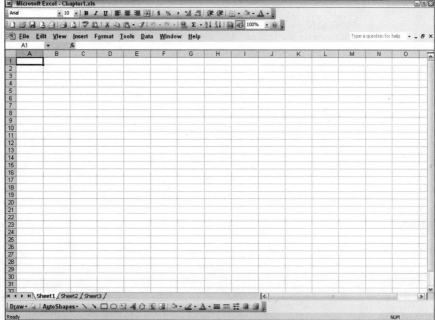

Figure 1-1:
Looking at a
workbook
and
worksheets.

At any given moment, one worksheet is always on top. In Figure 1-1, Sheet1 is on top. Another way of saying this is Sheet1 is the *active* worksheet. There is always one and only one active worksheet. To make another worksheet active, just click its tab.

Worksheet, spreadsheet, and just plain old sheet are used interchangeably to mean the worksheet.

Guess what's really cool? You can change the name of the worksheets. Names like Sheet1 and Sheet2 are just not exciting. How about Baseball Card Collection or Last Year's Taxes. Well actually Last Year's Taxes isn't too exciting either. The point is you can give your worksheets meaningful names. You have two ways to do this:

- ✔ Double-click the worksheet tab and then type in a new name.
- ✔ Right-click on the worksheet tab, select Rename from the pop-up list, and then type in a new name.

Figure 1-2 shows one worksheet name already changed and another about to be changed by right-clicking its tab.

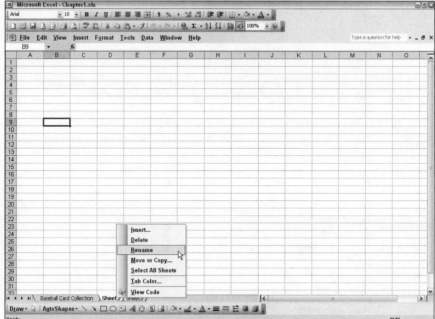

You can try changing a worksheet name on your own. Do it the easy way:

1. **Double-click a worksheet's tab.**

2. **Type in a new name and press Enter.**

You can change the color of worksheet tabs. Right-click on the tab and select Tab Color from the list.

To insert a new worksheet into a workbook, choose Insert ➪ Worksheet from the menu. To delete the active worksheet, choose Edit ➪ Delete Sheet from the menu. Yeah, we know. It would be easier if these were under the same menu. But in all likelihood, you will be inserting new worksheets more than deleting them.

Don't delete a worksheet unless you really mean to. You cannot get it back after it is gone. It does not go into the Windows Recycle Bin.

You can insert many new worksheets. The limit of how many is based on your computer's memory but you should have no problem inserting 200 or more. Of course we hope you have a good reason for having so many. Which brings us to the next point.

Worksheets organize your data. Use them wisely and you will find it easy to manage your data. For example, let's say you are the boss (We thought you'd like that!), and you have 30 employees that you are tracking information on over the course of a year. You might have 30 worksheets — one for each employee. Or you might have twelve worksheets — one for each month. Or you may just keep it all on one worksheet. How you use Excel is up to you, but Excel is ready to handle whatever you throw at it.

Excel has a default of how many worksheets appear in a new workbook. The default is usually three. You can change this number by choosing Tools ➪ Options from the menu and changing the "Sheets in new workbook" setting on the General tab in the Options dialog box.

Working with rows, columns, cells, and ranges

A worksheet contains cells. Lots of them. Millions of them. This might seem unmanageable but actually it's pretty straightforward. Figure 1-3 shows a worksheet filled with data. We use this figure to take a look at the components of a worksheet.

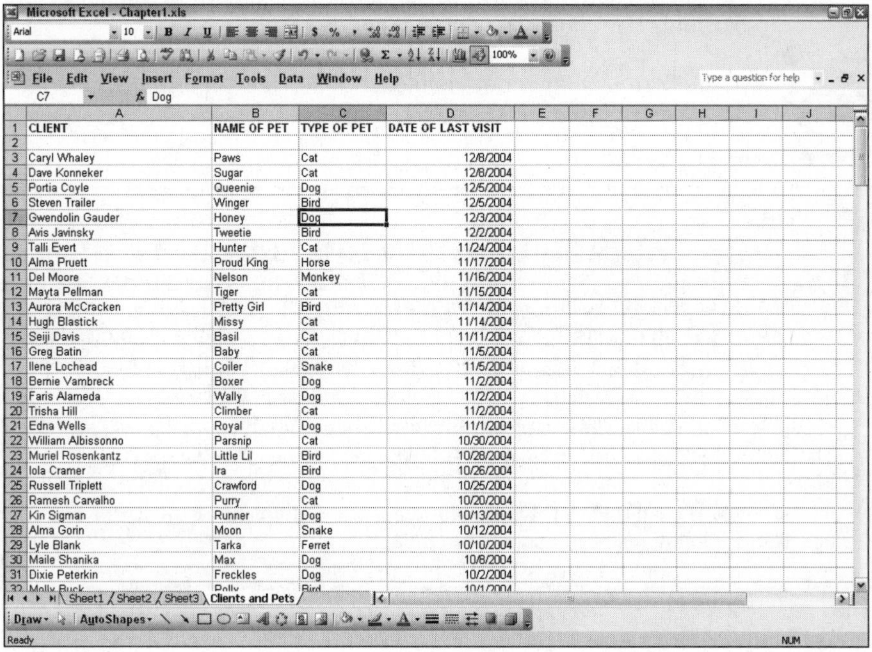

Figure 1-3: Looking at what goes into a worksheet.

Each cell can contain data or a formula. In Figure 1-3, the cells contain data. Some or even all the cells could contain formulas, but that's not the case here.

Columns have letter headers — A, B, C, and so on. These can be seen listed horizontally just above the area where the cells are. After you get past the 26th column, a double lettering system is used — AA, AB, and so on. Rows are listed vertically down the left side of the screen. Rows use a numbering system.

You find cells at the intersection of rows and columns. Cell A1 is the cell at the intersection of column A and row 1. A1 is the cell's *address*. There is always an *active* cell. That is, a cell in which any entry would go into should you start typing. The active cell has a border around it. Also the contents of the active cell are seen in the *Formula Bar*, which we will get to in a moment.

When we speak of or reference cells, we are referring to the address of the cell. The address is the intersection of a column and row. To talk about cell D20 means to talk about the cell that you find at the intersection of column D and row 20.

In Figure 1-3, the active cell is C7. You have a couple of ways to see this. For starters, Cell C7 has a border around it. Also notice that the column head C is shaded, as well as the row number 7. Just above the column headers are the Name Box and the Formula Bar. The Name Box is all the way to the left and shows the active cell's address of C7. To the right of the name box, the Formula Bar shows the contents of cell C7.

If the Formula Bar is not visible, choose View ⇨ Formula Bar from the menu to make it visible.

Getting to know the Formula Bar

You use the Formula Bar quite a bit as you work with formulas and functions. You use it to enter and edit formulas; it's the long entry box that starts in the middle of the bar. When you enter a formula into this box, you then click the little check mark button to finish the entry. The check mark button is only visible when you are entering a formula. The alternative is to enter formulas directly into the cell. Even so, the Formula Bar displays the contents of cells. When you want to see just the contents of a cell that has a formula, make that cell active and look at its contents in the Formula Bar. Cells that have formulas do not normally display the formula, but instead display the result of the formula. When you want to see the actual formula, the Formula Bar is the place to do it.

A *range* is a group of adjacent cells. Technically, even a single cell is a range. But we are talking about something bigger here. Make a range right now. Here's how:

1. **Position the mouse over the first cell.**

2. **Press and hold the left mouse button down.**

3. **Move the cursor to the last cell (this is called dragging).**

4. **Release the mouse button.**

Figure 1-4 shows the result. We selected a *range* of cells. The address of this range is A3:D21. Let's pick that address apart.

REMEMBER

A range address looks like two cell addresses put together, with a colon (:) in the middle. And that's what it is! A range address starts with the address of the cell in the upper-left of the range, then has a colon, and then ends with the address of the cell in the lower-right. Ranges are always rectangular in shape.

	A	B	C	D
1	CLIENT	NAME OF PET	TYPE OF PET	DATE OF LAST VISIT
2				
3	Caryl Whaley	Paws	Cat	12/8/2004
4	Dave Konneker	Sugar	Cat	12/6/2004
5	Portia Coyle	Queenie	Dog	12/5/2004
6	Steven Trailer	Winger	Bird	12/5/2004
7	Gwendolin Gauder	Honey	Dog	12/3/2004
8	Avis Javinsky	Tweetie	Bird	12/2/2004
9	Talli Evert	Hunter	Cat	11/24/2004
10	Alma Pruett	Proud King	Horse	11/17/2004
11	Del Moore	Nelson	Monkey	11/16/2004
12	Mayta Pellman	Tiger	Cat	11/15/2004
13	Aurora McCracken	Pretty Girl	Bird	11/14/2004
14	Hugh Blastick	Missy	Cat	11/14/2004
15	Seiji Davis	Basil	Cat	11/11/2004
16	Greg Batin	Baby	Cat	11/5/2004
17	Ilene Lochead	Coiler	Snake	11/5/2004
18	Bernie Vambreck	Boxer	Dog	11/2/2004
19	Faris Alameda	Wally	Dog	11/2/2004
20	Trisha Hill	Climber	Cat	11/2/2004
21	Edna Wells	Royal	Dog	11/1/2004
22	William Albissonno	Parsnip	Cat	10/30/2004
23	Muriel Rosenkantz	Little Lil	Bird	10/28/2004
24	Iola Cramer	Ira	Bird	10/26/2004
25	Russell Triplett	Crawford	Dog	10/25/2004
26	Ramesh Carvalho	Purry	Cat	10/20/2004
27	Kin Sigman	Runner	Dog	10/13/2004
28	Alma Gorin	Moon	Snake	10/12/2004
29	Lyle Blank	Tarka	Ferret	10/10/2004
30	Maile Shanika	Max	Dog	10/6/2004
31	Dixie Peterkin	Freckles	Dog	10/2/2004

Figure 1-4:
Selecting a range of cells.

One more detail about ranges — you can give them a name. This is a great feature because you can think about a range in terms of what is used for, instead of what its address is.

For example, say you have a list of clients on a worksheet. What's easier — thinking of exactly which cells are occupied, or thinking that there is your list of clients?

Throughout this book, we use ranges made of cell addresses and ranges, which have been given names. So it's time to get your feet wet creating a *named area*, as it's called. Here's what you do:

1. **Select an area of the worksheet.**

   To do this position the mouse over a cell, click and drag the mouse around. Release the mouse button when done.

2. **Choose Insert ➪ Name ➪ Define from the menu to open the Define Name dialog box.**

   Figure 1-5 shows you how it looks so far.

   Excel guesses that you want to name the area with the value it finds in the top cell of the range.

3. **Change the name if you need to and click the Add button.**

   Figure 1-6 shows an example of the name being changed to "Clients."

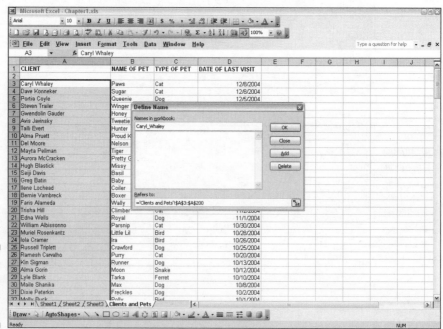

Figure 1-5:
Adding a name to the workbook.

Figure 1-6:
Completing
adding
a name.

4. **Click the Close button.**

That's it. Hey, you're already on your way to being an Excel pro!

Now that you have a named area, you can easily select your data at any time. Just go to the Name box and select it from the list. See Figure 1-7 for how to find the range named Clients. After you click the name, the worksheet area is selected.

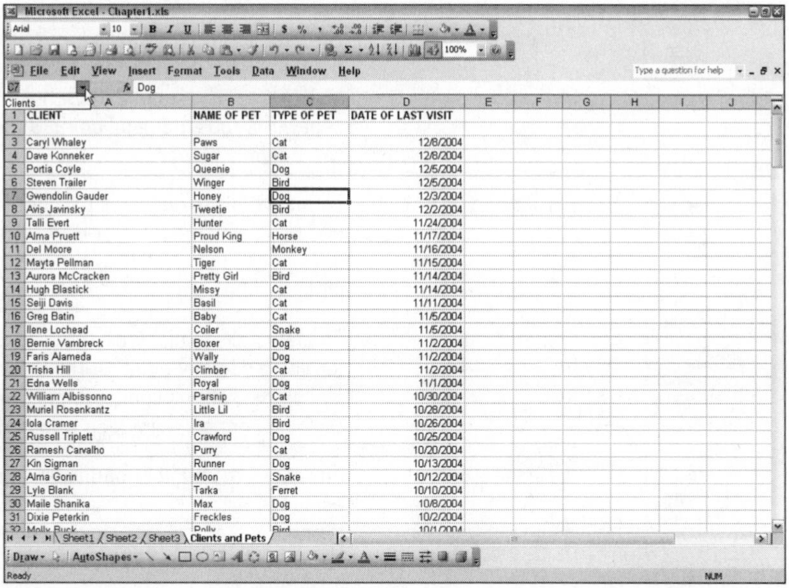

Figure 1-7:
Using the
name to
find the
data area.

Throughout the book are examples using rows, columns, cells, and ranges. Chapter 14 explains certain functions that work with these as well — ADDRESS, ROWS, COLUMNS, OFFSET, and more.

Formatting your data

Of course you will want to make your data look all spiffy and shiny. Bosses like that. If you see the number 98.6 — is this someone's temperature? Is it a score on a test? Or is it meant to be ninety-eight dollars and sixty cents? Is it a percentage? Any of these formats are correct:

- ✔ 98.6
- ✔ $98.60
- ✔ 98.6%

Excel lets you format your data in just they way you need. For starters, there is the Formatting toolbar. Imagine it, formatting is so important the makers of Excel made a toolbar for it. Table 1-1 shows some of the toolbar buttons and what they are used for.

Table 1-1		Formatting Toolbar Buttons
Tool	*Name*	*What It Does*
$	Currency Style	Formats cells to display the currency symbol defined in the Windows locale setting, and also to display the number with a thousands separator and a decimal point. Defaults to two decimal places.
%	Percent Style	Formats cells to display a percent sign (%) and to display the number as if 100 multiplied it. Thus, the value 0.5 displays as 50%, 0.8 as 80%, and 1.0 as 100%.
,	Comma Style	Formats cells to display a thousands separator and a decimal point. Defaults to two decimal places. This is similar to the Currency Style, except no dollar sign is included.
←.0 .00	Increase Decimal	Increases the number of displayed decimal positions.
.00 →.0	Decrease Decimal	Decreases the number of displayed decimal positions.

If the Formatting toolbar is not visible, choose View ➪ Toolbars from the menu to make it appear.

Figure 1-8 shows how formatting helps in the readability and understanding of a worksheet. Cell B1 has a monetary amount and is formatted as currency. Cell B2 is formatted as a percent. The actual value in cell B2 is .05. Cell B7 is also formatted as currency. The currency format displays a negative value in parenthesis. This is just one of the formatting options for currency. Chapter 5 explains further about formatting currency.

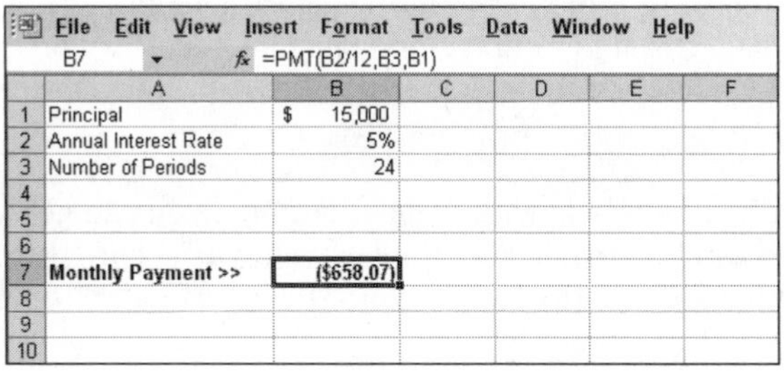

Figure 1-8: Formatting data.

Besides the Formatting toolbar, you have the Format Cells dialog box. This is the place to go for all your formatting needs beyond what's available on the toolbar. You can even create custom formats. Two ways to display the Format Cells dialog box are:

- Choose Format ➪ Cells from the menu.
- Right-click on any cell and select Format Cells from the pop-up list.

Figure 1-9 shows the Format Cells dialog box. So many settings are there it makes our heads spin! We discuss using this dialog box and formatting in general more extensively in Chapter 5.

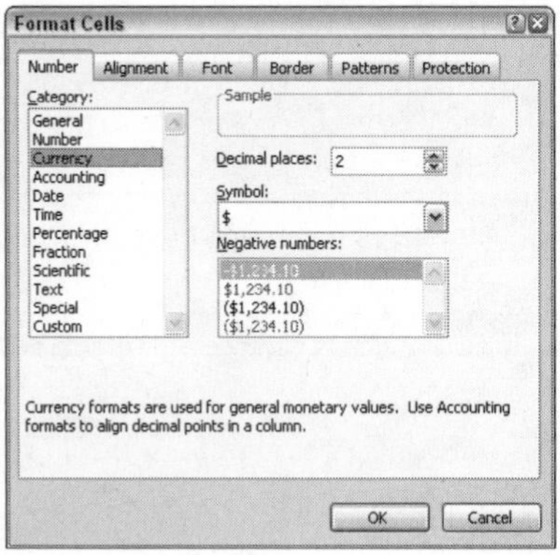

Figure 1-9: Using the Format Cells dialog box for advanced formatting options.

Getting help

Excel is complex, we can't deny that. And lucky for all of us, help is just a key press away. Yes, literally one key press — just press the F1 key. Try it now.

This starts up the Help system. From there you can search on a keyword or browse through the Help Table of Contents. Figure 1-10 shows how the help system was browsed through to find some specific help. Way on the right is the Help Table of Contents from which a specific help topic is selected and displayed.

Later on when you are working with Excel functions, you can get help on specific functions directly by clicking the <u>Help with This Function</u> link in the Insert Function dialog box. Chapter 2 covers the Insert Function dialog box in detail.

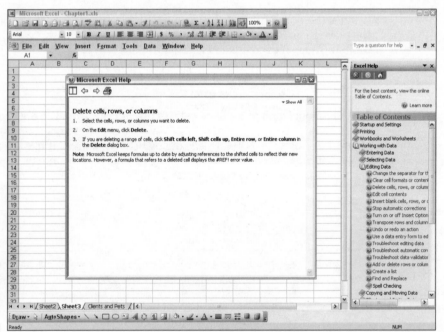

Figure 1-10:
Displaying
Help.

Gaining the Upper Hand on Formulas

Okay, get to the nitty gritty of what Excel is all about. Sure, you can just enter data and leave it as is, and even generate some pretty charts from it. But getting answers from your data, or creating a summary of your data, or applying what-if tests — all of this takes formulas.

To be specific, a formula in Excel calculates something, or returns some result based on data in the worksheet. Formulas are placed in cells and must start with an equal sign (=) to tell Excel that it is a formula and not data. Sounds simple, and it is.

Look at some very basic formulas. Table 1-2 shows a few formulas and tells you what they do.

We use the word "return" to refer to what displays after a formula or function does its thing. So to say "the formula returns a 7" is the same as saying "the formula calculated the answer to be 7."

Table 1-2	Basic Formulas
Formula	*What It Does*
=2 + 2	Returns the number 4.
=A1 + A2	Returns the sum of the values in cells A1 and A2, whatever those values may be. If either A1 or A2 has text in it, then an error is returned.
=D5	The cell that contains the formula ends up displaying the same value that is in cell D5. If you try to enter this formula into cell D5 itself, you create a condition called a circular reference. That is a no-no. You can read more about circular references in Chapter 4.
=SUM(A2:A5)	Returns the sum of the values in cells A2, A3, A4, and A5. Recall from above the syntax for a range. This formula uses the SUM function to sum up all the values in the range.

Entering your first formula

Ready to enter your first formula? Make sure Excel is running and a worksheet is in front of you, and then:

1. **Click an empty cell.**

2. **Type this in:** = 10 + 10.

3. **Press Enter.**

That was easy, wasn't it? You should see the *result* of the formula — the number 20.

Try another. This time you create a formula that adds together the value of two cells:

1. **Click a cell (any cell will do).**

2. **Type in a number.**

3. **Click another cell.**

4. **Type in another number.**

5. **Click a third cell.** This cell contains the formula.

6. **Type in an equal sign (=).**

7. **Click the first cell.**

   This is an important point in the creation of the formula. What is happening now is that the formula is being written by both your keyboard entry and clicking around with the mouse. The formula should now look about half complete. The formula should now be an equal sign immediately followed by the address of the cell you just clicked. Figure 1-11 shows what this looks like.

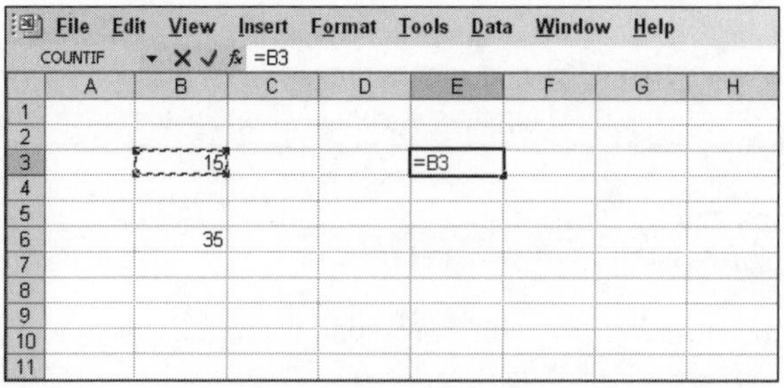

Figure 1-11:
Entering a
formula that
references
cells.

In the example, the value 15 has been entered into cell B3 and the value 35 into cell B6. The formula was started in cell E3. Cell E3 so far has =B3 in it.

8. Enter a plus sign (+).

9. Click the cell that has the second entered value.

In our example, this is cell B6. The formula in cell E3 now looks like this: =B3 + B6. You can see this is Figure 1-12.

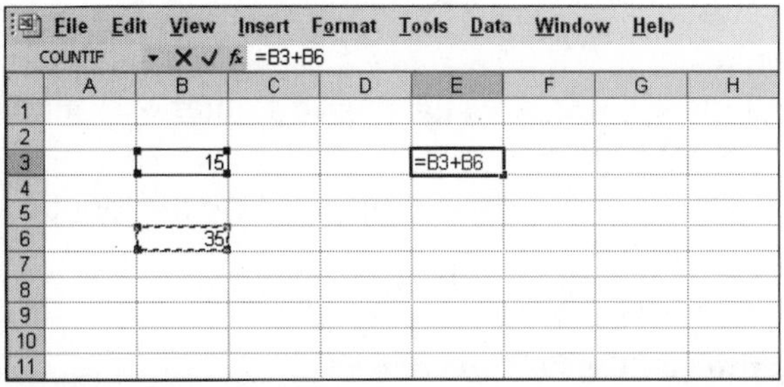

Figure 1-12:
Completing
the formula.

10. Press Enter. This ends the entry of the function. All done! Congratulations!

Figure 1-13 shows how our example ended up. Cell E3 displays the result of the calculation. Also notice that the Formula bar displays the contents of cell E3, which really is the formula.

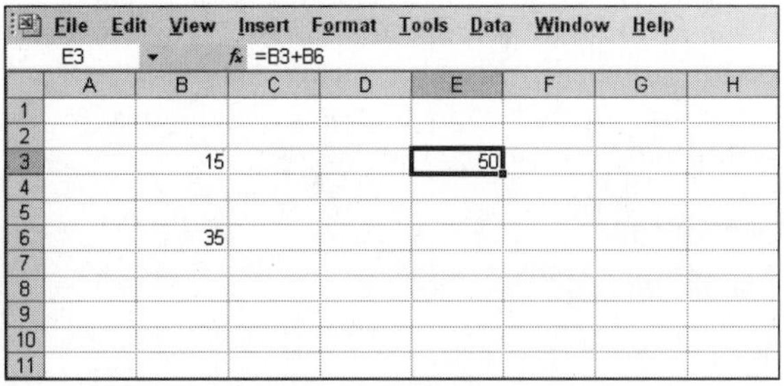

Figure 1-13:
A finished
formula.

Understanding references

References abound in Excel formulas. You can reference cells. You can reference ranges. You can even reference cells and ranges on other worksheets. You can reference cells and ranges in other workbooks. Formulas and functions are at their most useful when using references, so you need to understand them.

And if that isn't enough to stir the pot, you can use three types of cell references: relative, absolute, and mixed. Okay, one step at a time here. We can get to it all.

Try out a formula that uses a range. Formulas that use ranges often have a function in the formula, so use the SUM function here:

1. **Enter some numbers in a group of cells going down one column.**

2. **Click in another cell where you want the result to appear.**

3. **Enter =SUM(to start the function.**

4. **Click the first cell that has an entered value, and while holding the left mouse button down, drag the mouse pointer over all the cells that have the entered values.**

    You should see the range address appear where the formula and function are being entered.

5. **Enter a closing parenthesis.**

6. **Press Enter to end the function entry.**

Give yourself a pat on the back!

Wherever you drag the mouse to enter the range address into a function, you can also just type in the address of the range, if you know what it is.

Excel is dynamic when it comes to cell addresses. If you have a cell with a formula that references a cell address, and you copy the formula to another cell, the address of the reference inside the formula changes. Excel updates the reference inside the formula to match the number of rows and/or columns that separate the original cell (where the formula is being copied from) from the new cell (where the formulas is being copied to). This may be confusing so look at an example so you can see this for yourself:

1. **In cell B2, enter 100.**

2. **In cell C2, enter this:** =B2 * 2.

3. **Press Enter.**

    Cell C2 now returns the value 200.

4. **If C2 is not the active cell, click it once.**

5. **Copy the cell.**

    You can choose Edit ➪ Copy from the menu, or press Ctrl+C on the keyboard.

6. **Click cell C3.**

7. **To paste, choose Edit ➪ Paste from the menu, or press Ctrl+V on the keyboard.**

8. **If you see a strange moving line around cell C2, just press the ESC key on the keyboard to make it stop.**

Did you see a moving line stay over cell C2? That's called a *marquee*. It's a reminder that you are in the middle of a cut or copy operation, and the marquee goes around the cut or copied data.

Cell C3 should now be the active cell, but if it is not, just click it once. Look at the formula bar. The contents of cell C3 is =B3 * 2 and not the =B2 * 2 that you copied.

What happened? Excel, in its wisdom, assumed that if a formula in cell C2 references the cell B2 — one cell to the left, then the same formula put into cell C3 is supposed to reference cell B3 — also one cell to the left.

When copying formulas in Excel, relative addressing is usually what you want. That's why it is the default behavior. Sometimes you do not want relative addressing but rather *absolute* addressing. This is making a cell reference fixed to an absolute cell so that it does not change when the formula is copied.

In an absolute cell reference, a dollar sign ($) precedes both the column letter and the row number. You can also have a mixed reference in which the column is absolute and the row is relative or vice versa. Here's a summary of this. To create a mixed reference, you use the dollar sign in front of just the column letter or row number. Here are some examples:

Reference Type	Formula	What happens when you copy the formula
Relative	=A1	Either, or both, the column letter A and the row number 1 can change.
Absolute	=$A$1	The column letter A and the row number 1 won't change.
Mixed	=$A1	The column letter A won't change. The row number 1 can change.
Mixed	=A$1	The column letter A can change. The row number 1 won't change.

Copying formulas with the fill handle

As long as we're on the subject of copying formulas around, take a look at the fill handle. You're gonna love this one! The fill handle is a quick way to copy the contents of a cell to other cells with just a single click and drag.

The active cell always has a little square box in the lower-right side of its border. That is the fill handle. When you move the mouse pointer over the fill handle, the mouse pointer changes shape. If you click and hold down the mouse button, you can now drag up, down, or across over other cells. When you let go of the mouse button the contents of the active cell automatically copy to the cells you dragged over.

A picture is worth a thousand words, so take a look. Figure 1-14 shows a worksheet that adds some numbers. Cell E4 has this formula: =B4 + C4 + D4. This formula needs to be placed in cells E5 through E15. Look closely at cell E4. The mouse pointer is over the fill handle and it has changed to what looks like a small black plus sign. We are about to use the fill handle to drag that formula to the other cells.

Figure 1-14: Getting ready to drag the formula down.

	A	B	C	D	E	F	G	H	I	J
					=B4 + C4 + D4 (E4)					
1	Number of Orders									
2										
3		Retail	Mail Order	Internet	TOTAL BY MONTH					
4	January	1015	107	906	2028					
5	February	882	115	793						
6	March	960	150	907						
7	April	1020	141	1004						
8	May	1145	175	1015						
9	June	1287	199	1259						
10	July	1235	166	1181						
11	August	1044	135	1032						
12	September	994	122	851						
13	October	921	80	741						
14	November	742	55	652						
15	December	616	28	614						

Figure 1-15 shows what the worksheet looks like after the fill handle is used to get the formula into all the cells. This is a real timesaver. Also you can see that the formula in each cell of column E correctly references the cells to its left. This is the intention of using relative referencing. For example, the formula in cell E15 ended up with this formula: =B15 + C15 + D15.

Figure 1-15: Populating cells with a formula by using the Fill Handle.

	A	B	C	D	E	F	G	H	I	J
					=B15 + C15 + D15 (E15)					
1	Number of Orders									
2										
3		Retail	Mail Order	Internet	TOTAL BY MONTH					
4	January	1015	107	906	2028					
5	February	882	115	793	1790					
6	March	960	150	907	2017					
7	April	1020	141	1004	2165					
8	May	1145	175	1015	2335					
9	June	1287	199	1259	2745					
10	July	1235	166	1181	2582					
11	August	1044	135	1032	2211					
12	September	994	122	851	1967					
13	October	921	80	741	1742					
14	November	742	55	652	1449					
15	December	616	28	614	1258					

Assembling formulas the right way

There's a saying in the computer business — garbage in, garbage out. And that applies to how formulas are put together. If a formula is constructed the wrong way, it either returns an error or an incorrect result.

Two types of errors can occur in formulas. In one type, Excel can calculate the formula but the result is wrong. On the other type, Excel is not able to calculate the formula. Check out both of these.

A formula can work and still produce an incorrect result. Excel does not report an error because there is no error for it to find. This is almost always the result of not using parentheses properly in the formula. Take a look at some examples:

Formula	Result
=7 + 5 * 20 + 25 / 5	112
=(7 + 5) * 20 + 25 / 5	245
=7 + 5 *(20 + 25) / 5	52
=(7 + 5 * 20 + 25) / 5	26.4

All of these are valid formulas but the placement of parentheses makes a difference in the outcome. You must take into account the order of mathematical operators when writing formulas. The order is:

1. Parentheses

2. Exponents

3. Multiplication and division

4. Addition and subtraction

This is a key point of formulas. It is easy to just accept a returned answer. After all, Excel is so smart. Right? Wrong! Like all computer programs, Excel can only do what it is told. If you tell it to calculate an incorrect but structurally valid formula, it will do so. So watch your Ps and Qs! Er, rather your parentheses and mathematical operators when building formulas.

The second type of error is when there is a mistake in the formula or in the data the formula uses that prevents Excel from calculating the result. Excel makes your life easier by telling you when such an error occurs. To be precise:

✔ Excel displays a message when you attempt to enter a formula that is not constructed correctly.

✔ Excel returns an error message in the cell when there is something wrong with the result of the calculation.

First, let's see what happened when we tried to finish entering a formula that had the wrong number of parentheses. Figure 1-16 shows this.

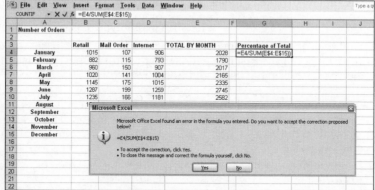

Figure 1-16: Getting a message from Excel.

Excel finds that there is an uneven number of open and closed parentheses. Therefore the formula cannot work (it does not make sense mathematically) and Excel tells you so. Watch for these messages, they often offer a solution.

On the other side of the fence are errors in returned values. If you got this far, then the formulas syntax passed muster, but something went awry nonetheless. Possible errors are:

- Attempting to perform a mathematical operation on text
- Attempting to divide a number by 0 (that's a mathematical no-no)
- Trying to reference a non-existent cell, range, worksheet, or workbook
- Entering the wrong type of information into an argument function

This is by no means an exhaustive list of possible error conditions, but you get the idea. So what does Excel do about it? There are a handful of errors that Excel places into the cell with the problem formula. These are:

Error Type	When it happens
#DIV/0!	When trying to divide by 0
#N/A!	When a formula or a function inside a formula cannot find the referenced data
#NAME?	When text in a formula is not recognized
#NULL!	When a space was used instead of a comma in formulas that reference multiple ranges (A comma is necessary to separate range references.)

Error Type	When it happens
#NUM!	When a formula has numeric data that is not valid for the type of operation
#REF!	When a reference is not valid
#VALUE!	When the wrong type of operand or function argument is used

Chapter 4 discusses catching and handling formula errors in detail.

Using Functions in Formulas

Functions are like little utility programs that do a single thing. For example, the SUM function sums up numbers, the COUNT function counts, and the AVERAGE function calculates an average.

There are functions to handle many different needs: working with numbers, working with text, working with dates and times, working with finance, and so on. Functions can be combined and nested (one goes inside another). Functions return a value, and this value can be combined with the results of a formula. The possibilities are nearly endless.

But functions do not exist on their own. They are always a part of a formula. Now that can mean that the formula is made up completely of the function or that the formula combines the function with other functions, data, operators, or references. But they must follow the formula golden rule: *Start with the equal sign*. Look at some examples.

Function/Formula	Result
=SUM(A1:A5)	Returns the sum of the values in the range A1:A5. This is an example of a function serving as the whole formula.
=SUM(A1:A5) /B5	Returns the sum of the values in the range A1:A5 divided by the value in cell B5. This is an example of mixing a function's result with other data.
=SUM(A1:A5) + AVERAGE(B1:B5)	Returns the sum of the range A1:A5 added with the average of the range B1:B5. This is an example of a formula that combines the result of two functions.

Ready to write your first formula with a function in it? Let's go! This function creates an average. Here's what you do:

1. **Enter some numbers in the cells of a column.**

2. **Click an empty cell where you want to see the result.**

3. **Enter =AVERAGE(to start the function.**

4. **Click the first cell with an entered value and then while holding the mouse button down, drag the mouse pointer over the other cells that have values.**

   An alternative to this is to just enter the range of those cells.

5. **Enter a closing parenthesis to end the function.**

6. **Press Enter.**

Wonderful! If all went well, your worksheet should look a little bit like ours, in Figure 1-17. Cell B11 has the calculated result, but look up at the formula bar and you can see the actual function as it was entered.

	File	Edit	View	Insert	Format	Tools	Data	Window	Help	

B11   ▼   *fx* =AVERAGE(B3:B7)

	A	B	C	D	E	F	G	H
1								
2								
3		6						
4		9						
5		22						
6		25						
7		35						
8								
9								
10								
11		19.4						
12								
13								

Figure 1-17: Entering the AVERAGE function.

Formulas and functions are dependent on the cells and ranges to which they refer. If you change the data in one of the cells, the result returned by the function updates. You can try this now. In the example you just did with making an average, click into one of the cells with the values and enter a different number. The returned average changes.

A formula can consist of nothing but a single function — preceded by an equal sign, of course!

Looking at what goes into a function

Most functions take inputs, called *arguments*, that specify the data the function is to use. (Another term for arguments is *parameters*.) Some functions take no arguments, some take one, and others take many — it all depends on the function. The argument list is always enclosed in parentheses following the function name. If there's more than one argument, they are separated by commas. Look at a few examples:

Function	*Comment*
=NOW()	Takes no arguments.
=AVERAGE(A6,A11,B7)	Take up to 30 arguments. Here, three cell references are included as arguments. The arguments are separated by commas.
=AVERAGE(A6:A10,A13:A19,A23:A29)	Arguments are range references instead of cell references. The arguments are separated by commas.
=IPMT(B5, B6, B7, B8)	Requires four arguments. Commas separate the arguments.

Some functions have required arguments and optional arguments. You must provide the required ones. The optional ones are well, optional. But you may want to include them if their presence helps the function return the value you need.

The IPMT function is a good example. Four arguments are required and two more are optional. You can read more about the IPMT function in Chapter 5. You can read about function arguments in general in Chapter 2.

Discovering usages of a function's arguments

Memorizing the arguments that every function takes would be a daunting task. We can only think that if you could pull that off you could be on television. But back to reality, you don't have to memorize them because Excel helps you select what function to use, and then tells you which arguments are needed.

Figure 1-18 shows the Insert Function dialog box. This great helper is accessed by choosing Insert ⇨ Function from the menu. The dialog box is where you select a function to use.

The dialog box contains a listing of all available functions — and there are a lot of them! So to make matters easier, the dialog box gives you a way to search for a function by a keyword, or you can filter the list of functions by category.

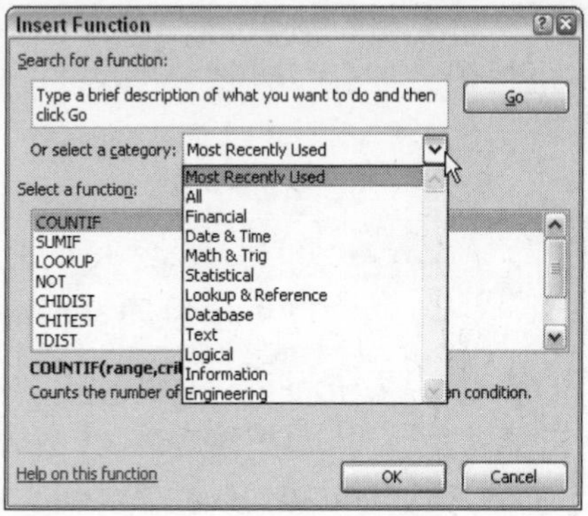

Figure 1-18:
Using the Insert Function dialog box.

Try it out! Here's an example of how to use the Insert Function dialog box to multiply together a few numbers:

1. **Enter three numbers in three different cells.**

2. **Click an empty cell where you want the result to appear.**

3. **Choose Insert ⇨ Function from the menu to open the Insert Function dialog box.**

   As an alternative, you can just click the little *fx* button on the Formula bar.

4. **In the dialog box, select All or Math & Trig as the category.**

5. **In the list of functions, find and select the PRODUCT function.**

6. **Click the OK button.**

   This closes the Insert Function dialog box and now displays the Function Arguments dialog box. See Figure 1-19.

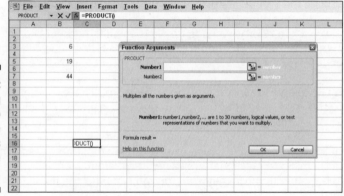

Figure 1-19:
Getting ready to enter some arguments to the function.

You can use the Function Arguments dialog box to enter as many arguments as needed. Initially it might not look like it can accommodate enough arguments. We need to enter three, but it looks like there is only room for two. This is like musical chairs!

More argument entry boxes appear as you need them. First though — how do you enter the argument? There are two ways. You can type in the numbers or cell references into the boxes, or you can use those funny looking squares to the right of the entry boxes. In Figure 1-19 there are two entry boxes ready to go. To the left of them are the names Number 1 and Number 2. To the right of the boxes are the little squares.

These squares are actually called RefEdit controls. They make argument entry a snap. All you do is click one, then click the cell with the value, and press Enter. To continue:

7. Click the RefEdit control to the right of the Number 1 entry box.

The Function Arguments dialog box shrinks to just the size of the entry box.

8. Click the cell with the first number.

Figure 1-20 shows what the screen looks like at this point.

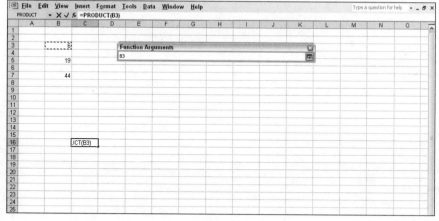

Figure 1-20:
Using RefEdit to enter arguments.

9. Press Enter.

The Function Arguments dialog box reappears with the argument entered into the box. The argument is not the value in the cell, but instead is the address of the cell with the value — exactly what you want.

10. Repeat Steps 7–9 to enter the other two cell references.

Figure 1-21 shows what the screen should now look like.

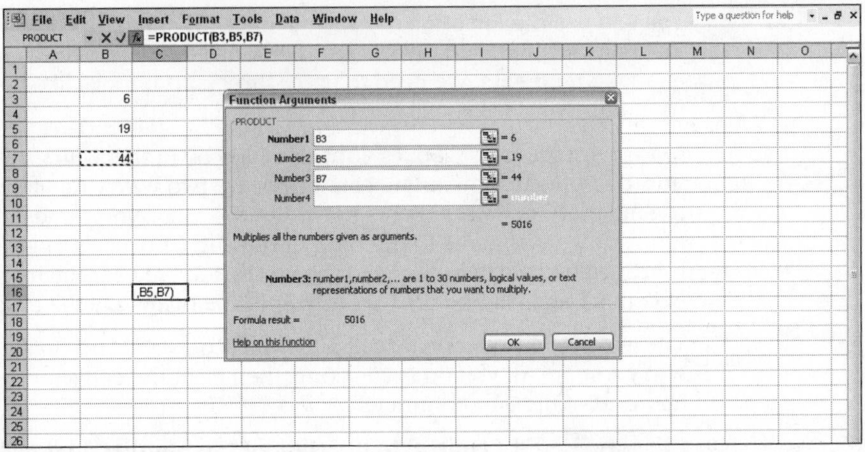

Figure 1-21:
Completing
the function
entry.

11. Click OK or just press Enter to complete the function.

Figure 1-22 shows the result of all this hooplah. The PRODUCT function returns the result of the individual numbers being multiplied together.

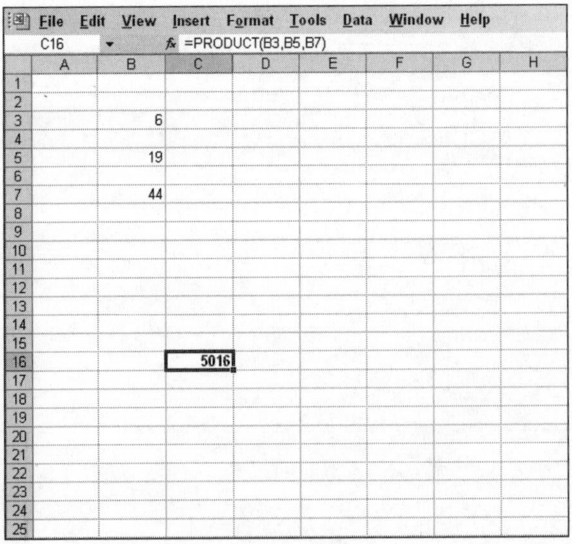

Figure 1-22:
Math was
never this
easy!

You do not have to use the Insert Function dialog box to enter functions into cells. It is there for convenience. As you become familiar with certain functions that you use repeatedly, you may find it faster to just type the function directly into the cell.

Nesting functions

Nesting is something a bird does, isn't it? Well, a bird expert would know the answer to that one but we do know how to nest Excel functions. A nested function is a function that is tucked inside another function — as one of its arguments. Nesting functions let you returns results you would have a hard time getting to otherwise.

Figure 1-23 shows the daily closing price for the S&P 500, for the month of September 2004. A possible analysis is to see how many times the closing price was higher than the average for the month. Therefore the average needs to be calculated first, before any single price can be compared. By embedding the AVERAGE function inside another function, the average is first calculated.

When a function is nested inside another, the inner function is calculated first. Then that result is used as an argument for the outer function.

File	Edit	View	Insert	Format	Tools	Data	Window	Help

D7   *fx* =COUNTIF(B5:B25, ">" & AVERAGE(B5:B25))

	A	B	C	D	E
1	S&P 500	Daily Close			
2					
3					
4	Date	Close			
5	1-Sep-04	1105.91			
6	2-Sep-04	1118.31			
7	3-Sep-04	1113.63		11	The number of times the closing price exceeded the monthly average
8	7-Sep-04	1121.3			
9	8-Sep-04	1116.27			
10	9-Sep-04	1118.38			
11	10-Sep-04	1123.92			
12	13-Sep-04	1125.82			
13	14-Sep-04	1128.33			
14	15-Sep-04	1120.37			
15	16-Sep-04	1123.5			
16	17-Sep-04	1128.55			
17	20-Sep-04	1122.2			
18	21-Sep-04	1129.3			
19	22-Sep-04	1113.56			
20	23-Sep-04	1108.36			
21	24-Sep-04	1110.11			
22	27-Sep-04	1103.52			
23	28-Sep-04	1110.06			
24	29-Sep-04	1114.8			
25	30-Sep-04	1114.58			

Figure 1-23: Nesting functions.

The COUNTIF function counts the number of cells in a range that meet a condition. The condition is that any single value in the range is greater than (>) the average of the range. The formula in cell D7 is:

```
=COUNTIF(B5:B25, ">" & AVERAGE(B5:B25))
```

The average function is evaluated first, and then the COUNTIF function is evaluated using the returned value from the nested function as an argument.

Nested functions are best entered directly. The Insert Function dialog box does not make it easy to enter a nested function. Try one out. In this example, you use the AVERAGE function to find the average of the largest values from two different sets of numbers. The nested function in this example is MAX. You enter the MAX function twice within the AVERAGE function:

1. **Enter a few different numbers in one column.**

2. **Enter a few different numbers in a different column.**

3. **Click empty cell where you want the result to appear.**

4. **Enter** =AVERAGE(**to start the function entry.**

5. **Enter** MAX(.

6. **Click the first cell in the first set of numbers and drag over all the cells of the first set.**

   The address of this range enters into the MAX function.

7. **Enter a closing parenthesis to end the first MAX function.**

8. **Enter a comma (,).**

9. **Once again, enter** MAX(.

10. **Click the first cell in the second set of numbers.**

    Keep the mouse button pressed and drag over all the cells of the second set. The address of this range enters into the MAX function.

11. **Enter a closing parenthesis to end the second MAX function.**

12. **Enter another closing parenthesis.**

    This one is to end the AVERAGE function.

13. **Press Enter.**

Figure 1-24 shows the result of our nested function. Cell C14 has this formula:

```
=AVERAGE(MAX(B4:B10),MAX(D4:D10))
```

When using nested functions, the outer function is preceded with an equal sign if it is the beginning of the formula. Any nested functions are not preceded with an equal sign.

Nested functions are used in examples in various places in the book. The COUNTIF, AVERAGE, and MAX functions are discussed in Chapter 9.

You can nest functions up to seven levels.

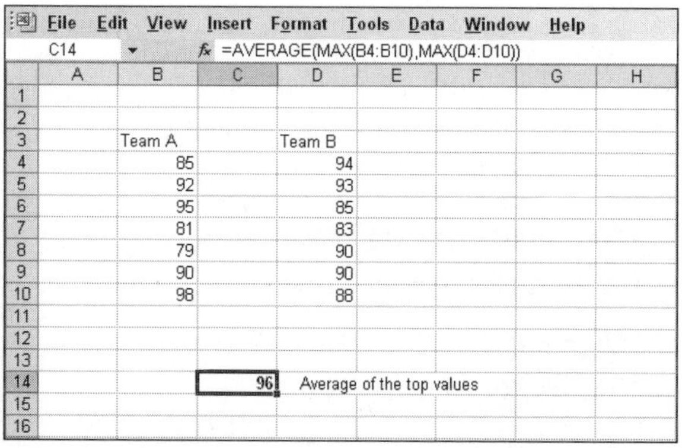

	File	Edit	View	Insert	Format	Tools	Data	Window	Help	
	C14	▼		*fx* =AVERAGE(MAX(B4:B10),MAX(D4:D10))						

	A	B	C	D	E	F	G	H
1								
2								
3		Team A		Team B				
4		85		94				
5		92		93				
6		95		85				
7		81		83				
8		79		90				
9		90		90				
10		98		88				
11								
12								
13								
14			96	Average of the top values				
15								
16								

Figure 1-24:
Getting a
result from
nested
functions.

Using array functions

Some functions return an array of data. An *array* is a collection of related data.
The output of an array function goes into multiple cells. To make this happen,
the function entry must follow a specific protocol, which we describe soon.

Figure 1-25 shows an example. In this worksheet, you have data on income for
months 1-6 and want to estimate what income will be for months 7-12 based
on this data. The TREND function, which is an array function, is designed for
just this task. We walk you through this example.

You must remember two details when using an array function:

- ✔ You start by selecting the *range* of cells where the array of results is
  to go.
- ✔ You enter the function in the usual way, but you must complete entry by
  holding down the Ctrl and Shift keys while you press Enter.

When you enter an array formula in this way, Excel knows it is an array formula and displays the results correctly. It won't work if you enter the formula
by pressing Enter alone.

Selecting the number of cells required to receive a returned value begins
entry of array functions. Entry of array functions is completed with the special Ctrl + Shift + Enter keystroke.

File	Edit	View	Insert	Format	Tools	Data	Window	Help

C12 ▾ *fx* {=TREND(C4:C9,B4:B9,B12:B17)}

	A	B	C	D	E	F
1						
2						
3		Month	Sales			
4		1	$ 14,000			
5		2	$ 15,525			
6		3	$ 19,000			
7		4	$ 17,300			
8		5	$ 20,750			
9		6	$ 23,100			
10						
11						
12		7	$ 24,227			
13		8	$ 25,926			
14		9	$ 27,625			
15		10	$ 29,325			
16		11	$ 31,024			
17		12	$ 32,723			
18						
19						
20						
21						
22						
23						
24						
25						

Figure 1-25: Viewing a trend returned with the TREND array function.

Here's how to enter and complete the array function demonstrated in Figure 1-25:

1. **Near the top of one column, enter the header "Month". In the next column to the right, in the same row, enter the header "Sales".**

2. **Under the Month header, enter the numbers 1 through 6, one number in each successive row.**

3. **Skipping one row, enter the numbers 7 through 12 going down through the column.**

4. **Under the Sales header, enter numeric values, such as those seen in Figure 1-25:** 14,000; 15,525; 19,000; 17,300; 20,750; **and** 23;100.

   You can enter other values if you want.

5. **At this point, the worksheet is set up with all the initial values needed to use the TREND function.**

   The TREND function is used to estimate the sales for months 7 through 12. It does this by evaluating a pattern from the first six months of values.

6. **Select the cells adjacent to the months numbered 7 through 12.**

7. **Enter =TREND(to start the function.**

8. **Click the cell that has the *sales* for month number 1 in it, keep the mouse button pressed, and drag down through the other sales amounts.**

9. **Enter a comma (,)**

10. **Click the cell that has the month number 1 in it, keep the mouse button pressed, and drag down through month number 6.**

11. **Enter a comma(,).**

12. **Click the cell that has the month number 7 in it, keep the mouse button pressed, and drag down through month number 12.**

13. **Enter a closing parenthesis.**

    Figure 1-26 shows what the worksheet should now look like. Notice that although entry appears to be going into one cell, all the selected cells receive a value when the entry is completed.

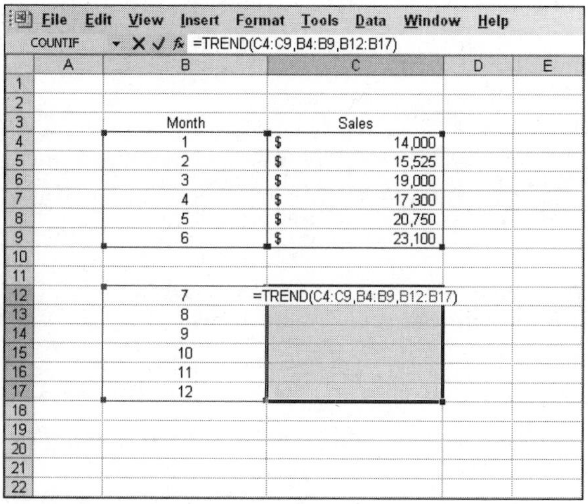

Figure 1-26: Completing the array function entry.

14. **Last but not least — do not press Enter to complete the entry. Press Ctrl+Shift+Enter. Go for it!**

And that's it! You now see the anticipated sales for months 7 through 12. This "trend" is based on an inherent trend found in the known values of the first six months.

Array functions are a bit confusing but mighty powerful. Chapter 3 is devoted to array formulas and functions. Chapter 11 discusses the TREND function.

Chapter 2

Saving Time with the Insert Function Dialog Box

. . . .

In This Chapter

▶ Displaying the Insert Function dialog box

▶ Finding the function you need

▶ Using functions that don't take arguments

▶ Getting help with functions

▶ Using the Function Arguments dialog box

. . . .

*E*xcel has so many functions that it's both a blessing and a curse. You can do many things with Excel functions — if you can remember them all! Even if you remember many function names, memorizing all the arguments the functions can use is a challenge.

Don't forget — arguments are pieces of information that functions use to calculate and return a value.

Never fear: Microsoft hasn't left you in the dark with figuring out which arguments to use. Excel has a great utility to help insert functions, and their arguments, into your worksheet. This makes it a snap to find and use the functions you need. You'll save both time and headaches, and make fewer errors to boot — so read on!

Getting Familiar with the Insert Function Dialog Box

The Insert Function dialog box (shown in Figure 2-1) is designed to simplify the task of using functions in your worksheet. The dialog box not only helps you locate the proper function for the task at hand, but also provides information about the arguments that the function takes. If you use the Insert Function dialog box, you don't have to type functions directly into worksheets cells. Instead the dialog box guides you through a (mostly) point-and-click procedure — a good thing, because if you're anything like us, you need all the help you can get!

In the Insert Function dialog box, you can browse functions by category, or scroll the complete alphabetical list. A search feature — where you type a phrase in the Search for a Function box, click the Go button, and see what comes up — is helpful. When you highlight a function in the Select a Function box, a brief description of what the function does is displayed under the list (ABS is selected in Figure 2-1). You can also click the Help on This Function link at the bottom of the dialog box to view more detailed information about the function.

Figure 2-1:
Use the
Insert
Function
dialog box
to easily
enter
functions
in a
worksheet.

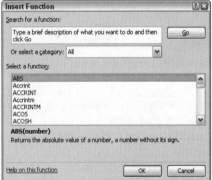

You can display the Insert Function dialog box in three ways:

✓ **Choose Insert ⇨ Function.**

✓ **On the Formula Bar, click the Insert Function button (which looks like *f*ₓ).**

✓ **On the Standard toolbar, click the AutoSum arrow-down next to the button and select More Functions (see Figure 2-2).** The AutoSum button has a list of commonly used functions that you can insert with a click. If you select More Functions, the Insert Function dialog box opens.

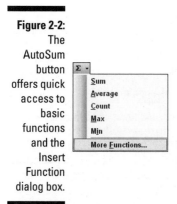

Figure 2-2:
The
AutoSum
button
offers quick
access to
basic
functions
and the
Insert
Function
dialog box.

Finding the Correct Function

The first step to using a function is finding the one you need! Even when you do know the one you need you may not remember all the arguments it takes. You can find a function in the Insert Function dialog box in two ways:

✔ **Search:** Type one or more keywords or a phrase into the Search for a Function box. Then click the Go button. If Excel is able to find any matches on your entry, the Select a Function list in the dialog box will be filled with the matched functions, and the Or Select a Category drop-down list will display Recommended, and the Select a Function box will display a list of the functions that match your search. If no match is made, the Or Select a Category drop-down list will display Most Recently Used functions, and the most recently used functions will appear in the Select a Function dialog box.

✔ **Browse:** Click the Or Select a Category down-arrow and from the drop-down list, select All or select an actual function category. When an actual category is selected, the Select a Function box will update to just the relevant functions. You can look through the list to find the function you want.

Table 2-1 lists the categories in the Or Select a Category drop-down list. Finding the function you need is different from knowing which function you need. Excel is great at giving you the functions, but you do need to know what to ask for.

Table 2-1	Function Categories in the Insert Function Dialog Box
Category	*Type of Functions*
Most Recently Used	The last several functions you used
All	The entire function list, sorted alphabetically
Financial	Functions for managing loans, analyzing investments, and so forth
Date & Time	Functions for calculating days of the week, elapsed time, and so forth
Math & Trig	A considerable number of mathematical functions
Statistical	Functions for using descriptive and inferential statistics
Lookup & Reference	Functions for obtaining facts about and data on worksheets
Database columns	Functions for selecting data in structured rows and
Text	Functions for manipulating and searching text values
Logical	Boolean functions (AND, OR, and so forth)
Information	Functions for getting facts about worksheet cells and the data therein
User Defined	Any available custom functions created in VBA code or from add-ins (*Note:* This category may not be listed.)
Engineering	Functions provided by the optional Analysis ToolPak (*Note:* This category may not be listed.)

Entering Functions Using the Insert Function Dialog Box

Now that you've seen how to search for or select a function, it's time to use the Insert Function dialog box to actually insert a function. The Insert Function dialog box makes it easy to both enter functions that take no arguments and functions that do take arguments. Either way the dialog box guides you through the process of entering the function.

Sometimes function arguments are not values but instead are references to cells or ranges. That this is also handled in the Insert Function dialog box makes it use so beneficial.

Selecting a function that takes no arguments

Some functions return a value, period. No arguments are needed for these ones. This means you don't have to have some arguments ready to go. What could be easier? Here's how to enter a function that does not take any arguments. For this example we are using the TODAY function:

1. **Position the cursor in the cell where you want the results to appear.**

2. **Choose Insert ⇨ Function to open the Insert Function dialog box.**

3. **Select All in the Or Select a Category drop-down list.**

4. **Scroll through the Select a Function list until you see the TODAY function and click it once.**

   We've been walking through these steps too and Figure 2-3 shows what our screen looks like.

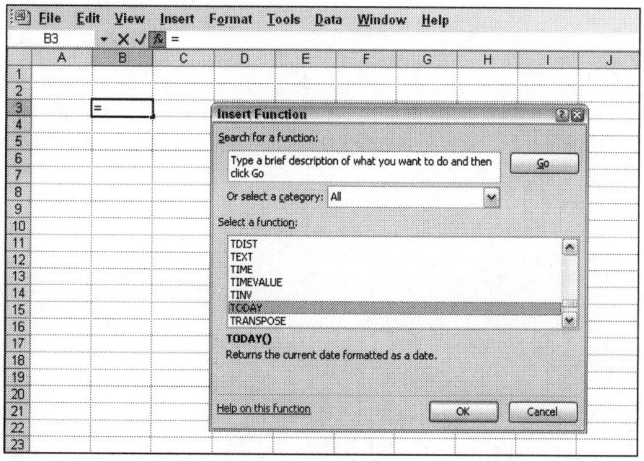

Figure 2-3: Selecting a function.

5. **Click the OK button.**

   The Insert Function dialog box closes and the Function Arguments dialog box opens. The dialog box tells you that function does not take any arguments. Figure 2-4 shows how the screen now looks.

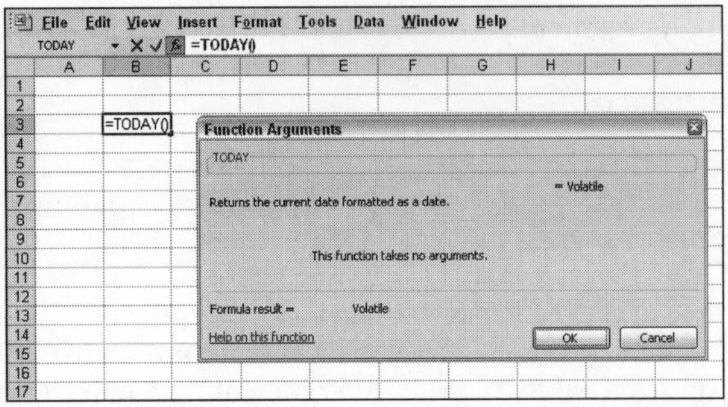

Figure 2-4:
Confirming
no
arguments
exist with
the Function
Arguments
dialog box.

	File	Edit	View	Insert	Format	Tools	Data	Window	Help		
TODAY		▾	✗ ✓	ƒ	=TODAY()						
	A	B	C	D	E	F	G	H	I	J

Function Arguments

TODAY

= Volatile

Returns the current date formatted as a date.

This function takes no arguments.

Formula result =   Volatile

Help on this function   OK   Cancel

6. **Click the OK button.**

   This closes the Function Arguments dialog box and the function entry is complete.

You may have noticed that the Function Arguments dialog box says the Formula result will equal "Volatile." This is nothing to be alarmed about! This just means the answer can be different each time you use the function.

Figure 2-5 shows how the result of the function has been returned to the worksheet. Cell B3 displays the date at the time we wrote this example. The date you see will be the current date.

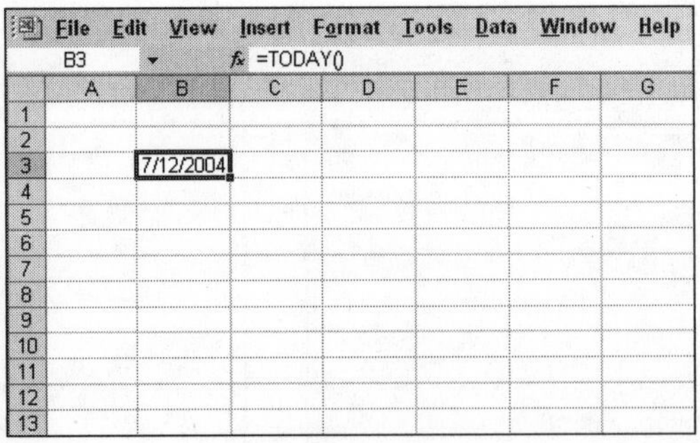

	File	Edit	View	Insert	Format	Tools	Data	Window	Help
B3		▾		ƒ	=TODAY()				
	A	B	C	D	E	F	G	
1								
2								
3		7/12/2004						
4								

Figure 2-5:
Populating a
worksheet
cell with
today's date.

Most functions do take arguments. The few that do not take arguments are able to return a result without needing any information to do so. For example the TODAY function just returns the current date. It doesn't need any information to figure this out.

Selecting a function that takes arguments

Most functions take arguments to provide the information the function needs to perform its calculation. Some functions take a single argument, others take many. Taking an argument means the function uses the argument. Taking arguments or using arguments means the same thing.

Most functions take arguments, but the number of arguments depends on the actual function. Some take a single argument and some can take up to 30.

In the following example, we show how to use the Insert Function dialog box to enter a function that does use arguments. The example uses the PRODUCT function. Here's how to enter the function and its arguments:

1. **Position the cursor in the cell where you want the results to appear.**

2. **Choose Insert ⇨ Function to open the Insert Function dialog box.**

3. **Select Math & Trig in the Or Select a Category drop-down list.**

4. **Scroll through the Select a Function list until you see the PRODUCT function and then click on it once.**

   We've been taking these steps too and Figure 2-6 shows what our screen now looks like.

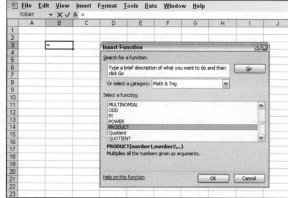

Figure 2-6: Preparing to multiply some numbers with the PRODUCT function.

5. **Click the OK button.**

   The Insert Function dialog box closes and the Function Arguments dialog box opens. Figure 2-7 shows what our screen looks like. The dialog box tells you that this function can take up to 30 arguments, yet there appears to be room for only 2. As you enter arguments the dialog box will expand to make room for more.

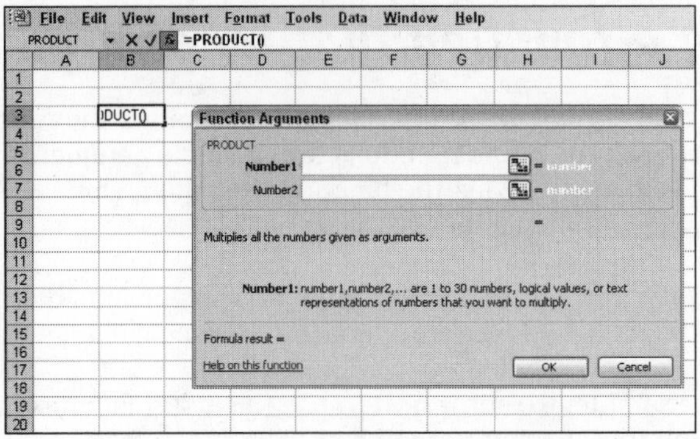

Figure 2-7:
Ready to
input
function
arguments.

6. **In the Function Arguments dialog box, enter a number in the Number 1 box and enter another number in the Number 2 box.**

   These are actual arguments you are entering. As you enter numbers the dialog box expands to allow additional arguments to be entered. Enter as many as you like, up to 30. Figure 2-8 shows how we entered 4 arguments. Also look at the bottom left of the dialog box. As you enter functions the Formula result is instantly calculated. Wouldn't it be nice to be that smart!

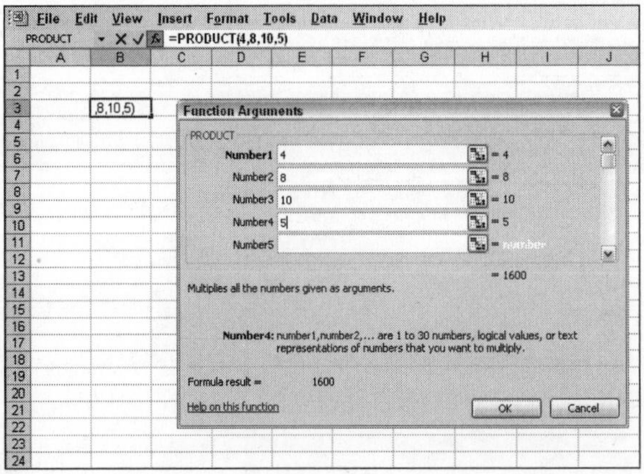

Figure 2-8:
Getting
instant
results in
the Function
Arguments
dialog box.

7. **Click OK to complete the function entry.**

   Figure 2-9 shows our worksheet with the returned result.

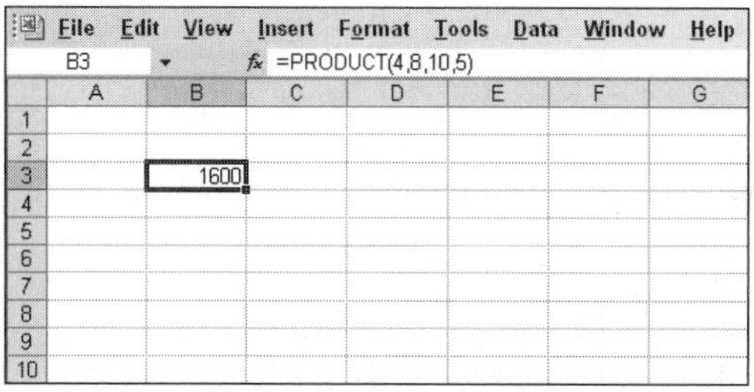

Figure 2-9:
Getting the
final answer
from the
function.

Entering cell and range references as function arguments

Excel is so cool. Not only can you provide single cell references as arguments, but in many cases you can enter an entire range reference into a single argument! And what's more, you can enter these arguments using either the keyboard or the mouse.

This example demonstrates using both single cell references and a range reference as arguments. For this example we use the SUM function. Here is how to use the Insert Function dialog box to enter the function and its arguments:

1. **Enter some values in a worksheet, at least ten values in a column.**

2. **Select the cell where you want the result to go.**

3. **Choose Insert ➪ Function to open the Insert Function dialog box.**

4. **In the dialog box, select the SUM function.**

   You may have to first select All or Math & Trig from the Or Select a Category drop-down list.

5. **Click OK.**

   The Function Arguments dialog box opens. To the right of each Number box is a small fancy button — a special Excel control sometimes called the RefEdit. It allows you to leave the dialog box, select a cell or range on the worksheet, and then go back into the dialog box. Whatever cell or range you click or drag over on the worksheet is brought into the entry box as a reference.

   You can type cell and range references directly into the Number boxes as well. The RefEdit controls are there for you to use if you want.

6. Click directly on the first RefEdit.

The dialog box shrinks so that the only thing visible is the field where you enter data.

7. Click a cell on the worksheet that has a number you entered previously.

8. Press the Enter key.

Your screen should look similar to the one shown in Figure 2-10. The area where you entered numbers and the cell you clicked on are likely to be different, but you should see that the Function Arguments dialog box now has its first argument — as a cell reference.

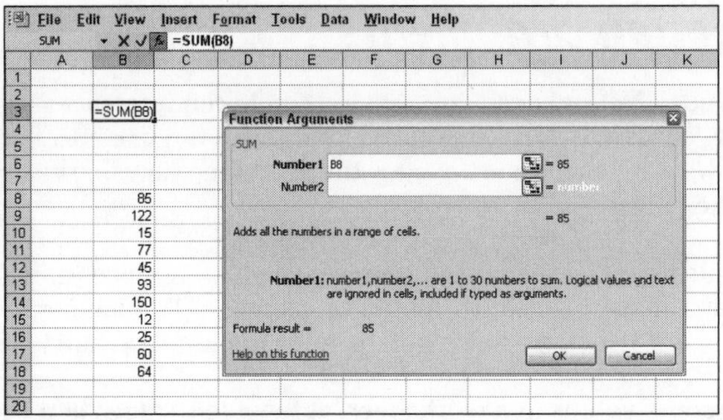

Figure 2-10:
Entering a single cell reference as a function argument.

9. Use the RefEdit control of the second Number box to click another cell that has a number.

10. Press the Enter key.

The Function Arguments dialog box opens again. Your screen should now look similar to that in Figure 2-11.

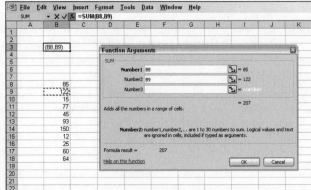

Figure 2-11:
Entering more function arguments.

11. Click the third RefEdit control.

12. To input a range as a function argument, click on a cell and hold down the mouse button; drag over several cells that are filled with numbers.

13. Press the Enter key.

Your screen should look similar to that in Figure 2-12. The Function Arguments dialog box should show two individual cell references and one range reference.

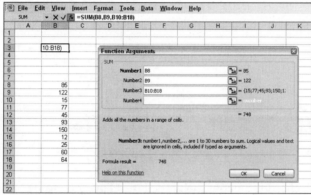

Figure 2-12: Calculating a sum based on cell and range references.

14. Click the OK button in the Function Arguments dialog box to close it and populate the active cell with the result.

Congratulations! You did it. You successfully inserted a function that took both cell and range references. You're harnessing the power of Excel. Look at the result — the sum of the numbers in all the cells, both the individual cells and those in the range. Just imagine how much summing you can do. You can have up to 30 inputs, with each one being a range of cells.

You can use the Insert Function dialog box at any time during the entry of a formula. This is helpful for when the formula uses some values and references in addition to a function. Just open the Insert Function dialog box when the formula entry is at the point where the function goes.

Getting Help while Using the Insert Function Dialog Box

The number of functions and their exhaustive capabilities gives you the power to do great things in Excel. However, from time to time, you may need guidance on how to get functions to work. Lucky for you, help is just a click away.

Both the Insert Function and Function Arguments dialog boxes have a link to the Help system. At any time, you can click the <u>Help on This Function</u> link in the lower-left corner of the dialog box and get help on the function you're using. The Help system has many examples; often, reviewing how a function works leads you to other similar functions that may be better suited to your situation.

Using the Function Arguments Dialog Box to Edit Functions

Excel makes entering functions with the Insert Function dialog box easy. But what about when you need to change a function that has already been entered into a cell? Maybe you have to add more arguments or take some away. Well, there is an easy way to do this!

Position the cursor in the cell with the existing function before going to display the Insert Function dialog box. The Function Argument dialog box appears. This dialog box is already set to work with your function. In fact, the arguments that have already been entered into the function are displayed in the dialog box as well! You can add, edit, and delete arguments. Click OK when you're finished, and the function will be updated with your changes.

Chapter 3

Understanding Array Formulas and Functions

In This Chapter

▶ Understanding arrays

▶ Creating formulas that use arrays

▶ Using functions that return arrays of data

*E*xcel is really quite sophisticated — its many built-in functions make your work easier. On top of that, Excel allows you to tell functions to work on entire sets of values, called *arrays,* which makes for even more clever analysis.

An array is a set of two or more values (for example, the contents of two or more worksheet cells, or even the contents of two or more worksheet ranges). Certain functions use arrays for arguments.

You may be thinking, "Hey, how is this different than just entering a bunch of arguments?" You're right in the comparison. For example, the SUM function can take up to 30 arguments. Isn't this the same as giving the function an array with 30 values? Well, yes and no. It's the same idea, but the way you apply the array can produce different results, as you will soon see.

There is even another side to array functions. Some of the functions *return* an array. Yes, that's right. Most of the time a function returns a single value into a single cell. In this chapter, we show you how some functions return a group of values into multiple cells.

Discovering Arrays

An array is like a box. It can hold a number of items. In Excel, an array holds a collection of values or cell references. These arrays are used exclusively in formulas and functions. That is, the association of some values as one cohesive group exists just for the purpose of calculating results. An array differs from the named areas (a range of cells) that you can create in Excel. Named areas become part of the worksheet and can referenced at anytime.

Named areas are set using the Define Name dialog box, shown in Figure 3-1. In contrast, there is no such dialog box or method to create arrays that can be referenced from functions or formulas. Arrays, instead, are embedded in formulas.

Figure 3-1:
Creating a
named area
with the
Define
Name
dialog box.

Named areas are easily referenced in formulas. For example if a workbook contains a named area "Sales," then the values of all the cells in "Sales" can be summed up like this:

```
=SUM(Sales)
```

Let's assume that "Sales" contains three cells with these values — 10, 15, and 20. These values of course can be directly entered in the SUM function like this:

```
=SUM(10,15,20)
```

This is almost an array, but not quite. Excel recognizes a group of values to be an array when they are enclosed with braces ({ and }). Therefore to enter the array of values into the function, the entry looks like this:

```
=SUM({10,15,20})
```

Essentially the braces tell Excel to treat the group of values as an array. So far, you may be wondering about the usefulness of an array, but in the next section, we show you how using arrays with standard functions such as SUM can provide sophisticated results.

To enter values as an array within a function, enclose them with braces.

Using Arrays in Formulas

You can use arrays when entering formulas and functions. Typically the arguments to a function are entered in a different manner, which we demonstrate in this section. Using arrays can save entry steps and deliver an answer in a single formula. This is useful in situations that normally require a set of intermediate calculations from which the final result is calculated .We don't know about you but we like shortcuts, especially when we have too much to do!

Here's an example. The SUM function is normally used to add a few numbers together. Summing up a few numbers doesn't require an array formula per se, but what about summing up the results of other calculations? This next example shows how using an array simplifies getting to the final result.

Figure 3-2 shows a small portfolio of stocks. Column A has the stock symbols, Column B has the number of shares per security, and Column C has recent prices for each.

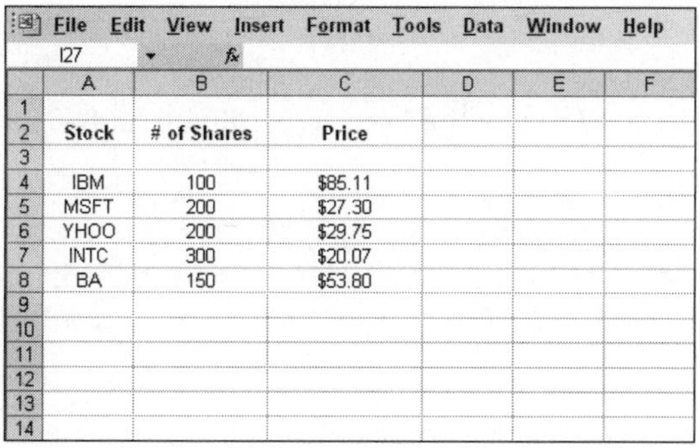

Figure 3-2:
A stock portfolio.

The task is to find out the total value of the portfolio. The typical way to do this is to:

1. **Multiply the number of shares for each stock by its price.**

2. **Sum up the results from Step 1.**

Figure 3-3 shows a very common way to do this. Column D contains formulas to calculate the value of each stock in the portfolio. This is done by multiplying the number of shares for each stock by its price. For example, cell D4 contains the formula =B4*C4. Cell D10 sums up the interim results with the formula =SUM(D4:D8).

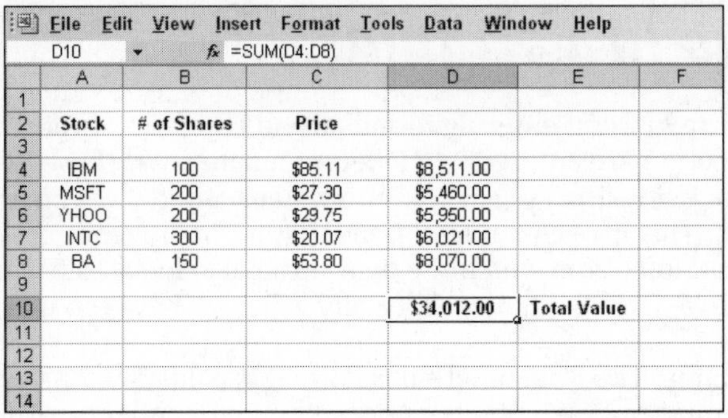
File Edit View Insert Format Tools Data Window Help

D10 =SUM(D4:D8)

	A	B	C	D	E	F
1						
2	Stock	# of Shares	Price			
3						
4	IBM	100	$85.11	$8,511.00		
5	MSFT	200	$27.30	$5,460.00		
6	YHOO	200	$29.75	$5,950.00		
7	INTC	300	$20.07	$6,021.00		
8	BA	150	$53.80	$8,070.00		
9						
10				$34,012.00	Total Value	
11						
12						
13						
14						

Figure 3-3: Calculating the value of a stock portfolio, the old-fashioned way.

The method shown in Figure 3-3 requires creating additional calculations — those in Column D. These are necessary if you need to know the value of each stock, but not if all you need to know is the value of the portfolio as a whole.

Fortunately, alternatives to this old-fashioned approach exist. One is to embed the separate multiplicative steps directly inside the SUM function, like this:

```
=SUM(B4*C4,B5*C5,B6*C6,B7*C7,B8*C8)
```

That works, but it's bloated to say the least. What if you had 20 stocks in the portfolio? Forget it!

Another alternative is the SUMPRODUCT function. This function sums the products, just as the other methods shown here also do. The limitation, however, is that SUMPRODUCT can only be used for summing. It cannot, for example, give you an average.

In many situations such as this one, your best bet is to use an array function. Figure 3-4 shows the correct result from using the SUM function entered as an array function.

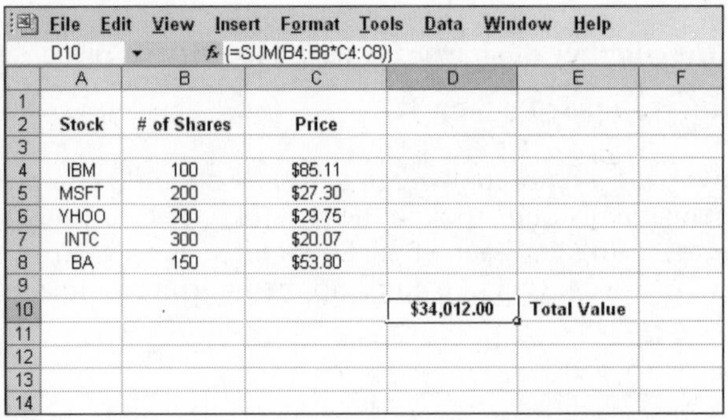
File Edit View Insert Format Tools Data Window Help

D10 {=SUM(B4:B8*C4:C8)}

	A	B	C	D	E	F
1						
2	Stock	# of Shares	Price			
3						
4	IBM	100	$85.11			
5	MSFT	200	$27.30			
6	YHOO	200	$29.75			
7	INTC	300	$20.07			
8	BA	150	$53.80			
9						
10				$34,012.00	Total Value	
11						
12						
13						
14						

Figure 3-4: Calculating the value of a stock portfolio using an array function.

The syntax is important. Two ranges are entered into the function: One contains the cells that hold the number of shares, and the other contains the cells that have the stock prices. These are multiplied in the function by entering the multiplication operator (*):

```
{=SUM(B4:B8*C4:C8)}
```

Of course Ctrl+Shift+Enter had been pressed to turn the whole thing into an array function.

Use Ctrl+Shift+Enter to turn a formula into an array formula. You must use the key combination after entering the formula but before pressing the Enter key. The key combination takes the place of the standard Enter key press.

Try this out. Here's how you use an array with the SUM function:

1. **Enter two columns of values.**

   The two lists must be the same size.

2. **Position the cursor in the cell where you want the result to appear.**

3. **Enter =SUM(to start the function.**

4. **Click on the first cell in the first list and drag the mouse over the first list. Then release the mouse button.**

5. **Enter the multiplication sign (*).**

6. **Click on the first cell in the second list and drag the mouse over the second list. Then release the mouse button.**

7. **Enter a closing parenthesis.**

8. **Press Ctrl+Shift+Enter to end the function.**

Array functions are useful for saving steps in mathematical operations. Therefore you can apply these examples to a number of functions, such as AVERAGE, MAX, MIN, and so on.

As another example, suppose you run a fleet of taxis and you need to calculate the average cost of gasoline per mile driven. This is easy to calculate for a single vehicle. You just divide the total miles driven by the total spent on gasoline, for a given period of time. The calculation looks like this:

cost of gasoline per mile = amount spent on gasoline ÷ miles driven

How can you easily calculate this for a fleet of vehicles? Figure 3-5 shows how this is done. The vehicles are listed in Column A, the total miles driven for the month appear in Column B, and the total amounts spent on gasoline appear in Column C.

	File	Edit	View	Insert	Format	Tools	Data	Window	Help		

C21   ▾   *fx* (=AVERAGE(C6:C17/B6:B17))

	A	B	C	D	E
1	*The Happy Taxi Company*				
2	*Mileage and Gasoline for October 2004*				
3					
4					
5	*TAXI*	*MILES DRIVEN*	*AMOUNT SPENT ON GAS*		
6	Taxi 1	1155	$193.42		
7	Taxi 2	1722	$356.84		
8	Taxi 3	1295	$265.10		
9	Taxi 4	1785	$481.25		
10	Taxi 5	2627	$394.43		
11	Taxi 6	2014	$323.32		
12	Taxi 7	965	$122.29		
13	Taxi 8	1828	$205.94		
14	Taxi 9	1751	$369.39		
15	Taxi 10	1749	$327.47		
16	Taxi 11	1333	$244.38		
17	Taxi 12	1610	$285.65		
18					
19					
20					
21	**Average Gasoline Expense per Mile Driven:**		$0.18		
22					
23					

Figure 3-5: Making an easy calculation using an array formula.

One single formula in cell C21 answers the question. By using the AVERAGE function in an array formula, the result is returned without the need for any intermediate calculations. The formula looks like this:

```
{=AVERAGE(C6:C17/B6:B17)}
```

Working with Functions That Return Arrays

A few functions actually return arrays of data. Instead of providing a single result, as most functions do, these functions return several values. The number of actual returned values is directly related to the function's arguments. The returned values go into a range of cells.

Excel array functions are special functions that accept arrays as arguments and possibly return arrays of data.

A good example of this is the TRANSPOSE function. This interesting function is used to reorient data. Data situated a given way in columns and rows is transposed (changed to be presented instead in rows and columns). Figure 3-6 shows how this works.

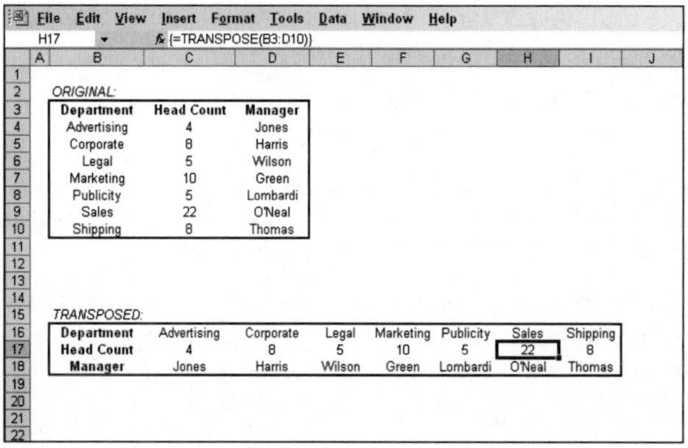

Figure 3-6:
Transposing
data.

Cells B3 through D10 contain information about departments in a company. Departments are listed going down Column B. Note that the area of B3 through D10 specifically occupies three columns and eight rows. The header row is included in the area.

Cells B16 through I18 contain the transposed data. It is the same data, but now it occupies eight columns and three rows. In total number of cells, this is the same size as the original area. Just as important is that the area is made up of the same dimensions, just reversed. That is, a 3-by-8 area became an 8-by-3 area. The number of cells remains at 24. However the transposed area has not been altered to be 6 by 3 or 2 by 12, or any other two dimensions that cover 24 cells.

Every single cell in the B16:I18 range contains the same formula — {=TRANSPOSE(B3:D10)} — however the function was entered only once.

In detail, here is how you can use the TRANSPOSE function:

1. **Enter some data that occupies at least two adjacent cells at a minimum.**

   Creating an area of data that spans multiple rows and columns is best for seeing the how useful the function is.

2. **Elsewhere on the worksheet, select an area that covers the same number of cells, but has the length of the sides of the original area reversed.**

   For example:

   • If the original area is two columns and six rows then select an area that is six columns and two rows.

- If the original area is one column and two rows then select an area that is two columns and one row.

- If the original area is 200 columns and 201 rows then select an area that is 201 columns and 200 rows.

- If the original area is five columns and five rows then select an area that is five columns and five rows. (A square area is transposed into a square area.)

Figure 3-7 shows an area of data and a selected area ready to receive the transposed data. The original data area occupies 11 columns and 3 rows. The selected area is 3 columns by 11 rows.

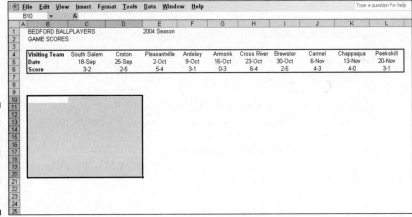

Figure 3-7:
Preparing
an area to
receive
transposed
data.

3. **Enter** =TRANSPOSE(**to start the function.**

4. **Click on the first cell in the original data and drag the mouse over the entire original data area while keeping the mouse button down.**

   The function now shows the range of the area. Figure 3-8 shows how the entry should appear at this step.

5. **Enter a closing parenthesis.**

6. **Press Ctrl+Shift+Enter to end the function.**

Note: The transposed data does not take on the formatting of the original area. You need to format the area as needed. Figure 3-9 shows the result of using TRANSPOSE *and* then formatting the transposed data.

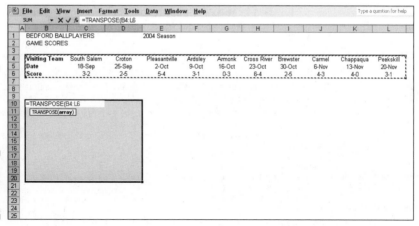

Figure 3-8:
Completing
the function.

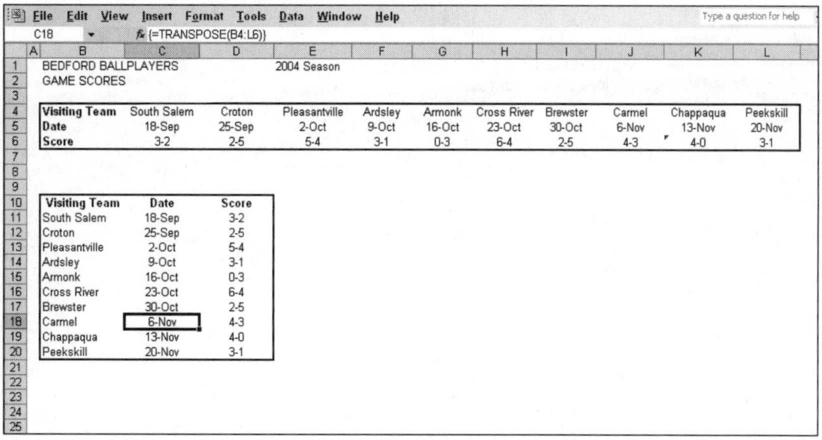

Figure 3-9:
Transposed
data after
formatting.

Wait! Isn't this a waste of time? Excel can easily transpose data using the Paste Special dialog box. Simply copying a range of data and using this dialog box to paste the data gives the same result as the TRANSPOSE function. Or does it?

Figure 3-10 shows the Paste Special dialog box with the Transpose check box checked. This will transpose the data. You don't even have to select the area first!

However, when data is transposed with the Paste Special dialog box, the actual data is copied to the new area. By contrast the TRANSPOSE function pastes a formula that references the original data — and that is the key point.

When data is changed in the original area, the change is reflected in the new, transposed area, if the TRANSPOSE function was used.

You can transpose data in two ways. The TRANSPOSE function references the original data and will update as original data is changed. Using the Paste Special dialog box to transpose data creates values that do not update when the original data changes.

Figure 3-10:
Using the
Paste
Special
dialog box
to transpose
data.

Chapter 4

Correcting Formulas

. . . .

In This Chapter

▶ Preventing errors with Excel

▶ Following the flow of cell and range references to and from formulas

▶ Using Excel's array of tools to correct formulas

. . . .

*E*xcel would be nothing if it didn't allow you to create formulas. Creating formulas is, after all, the real purpose of a worksheet — to allow you to build a solution that pertains to your specific needs. Without formulas, Excel would be no more than a place to store information.

Excel allows formulas up to 1,024 characters in length. This means you can create some monster formulas! Formulas can reference cells that have formulas that reference other cells that have formulas that reference . . . well, you get the idea!

Ah, but this comes with a price — how can you track down errors in long formulas? How can you avoid them in the first place? In this chapter, we explain how Excel steers you away from entering problematic formulas, and how to correct completed formulas that are not working in the way you intended.

Catching Errors as They're Entered

Excel is keeping an eye on you when you enter formulas. Don't be worried! This is a good thing. You aren't being graded. Excel is helping you, not testing you.

All formulas start with an equal sign. When you complete an entry by pressing Enter or Tab (or clicking into another cell), Excel scans the entry. If the entry did indeed start with an equal sign, then Excel immediately looks for three major problems:

- Do the number of open and closed parentheses match?

- Does the formula reference the same cell it is entered in? For example what if cell A1 has this formula: =A1*5. You could send Excel into an endless loop, called a *circular reference.* This is a bit like a dog chasing its tail.

- Does the formula refer to a nonexistent reference?

Each of the problems is handled differently. Excel will offer a fix for mismatched parentheses but will only *warn* you about formulas that reference the cell they are entered in. For nonexistent references, Excel will ask you where to find them. Excel will display an Open File type of dialog box that you use to browse to the reference, assuming the reference is meant to come from an external workbook. If a reference to an external workbook was not the intention, then the dialog box won't make sense. In this case, dismiss the dialog box and edit the formula.

Getting parentheses to match

In a mathematical formula, each open parenthesis must have a matching closing parenthesis. Excel checks your formulas to make sure they comply. Figure 4-1 shows a simple business calculation that requires parentheses to make sense. The result is based on multiplying units by price per unit, adding an additional purchase amount to that, then applying a discount, and finally applying tax.

	File Edit View Insert Format Tools Data Window Hel
	B14 ▼ *f* =(B3*B4+B6) * B8 * (1 + B9)

	A	B	C	D	E
1					
2					
3	Units Sold	100			
4	Price Per Unit	$4.95			
5					
6	Additional Purchases	$125			
7					
8	Discount	40%			
9	Tax	0.0825			
10					
11					
12					
13					
14	TOTAL PRICE:	268.46			
15					
16					
17					

Figure 4-1:
Using parentheses in a formula.

In math terms, here is how the formula works:

$$(\text{Units Sold} \times \text{Price Per Unit} + \text{Additional Cost}) \times \text{Discount} \times (1 + \text{Tax Rate})$$

The placement of the parentheses is critical to making the formula work. Excel won't sense a problem if any particular parenthesis is in the wrong place, as long as there is a matching number of open and closed parentheses. For example, using the cells and values from Figure 4-1, here are some possibilities of valid formulas that return incorrect answers:

Formula	Result
=B3*(B4+B6) * B8 * (1 + B9)	5626.84
=B3*B4+(B6 * B8) * (1 + B9)	549.13
=(B3*B4+B6 * B8) * (1 + B9)	589.96
=(B3*B4+B6) * (B8 * 1 + B9)	299.15

Correct parentheses placement and a firm understanding of mathematical-operator precedence are critical to calculating correct answers. We suggest a brush-up on these basic math concepts if you aren't sure how to construct your formulas.

What if, during entry, a parenthesis is left out? When you try to complete the entry, Excel will pop up a warning and a suggestion. In this example, the first close parenthesis is purposely left out. Here is the *incorrect* formula:

```
=(B3*B4+B6*B8*(1+B9)
```

Figure 4-2 shows how Excel catches the error and offers a solution.

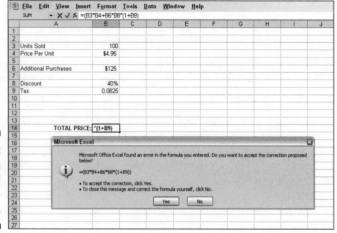

Figure 4-2:
Fixing mismatched parentheses.

Don't be hasty! The correction proposed by Excel will correct the mismatched parentheses but will not create the correct formula. Look closely at the following example of a proposed correction by Excel:

```
=(B3*B4+B6*B8*(1+B9))
```

But what you really need is this:

```
=(B3*B4+B6)*B8*(1+B9)
```

Excel simply added the missing parenthesis to the end of the formula. A good idea, but not good enough. If the proposed correction were accepted, a result of $549.13 would be returned in this example. The correct answer is $268.46 for this example. In this case, you should reject the proposal and fix the formula yourself.

Do not assume Excel's proposed formula corrections are correct for what you need. Carefully review the proposed correction and accept or reject accordingly.

Avoiding circular references

A *circular reference* occurs when a cell refers to itself, whether directly or indirectly. For example, if =100 + A2 is entered into cell A2, then a direct circular reference has been created. An indirect circular reference is when the formula in a given cell refers to one or more other cells that in return refer back to the original cell. For example a formula in A1 refers to cell A2, A2 refers to A3, and A3 refers back to A1.

Figure 4-3 shows a worksheet that has a direct circular reference. Cell D10 is meant to sum the values above it but mistakenly includes itself in the sum: =SUM(D4:D10). Excel reports the problem in the message box shown in Figure 4-3.

If Automatic Calculation is turned off, then the circular reference is unnoticed until a manual calc is done (by pressing F9) or the setting is changed to Automatic Calculation.

Figure 4-4 shows the Calculation tab on the Options dialog box. Here is where the calculation setting — automatic or manual — is set. Note that the Iteration check box is here as well. When this is set, circular references are allowed. How they calculate values in this case is dependent on the Maximum Iterations and Maximum Change settings.

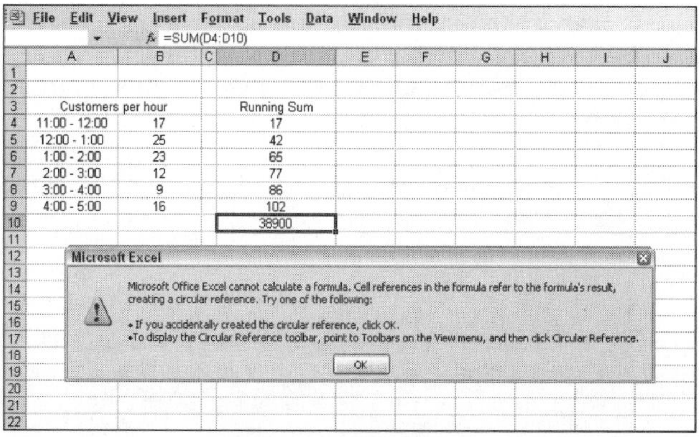

Figure 4-3:
Correcting a
circular
reference.

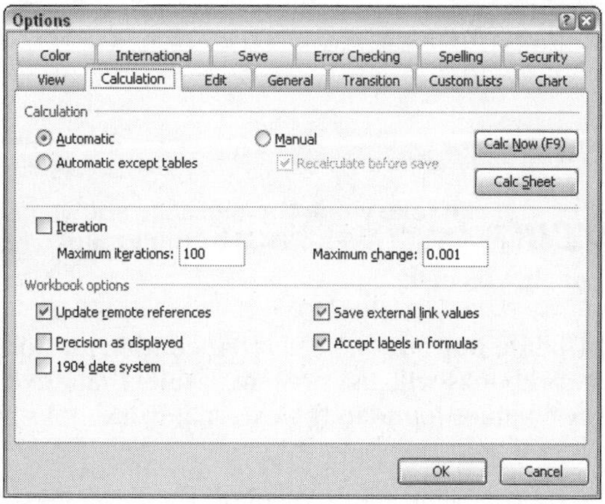

Figure 4-4:
Setting
calculation
and iteration
settings.

Checking and applying iterations on the Calculation tab of the Options dialog box allows you to use circular references in your formulas, useful for certain advanced calculations that are beyond the scope of this book. (See Excel's Help for more information.)

Mending broken links

Formulas can reference external workbooks. As an example, a formula could be written like this: ='C:\Inventory\[Inventory.xls]Engine Parts'!$D$8. The formula uses the value found in the external workbook Inventory.xls. What if the workbook is not found?

Links become broken when external workbooks have been moved, deleted, or renamed. When a workbook that contains an external reference is opened but cannot find the other workbook(s) referenced in one or more formulas, then an error occurs.

Figure 4-5 shows the error message that pops up when a link is broken.

Figure 4-5:
Deciding what to do when formulas reference unfound external workbooks.

There are three choices you can take when the message shown in Figure 4-5 appears. One is Help — you can find out more about links and what to do. More to the point, though, you can:

- **Click the Don't Update button.** The cells that contain formulas that reference external workbooks will just present results that are calculated with the last known values found in the external workbooks from previous sessions.

- **Click the Update button.** This action displays the Edit Links dialog box shown in Figure 4-6. This dialog box offers a number of choices of how to handle the broken links.

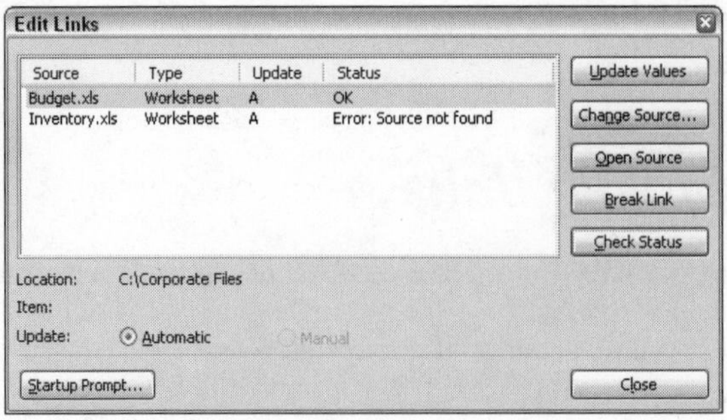

Figure 4-6:
Using the Edit Links dialog box to correct external reference problems.

The Edit Links dialog box gives you options on how to handle broken links. The buttons along the right side of the dialog box work like this:

- ✔ **Update Values:** When external workbooks are where they should be, this action gets the values from the external workbooks, and the cells with those formulas are recalculated. When there are broken links, an Open File type of dialog box appears from which you browse to a file from which to get the values. This does not necessarily have to be the missing workbook — it could be another workbook. A point to be aware of is that using Update Values in this manner does not fix the link. It helps you get values but does not change the way formulas are written. Instead use the Change Source option, listed next.

- ✔ **Change Source:** This option displays an Open File type of dialog box that lets you select an external workbook to use. Selecting a workbook in this dialog box actually alters the formula that references the external workbook. So, this is the best course to take to permanently fix a broken link.

- ✔ **Open Source:** In the case of broken links, this action does nothing, because the source (the external workbook) cannot be found. An error message will confirm this. In the case of working links, this action opens the workbook referenced in the link.

- ✔ **Break Link:** This action converts formulas that contain external links to the calculated values. In other words, the cells that contain formulas with external links are replaced with a value and the formulas are removed. Make sure this is what you want to do. You cannot undo this action, and it can be a serious mistake if you did this unintentionally. Excel displays a confirmation of this, shown in Figure 4-7.

- ✔ **Check Status:** Provides status about links. A number of values are possible (such as: OK, Unknown, Error: Source not found, Error: Worksheet not found, and so on). In the Edit Links dialog box (refer to Figure 4-6), Status is a column in the middle of the dialog box. Each link receives its own status.

Figure 4-7:
Confirming
that you
mean to
break links.

The Edit Links dialog box shown in Figure 4-6 also has the StartUp Prompt button in the lower left. Clicking this button leads to a choice of what the workbook should do when opened and there are no external links. The choices are:

- ✔ Let users choose to display the alert or not.
- ✔ Don't display the alert and don't update automatic links.
- ✔ Don't display the alert and update automatic links.

Using the formula error checker

Some errors are immediately apparent, such as mismatched parentheses explained earlier. Other types of entries are not blatant errors, but instead *resemble* errors. In this case, Excel alerts you to the possible problem and lets you choose how to handle it.

Figure 4-8 shows a few numbers and a sum at the bottom. The formula in cell B10 is =SUM(B4:B9). There is nothing wrong here, no possible error yet.

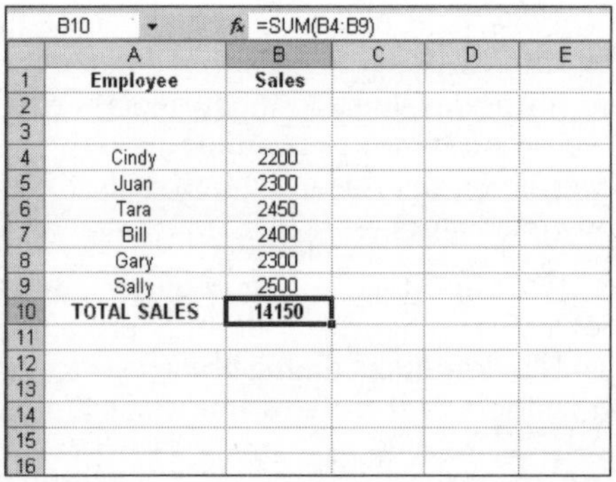

Figure 4-8: Calculating a sum, no possible error.

	A	B	C	D	E
1	Employee	Sales			
2					
3					
4	Cindy	2200			
5	Juan	2300			
6	Tara	2450			
7	Bill	2400			
8	Gary	2300			
9	Sally	2500			
10	TOTAL SALES	14150			
11					
12					
13					
14					
15					
16					

B10   *fx* =SUM(B4:B9)

Note that, in Figure 4-8, the headings row is not adjacent to the rows of information. Rows 2 and 3 are in between the headings and the data. This is not unusual, because this leads to a clean looking report.

However, watch what happens if a value is accidentally entered into the area between the headings and the data. The formula in cell B10 calculates values starting in Row 4. When a value is entered in cell B3, Excel alerts you that there *may* be an error. You can see this in Figure 4-9. A small triangle is now visible in the upper-left corner of cell B10 — which just happens to be the cell with the formula.

B3	▼	*fx*	2450			
	A		B	C	D	E
1	Employee		Sales			
2						
3			2450			
4	Cindy		2200			
5	Juan		2300			
6	Tara		2450			
7	Bill		2400			
8	Gary		2300			
9	Sally		2500			
10	TOTAL SALES		14150			
11						
12						
13						
14						
15						
16						

Figure 4-9:
Excel
senses a
possible
error.

Clicking back into cell B10, and moving the pointer over the triangle, causes a small symbol with an exclamation point to appear. Clicking the symbol displays a list of choices, shown in Figure 4-10.

An error is represented by a triangle in the upper-left corner of a cell. A smart tag is represented by triangle in the lower-right corner of a cell. Smart tags lead to helpful options based on the contents of the cell. See the Excel Help system for more information on Smart Tags.

	File	Edit	View	Insert	Format	Tools	Data	Window	Help	
	B10	▼	*fx*	=SUM(B4:B9)						
	A		B	C	D	E	F	G		
1	Employee		Sales							
2										
3			2450							
4	Cindy		2200							
5	Juan		2300							
6	Tara		2450							
7	Bill		2400							
8	Gary		2300							
9	Sally		2500							
10	TOTAL SAL	◇ ▾	14150							
11										
12		Formula Omits Adjacent Cells								
13		Update Formula to Include Cells								
14		Help on this error								
15										
16		Ignore Error								
17		Edit in Formula Bar								
18										
19		Error Checking Options...								
20		Show Formula Auditing Toolbar								
21										
22										
23										
24										
25										

Figure 4-10:
Deciding
what to do
with the
possible
error.

The first item in the list is just a statement of the problem. In this example, the statement is "Formula Omits Adjacent Cells." Sure enough, it does just that! But is it an error? Did you mean to enter the extra value in cell B3? Perhaps it has some other meaning or use.

The other items in the list give you options for what to do:

- **Update Formula to Include Cells:** Automatically changes the formula to include the extra cell in this example. So the formula in cell B10 changes from =SUM(B4:B9) to =SUM(B3:B9). And, of course, the calculated sum will change as well.

- **Help on This Error:** Steers you to Excel's Help system.

- **Ignore Error:** Removes the list and returns you to the worksheet. The triangle is removed from the cell in question. You've told Excel that you know what you're doing and you want Excel to butt out. Good job!

- **Edit in Formula Bar:** Puts the cell into an edit mode so you can work on the formula. The formula is displayed in the formula bar.

- **Error Checking Options:** Displays the Error Checking tab from Excel's Options dialog box (as shown in Figure 4-11). In this tab, you set options on how Excel handles errors.

- **Show Formula Auditing Toolbar:** Displays the Formula Auditing toolbar, which we cover in the next section.

Figure 4-11:
Setting
options
on error
handling.

Auditing Formulas

Excel can be used to create some fairly complex solutions. A cell can contain a formula that uses values from multitudes of other cells and ranges. Working through long, complex formulas to track down problems can be quite tedious. The good news is that Excel has a way to help!

Formulas may contain precedents and may serve as dependents to other formulas:

- A *precedent* is a cell or range that is referred to in the formula of a given cell.

- A *dependent* is a cell or range that is referred to in the formula of another cell.

It's all relative! A cell often serves as both a precedent and a dependent. Figure 4-12 shows a simple worksheet with some values and some calculations. Cell B9 contains the formula =SUM(B3:B8). Cell B21 contains the formula =SUM(B15:B20). Cell E25 contains the formula =B9-B21.

- Cells B3:B8 are precedents of B9, but at the same time cell B9 is dependent on all the cells in B3:B8.

- Cells B15:B20 are precedents of B21, but at the same time cell B21 is dependent on all the cells in B15:B20.

- Cells B9 and B21 are precedents of E25, but at the same time cell E25 is dependent on cells B9 and B21.

	A	B	C	D	E	F	G	H
1	Employee	Sales						
2								
3	Cindy	2200						
4	Juan	2300						
5	Tara	2450						
6	Bill	2400						
7	Gary	2300						
8	Sally	2500						
9	TOTAL SALES	14150						
10								
11								
12								
13	Employee	Returns						
14								
15	Cindy	0						
16	Juan	100						
17	Tara	350						
18	Bill	50						
19	Gary	0						
20	Sally	0						
21	TOTAL RETURNS	500						
22								
23								
24								
25				TOTAL NET SALES	13650			
26								
27								
28								

E25 =B9-B21

Figure 4-12: Understanding precedents and dependents.

To help follow and fix formulas, Excel provides the Formula Auditing toolbar. This toolbar provides a variety of buttons to help follow how the formulas in your workbook interact. To display it, choose Formula Auditing ⇨ Show Formula Auditing Toolbar from the Tools menu. The toolbar lets you trace precedents and dependents, evaluate formulas, and more. Figure 4-13 shows the worksheet from Figure 4-12 with the Formula Auditing toolbar visible, as well as tracing arrows showing precedents and dependents. The second and fourth buttons on the toolbar are used to show precedents and show dependents.

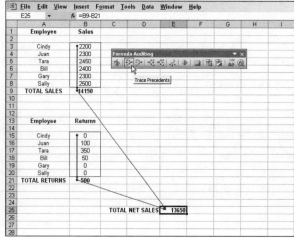

Figure 4-13: Tracing formulas.

In Figure 4-13, cells B9 and B21 have arrows that originate in the cells above. This shows the flow of precedents into the given cells. The arrow head rests in the cell that has the formula that contains the references to the precedents.

On the other hand, cells B9 and B21 themselves then have lines coming from them and ending as arrow heads in cell E25. Therefore, B9 and B21 serve as precedents to cell E25. Or, said another way, cell E25 is dependent on cells B9 and B21.

Double-clicking on a tracer arrow activates the cell on one end of the line. Double-clicking again activates the cell on the other end.

The toolbar itself has a number of buttons on it. Moving from left to right, Table 4-1 lists each and what it is used for. Some of the features are presented in greater detail following the table.

Table 4-1	Using the Formula Auditing Toolbar
Button	**Use**
Error Checking	Cycles through all errors on the worksheet and provides a dialog box to work through each error.
Trace Precedents	Displays tracer arrows from the active cell or range to precedents.

Button	Use
Remove Precedent Arrows	Removes any tracer arrows leading to precedents.
Trace Dependents	Displays tracer arrows from the active cell or range to dependents.
Remove Dependent Arrows	Removes any tracer arrows leading to dependents.
Remove All Arrows	Removes all tracer arrows.
Trace Error	Displays tracer arrows from the active cell to precedents if the active cell has an error (such as #DIV/0!). Similar in use to the Trace Dependents button.
New Comment	Allows a comment to be added to the active cell. More useful for note taking, not for tracing an error.
Circle Invalid Data	If an area of a worksheet has been set for validation, this feature will circle cells that violate the validation. Used for validating data, not formulas.
Clear Validation Circles	Removes any circles over non-valid data.
Show Watch Window	Displays the Add Watch dialog box.
Evaluate Formula	Displays the Evaluate Formula dialog box.

Tracing precedents and dependents can lead to some interesting conclusions about a worksheet. Complex formulas can be difficult to follow, but by displaying tracer arrows, you can better see what is going on. Figure 4-14 shows a piece of a worksheet used in a comprehensive financial solution. The active cell, X22, has a complex formula in it, as you can see by looking at the Formula Bar. The tracer arrows show that numerous precedents are feeding the formula in the active cell.

The tracer arrows make it easy to see the values that are feeding the formula and, therefore, make it easier to look for the source of a problem. For example, cell X22 may be returning a negative number as an answer. The formula multiples certain values together. A positive number multiplied by a negative number returns a negative number as the answer. Therefore, just looking for a negative number among the values at the end of the tracer arrows may help identify the problem, perhaps within just a few seconds!

The Watch Window lets you watch the calculated results of a formula, but without the limitation of having the cell be in the viewing area of Excel. This is helpful when you're working on correcting formulas that use precedents that are scattered about the worksheet or workbook.

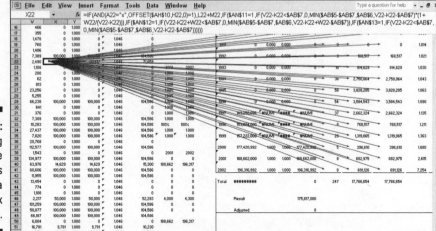

Figure 4-14:
Examining
the
components
of a
complex
formula.

First, to set up a watch, follow these steps:

1. **Click the Show Watch Window on the Formula Auditing Toolbar.**

2. **In the Watch Window, click the Add Watch button.**

3. **Use the RefEdit control (the little square button to the right of the entry box) to specify the cell(s), or type in the cell address or range.**

4. **Click the Add button to complete setting up the watch.**

Figure 4-15 shows the Watch Window with a watch already in place. Cell C6 on the Costs worksheet is being watched. The formula uses precedents from both the Orders and Shipping worksheets. The Watch Window sits on top of the workbook and stays visible regardless of which worksheet is active. This means, for example, that you could try out different values on the Orders worksheet and see the result in the calculation in Costs!C6, but without having to bounce around the worksheets to see how new values alter the calculated result.

Figure 4-15:
Using the
Watch
Window to
keep an
eye on a
formula's
result.

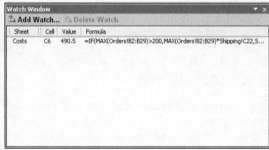

You can add a cell to the Watch Window by simply right-clicking on the cell and choosing Add Watch from the list of options.

The Watch Window also lets you delete a watch. That's a good thing or else you would end up with a bunch of watches you no longer need! To delete a watch:

1. **Select a watch from the list of watches in the Watch Window.**

2. **Click on the Delete Watch window.**

The Evaluate Formula dialog box walks you through the sequential steps used in calculating a result from a formula. This is useful to track down errors in formulas that are long, or have precedents. For example, the formula =IF(MAX(Orders!B2:B29)>200,MAX(Orders!B2:B29)*Shipping!C22, Shipping!C24) refers to different worksheets. Using the Evaluate Formula dialog box makes it easy to see how this formula is worked out by Excel. The step-by-step approach lets you see what is done at each step.

Figure 4-16 shows the Evaluate Formula dialog box at the start of evaluating the formula. With each successive click on the Evaluate button, the Evaluation box displays the interim results. The Step In and Step Out buttons are enabled during the steps that work on the precedents.

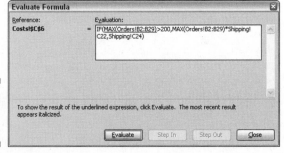

Figure 4-16:
Evaluating a
formula.

The Evaluate Formula dialog box is great for really seeing how each little step feeds into the final calculated result. Using this dialog box lets you pinpoint exactly where a complex formula has gone sour.

Part II

Evaluating Loans and Investments

The 5th Wave   By Rich Tennant

"The first thing we should do is get you two into a good mutual fund. Let me get out the 'Magic 8-Ball' and we'll run some options."

In this part . . .

Are you a money minded person? We have just the thing for you. Part II is all about loans, investments, depreciation, and internal rates of return. Chapter 5 explains how Excel works with and formats monetary values. Did you know that Excel is so smart it can work with your local currency? Following next is the ever useful basic financial functions of Excel. Keeping tabs on loans has never been easier. Heck, you can even figure whether a loan is worth it in the first place! Chapter 6 takes this up a notch to demonstrate advanced financial functions that calculate depreciation and internal rates of returns. The kind of stuff you would think to ask an accountant about. Only now you can figure it out yourself!

Chapter 5

Calculating Loan Payments and Interest Rates

There is a saying — a penny saved is a penny earned. A penny by itself is not much. But add a little savings here and there over the life of a loan, and the sum could be significant! Just think of what you can do with the extra money — extend a vacation, give it to charity, or save it for a rainy day.

Taking out a car loan, a mortgage, or another type of loan involves planning how you want to manage the loan payments. In the simplest terms, all you may need to know is the amount of your monthly payment. But knowing the components of a loan and being able to compare one loan with another can help you to manage your financial resources in your own best interest.

Consider an auto loan, one of the most common loan types. The factors involved include the cost of the vehicle, the down payment, the length of the loan, and the interest rate. Excel can help you see how all these factors affect your bottom line, letting you make the best decision (I would love to get the Ferrari, but the Hyundai will have to do).

You can use the financial functions in Excel to crunch the numbers for your loans. You supply these functions with the relevant numbers: the principal amount, the interest rate, the *period* (how often you make a payment), and the length of the loan. Then, the functions return an answer such as your payment amount. In this chapter, we show you how to use these functions to turn your finance figures into meaningful results.

The *principal* is the amount being borrowed. The *interest rate* is the annual percentage that the lender charges for lending the money. Your total payments will equal the principal plus the sum of all interest charges.

Understanding How Excel Handles Money

Excel is a lot more than a simple adding machine. It has great tools for working with money values, and a number of ways of presenting the amounts. For example, Excel makes it easy for you to make sure your financial amounts are displayed with two decimal points. You can even work with different currencies from around the world. You need to understand how to use the features before we get to the fun part of the chapter.

Going with the cash flow

Excel works with money on a cash flow basis. In other words, money amounts are treated either as a cash flow *in* (money you receive) or a cash flow *out* (money you pay out). Yes, we know, there always seems to be too many of the latter and not enough of the former — but hey, you can't blame Excel for that!

Excel represents cash flow in as positive numbers and cash flow out as negative numbers. For example, when you calculate the payments on a loan, the situation is as follows:

- ✔ The amount of the loan is entered as a positive value, because this is the money you'll receive from the bank or whoever is giving you the loan.

- ✔ The monthly payment that Excel calculates is a negative value because this is money that you'll be paying out.

Formatting for dollars

One of Excel's shining strengths is accepting, manipulating, and reporting on monetary data. As such, Excel provides robust formatting for numeric data, including the ability to control the placement of commas and decimals, and even how to format negative values.

People are used to seeing money amounts formatted with a currency symbol and a certain number of decimal places. In the U.S. and Canada, that is the dollar sign and two decimal places. Let's face it — $199.95 looks like money but 199.950 does not. Excel makes formatting cells to display money amounts as easy as clicking a button. To format amounts as dollars, follow these steps:

1, **Select the cell or cells you want to format.**

2. **Click the Dollar ($) button on the toolbar.**

This technique assigns Excel's default currency format to the selected cells. In the U.S., the default currency format is:

- ✔ Dollar sign

- ✔ Two decimal places

- ✔ Negative numbers enclosed in parentheses

The default format depends on your locale, which is a setting of the operating system. If you're in Italy, for example, the locale should be set so that the default currency format is the euro (€).

But suppose you don't want the default currency formatting — perhaps you're in the U.S. and working on a spreadsheet for the London office. You can specify the currency symbol, the number of decimal places, and how negative values are shown by following these steps:

1. **Select the cell or cells you want to format.**

2. **Choose Format ⇨ Cells from the menu to open the Format Cells dialog box.**

3. **In the Format Cells dialog box, select the Number tab, as shown in Figure 5-1.**

4. **Click Currency in the Category list.**

5. **Select the desired number of decimal places from the Decimal Places drop-down list.**

6. **Select the desired currency symbol from the Symbol drop-down list.**

7. **Select the desired format for negative numbers from the Negative Numbers list.**

8. **Click OK to apply the formatting.**

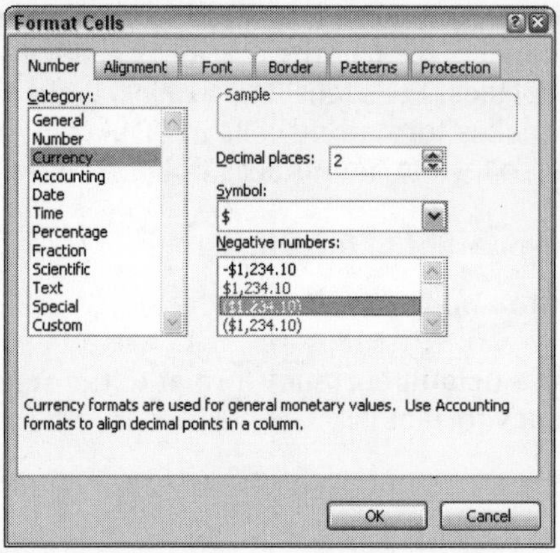

Figure 5-1:
Using the
Format Cells
dialog box
to control
numeric
display.

Choosing your separators

When numbers are formatted as currency, two separator symbols are typically used — one to separate thousands and the other to separate the decimal part of the value. In the U.S., commas are used for thousands and the period for the decimal:

$12,345.67

Other countries have different ways of doing this. In many European countries, for example, the period is used to separate thousands and the comma is used for the decimal. In addition, the currency symbol is often at the end of the number. An amount in euros, for example, may be formatted as follows:

12.345,67€

In almost all situations, the operating system's locale settings will result in the proper separators being used automatically. If you need to change the separators from the defaults, following these steps:

1. **Choose Tools ⇨ Options to open the Options dialog box.**

2. **In the Options dialog box, click the International tab, as shown in Figure 5-2.**

3. **In the Number Handling section, uncheck the Use System Separators check box.**

4. **Enter the desired separators in the Decimal Separator and Thousands Separator boxes.**

5. **Click OK to apply your settings.**

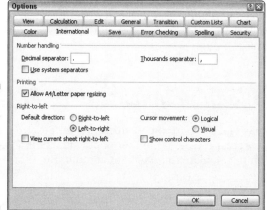

Figuring the Numbers on Your Loans

Loans are part of almost everyone's life. At the personal level, you may need to deal with car loans, education loans, and a home mortgage. From a business perspective, companies from the smallest to the largest often use loans to fund new equipment, expansion, and so on. No matter what kind of loan you need, Excel has the tools that permit you to evaluate loans and calculate specific details.

Most loans have the following five factors to deal with:

- ✔ **Loan principal:** The amount you're borrowing. For example if you are interested in a loan for $5,000, the loan principal *is* $5,000.

- ✔ **Interest rate:** The cost to borrow the principal. This is how lenders make money. The interest rate is a fee, so to speak, that a borrower pays to a lender. Usually, but not always, the interest rate is expressed as a percent per year.

- ✔ **Payment period:** Loans are usually paid back by paying a periodic amount. Most often the period is monthly.

- ✔ **Duration of the loan:** This is the count of payment periods. For example a loan may have 36 monthly payments.

- ✔ **Payment:** The amount you pay each payment period.

Each of these factors is related to all the others. If you borrow more, your monthly payments will be higher —that's no surprise. If you get a low interest rate, you may be able to pay off your loan in less time — that may be something to consider!

The functions used to calculate loan factors work with the same group of inputs, namely the five factors just listed. The functions typically accept three or four inputs as data and then calculate the desired value, kind of like the way algebra works.

Calculating loan payments with PMT

The PMT function tells you the periodic payment amount for your loan. If you know the principal, interest rate, and number of payments for a loan, you can use the PMT function to calculate the payment amount. But first, a word about interest rates.

Most loan interest rates are expressed as an annual rate. However, Excel needs the interest rate per payment *period* in order to calculate properly. For example, if you're calculating for a loan with monthly payments, you need the monthly interest rate. You can easily get this number by dividing the annual interest rate by 12, the number of months in a year. To calculate a loan payment, follow these steps:

1. **Enter the loan principal, annual interest rate, and number of payment periods in separate cells within the worksheet.**

   You can add labels to adjacent cells to identify the values, if desired.

2. **Position the cursor in the cell where you want the results to display.**

3. **Enter =PMT(to begin the function entry.**

4. **Click the cell where you entered the interest rate, or just enter the cell address.**

5. **Enter /12 to divide the annual interest rate to get the monthly interest rate.**

6. **Enter a comma (,).**

7. **Click the cell where you entered the number of payments, or just enter the cell address.**

8. **Enter a comma (,).**

9. **Click the cell where you entered the principal amount, or just enter the cell address.**

10. **Enter a closing parenthesis to end the function, and press Enter.**

Watch those percents! Remember that a percent is really one one-hundredth, so 5 percent is really the numerical value 0.05. Although you can format values to display as percents in Excel, remember to enter the proper value.

Figure 5-3 shows how we set up a worksheet with values and returned the periodic payment amount for a loan. The amount is expressed as a negative number because payments are a cash flow out.

For example, you may be considering taking a loan out from the bank for some house additions. Using real numbers, the loan may be structured like this:

✔ A loan amount of $15,000 (the principal)

✔ An annual interest rate of 5 percent

✔ A monthly payment period

✔ A payment period of 24 payments

This summarizes four of the key parameters. The PMT function figures out the fifth — the periodic payment.

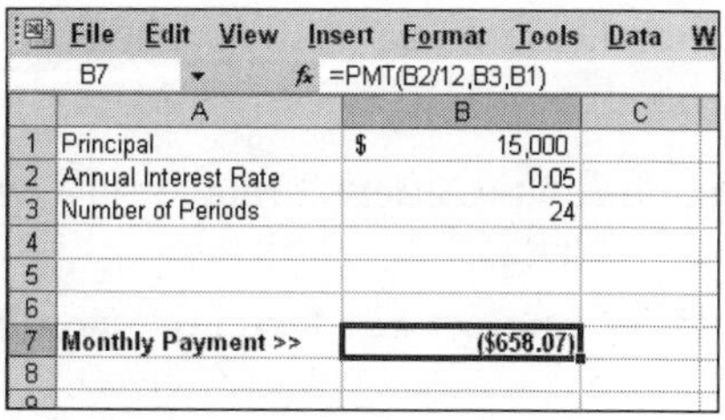

Figure 5-3:
The PMT function calculates the loan payment amount.

Although the PMT function returns the constant periodic payback amount for a loan, note that each payment actually consists of two portions. One portion goes toward reducing the principal, and the other portion is the interest payment. As if this weren't already confusing enough!

You may notice some new terms when using this function: PV, FV, and NPer. In financial terminology, *present value* (PV) refers to the value of a transaction at the present moment. When dealing with a loan, for example, the present value is the amount you receive from the loan — in other words the principal. The term *future value* (FV) refers to the value of a transaction at some point in the future, such as the amount you'll accumulate by saving $50 a month for five years. *NPer* stands for the number of payment periods in the loan.

Using IPMT to calculate interest payments

The IPMT function tells you the interest payment for a given period. In each payment period during a typical loan, the payment consists of a portion set to reduce the principal of the loan, with the other portion of the payment being the interest on the principal. The amount of interest varies payment by payment. In a typical loan, the portion of the payment that is interest is highest in the first period and is reduced in each successive period.

The IPMT function takes four inputs: the principal, the interest rate, the number of payments for the loan, and the number of the payment you're interested in. For example, a loan may have 24 payments and you're interested in how much interest is included in the 12th payment. For some types of loans, the interest is tax deductible, so this information may literally be worth something! Here are the steps to use the IMPT function:

1. **Enter the loan principal, the annual interest rate, the number of payment periods, and the number of the actual period for which you want to calculate the interest in separate cells within a column on the worksheet.**

   You can add labels to adjacent cells to identify the values, if desired.

2. **Position the cursor in the cell where you want the results to appear.**

3. **Enter =IPMT(to begin the function entry.**

4. **Click the cell where you entered the interest rate, or just enter the cell address.**

5. **Enter /12 to divide the annual interest rate to get the monthly interest rate.**

6. **Enter a comma (,).**

7. **Click the cell where you entered the number of the payment to analyze, or just enter the cell address.**

8. **Enter a comma (,).**

9. **Click the cell where you entered the number of payments, or just enter the cell address.**

10. **Enter a comma (,).**

11. **Click the cell where you entered the principal amount, or just enter the cell address.**

12. **Enter a closing parenthesis to end the function, and press Enter.**

The IPMT function returns the amount of the specified payment that is interest. This amount will be smaller than the full periodic payment amount. How much smaller depends on which sequential payment is being examined. The remainder of the payment — the part that is not interest — goes to reduce the principal.

You can use two optional arguments with IPMT:

- **Future Value:** The amount you wish the loan to be worth at the end of its life. The default is 0.

- **Type:** This tells the function whether payments are applied at the end of the period or the beginning of the period. A value of 0 indicates the end of the period. A value of 1 indicates the beginning of the period. The default is 0.

These optional arguments when used become the respective fifth and sixth arguments.

Using PPMT to calculate payments toward principal

The PPMT function tells you the payment on principal for a given period. In each payment period during a typical loan, the payment consists of a portion that goes toward reducing the principal of the loan and another portion that is interest. With the PPMT function, you can find out the amount that reduces the principal.

The ratio of the interest portion to the payment on principal portion varies payment by payment. In a typical loan, the portion of the payment that is interest is highest in the first period and is reduced in each successive period. Turning that around, the last payment is almost all toward paying down the principal.

The PPMT function takes four inputs: the principal, the interest rate, the number of payments for the loan, and the number of the payment in question. For example, a loan may have 36 payments and you're interested in how much principal is included in just the last payment. Here are the steps to use this function:

1. **Enter the loan principal, the annual interest rate, the number of payment periods, and the number of the actual period for which the interest is to be calculated in separate cells within the worksheet.**

    You can add labels to adjacent cells to identify the values, if you want.

2. **Position the cursor in the cell where you want the results to appear.**

3. **Enter** =PPMT(**to begin the function entry.**

4. **Click the cell where you entered the interest rate, or just enter the cell address.**

5. **Enter /12 to divide the annual interest rate to get the monthly interest rate.**

6. **Enter a comma (,).**

7. **Click the cell where you entered the number of the payment to analyze, or just enter the cell address.**

8. **Enter a comma (,).**

9. **Click the cell where you entered the number of payments, or just enter the cell address.**

10. **Enter a comma (,).**

11. **Click the cell where you entered the principal amount, or just enter the cell address.**

12. **Enter a closing parenthesis to end the function, and press Enter.**

The PPMT function returns the amount of the payment that reduces the principal. This amount will be smaller than the full periodic payment amount. How much smaller depends on which sequential payment is being examined. The remainder of the payment, of course, is the interest charge.

The PMT function tells how much each payment is. The IPMT function tells you the interest portion. The PPMT tells you the principal function. For any given payment period, the amounts returned by IPMT and PPMT should equal the amount returned by PMT.

You can use two optional arguments with PPMT:

✔ **Future Value:** The amount you want the loan to be worth at the end of its life. The default is 0.

✔ **Type:** This tells the function whether payments are applied at the end of the period or the beginning of the period. A value of 0 indicates the end of the period. A value of 1 indicates the beginning of the period. The default is 0.

These optional arguments, when used, become the respective fifth and sixth arguments.

Calculating the number of payments with NPER

The NPER function tells you how many payments are necessary to pay off a loan. This is useful when you know how much you can afford to pay per month, and need to know how long it will take to pay off the loan. The inputs for this function are the principal, the interest rate, and the periodic payment amount.

Here's how to use the NPER function:

1. **Enter the loan principal, the annual interest rate, and the periodic payment amount (the amount you can afford to pay) into separate cells on your worksheet.**

   Enter the periodic payment amount as a negative number, because payments are a cash flow out. You can add labels to adjacent cells to identify the values, if you want.

2. **Position the cursor in the cell where you want the results to display.**

3. **Enter =NPER(to begin the function entry.**

4. **Click the cell where you entered the interest rate, or just enter the cell address.**

5. **Enter /12 to divide the annual interest rate to get the monthly interest rate.**

6. **Enter a comma (,).**

7. **Click the cell where you entered the periodic payment amount, or just enter the cell address.**

8. **Enter a comma (,).**

9. **Click the cell where you entered the principal amount, or just enter the cell address.**

10. **Enter a closing parenthesis to end the function, and press Enter.**

Figure 5-4 shows how we set up a worksheet with values and used the NPER function to find out how many payments are necessary to pay off a loan. In our example, we assume you can afford to pay $200 per month for a loan. The amount you need is $4,000, and you're able to get a 6 percent interest rate.

Figure 5-4:
The NPER
function
calculates
the number
of payments
for a loan.

	File	Edit	View	Insert	Format	Tools	Data	Wi
	B7	▾		*fx*	=NPER(B2/12,B3,B1)			

	A	B	C
1	Principal	$ 4,000	
2	Annual Interest Rate	0.06	
3	Affordable Monthly Payment	$ (200)	
4			
5			
6			
7	**Number of Payments >>**	21.12	
8			
9			
10			

With this set of assumptions, the NPER function tells returns a value of 21.12 months to pay off the loan. We don't think anyone will mind if you round that off to 21 months. Knowing you'll pay off the loan in less than two years may very well allow you to plan ahead for some other activity at that time. Did someone say "Las Vegas"!?

You can use two optional arguments with NPER:

✔ **Future Value:** The amount you want the loan to be worth at the end of its life. The default is 0.

✔ **Type:** This tells the function whether payments are applied at the end of the period or the beginning of the period. A value of 0 indicates the end of the period. A value of 1 indicates the beginning of the period. The default is 0.

These optional arguments, when used, become the respective fifth and sixth arguments.

Using RATE to calculate the interest rate

The RATE function tells you what the interest rate is on a loan. This function is great for comparing loan offers. Although a loan offer will always include an interest rate, you may want to use Excel to double-check and ensure that some other fees are not included in the payments. Then you can compare different loan scenarios to see which one offers the true lowest interest rate. We don't think anyone wants to pay more than he has to!

Some lenders charge fees as well as an annual interest rate. When these fees are figured in, the *effective interest rate* will be higher than the stated interest rate. You can use the RATE function to determine the effective interest rate for a loan. If it's the same as the stated interest rate, then you know no fees are being added.

The inputs for this function are the principal, the number of payments, and the fixed amount of the periodic payment. Here's how to use the RATE function:

1. **Enter the loan principal, the number of payment periods, and the amount that you will pay each month in separate cells within the worksheet.**

   Enter the monthly payment amount as a negative number, because it is a cash flow out. You can add labels to adjacent cells to identify the values, if you want.

2. **Position the cursor in the cell where you want the results to appear.**

3. **Enter =RATE(to begin the function entry.**

4. **Click the cell where you entered the number of periods, or just enter the cell address.**

5. **Enter a comma (,).**

6. **Click the cell where you entered the monthly payment amount, or just enter the cell address.**

7. **Enter a comma (,).**

8. **Click the cell where you entered the principal amount, or just enter the cell address.**

9. **Enter a closing parenthesis to end the function, and press Enter.**

The RATE function returns the interest rate *per period.* This number can be misleading. The periodic interest amount may be small enough that it is displayed as 0 percent if the formatting in the cell isn't set to display enough decimal points.

To find out the annual rate, you simply need to take the number returned by RATE and multiply it by 12. To do this:

1. **Position the cursor in the cell where you want the annual interest rate to appear.**

2. **Enter the equal sign (=).**

3. **Click the cell where the RATE function returned the periodic interest rate.**

4. **Enter the multiplication symbol ($\times$).**

5. **Enter 12.**

6. **Press Enter.**

As an example, assume a loan principal of $15,000 with a monthly payment of $650. The loan is to be paid off in 24 months. Figure 5-5 shows a worksheet with these figures. The periodic interest rate is calculated with the RATE function, and then the annual rate is calculated by multiplying the periodic interest rate by 12.

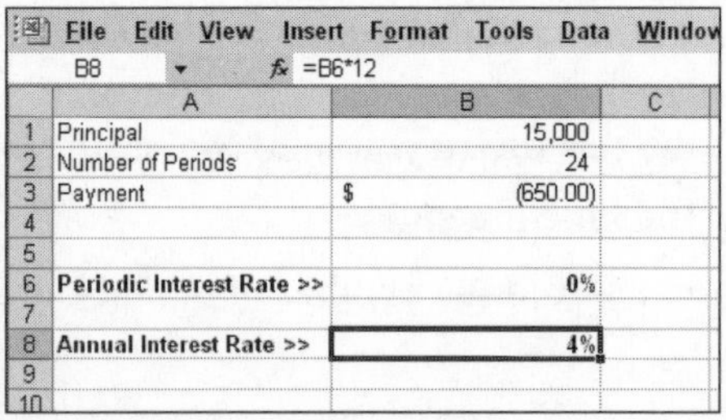

Figure 5-5:
The RATE function calculates the periodic interest rate.

You can use three optional arguments with RATE:

- **Future Value:** The amount you want the loan to be worth at the end of its life. The default is 0.

- **Type:** This tells the function whether payments are applied at the end of the period or the beginning of the period. A value of 0 indicates the end of the period. A value of 1 indicates the beginning of the period. The default is 0.

- **Guess:** An estimate of what the interest rate should be. It is possible the function will need this value to determine a result. (See Excel's Help system for further information.) The default value is .1 (for 10 percent).

These optional arguments, when used, become the respective fourth, fifth, and sixth arguments.

Using PV to calculate the principal on a loan

The PV function tells you what the principal amount of a loan is when you know the other loan factors, such as the interest rate and the number of payment periods. You can use PV to determine how much you can borrow when you already know how much you can pay each month and how long you can make payments.

The inputs for this function are the interest rate, the number of payment periods, and the monthly payment amount. The interest rate used in the function is the periodic rate, not the annual rate. Here's how to use the PV function:

1. **Enter the annual interest rate, the number of payment periods, and the periodic payment amount into separate cells on your worksheet.**

   Enter the periodic payment amount as a negative number, because payments are a cash flow out. You can add labels to adjacent cells to identify the values, if desired.

2. **Position the cursor in the cell where you want the results to appear.**

3. **Enter =PV(to begin the function entry.**

4. **Click the cell where you entered the interest rate, or just enter the cell address.**

5. **Enter /12 to divide the annual interest rate to get the monthly interest rate.**

6. **Enter a comma (,).**

7. **Click the cell where you entered the number of payments, or just enter the cell address.**

8. **Enter a comma (,).**

9. **Click the cell where you entered the periodic payment amount, or just enter the cell address.**

10. **Enter a closing parenthesis to end the function, and press Enter.**

As an example, assume a monthly payment amount of $600 The annual interest rate is 5 percent. There are 24 monthly payments. Figure 5-6 shows a worksheet with these figures.

With these assumptions, the loan principal is $13,676. Altering any of the parameters will cause PV to return a different amount of principal. For example, raising the interest rate to 7.5 percent tells you that you can only borrow $13,333. Although you may often think of how much you're borrowing, having interest in the interest is just as important!

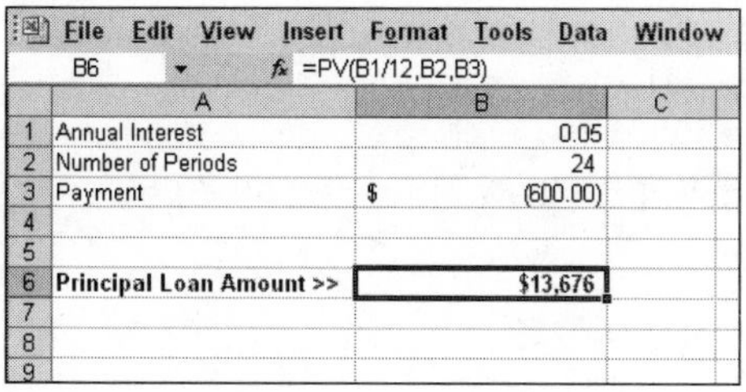

Figure 5-6:
The PV function calculates the principal amount of a loan.

You can use two optional arguments with PV:

- **Future Value:** The amount you want the loan to be worth at the end of its life. The default is 0.

- **Type:** This tells the function whether payments are applied at the end of the period or the beginning of the period. A value of 0 indicates the end of the period. A value of 1 indicates the beginning of the period. The default is 0.

These optional arguments, when used, become the respective fifth and sixth arguments.

Chapter 6

Performing Advanced Financial Calculations

In This Chapter

▶ Determining what an investment is worth

▶ Using different depreciation methods

▶ Evaluating business opportunities

Money makes the world go 'round, so the saying goes. We have a new one: Excel functions make the money go 'round. Excel has functions that let you figure out what an investment will be worth at a future date. We all know it's a good thing to look for a good interest rate on an investment. With the FV function, you can take this a step further and know how much the investment will be worth down the road.

Have you ever wondered what to do with some extra money? You can put it in the bank, you can pay off a debt, or you can purchase something. Excel helps you figure out the best course of action by using the IRR function. The IRR function lets you boil down each option to a single value that you can then use to compare opportunities and select the best one.

For the business set, Excel has a number of functions to help create depreciation schedules. Look no further than the SLN, SYD, DB, and DDB functions for help in this area. Brush up on these and you can talk shop with your accountant!

Looking into the Future with FV

The FV function tells you what an investment will be worth in the future. The function takes an initial amount of money and also takes into account additional periodic fixed payments. You also specify a rate of return — the interest rate — and the returned value tells you what the investment will be worth after a specified period of time.

For example, you start a savings account with a certain amount, say $1,000. Every month you add an additional $50 to the account. The bank pays an annual interest rate of 5percent. At the end of two years, what is value of the account?

This is the type of question the FV function answers. The function takes five arguments:

✔ **Interest rate:** This is the annual interest rate. When entered in the function, it needs to be divided by the number of payments per year — presumably 12, if the payments are monthly.

✔ **Number of payments:** This is the total number of payments in the investment. These payments are the ones beyond the initial investment; don't include the initial investment in this figure. If payments occur monthly and the investment is for 3 years, then there are 36 payments.

✔ **Payment amount:** This is the fixed amount contributed to the investment each payment period.

✔ **Initial investment (also called PV or present value):** This is the amount the investment starts with. A possible value is 0, which means no initial amount is used to start the investment. This is an optional argument. If left out, 0 is assumed.

✔ **How payments are applied:** The periodic payments may be applied at either the beginning of each period or the end of each period. This affects the result to a small but noticeable degree. Either a 0 or a 1 can be entered. A 0 tells the function that payments occur at the end of the period. A 1 tells the function that payments occur at the start of the period. This is an optional argument. If left out, 0 is assumed.

 When using the FV function, be sure to enter the initial investment amount and the periodic payment amount as negative numbers. Although you're investing these monies, you're essentially paying out (even if it's into your own account). Therefore, these are cash flows out.

Here's how to use the FV function:

1. **Enter the annual interest rate, the number of payment periods, the periodic payment amount, and the initial investment amount in separate cells within the worksheet.**

   You can add labels to adjacent cells to identify the values, if desired.

2. **Position the cursor in the cell where you want the results to appear.**

3. Enter =FV(to begin the function entry.

4. Click on the cell where you entered the annual interest rate, or enter the cell address.

5. Enter /12 to divide the annual interest rate to get the monthly interest rate.

6. Enter a comma (,).

7. Click on the cell where you entered the total number of payments, or enter the cell address.

8. Enter a comma (,).

9. Click on the cell where you entered the periodic payment amount, or enter the cell address.

10. Enter a comma (,).

11. Click on the cell where you entered the initial investment amount, or enter the cell address.

12. Optionally, enter a comma (,), and then enter either 0 or 1 to identify whether payments are made at the beginning of the period (0) or at the end of the period (1).

13. Enter a closing parenthesis to end the function, and press Enter.

Figure 6-1 shows how much an investment is worth after two years. The investment is begun with $1,000 and an additional $50 is added each month. The interest rate is 5percent. The value of the investment at the end is $2,364.24. The actual layout was $2,200 ($1,000 + [$50 × 24]). The account has earned $164.24.

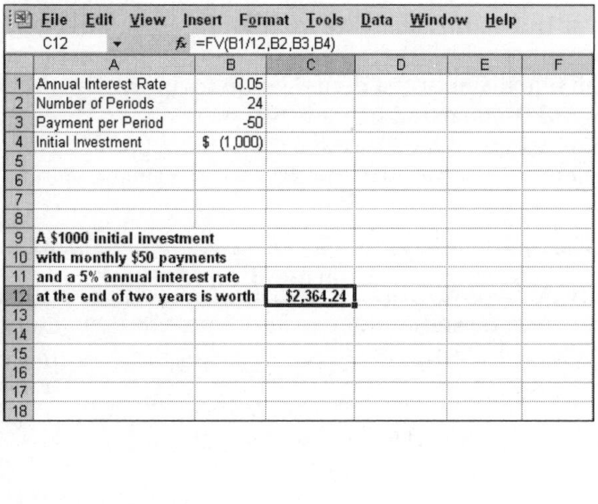

Figure 6-1:
Earning
extra money
in an
investment.

Depreciating the Finer Things in Life

Depreciation is the technique of allocating the cost of an asset over the useful period that the asset is used. Depreciation is applied to *capital assets,* tangible goods that provide usefulness for a year or more.

Vehicles, buildings, and equipment are the type of assets that depreciation can be applied to. A tuna sandwich is not a capital asset, because its usefulness is going to last for just the few minutes it takes someone to eat it — although the person eating it may expect to capitalize on it!

Let's take the example of a business purchasing a delivery truck. The truck costs $35,000. It's expected to be used for 12 years; this is known as the *life* of the asset. At the end of 12 years, the vehicle's estimated worth will be $8,000. These figures follow certain terminology used in the depreciation formulas:

- ✔ **Cost:** This is the initial cost of the item ($35,000). This could include not just the price of the item, but costs associated with getting and installing the item, such as delivery costs.

- ✔ **Salvage:** This is the value of the item at the end of the useful life of the item ($8,000).

- ✔ **Life:** This is the number of periods that the depreciation is applied to. This is usually expressed in years (in this case, 12 years).

Depreciation is calculated in different ways. Some techniques assume that an asset provides the majority of its usefulness during the earlier periods of its life. Depreciation in this case is applied on a sliding scale from the first period to the last. The bulk of the depreciation gets applied in the first few periods. This is known as an *accelerated depreciation schedule.* Sometimes the depreciation amount runs out sooner than the asset's life. Alternatively, depreciation can be applied evenly over all the periods. In this case, each period of the asset's life has an equal amount of depreciation to apply. The different depreciation methods are summarized in Table 6-1.

The depreciable cost is the original cost minus the salvage value.

Table 6-1	Depreciation Methods	
Method	*Comments*	*Excel Function That Uses the Method*
Straight Line	Evenly applies the depreciable cost (Cost – Salvage) among the periods. Uses the formula (Cost – Salvage) ÷ Number of Periods.	SLN

Method	Comments	Excel Function That Uses the Method
Sum of Years' Digits	First sums up the periods, literally. For example, if there are five periods, then the method first calculates the sum of the years' digits as: $1 + 2 + 3 + 4 + 5 = 15$. Creates an accelerated depreciation schedule. See Excel Help for more information.	SYD
Double Declining Balance	Creates an accelerated depreciation schedule by doubling the Straight Line depreciation rate, but then applies it to the running declining balance of the asset cost, instead of to the fixed depreciable cost.	DDB, DB

Figure 6-2 shows a worksheet with a few different depreciation methods. The methods use the example of a delivery truck that costs $35,000, is used for 12 years, and has an ending value of $8,000. An important calculation in all these methods is the depreciable cost, which is the original cost minus the salvage value. In this example, the depreciable cost is $27,000, calculated as $35,000 − $8,000.

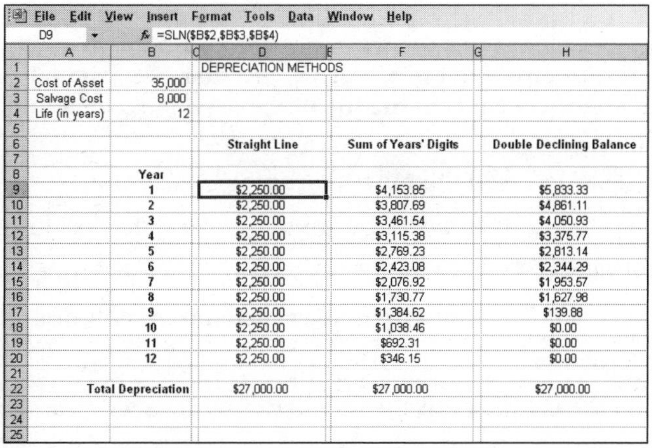

Figure 6-2: Depreciating an asset.

In the three depreciation methods shown in Figure 6-2 — straight line, sum of the years' digits, and double declining balance — all end having the accumulated depreciation at the end of life equal to the depreciable cost, or the cost minus the salvage.

However each method arrives at the total in a different way. The Straight Line method simply applies an even amount among the periods. The Sum of Years' Digits and Double Declining Balance methods accelerate the depreciation. In fact the Double Declining Balance method does it to such a degree that all the depreciation is accounted for before the asset's life is over.

Calculating straight line depreciation

The SLN function calculates the depreciation amount for each period of the life of the asset. The arguments are simple; just the cost, salvage, and the number of periods. In Figure 6-2, each cell in the range D9:D20 has the same formula: =SLN($B$2,$B$3,$B$4). Because straight line depreciation provides an equal amount of depreciation to each period, it makes sense that each cell uses the formula verbatim. The answer is the same regardless of the period (this approach differs from the accelerated depreciation methods that follow).

Using dollar signs ($) in front of column and row indicators fixes the cell address so it won't change.

Here's how to use the SLN function:

1. **Enter three values in a worksheet — the cost of an asset, the salvage value (make sure that the salvage is less than the original cost), and the number of periods in the life of the asset (usually a number of years).**

2. **Enter =SLN(to begin the function entry.**

3. **Click on the cell that has the original cost, or enter its address.**

4. **Enter a comma (,).**

5. **Click on the cell that has the salvage amount, or enter its address.**

6. **Enter a comma (,).**

7. **Click on the cell that has the number of periods, or enter its address.**

8. **Enter a closing parenthesis to end the function, and press Enter.**

The returned value is the amount of depreciation per period. Each period has the same depreciation amount.

Using the SYD function for accelerated depreciation

The SYD function creates an accelerated depreciation schedule (that is, more depreciation is applied in the earlier periods of the asset's life). The method uses an interesting technique of first summing up the years' digits. So for a depreciation schedule that covers 5 years, a value of 15 is first calculated as $1 + 2 + 3 + 4 + 5 = 15$. If the schedule is for 10 years, then the first step of the method is to calculate the sum of the digits 1 through 10, like this: $1 + 2 + 3 + 4 + 5 + 6 + 7 + 8 + 9 + 10 = 55$.

The years' digit sum is then used as the denominator in calculations with the actual digits themselves to determine a percentage per period. The digits in the calculations are the reverse of the actual periods. In other words, in a five-year depreciation schedule, the depreciation for the first period is calculated as $(5 \div 15) \times$ Depreciable Cost. The second period depreciation is calculated as $(4 \div 15) \times$ Depreciable Cost. The following table makes it clear, with an assumed 5-year depreciation on a depreciable cost of $6,000:

Period	Calculation	Result
1	$(5/15) \times 6000$	$2,000
2	$(4/15) \times 6000$	$1,600
3	$(3/15) \times 6000$	$1,200
4	$(2/15) \times 6000$	$800
5	$(1/15) \times 6000$	$400

Guess what? You don't even need to know how this works! Excel does all the figuring out for you. The SYD function takes four arguments: the cost, the salvage, the life (the number of periods), and the period to be calculated.

SYD returns the depreciation for a single period. Earlier, we showed you that the SLN function also returns the depreciation per period, but because all periods are the same, the SLN function didn't need to have an actual period entered as an argument.

The SYD function returns a different depreciation amount for each period, so the period must be entered as an argument. In Figure 6-2, each formula in the range F9:F20 uses the SYD function but has a different period as the fourth argument. For example, cell F9 has the formula =SYD($B$2,$B$3,$B$4,B9) and cell F10 has the formula =SYD($B$2,$B$3,$B$4,B10). The last argument provides a different value.

Here's how to use the SYD function to calculate the depreciation for one period:

1. **Enter three values in a worksheet: the cost of an asset, the salvage value (make sure that the salvage is less than the original cost), and the number of periods in the life of the asset (usually a number of years).**

2. **Enter =SYD(to begin the function entry.**

3. **Click on the cell that has the original cost, or enter its address.**

4. **Enter a comma (,).**

5. **Click on the cell that has the salvage amount, or enter its address.**

6. **Enter a comma (,).**

7. **Click on the cell that has the number of periods, or enter its address.**

8. **Enter a comma (,).**

9. **Enter a number for the period for which to calculate the depreciation.**

10. **Enter a closing parenthesis to end the function, and press Enter.**

The returned value is the amount of depreciation for the entered period. To calculate the depreciation for the entire set of periods, you need to enter a formula with the SYD function into the same number of cells as there are periods. In this case, each cell would have a different period entered for the fourth argument (refer to Figure 6-2).

Creating an accelerated depreciation schedule with the DDB function

The Double Declining Balance method provides an accelerated depreciation schedule but calculates the amounts differently than the Sum of Years' Digits method.

Although rooted in the doubling of the Straight Line method (which is not an accelerated method), the calculation for each successive period is based on the remaining value of the asset after each period instead of to the depreciable cost. Because the remaining value is reduced each period, the schedule for each period is different.

The DDB function takes five arguments. The first four are required. These are the cost, the salvage, the life (the number of periods), and the period for which the depreciation is to be calculated. The fifth argument is the factor. A factor of 2 tells the function to use the Double Declining Balance method. Other values can be used, such 1.5. The factor is the rate at which the balance declines. A smaller value (than the default of 2) results in a longer time for the balance to decline. When the fifth argument is omitted, the value of 2 is the default.

The DDB function returns a different depreciation amount for each period, so the period must be entered as an argument. In Figure 6-2, each formula in the range H9:H20 uses the DDB function but has a different period as the fourth argument. For example, cell H9 has the formula =DDB($B$2,$B$3,$B$4,B9) and cell H10 has the formula =DDB($B$2,$B$3,$B$4,B10). The last argument provides a different value.

As shown in Figure 6-2 earlier, the Double Declining Balance method provides an even more accelerated depreciation schedule than the Sum of Years' Digits method. In fact, the depreciation is fully accounted for before the asset has reached the end of its life.

Here's how to use the DDB function to calculate the depreciation for one period:

1. **Enter three values in a worksheet: the cost of an asset, the salvage value (make sure that the salvage is less than the original cost), and the number of periods in the life of the asset (usually a number of years).**

2. **Enter =DDB(to begin the function entry.**

3. **Click on the cell that has the original cost, or enter its address.**

4. **Enter a comma (,).**

5. **Click on the cell that has the salvage amount, or enter its address.**

6. **Enter a comma (,).**

7. **Click on the cell that has the number of periods.**

8. **Enter a comma (,).**

9. **Enter a number for the period for which to calculate the depreciation.**

10. **If a variation on the Double Declining Balance method is desired, then enter a comma (,) and a numeric value other than 2.**

11. **Enter a closing parenthesis to end the function, and press Enter.**

The returned value is the amount of depreciation for the entered period. To calculate the depreciation for the entire set of periods, you need to enter a formula with the DDB function into the same number of cells as there are periods. In this case, each cell would have a different period entered for the fourth argument (refer to Figure 6-2).

There is no hard-and-fast rule for selecting the best depreciation method. However, it makes sense to use one that matches the depreciating value of the asset. For example, cars lose a good deal of their value in the first few years, so applying an accelerated depreciation schedule makes sense.

Calculating a depreciation schedule that starts in the middle of a year

Most assets are not purchased, delivered, and put into service on January 1. So Excel provides a depreciation formula, DB, that accounts for the periods being offset from the calendar year. The DB takes five arguments. The first four are the typical ones: the cost, the salvage, the life (the number of periods), and the period for which the depreciation is to be calculated. The fifth argument is the number of months in the first year. The fifth argument is optional, but when left out, the function will use 12 as a default.

For the fifth argument, a value of 3 means the depreciation starts in October (October through December is 3 months), so the amount of depreciation charged in the first calendar year is small. A value of 11 means the depreciation starts in February (February through December is 11 months).

Figure 6-3 shows a depreciation schedule created with the DB function. Note that the life of the asset is 12 years (in cell B4) but that the formula is applied to 13 different periods. Including an extra year is necessary because the first year is partial. The remaining handful of months must spill into an extra calendar year. The depreciation periods and the calendar years are offset from each other.

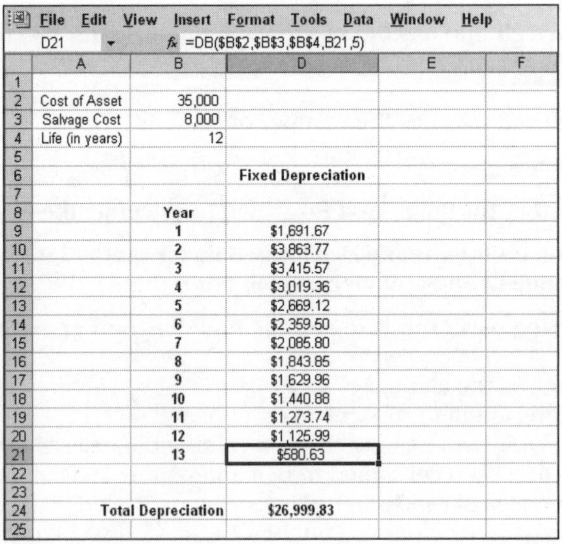

Figure 6-3: Offsetting depreciation periods from the calendar.

File Edit View Insert Format Tools Data Window Help				
D21 ▼	fx =DB($B$2,$B$3,$B$4,B21,5)			

	A	B	D	E	F
1					
2	Cost of Asset	35,000			
3	Salvage Cost	8,000			
4	Life (in years)	12			
5					
6			Fixed Depreciation		
7					
8		Year			
9		1	$1,691.67		
10		2	$3,863.77		
11		3	$3,415.57		
12		4	$3,019.36		
13		5	$2,669.12		
14		6	$2,359.50		
15		7	$2,085.80		
16		8	$1,843.85		
17		9	$1,629.96		
18		10	$1,440.88		
19		11	$1,273.74		
20		12	$1,125.99		
21		13	$580.63		
22					
23					
24		Total Depreciation	$26,999.83		
25					

The example in Figure 6-3 is for an asset put into service in August. Cell D9 has the formula =DB($B$2,$B$3,$B$4,B9,5). The fifth argument is 5, which indicates the first year depreciation covers 5 months — August, September, October, November, and December.

Here's how to use the DB function to calculate the depreciation for one period:

1. **Enter three values in a worksheet: the cost of an asset, the salvage value (make sure that the salvage is less than the original cost), and the number of periods in the life of the asset (usually a number of years).**

2. **Enter =DB(to begin the function entry.**

3. **Click on the cell that has the original cost, or enter its address.**

4. **Enter a comma (,).**

5. **Click on the cell that has the salvage amount, or enter its address.**

6. **Enter a comma (,).**

7. **Click on the cell that has the number of periods.**

8. **Enter a comma (,).**

9. **Enter a number for the period for which to calculate the depreciation.**

10. **Enter a comma (,).**

11. **Enter the number of months within the first year that the depreciation is applied to.**

12. **Enter a closing parenthesis to end the function, and press Enter.**

The returned value is the amount of depreciation for the entered period. To calculate the depreciation for the entire set of periods, you need to enter a formula with the DB function in the same number of cells as there are periods. However, you should make space for an additional period (refer to Figure 6-3).

Measuring Your Internals

Which is better to do — pay off your credit card or invest in Uncle Ralph's new business venture? You're about to finance a car. Should you put down a large down payment? Or should you put down a small amount and invest the rest? How can you make decisions about alternative financial opportunities like these?

The Internal Rate of Return (IRR) method helps answer these types of questions. The IRR function analyzes the cash flows in and out of an investment and calculates an interest rate that is the effective result of the cash flows. In other words, all the various cash flows are accounted for and one interest rate is returned. Then you can compare this figure to other financial opportunities.

Perhaps Uncle Ralph's business venture will provide a 10 percent return on your investment. On the other hand, the credit-card company charges you 12 percent on your balance. In this case, paying off the credit card is wiser. Why? Because earning 10 percent is pointless when you're just losing 12 percent elsewhere. Uncle Ralph will understand, won't he?

The IRR function takes two arguments. The first is required, the second is optional in some situations and required in others.

The first argument is an array of cash flows. Following the cash-flows standard, money coming in is entered as a positive value and money going out is entered as a negative value. Assuming the particular cash flows in and out are entered on a worksheet, the first argument to the function is the range of cells.

The second argument is a guess at what the result should be. We know this sounds crazy, but Excel may need your help here (though most times it won't). The IRR function works by starting with a guess at the result and calculating how closely the guess matches the data. Then it adjusts the guess up or down and repeats the process (a technique called *iteration*) over and over until it arrives at the correct answer. If it doesn't figure it out in 20 tries, then the #NUM! error is returned. In this case, you could enter a guess into the function to help it along. For example, 0.05 indicates a guess of 5 percent, 0.15 indicates a guess of 15 percent and so on. You can enter a negative number, too. For example, entering –0.05 tells the function you expect a 5 percent loss. If you don't enter a guess, Excel assumes 0.1 (10 percent).

Figure 6-4 shows a business venture that has been evaluated using IRR. The project is to create a music CD and market it. Assorted costs such as studio time are cash flows out, entered as negative numbers. The one positive value in cell B7 is the expected revenue.

The IRR function has been used to calculate an expected rate of return. The formula in cell B10 is =IRR(B3:B7). The entered range includes all the cash flows, in and out.

This project has an internal rate of return of 11 percent. By the way, the investment amount in this case is the sum of all the cash flows out — $8,400. Earning back $11,960 makes this a good investment. The revenue is significantly higher than the outlay.

Figure 6-4:
Calculating
the return
on a
business
venture.

	File	Edit	View	Insert	Format	Tools	Data	Window	Help	
B10			▼	*fx* =IRR(B3:B7)						
	A	B	C	D	E	F	G	H		
1										
2										
3		-5000		Studio Time						
4		-1000		Pressing CDs						
5		-2000		Marketing						
6		-400		Administrative Costs						
7		11960		Expected Revenue						
8										
9										
10		11%		Internal Rate of Return						
11										
12										

Even though a business opportunity seems worthy after IRR has been applied, you must consider other factors. For example you may have to *borrow* the money to invest in the business venture. The real number to look at is the IRR of the business venture less the cost of borrowing the money to invest.

However, the project can now be compared to other investments. Another project might calculate to a higher internal rate of return. Then the second project would make sense to pursue. Of course, don't forget the fun factor. Making a CD may be worth giving up a few extra points!

Figure 6-5 compares the business venture in Figure 6-4 with another investment opportunity. The second business venture is to start up a video-taping business for weddings and other affairs. There is a significant outlay for equipment and marketing. An internal rate of return is calculated for the first year, and then for the first and second year together. Cell H10 has the formula =IRR(H3:H5), and cell H11 has the formula =IRR(H3:H6). It's clear that even within the first year the second business venture surpasses the first.

Figure 6-5:
Comparing
business
opportun-
ities.

	File	Edit	View	Insert	Format	Tools	Data	Window	Help					Type a question for help ▼ _ ₽ ×
H10	▼		*fx* =IRR(H3:H5)											
	A	B	C D	E	F	G	H	I J	K	L	M	N	O	P
1		Business Venture 1					Business Venture 2							
2														
3		-5000	Studio Time				-9000	Purchase of Video Equipment						
4		-1000	Pressing CDs				-6500	Marketing						
5		-2000	Marketing				26000	First Year Expected Revenue						
6		-400	Administrative Costs				54000	Second Year Expected Revenue						
7		11960	Expected Revenue within one year											
8														
9														
10		11%	Internal Rate of Return				38%	Internal Rate of Return after 1 year						
11							107%	Internal Rate of Return after 2 years						
12														
13														
14														
15														

This is how to use the IRR function:

1. **Enter a series of cash flow values: Money paid out, such as the initial investment, is entered as a negative value; money coming in, such as revenue, is entered as a positive value.**

2. **Enter =IRR(to begin the function entry.**

3. **Drag the cursor over the range of cells containing the cash flows, or enter the range address.**

4. **Optionally, enter a guess to help the function.**

   To do this enter a comma (,) and then enter a decimal value to be used as a percentage, such as .2 for 20percent. You can enter a positive or negative value.

5. **Finally, enter a closing parenthesis to end the function, and press Enter.**

Considering that IRR is based on cash flows, in and out, it's prudent to include paying yourself, as well as accounting for investments back in the business. Salary is a cash flow out, investment is a cash flow in.

Figure 6-6 expands on the video-taping business with a detailed example. As a business, there are various cash flows in and out — investment, utility payments, fees to the accountant and lawyer, advertising, salary, and so on.

	File	Edit	View	Insert	Format	Tools	Data	Window	Help		

	E2	▼	*fx* =IRR(B6:B45,-0.2)			
	A	B	C	D	E	F
1						
2	Internal Rate Of Return (for January - June, 2005)				-11.5%	
3						
4						
5	Date	Amount		Item		
6	1/10/2005	13000		Initial Cash Investment		
7	1/15/2005	-9000		Purchase of Video Equipment		
8	1/17/2005	-325		Office Supplies		
9	1/18/2005	-700		Advertising		
10	1/28/2005	-450		Professional Fees		
11	2/1/2005	500		Cash Investment		
12	2/10/2005	1800		Payment for Job		
13	2/21/2005	2400		Payment for Job		
14	2/28/2005	-3000		Salary		
15	3/5/2005	500		Cash Investment		
16	3/7/2005	1295		Payment for Job		
17	3/8/2005	1600		Payment for Job		
18	3/12/2005	-350		Additional Video Equipment		
19	3/15/2005	-225		Insurance		
20	3/15/2005	-140		Phone and Utilities		
21	3/19/2005	2650		Payment for Job		
22	3/24/2005	1725		Payment for Job		
23	3/26/2005	-1000		Advertising		
24	3/31/2005	-4500		Salary		
25	4/1/2005	500		Cash Investment		
26	4/10/2005	-550		Additional Video Equipment		
27	4/12/2005	2000		Payment for Job		
28	4/16/2005	-140		Phone and Utilities		
29	4/19/2005	2200		Payment for Job		
30	4/24/2005	1600		Payment for Job		

Figure 6-6:
Calculating
IRR with
several
cash flows.

The Internal Rate of Return for the first six months of the business is displayed in cell E2. The formula is =IRR(B6:B45,-0.2). By the way, this one needed a guess to return the answer. The guess is –0.2. The internal rate or return is –11.5percent. The video-taping business is not a moneymaker after six months, but this is true of many startups.

Note that this example includes dates. The IRR function works with an assumption that cash flows are periodic, which they aren't in this example. There is a function, XIRR, that handles dates in its calculation of the internal rate of return. This function is available in the Analysis ToolPak add-in. See Chapter 20 for more information on the Analysis ToolPak add-in.

Part III
Working with Numbers

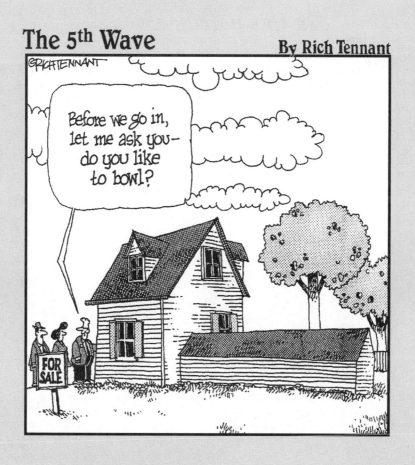

The 5th Wave   By Rich Tennant

Before we go in, let me ask you— do you like to bowl?

FOR SALE

In this part . . .

Excel is a math-loving, number-crunching lean, mean machine. Part III is going to show just how much this is true! Basic math — no sweat. How about combinations, permutations, subtotals, and summing up condition-based values. Hey, now we are talking some cool math here. Ever try to work your way through a book on statistics? Boring! Part III does it better. We show you how to use the statistical functions with examples. Right to the point. Discover a couple of these and impress the boss. You can even use an Excel statistical function to calculate the probability of getting a raise!

Chapter 7

Using Math Functions to Figure Basic Math Answers

In This Chapter

▶ Summing, rounding, and truncating values

▶ Using a value's sign in a calculation

▶ Removing the sign from a number

Excel is excellent for working with advanced math and complex calculations. You can do so many complex things with Excel that it's easy to forget that Excel is great at basic math, too.

Need the sum of a batch of numbers? No problem. Need to round a number? Read on! In this chapter, we show you not just how to sum and round numbers, but how to use these methods in ways that give you just the answers you need.

Adding It All Together with the SUM Function

Just adding numbers together is something Excel is great at. Oh, you can use your calculator to add numbers as well, but think about it: On a calculator you enter a number, then press the + button, then enter another number, then press the + button, and so on. Eventually you press the = button and you get your answer. But if you made an entry mistake in the middle, you have to start all over!

The SUM function in Excel adds numbers together in a more efficient way. First, you list all your numbers on the worksheet. You can see them all and verify that they're correct. Then you use the SUM function to add them all together. Here's how:

1. **Enter some numbers in a worksheet.**

   These numbers can be both integer and real (decimal) values. You can add labels to adjacent cells to identify the values, if you want.

2. **Position the cursor in the cell where you want the results to appear.**

3. **Enter =SUM (to begin the function entry.**

4. **Click a cell where you entered a number.**

5. **Enter a comma (,).**

6. **Click a cell where you entered another number.**

7. **Repeat Steps 5 and 6 until all the numbers have been entered into the function.**

8. **Enter a closing parenthesis to end the function, and press Enter.**

Figure 7-1 shows an example of how these steps help sum up amounts that are not situated next to each other on a worksheet. Cell F6 contains the sum of values found in cells C2, E2, G2, and I2.

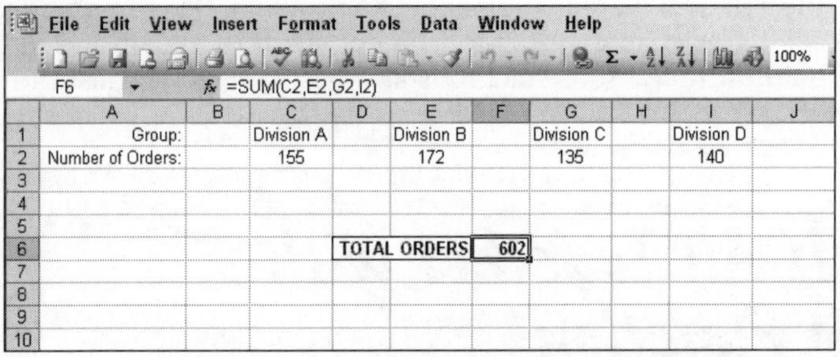

Figure 7-1: Using the SUM function to add noncontiguous numbers.

Using SUM is even easier when the numbers you're adding are next to each in a column or row. The SUM function lets you enter a range of cells in place of single cells in the arguments of the function. So adding a list of contiguous numbers is as easy as giving SUM a single argument. Here's how you enter a range as a single argument:

1. **Enter some numbers in a worksheet.**

   Be sure the numbers are continuous in a row or column. You can add labels to adjacent cells to identify the values, if desired, but this doesn't affect the SUM function.

2. **Position the cursor in the cell where you want the results to appear.**

3. **Enter =SUM(to begin the function entry.**

4. **Enter the range address that contains the numbers, or drag the mouse over the range of cells.**

5. **Enter a closing parenthesis to end the function, and press Enter.**

Using a range address in the function is a real timesaver — and is easier on the fingers, too. Figure 7-2 shows how a single range is used with the SUM function. Look at the formula bar and you'll see the entire function's syntax is =SUM(B6:B12). A single range takes the place of multiple individual cell addresses.

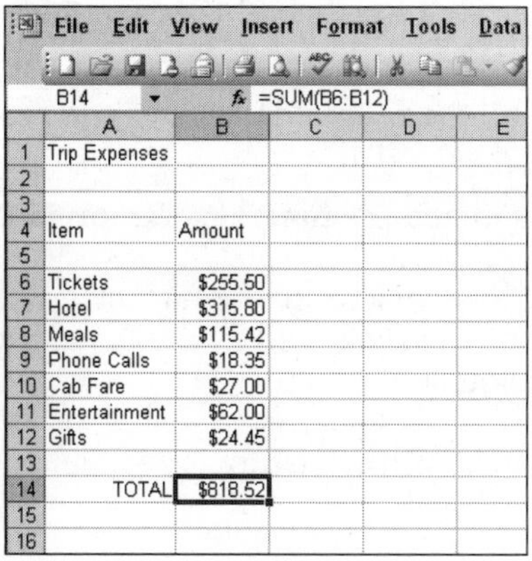

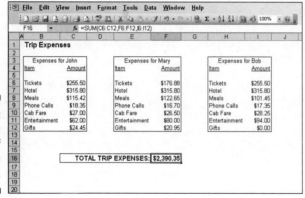

Figure 7-2: Calculating a sum from a range of cells.

You can sum multiple ranges in a single formula, which is great when multiple distinct contiguous cell ranges all must feed a grand total. Figure 7-3 shows just such a situation.

Figure 7-3: Calculating a sum of multiple ranges.

Here's how you use SUM to add the values in multiple ranges:

1. **Enter some lists of numbers in a worksheet.**

   You can add labels to adjacent cells to identify the values, if desired.

2. **Position the cursor in the cell where you want the results to appear.**

3. **Enter =SUM(to begin the function entry.**

4. **Click the first cell in a range and, while holding down the mouse button, drag the mouse over all the cells in the range, then release the mouse button.**

5. **Enter a comma (,).**

6. **Click the first cell in another range and, while holding down the mouse button, drag the mouse over all the cells in this range, then release the mouse button.**

7. **Repeat Steps 5 and 6 until all the ranges have been entered into the function.**

8. **Enter a closing parenthesis to end the function, and press Enter.**

The completed function entry should look similar to the entry shown in the formula bar in Figure 7-3. Each range is separated by a comma, and a grand sum is in the cell where the function was entered.

When entering ranges into a formula, you can either type them in, or use the mouse to drag over the range.

Excel has a special button, the AutoSum button, that makes it easier to use the SUM function. Find the AutoSum button on the Standard toolbar. The AutoSum feature works best with numbers that are in a vertical or horizontal list. In a nutshell, AutoSum creates a range reference for the SUM function to use. AutoSum makes its best guess of what the range should be. Often, it gets it right — but sometimes you have to help it along.

So where is the AutoSum anyway? Figure 7-4 shows it being used to sum up a column of numbers. To better show how this works, the Standard toolbar has been pulled down to the middle of the worksheet. The mouse pointer is on the AutoSum button.

Using AutoSum is a two-click operation. The first click gets AutoSum to guess a range of cells to be summed. Figure 7-4 shows how AutoSum looks after the first click. The range address can be edited, or you can use the mouse to drag over a different range of cells. If you use AutoSum in the first empty cell below a column of numbers, it will select the entire column above it.

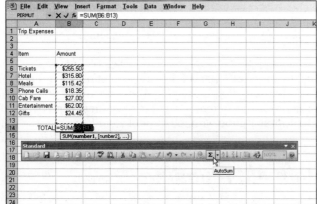

Figure 7-4:
Using
AutoSum to
guess a
range for
the SUM
function.

A second mouse click ends using AutoSum. Often, you just double-click through using AutoSum, without considering if you have to edit the range that AutoSum guessed. As you use it more and more, you'll know how it guesses ranges. To use AutoSum:

1. **Enter some lists of numbers in a worksheet.**

   You can add labels to adjacent cells to identify the values, if desired.

2. **Position the cursor in the cell where you want the results to appear.**

3. **Click the AutoSum button.**

   AutoSum has entered a suggested range into the SUM function.

4. **Change the suggested range, if necessary, either by entering it with the keyboard or using the mouse to drag over a range of cells.**

5. **Click the AutoSum button again to complete the function.**

Rounding Out Your Knowledge of Rounding Functions

Excel calculates answers to many decimal places. Unless you're doing rocket science, you probably don't need such precise answers. Excel has a great set of functions for rounding numbers so they're usable for the rest of us.

Excel's rounding functions are really helpful. The other day, Ken's son had a couple of his friends over. We ordered a large pizza for their lunch. That's eight slices for three hungry boys. How many slices does each boy get? Presto magic, we went over to the computer where Excel was already running (okay, we are Excel nuts after all), and we entered this simple formula =8/3.

Of course, Excel gave us the perfect answer. Each boy gets 2.66667 slices. Have you ever tried to cut 66,667/100,000ths of a slice of pizza? Not easy! This is the type of answer that rounding is used for. Although, to tell you the truth, we did solve the pizza problem a different way. We gave them each two slices, and we ate the last two (pretty good with mushrooms!).

Just plain old rounding

Easy to use, the ROUND function is the old tried-and-true method for rounding off a number. It takes two arguments — one argument is the number to round, and the other argument indicates how many decimal places to round to.

The ROUND function rounds up or down depending on the number being rounded. When the value is less than the halfway point of the next significant digit, then the number is rounded down. When the value is at or greater than the halfway point, then the number is rounded up. For example:

✔ 10.4 rounds down to 10.

✔ 10.6 rounds up to 11.

✔ 10.5 also rounds up to 11.

Table 7-1 shows some examples of the ROUND function.

Table 7-1	Using the ROUND Function	
Example of Function	*Result*	*Comment*
=ROUND(12.3456,1)	12.3	The second argument is 1. The result is rounded to a single decimal place.
=ROUND(12.3456,2)	12.35	The second argument is 2. The result is rounded to two decimal places. Note that the full decimal of .3456 becomes .35. This is because the .0456 portion of the decimal value rounds to the closest second place decimal, which is .05.

Example of Function	Result	Comment
=ROUND(12.3456,3)	12.346	The second argument is 3. The result is rounded to three decimal places. Note that the full decimal or .3456 becomes .346. This is because the .0056 portion of the decimal value rounds to the closest third place decimal, which is .006.
=ROUND(12.3456,4)	12.3456	The second argument is 4. There are four decimal places. No rounding takes place.
=ROUND(12.3456,0)	12	When the second argument is 0, the number is rounded to the nearest integer. Because 12.3456 is closer to 12 than to 13, the number rounds to 12.
=ROUND(12.3456,-1)	10	When negative values are used in the second argument, the rounding occurs on the left side of the decimal (the integer portion). A second argument value of –1 tells the function to round to the closest value of 10. In this example, that value is 10 because 12 is closer to 10 than 20.

Here's how to use the ROUND function:

1. **Position the cursor in the cell where you want the results to appear.**
2. **Enter** =ROUND(**to begin the function entry.**
3. **Click a cell where you entered a number.**
4. **Enter a comma (,).**
5. **Enter a number to indicate how many decimal places to round to.**
6. **Enter a closing parenthesis to end the function, and press Enter.**

Rounding in one direction

Excel has a handful of functions that round numbers either always up or always down. That is, when rounding a number, the functions that round down will always give a result that is lower than the number itself. Functions that round up, of course, always give a higher number. These functions are useful when letting the good ol' ROUND function determine which way to round just isn't going to do.

A few of these rounding functions not only round in the desired direction, but even allow you to specify some additional ways of rounding. The EVEN and ODD functions, for example, round respectively to the closest even or odd number. The CEILING and FLOOR functions let you round to a multiple. EVEN, ODD, CEILING, and FLOOR are discussed later in this section.

Directional rounding, pure and simple

ROUNDUP and ROUNDDOWN are similar to the ROUND function. The first argument to the function is the number to be rounded. The second argument indicates the number of decimal places to round to. But unlike the plain old ROUND, the rounding direction is not based on the halfway point of the next significant digit but rather on which function you use.

So for example, =ROUND(4.22,1) returns 4.2, but =ROUNDUP(4.22,1) returns 4.3. ROUNDDOWN however returns 4.2, because 4.2 is less than 4.22. Table 7-2 shows some examples of ROUNDUP and ROUNDDOWN.

Table 7-2	Using the ROUNDUP and ROUNDDOWN Functions	
Example of Function	*Result*	*Comment*
=ROUNDUP(150.255,0)	151	The second argument is 0. The result is rounded up to the next higher integer, regardless of the fact that that the decimal portion would normally indicate the rounding would go to the next lower integer.
=ROUNDUP(150.255,1)	150.3	The second argument is 1. The result is rounded to a single decimal point. Note that the full decimal of .255 rounds up to.3. This would also happen with the standard ROUND function.
=ROUNDUP(150.255,2)	150.26	The second argument is 2, the result is rounded to two decimal places. Note that the full decimal or .255 becomes .26. This would also happen with the standard ROUND function.

Example of Function	Result	Comment
=ROUNDUP(150.255,3)	150.255	The second argument is 3, and there are three decimal places. No rounding takes place.
=ROUNDDOWN(155.798,0)	155	The second argument is 0. The result is rounded down to the integer portion of the number, regardless of the fact that that the decimal portion would normally indicate that the rounding would go to the next higher integer.
=ROUNDDOWN(155.798,1)	155.7	The second argument is 1. The result is rounded to a single decimal place. Note that the full decimal of .798 rounds down to .7. The standard ROUND function would round the decimal up to .8.
=ROUNDDOWN(155.798,2)	155.79	The second argument is 2. The result is rounded to two decimal places. Note that the full decimal or .798 becomes .79. The standard ROUND function would round the decimal up to .8.
=ROUNDDOWN(155.798,3)	155.798	The second argument is 3, and there are three decimal places. No rounding takes place.

Here's how to use either the ROUNDUP or ROUNDDOWN function:

1. **Position the cursor in the cell where you want the results to appear.**

2. **Enter either** =ROUNDUP(**or** =ROUNDDOWN(**to begin the function entry.**

3. **Click a cell where you entered a number, or enter a number.**

4. **Enter a comma (,).**

5. **Enter a number to indicate how many decimal places to round to.**

6. **Enter a closing parenthesis to end the function, and press Enter.**

Rounding to the multiple of choice

The FLOOR and CEILING functions take directional rounding to a new level. With these functions, the second argument is a multiple to which to round to. What does that mean?

Well, imagine this: You're a human resources manager and you need to prepare a summary report of employee salaries. You don't need the figures to be reported down to the last penny, just rounded to the closest $250 multiple. Either FLOOR or CEILING can be used to do this. For this example, FLOOR can be used to round down to the closest $250 less than the salary, or CEILING can be used to round up to the next $250 multiple greater than the salary. Figure 7-5 shows how both FLOOR and CEILING return rounded values.

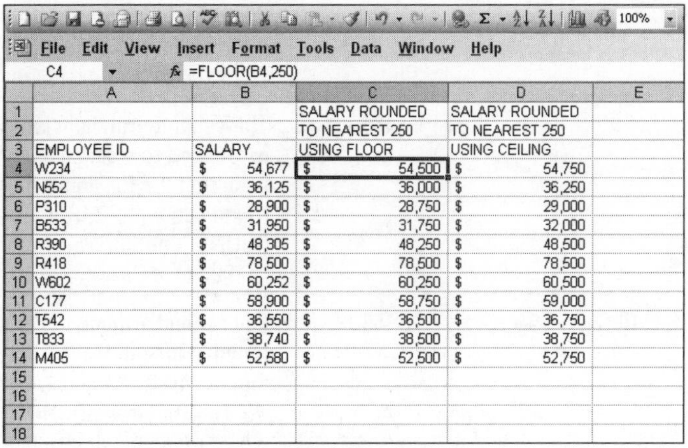

	A	B	C	D	E
1			SALARY ROUNDED	SALARY ROUNDED	
2			TO NEAREST 250	TO NEAREST 250	
3	EMPLOYEE ID	SALARY	USING FLOOR	USING CEILING	
4	W234	$ 54,677	$ 54,500	$ 54,750	
5	N552	$ 36,125	$ 36,000	$ 36,250	
6	P310	$ 28,900	$ 28,750	$ 29,000	
7	B533	$ 31,950	$ 31,750	$ 32,000	
8	R390	$ 48,305	$ 48,250	$ 48,500	
9	R418	$ 78,500	$ 78,500	$ 78,500	
10	W602	$ 60,252	$ 60,250	$ 60,500	
11	C177	$ 58,900	$ 58,750	$ 59,000	
12	T542	$ 36,550	$ 36,500	$ 36,750	
13	T833	$ 38,740	$ 38,500	$ 38,750	
14	M405	$ 52,580	$ 52,500	$ 52,750	
15					
16					
17					
18					

Figure 7-5: Using FLOOR or CEILING to round to a desired multiple.

FLOOR and CEILING exceed the rounding ability of ROUND, ROUNDUP, and ROUNDDOWN. These three functions can use the positioning of digit placeholders in how they work. For example, `=ROUND(B4,-3)` tells the ROUND function to round on the thousandth position. On the other hand, FLOOR and CEILING can round to whatever specific multiple you set.

The FLOOR function rounds toward 0, returning the closest multiple of the second argument that is lower than the number itself.

The CEILING function works in the opposite direction. CEILING will round its first argument, the number to be rounded, to the next multiple of the second number that is in the direction away from 0.

Certainly, a few examples will make this clear! Table 7-3 shows ways that FLOOR and CEILING can be used.

Table 7-3	Using FLOOR and CEILING for Some Sophisticated Rounding	
Example of Function	*Result*	*Comment*
=FLOOR(30.17,0.05)	30.15	The second argument says to round to the next 0.05 multiple, in the direction of 0.
=FLOOR(30.17,0.1)	30.1	The second argument says to round to the next 0.1 multiple, in the direction of 0.
=FLOOR(-30.17,-0.1)	−30.1	The second argument says to round to the next 0.1 multiple, in the direction of 0.
=CEILING(30.17,0.05)	30.2	The second argument says to round to the next 0.05 multiple, away from 0.
=CEILING(30.17,0.1)	30.2	The second argument says to round to the next 0.1 multiple, away from 0.
=CEILING(-30.17,-0.1)	−30.2	The second argument says to round to the next 0.1 multiple, away from 0.

FLOOR and CEILING can be used to round negative numbers. FLOOR rounds toward 0, and CEILING rounds away from 0. FLOOR decreases a positive number as it rounds it towards 0, and also decreases a negative number toward 0, although in absolute terms, FLOOR actually increases the value of a negative number. Weird, huh?

CEILING does the opposite. It increases a positive number away from 0 and also increases a negative number away from 0, which in absolute terms means the number is getting smaller.

For both the FLOOR and CEILING functions, the first and second arguments must match signs. Trying to apply a positive number with a negative multiple, or vice versa, results in an error.

Here's how to use either the FLOOR or CEILING function:

1. **Position the cursor in the cell where you want the results to appear.**

2. **Enter either =FLOOR(or =CEILING(to begin the function entry.**

3. **Click a cell where you entered a number, or enter a number.**

4. **Enter a comma (,).**

5. **Enter a number that is the next multiple you want to round the number to.**

6. **Enter a closing parenthesis to end the function, and press Enter.**

Rounding to the next even or odd number

The EVEN and ODD functions round numbers away from 0. The EVEN function will round a number to the next highest even integer. ODD rounds a number to the next highest odd integer.

Table 7-4 has examples of how these functions work.

Table 7-4	Rounding to Even or Odd Integers	
Example of Function	*Result*	*Comment*
=EVEN(3)	4	Rounds to the next even integer, moving away from 0.
=EVEN(4)	4	Because 4 is an even number, no rounding takes place. The number 4 itself is returned.
=EVEN(4.01)	6	Rounds to the next even integer, moving away from 0.
=EVEN(-3.5)	−4	Rounds to the next even integer, moving away from 0.
=ODD(3)	3	Because 3 is an odd number, no rounding takes place. The number 3 itself is returned.
=ODD(4)	5	Rounds to the next odd integer, moving away from 0.
=ODD(5.01)	7	Rounds to the next odd integer, moving away from 0.
=ODD(-3.5)	−5	Rounds to the next odd integer, moving away from 0.

The EVEN function is helpful in calculations that depend on multiples of two. For example, let's say you're in charge of planning a school trip. You need to figure out how many bus seats are needed for each class. A seat can fit two children. When a class has an odd number of children, you still have to count that last seat as taken, even though only one child will sit there.

Let's say the class has 17 children. This formula tells you how many seats are needed:

```
=EVEN(17)/2
```

The EVEN function returns the number 18 (the next higher integer), and that result is divided by 2, because two children fit on each seat. The answer is 9 seats are needed for a class of 17.

Here's how to use either the EVEN or ODD function:

1. **Position the cursor in the cell where you want the results to appear.**
2. **Enter either =EVEN(or =ODD(to begin the function entry.**
3. **Click a cell where you entered a number, or enter a number.**
4. **Enter a closing parenthesis to end the function, and press Enter.**

Leaving All the Decimals Behind with the INT Function

The INT function rounds a number down to the next lowest integer. The effect is as if the decimal portion is just dropped, and often INT is used to facilitate just that — dropping the decimal.

INT comes in handy when all you need to know is the integer part of a number or the integer part of a calculation's result. For example, you may be estimating what it will cost to build a piece of furniture. You have the prices for each type of raw material, and you just want a ballpark total.

Figure 7-6 shows a worksheet in which a project has been set up. Column A contains item descriptions, and Column B has the price for each item. Columns C and D contain the parameters for the project. That is, Column C contains the count of each item needed, and Column D has the amount of how much will be spent for each item.

The sums to be spent are then summed into a project total. If you added the item sums as they are — 83.88, 176.76, and 19.96 — you get a total of $211.60. Instead, the INT function is used to round the total to a ballpark figure of $211.

In cell D8, INT is applied to the total sum, like this:

```
=INT(SUM(D3:D5))
```

The INT function effectively drops the decimal portion, .60, and just returns the integer part, 211. The project estimate is $211.

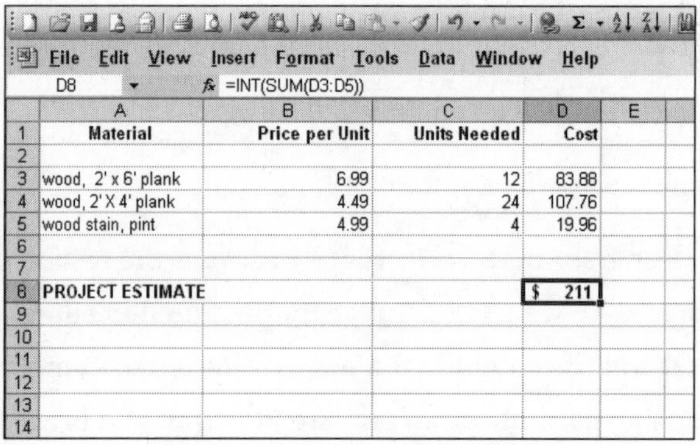

Figure 7-6:
Using INT
to drop
unnecessary
decimals.

INT takes only the number as an argument. INT can work on positive or negative values, but works a little differently with negative numbers. INT actually rounds down a number to the next lower integer. When working with positive numbers the effect appears the same as just dropping the decimal. With negative numbers the effect is dropping the decimal portion then subtracting 1.

With negative numbers, the function produces an integer that is further away from 0. Therefore, a number such as –25.25 becomes –26. Here are some examples:

- INT(25.25) returns 25.
- INT(25.75) returns 25.
- INT(-25.25) returns –26.
- INT(-25.75) returns –26.

Here's how to use the INT function:

1. **Position the cursor in the cell where you want the results to appear.**

2. **Enter =INT(to begin the function entry.**

3. **Click a cell where you entered a number, or enter a number.**

4. **Enter a closing parenthesis to end the function, and press Enter.**

INT can also be used to return just the decimal part of a number. Subtracting the integer portion of a number from its full value leaves just the decimal as the answer. For example, `10.95-INT(10.95) = 0.95`.

Leaving Some of the Decimals behind with the TRUNC Function

The TRUNC function drops a part of a number. The function takes two arguments. The first argument is the number to be changed. The second argument indicates how much of the number is to be dropped. A value of 2 for the second argument says to leave 2 decimal places remaining. A value of 1 for the second argument says to leave 1 decimal place remaining.

TRUNC does no rounding as it truncates numbers. Here are some examples:

```
=TRUNC(212.65, 2) returns 212.65
=TRUNC(212.65, 1) returns 212.6
=TRUNC(212.65, 0) returns 212
```

You can even use TRUNC to drop a portion of the number from the integer side. To do this, you enter negative values for the second argument, like this:

```
=TRUNC(212.65, -1) returns 210
=TRUNC(212.65, -2) returns 200
```

The INT and TRUNC functions work exactly the same way for positive numbers. The only difference is when negative numbers are being changed. Then INT's rounding produces a different result than TRUNC's truncation.

Looking for a Sign

Excel's SIGN function tells you whether a number is positive or negative. The SIGN function does not alter the number in any way but instead is used to find out information about the number.

SIGN does actually return a number, but it isn't a variation of the number being tested in the function. SIGN returns only three different numbers:

- 1 if the number being tested is positive
- –1 if the number being tested is negative
- 0 if the number being tested is 0

For example,

- ✔ `=SIGN(5)` returns 1.
- ✔ `=SIGN(-5)` returns –1.
- ✔ `=SIGN(0)` returns 0.

USING SIGN in combination with other functions presents sophisticated ways of working with your information. As an example, you may be tallying up a day's receipts from your store. You want to know the total value of sold merchandise and the total value of returned merchandise. Sales are recorded as positive amounts, and returns are recorded as negative amounts.

Figure 7-7 shows a worksheet with these facts. Column A shows individual transaction amounts. Most are sales and are positive. A few returns occurred during the day, entered as negative amounts.

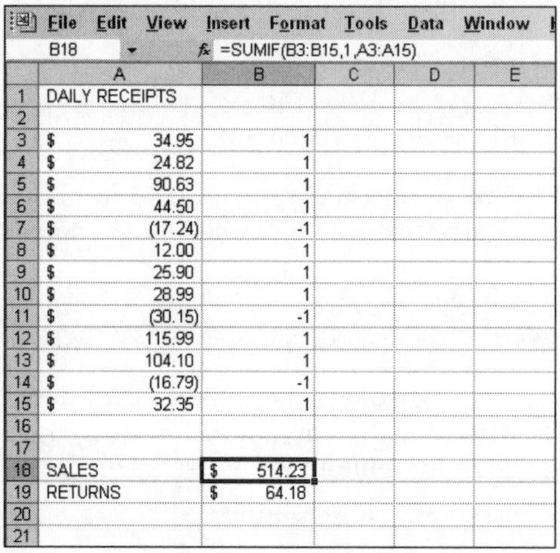

Figure 7-7:
Using SIGN
to help
correctly
sum
amounts.

	File	Edit	View	Insert	Format	Tools	Data	Window	
B18			*fx* =SUMIF(B3:B15,1,A3:A15)						

	A	B	C	D	E
1	DAILY RECEIPTS				
2					
3	$ 34.95	1			
4	$ 24.82	1			
5	$ 90.63	1			
6	$ 44.50	1			
7	$ (17.24)	-1			
8	$ 12.00	1			
9	$ 25.90	1			
10	$ 28.99	1			
11	$ (30.15)	-1			
12	$ 115.99	1			
13	$ 104.10	1			
14	$ (16.79)	-1			
15	$ 32.35	1			
16					
17					
18	SALES	$ 514.23			
19	RETURNS	$ 64.18			
20					
21					

Just summing the whole transaction list would calculate the net revenue of the day, but often a business needs better information. Instead, two sums are calculated: the sum of sales and the sum of returns.

For each value in Column A, there is a value in Column B. The Column B values are the result of using the SIGN function. For example, cell B3 has this formula:

```
=SIGN(A3)
```

As shown in Figure 7-7, values in Column B equal 1 when the associated value in Column A is positive. Column B displays –1 when the associated value is negative. This information is then used in a SUMIF function, which selectively sums information from Column A.

In cell B18 is this formula:

```
=SUMIF(B3:B15,1,A3:A15)
```

In cell B19 is this formula:

```
=ABS(SUMIF(B3:B15,-1,A3:A15))
```

The SUMIF function is used to indicate a criterion to use in determining which values to sum. For the sum of sales in cell B18, the presence of the value 1 in Column B determines which values to sum in Column A. For the sum of returns in cell B19, the presence of the value –1 in Column B determines which values to sum in Column A.

Also, the Absolute function (ABS) is used to present the number in cell B19 as a positive number. The answer in cell B19 is the sum of merchandise returns. You would say there was $64.18 (not –$64.18) in returned merchandise, if you were asked.

The SUMIF function is covered in Chapter 7. The ABS function is covered next in this chapter.

Here's how to use the SIGN function:

1. **Position the cursor in the cell where you want the results to appear.**
2. **Enter =SIGN(to begin the function entry.**
3. **Click a cell where you entered a number, or enter a number.**
4. **Enter a closing parenthesis to end the function, and press Enter.**

Ignoring Signs

THE ABS function returns the absolute value of a number. The absolute number is always a positive. The absolute of a positive number is the number itself. The absolute of a negative number is the number, but with the sign changed to positive. For example, =ABS(100) returns 100, as does =ABS(-100).

The ABS function is handy in a number of situations. For example, sometimes imported data comes in as negative values and needs to be converted to their positive equivalents. Or, for example, when working with cash flows as discussed in Chapter 3, the ABS function can be used to present cash flows as positive numbers.

A common use of the ABS function is to calculate the difference between two numbers, when you don't know which number has the greater value to begin with. Let's say you need to calculate the difference between scores for two contestants. Score 1 is in cell A5 and score 2 is in cell B5. The result goes in cell C5. The formula in cell C5 would then be:

```
=A5-B5
```

Plugging in some numbers, assume score 1 is 90 and score 2 is 75. The difference is 15. Okay, that's a good answer. What happens when score 1 is 75 and score 2 is 90? The answer is –15. This answer is mathematically correct but not presented in a useful way. The difference is still 15, not –15. By using the ABS function, the result is always returned as positive. Therefore for this example, the best coding of the formula is like this:

```
=ABS(A5-A6)
```

Now either way, whether score 1 is greater than score 2 or score 2 is greater than score 1, the correct difference is returned.

Here's how to use the ABS function:

1. **Position the cursor in the cell where you want the results to appear.**

2. **Enter** =ABS(**to begin the function entry.**

3. **Click a cell where you entered a number, or enter a number.**

4. **Enter a closing parenthesis to end the function, and press Enter.**

Chapter 8

Getting More Advanced with Math

*I*n this chapter, we show you some of the more-advanced math functions. You won't use these functions everyday, but they're just the right thing when you need them. Some of this will come back to you because you probably learned most of this in school.

Using the PI Function to Calculate Circumference and Diameter

Pi is the ratio of a circle's circumference to its diameter. A circle's *circumference* is its outer edge and is equal to the complete distance around the circle. A circle's *diameter* is the length of a straight line spanning from one side of the circle, through the middle, and reaching the other side.

Dividing a circle's circumference by its diameter returns a value of approximately 3.141, known as *pi*. Pi is represented with the Greek letter pi and the symbol π.

Mathematicians have proven that pi is an *irrational number* — in other words, it has an infinite number of decimal places. They have calculated the value of pi to many thousands of decimal places, but you don't need that level of precision in most calculations. Many people use the value 3.14159 for pi, but the PI function in Excel does a bit better than that. Excel returns a value of pi accurate to 15 digits — that is 14 decimal places in addition to the integer 3. This function has no input arguments. The function uses the syntax:

```
=PI()
```

In Excel, the PI function always returns 3.14159265358979, but initially it may look like some of the decimal points are missing. Change the formatting of the cell to display numbers with 14 decimal places to see the entire number.

If you know the circumference of a circle, you can calculate its diameter with this formula:

Diameter = Circumference ÷ Pi

If you know the diameter of a circle, you can calculate its circumference with this formula:

Circumference = Diameter × Pi

If you know the diameter of a circle, you can calculate the area of the circle. A component of this calculation is the *radius,* which equals one-half of the diameter. The formula is:

Area = (Diameter × 0.5)^2 × Pi

Generating and Using Random Numbers

Random numbers are, by definition, unpredictable. That is, given a series of random numbers, you can't predict the next number from what has come before. Random numbers are quite useful for trying out formulas and calculations. Suppose you're creating a worksheet to perform various kinds of data analysis. You may not have any real data yet, but you can generate random numbers to test the formulas and charts in the worksheet.

For example, an actuary may want to test some calculations based on a distribution of people's ages. Random numbers that vary between 18 and 65 could be used for this task. You don't have to manually enter fixed values between 18 and 65, because Excel can generate them automatically using the RAND function.

The RAND function is simple — it takes no arguments and returns a decimal value between 0 and 1. That is, RAND never actually returns 0 or 1; the value is always in between these two numbers. The function is entered like this:

```
=RAND()
```

The RAND function returns values such as 0.136852731, 0.856104058, or 0.009277161. "Yikes!" you may be thinking. "How do these numbers help if you need values between 18 and 65." Actually it's easy with a little extra math.

There is a standard calculation for generating random numbers within a determined range. The calculation is:

```
= RAND() * (high number - low number) + low number
```

Using 18 and 65 as a desired range of numbers, the formula looks like `=RAND()*(65-18)+18`. Some sample values that are returned with this formula are:

> 51.71777896
>
> 27.20727871
>
> 24.61657068
>
> 55.27298686
>
> 49.93632709
>
> 43.60069745

Almost usable! But what about the long decimal portions of these numbers? Some people lie about their ages, but I've never heard someone say he's 27.2 years old!

All that is needed now for this 18-to-65 age example is to include the INT or ROUND function. INT simply discards the decimal portion of a number. ROUND allows control over how to handle the decimal portion.

The syntax for using the INT function with the RAND function is

```
= INT((high number - low number + 1) * RAND() + low number)
```

The syntax for using the ROUND function with the RAND function is

```
=ROUND(RAND() * (high number-low number) + low number,0)
```

Try it yourself! Here's how to use RAND and INT together:

1. **Position the cursor in the cell where you want the results displayed.**

2. **Enter =INT((to begin the formula.**

3. **Click the cell that has the highest number to be used, or enter such a value.**

4. **Enter – (a minus sign).**

5. **Click the cell that has the lowest number to be used, or enter such a value.**

6. **Enter +1) * RAND() + .**

7. **Click again on the cell that has the lowest number to be used, or enter the value again.**

8. **Finally, enter a closing parenthesis to end the formula, and press Enter.**

A random number, somewhere in the range of the low and high number, is returned.

Table 8-1 shows how returned random numbers can be altered with the INT and ROUND functions.

Table 8-1	Using INT And ROUND to Process Random Values	
Value	*Value returned with INT*	*Value returned with ROUND*
51.71777896	51	52
27.20727871	27	27
24.61657068	24	25
55.27298686	55	55
49.93632709	49	50
43.60069745	43	44

Table 8-1 points out how the INT and ROUND functions return different numbers. For example, 51.71777896 is more accurately rounded to 52. Bear in mind that the second argument in the ROUND function, 0 in this case, has an effect on how the rounding works. A 0 tells the ROUND function to round the number to the nearest integer, up or down to whichever integer is closest to the number.

Random values are volatile. Each time a worksheet is recalculated the random values change. This behavior can be avoided by typing the formula directly into the Formula Bar and pressing the F9 key.

A last but not insignificant note about using the RAND function: It is subject to the recalculation feature built into worksheets. In other words, each time the worksheet calculates, the RAND function is rerun and returns a new random number. The calculation setting in your worksheet is probably set to automatic. You can check this by choosing Tools ⇨ Options and selecting the Calculation tab. Figure 8-1 shows the calculation setting. On a setting of Automatic, the worksheet recalculates with every action. The random generated numbers keep changing, which can become quite annoying — not to mention the fact that it can ruin your work!

Luckily, you can generate a random number but have it remain fixed regardless of the calculation setting. The method is to type the RAND function, along with any other parts of a larger formula, directly into the Formula Bar. The Formula Bar sits just above the column headings. If you can't see it, choose View ⇨ Formula Bar to have it appear. After you type your formula in, *press the F9 key*. This tells Excel to calculate the formula and enter the returned random number as a fixed number instead of a formula. If you press the Enter key or finish the entry in some way other than using the F9 key, you'll have to enter it again.

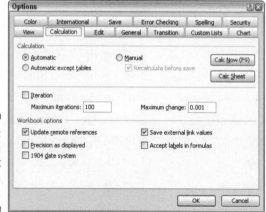

Figure 8-1:
Setting
worksheet
calculation
options.

Determining the Ways Items Can Be Ordered

Remember the Beatles? John, Paul, George, and Ringo? If you're a drummer, you may think of the Beatles as Ringo, John, Paul, and George. The order of items in a list is known as a *permutation*. The more items in a list, the more possible permutations exist.

Excel provides the PERMUT function. It takes two arguments — the total number of items to choose from and the number of items to be used in determining the permutations. The function returns a single whole number. The syntax of the function is:

```
=PERMUT(total number of items, number of items to use)
```

Permutations are used when the order of items is important.

The total number of items must be the same as or greater than the number of items to use, or else an error is generated.

You may be confused about why the function takes two arguments. On the surface, it seems that the first argument is sufficient. Well, not quite. Getting back to the Beatles (anyone have a copy of *Abbey Road* we can borrow?). If we plug in 4 as the number for both arguments, like this — =PERMUT(4,4) — 24 permutations are returned:

- John Paul George Ringo
- John Paul Ringo George
- John George Paul Ringo
- John George Ringo Paul
- John Ringo Paul George
- John Ringo George Paul
- Paul John George Ringo
- Paul John Ringo George
- Paul George John Ringo
- Paul George Ringo John
- Paul Ringo John George
- Paul Ringo George John
- George John Paul Ringo
- George John Ringo Paul
- George Paul John Ringo
- George Paul Ringo John
- George Ringo John Paul
- George Ringo Paul John
- Ringo John Paul George
- Ringo John George Paul
- Ringo Paul John George
- Ringo Paul George John
- Ringo George John Paul
- Ringo George Paul John

Altering the function to use 2 items at a time from the total of 4 items — PERMUT(4,2) — returns just 12 permutations:

- ✔ John Paul
- ✔ John George
- ✔ John Ringo
- ✔ Paul John
- ✔ Paul George
- ✔ Paul Ringo
- ✔ George John
- ✔ George Paul
- ✔ George Ringo
- ✔ Ringo John
- ✔ Ringo Paul
- ✔ Ringo George

Just for contrast, using the number 2 for both arguments — PERMUT(2,2) — returns just two items! When using PERMUT, make sure you've selected the correct numbers for the two arguments; otherwise, you'll end up with an incorrect result and may not be aware of the mistake. The PERMUT function simply returns a number. The validity of the number is in your hands.

Combining Items with the COMBIN Function

Combinations are similar to permutations but with a distinct difference. The order of items is intrinsic to permutations. Combinations, however, are groupings of items when the order doesn't matter. For example, "John Paul George Ringo" and "Ringo George Paul John" are two distinct permutations but identical combinations.

Combinations are grouping of items, regardless of the order of the items.

The syntax for the function is:

```
=COMBIN(total number of items, number of items to use)
```

The first argument is the total number of items to choose from, and the second argument is the number of items to be used in determining the combinations. The function returns a single whole number. The arguments for the COMBIN function are the same as those for the PERMUT function. The first argument must be equal to or greater then the second argument.

Plugging in the number 4 for both arguments — COMBIN(4,4) — returns 1. Yes, there is just one combination of four items selected from a total of four items! Using the Beatles once again, just one combination of the four musicians exists, because the order of names doesn't matter.

Selecting to use two items from a total of four — COMBIN(4,2) — returns 6. Selecting two items out of two — COMBIN(2,2) — returns 1. In fact, whenever the two arguments to the COMBIN function are the same, the result is always 1.

Raising Numbers to New Heights with the POWER Function

There is an old tale about a king who loved chess so much he decided to reward the inventor of chess with any request he had. The inventor asked for a grain of wheat for the first square of the chessboard on Monday, two grains for the second square on Tuesday, four for the third square on Wednesday, eight for the fourth square on Thursday, and so on, each day doubling the amount until the 64th square was filled with wheat. The king thought this was a silly request. The inventor could have asked for riches!

What happened is that the kingdom quickly ran out of wheat. By the 15th day, the number equaled 16,384. By the 20th day, the number was 524,288. On the 64th day, the number would have been an astonishing 9,223,372,036,854,780,000, but the kingdom had run out of wheat at least a couple of weeks earlier!

This "powerful" math is literally known as raising a number to a power. The *power,* in this case, means how many times a number is to be multiplied by itself. The notation is typically seen as a superscript (2^3 for example). Another common way of noting the use of a power is with the carat symbol: 2^3. The verbiage for this is *two to the third power.*

In the chess example, each day, 2 is raised to a higher power. Table 8-2 shows the first 10 days.

Table 8-2		The Power of Raising Numbers to A Power		
Day	Power That 2 Is Raised To	Power Notation	Basic Math Notation	Result
1	0	2^0	1	1
2	1	2^1	2	2
3	2	2^2	2×2	4
4	3	2^3	$2 \times 2 \times 2$	8
5	4	2^4	$2 \times 2 \times 2 \times 2$	16

Day	Power That 2 Is Raised To	Power Notation	Basic Math Notation	Result
6	5	2^5	$2 \times 2 \times 2 \times 2 \times 2$	32
7	6	2^6	$2 \times 2 \times 2 \times 2 \times 2 \times 2$	64
8	7	2^7	$2 \times 2 \times 2 \times 2 \times 2 \times 2 \times 2$	128
9	8	2^8	$2 \times 2 \times 2 \times 2 \times 2 \times 2 \times 2 \times 2$	256
10	9	2^9	$2 \times 2 \times 2 \times 2 \times 2 \times 2 \times 2 \times 2 \times 2$	512

The concept is easy enough. Each time the power is incremented by one, the result doubles. Note that the first entry raises 2 to the 0 power. Isn't that strange? Well, not really. Any number raised to the 0 power = 1. Also note that any number raised to the power of 1 equals the number itself.

Excel provides the POWER function. The syntax is:

```
=POWER(number, power)
```

Both the number and power arguments can be integer or real numbers, and negative numbers are allowed.

In a worksheet, either the POWER function or the carat can be used. For example, in a cell you can enter =POWER(4,3), or =4^3. The result is the same either way. The carat is inserted by holding Shift and pressing the number 6 key on the keyboard.

Multiplying Multiple Numbers with the PRODUCT function

The PRODUCT function is useful for multiplying up to 30 numbers at once. The syntax is:

```
=PRODUCT (number1, number2,...)
```

Cell references can be included in the argument list, as well as actual numbers, and, of course, they can be mixed. Therefore, all these variations work:

```
=PRODUCT(A2, B15, C20)
=PRODUCT(5, 8, 22)
=PRODUCT(A10, 5, B9)
```

In fact, you can use arrays of numbers as the arguments. In this case, the notation looks like this:

```
=PRODUCT(B85:B88,C85:C88, D86:D88)
```

Here's how to use the PRODUCT function:

1. **Enter some values on a worksheet.**

   You can include many values, going down columns or across in rows.

2. **Position the cursor in the cell where you want the results displayed.**

3. **Enter =PRODUCT(to begin the function.**

4. **Click a cell that has a number or drag the mouse over a range of cells with numbers.**

5. **Enter a comma (,).**

6. **Repeat Steps 4 and 5 up to 30 times.**

7. **Finally, enter a closing parenthesis to end the function, and press Enter.**

The result you see is calculated by multiplying all the numbers you selected. Your fingers would probably hurt if you had done this on a calculator.

Figure 8-2 shows this on a worksheet. Cell C10 shows the result of multiplying 12 numbers, although only three arguments, as ranges, have been used in the function.

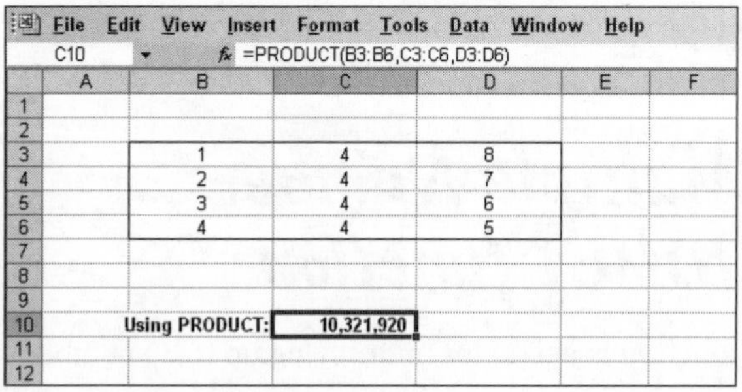

Figure 8-2: Putting the PRODUCT function to work.

A	B	C	D	E	F
	1	4	8		
	2	4	7		
	3	4	6		
	4	4	5		
	Using PRODUCT:	10,321,920			

C10 =PRODUCT(B3:B6,C3:C6,D3:D6)

Using SUMPRODUCT to Multiply and Sum Positional Values in One Step

The SUMPRODUCT function provides a sophisticated way to add together various products — across ranges of values. It doesn't just add together the products of separate ranges, it produces products of the values that are positioned in the same place in each range, then sums up those products. The syntax for the function is:

```
=SUMPRODUCT(Range1, Range2, ...)
```

The arguments to SUMPRODUCT must be ranges, although a range can be a single value. What is required is that all the ranges are the same size, both row- and column-wise. Up to 30 ranges are allowed, and at least 2 are required.

SUMPRODUCT works by first multiplying elements, by position, across the ranges, then adding all the results. To see how this works, take a look at Figure 8-3. There are three ranges of values. We have put letters in the ranges instead of numbers to make this easier to explain. Suppose you entered the following formula in the worksheet:

```
=SUMPRODUCT(B2:C4, E2:F4, H2:I4)
```

The result would be calculated by

1. **Multiplying A times H times N and saving the result.**

2. **Multiplying D times K times Q and saving the result.**

3. **Multiplying B times I times O and saving the result.**

4. **Multiplying E times L times R and saving the result.**

5. **Multiplying C times J times P and saving the result.**

6. **Multiplying F times M times S and saving the result.**

7. **Adding all six results to get the final answer.**

Figure 8-3:
Following
the steps
used by
SUM
PRODUCT.

	File	Edit	View	Insert	Format	Tools	Data	Window	Help	
	M27	▼		*fx*						
	A	B	C	D	E	F	G	H	I	J
1										
2		A	D		H	K		N	Q	
3		B	E		I	L		O	R	
4		C	F		J	M		P	S	
5										
6										
7										
8										
9										

Be careful when you're using the SUMPRODUCT function. It's easy to mistakenly assume the function will add together products of individual ranges. It won't. SUMPRODUCT returns the sums of products across positional elements.

As confusing as SUMPRODUCT seems, it actually has a sophisticated use. Imagine you have a list of units sold by product, and another list of the products' prices. You need to know total sales (that is, the sum of the amounts), where an amount is units sold times the unit price.

In the old days of spreadsheets, you would use an additional column to first multiply each unit sold figure by its price. Then you would sum those intermediate values.

Now, with SUMPRODUCT, the drudgery is over. The single use of SUMPRODUCT gets the final answer in one step. Figure 8-4 shows how one cell contains the needed grand total. No intermediate steps were necessary.

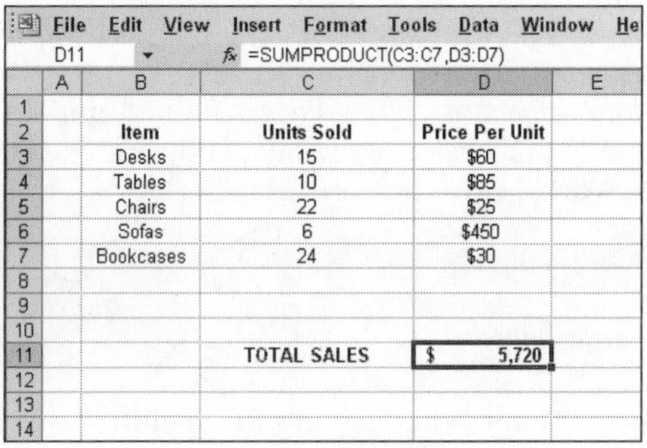

	A	B	C	D	E
1					
2		Item	Units Sold	Price Per Unit	
3		Desks	15	$60	
4		Tables	10	$85	
5		Chairs	22	$25	
6		Sofas	6	$450	
7		Bookcases	24	$30	
8					
9					
10					
11			TOTAL SALES	$ 5,720	
12					
13					
14					

Figure 8-4: Being productive with SUM PRODUCT.

Using What Remains with the MOD Function

The MOD function returns the remainder from an integer division operation. This is called the *modulus,* hence the function's name. The function has two arguments: the number being divided, and the number being used to divide the first argument. The second argument is the divisor. The syntax of the function is:

```
=MOD(number, divisor)
```

Some examples of the MOD function are

`=MOD(12,6)` returns 0

`=MOD(14,5)` returns 4

`=MOD(27,7)` returns 6

`=MOD(-25,10)` returns 5

`=MOD(25,-10)` returns -5

`=MOD(15.675,8.25)` returns 7.425

The returned value is always the same sign as the divisor.

You can use MOD to tell if a number is odd or even. By simply using a number 2 as the second argument, the returned value will be 0 if the first argument is an even number and 1 if it is not.

But what's so great about that? You can just look at a number and tell whether it's odd or even. The power of the MOD function is apparent when testing a reference or formula, such as `=MOD(D12 - G15,2)`. In a complex worksheet with many formulas, you many not be able to tell when a cell will contain an odd or even number.

Taking this a step further, the MOD function can be used to identify cells in a worksheet that are multiples of the divisor. Figure 8-5 shows how this works.

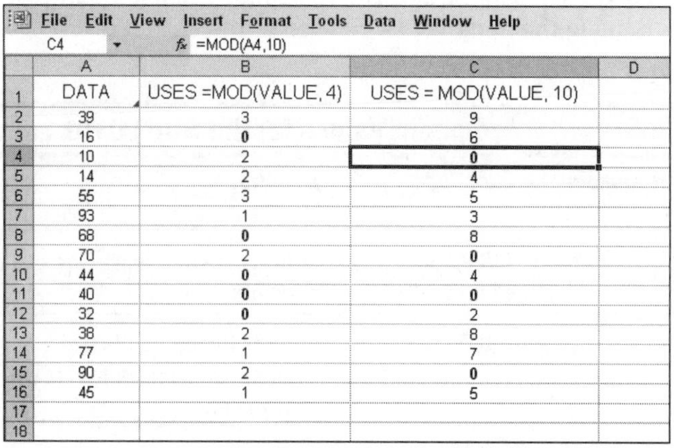

	A	B	C	D
1	DATA	USES =MOD(VALUE, 4)	USES = MOD(VALUE, 10)	
2	39	3	9	
3	16	0	6	
4	10	2	0	
5	14	2	4	
6	55	3	5	
7	93	1	3	
8	68	0	8	
9	70	2	0	
10	44	0	4	
11	40	0	0	
12	32	0	2	
13	38	2	8	
14	77	1	7	
15	90	2	0	
16	45	1	5	
17				
18				

Figure 8-5: Using MOD to find specific values.

In row 1 of the worksheet in Figure 8-5, the example formulas are entered into the successive rows of columns B and C. Column A contains numbers that will be tested with the MOD function. If looking for multiples of 4, the MOD function will have 4 as the divisor, and when a value is a multiple of 4, MOD returns 0. This is evident by comparing the numbers in column A with the returned values in column B.

The same approach is used in column C, only here the divisor is 10, so multiples of 10 are being tested for in column A. Where a 0 appear in column C, the associated number in Column A is a multiple of 10.

In this way, the MOD function can be used to find meaningful values in a worksheet.

Getting Just the Answer You Need with SUBTOTAL

The SUBTOTAL function is very flexible. It doesn't perform just one calculation, but rather it can do any one of 11 different calculations depending on what you need. What's more, SUBTOTAL can perform these calculations on up to 29 ranges of numbers. This gives you the ability to get exactly the type of summary you need without creating a complex set of formulas. The syntax for the function is:

```
=SUBTOTAL(function number, range1, range2,...)
```

The first argument determines which calculation is performed. It can be any of the values shown in Table 8-3. The remaining arguments identify the ranges containing the numbers to be used in the calculation.

Table 8-3	Argument Values for the SUBTOTAL Function	
Function Number for First Argument	**Function**	**Description**
1	AVERAGE	Returns the average value of a group of numbers
2	COUNT	Returns the count of cells that contain numbers and also numbers within the list of arguments
3	COUNTA	Returns the count of cells that are not empty and only non-empty values within the list of arguments
4	MAX	Returns the maximum value found in a group of numbers
5	MIN	Returns the minimum value found in a group of numbers
6	PRODUCT	Returns the product of a group of numbers
7	STDEV	Returns the standard deviation from a sample of values
8	STDEVP	Returns the standard deviation from a whole group of values, including text and logical values

Function Number for First Argument	Function	Description
9	SUM	Returns the sum of a group of numbers
10	VAR	Returns variance based on a sample
11	VARP	Returns variance based on an entire population

Figure 8-6 exemplifies a few uses of the SUBTOTAL function. Raw data values are listed in Column A. The results of using the function in a few variations are listed in Column C. Column D displays the actual function entries that returned the respective results in Column C.

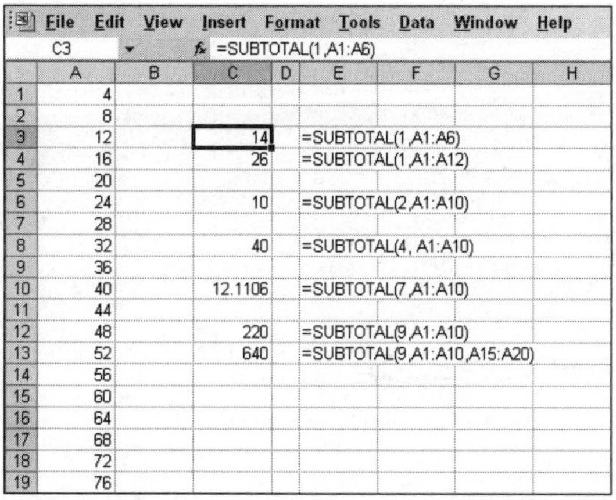

Figure 8-6:
Working with the SUBTOTAL function.

	File	Edit	View	Insert	Format	Tools	Data	Window	Help	
	C3		▼	*fx*	=SUBTOTAL(1,A1:A6)					
	A	B	C	D	E	F	G	H		
1	4									
2	8									
3	12		14		=SUBTOTAL(1,A1:A6)					
4	16		26		=SUBTOTAL(1,A1:A12)					
5	20									
6	24		10		=SUBTOTAL(2,A1:A10)					
7	28									
8	32		40		=SUBTOTAL(4, A1:A10)					
9	36									
10	40		12.1106		=SUBTOTAL(7,A1:A10)					
11	44									
12	48		220		=SUBTOTAL(9,A1:A10)					
13	52		640		=SUBTOTAL(9,A1:A10,A15:A20)					
14	56									
15	60									
16	64									
17	68									
18	72									
19	76									

Using named ranges with the SUBTOTAL function is useful. For example, =SUBTOTAL(1, October_Sales, November_Sales, December_sales) makes for an easy way to calculate the average sale of the fourth quarter.

Using SUMIF to Tally Only What's Needed

SUMIF is one of the real gemstones of Excel functions. It calculates the sum of a range of values, including only those values that meet a specified criterion. The criterion can be based on the same column that is being summed, or it can be based on an adjacent column.

Suppose you use a worksheet to keep track of all your food-store purchases. For each shopping trip, you put the date in Column A, the amount in Column B, and the name of the store in column C. You can use the SUMIF function to tell Excel to add all the values in Column B only where Column C contains "Great Grocery." That's it. SUMIF gives you the answer. Neat!

Figure 8-7 shows this example. The date of purchase, place of purchase, and amount spent are listed in three columns. SUMIF calculates the sum of purchases at Great Grocery. Here is how the function is written for the example:

```
=SUMIF(C3:C15,"Great Grocery",B3:B15)
```

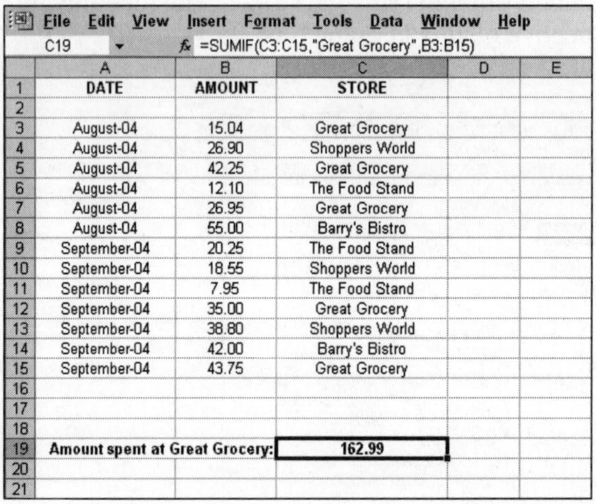

File Edit View Insert Format Tools Data Window Help

C19 =SUMIF(C3:C15,"Great Grocery",B3:B15)

	A	B	C	D	E
1	DATE	AMOUNT	STORE		
2					
3	August-04	15.04	Great Grocery		
4	August-04	26.90	Shoppers World		
5	August-04	42.25	Great Grocery		
6	August-04	12.10	The Food Stand		
7	August-04	26.95	Great Grocery		
8	August-04	55.00	Barry's Bistro		
9	September-04	20.25	The Food Stand		
10	September-04	18.55	Shoppers World		
11	September-04	7.95	The Food Stand		
12	September-04	35.00	Great Grocery		
13	September-04	38.80	Shoppers World		
14	September-04	42.00	Barry's Bistro		
15	September-04	43.75	Great Grocery		
16					
17					
18					
19	Amount spent at Great Grocery:		162.99		
20					
21					

Figure 8-7: Using SUMIF for targeted tallying.

The dates in this example aren't used, but asking SUMIF to tell how much is spent on a given day (or range of dates) instead of which store would be easy enough.

A couple of important points about the SUMIF function:

- The second argument can accommodate several variations of expressions, such as including greater than (>) or less than (<) signs or other operators. For example, if a column has regions such as North, South, East, and West; the criteria could be `<>North`, which would return the sum of rows that are *not* for the North region.
- Unpredictable results will occur if the ranges in the first and third arguments do not match in size.

Try it yourself! Here's how to use the SUMIF function:

1. **Enter two ranges of data in a worksheet.**

   At least one should contain numerical data. Make sure both ranges are the same size.

2. **Position the cursor in the cell where you want the results displayed.**

3. **Enter =SUMIF(to begin the function.**

4. **Click and drag the mouse over one of the ranges.**

   This is the range that can be other than numerical data.

5. **Enter a comma (,).**

6. **Click on one of the cells in the first range.**

   This is the criteria.

7. **Enter a comma (,).**

8. **Click and drag the mouse over the second range.**

   This is the range that must contain numerical data.

9. **Enter a closing parenthesis to end the function, and press Enter.**

The result you see is a sum of the numeric values where the items in the first range matched the selected criteria.

Chapter 9

Using Descriptive Statistical Functions

*J*ust pick up the newspaper, or turn on the television or the radio. We're bombarded with interesting facts and figures that are the result of statistical work: There is a 60 percent chance of rain; the Dow Jones Industrial Average gained 2.8 percent; the Yankees are favored over the Red Sox, 4-3; and so on.

Statistics are used to tell us facts about the world around us. Statistics are also used to give us lies about our world. Statistics can be used to confuse or obscure information. Imagine you try a new candy bar and you like it. Well, then you can boast that 100 percent of the people who tried it liked it!

Sometimes statistics produce odd conclusions — to say the least! Imagine this: Bill Gates helps out at a homeless shelter. The average wealth of the 40 or so people in the room is $1 billion. How about this: You hear on the news that the price of gasoline dropped 6 percent. Hurray! Let's go on a trip. But what is that 6 percent decrease based on? Is it a comparison to last week's price, last month's price, or last year's price? Perhaps the price of gasoline dropped 6 percent, compared to last month. But still prices are 20 percent higher than last year. Is this good news?

Deciding Where the Middle Is with AVERAGE, MEDIAN, and MODE

Are you of average height? Do you earn an average income? Are your children getting above-average grades? There is more than a single way to determine the middle value from a group of values. There are actually three common statistical functions to describe the center value from a population of values. These are the mean, the median, and the mode.

A population is an entire set of values. Often this is a large set of observed or recorded values, such as 10,000 sales transactions, or the scores on 150,000 history tests.

The term *average* is often meant to be the mean value, but in common language *average* can also mean the median or the mode, instead of the mean. This leads to all sorts of wonderful claims from advertisers and anyone else who wants to make a point.

Here's some clarification of these terms:

- **Mean:** The mean is a calculated value. It's the result of summing the values in a list or set of values, and then dividing the sum by the number of values. For example the average of the numbers 1, 2, and 3 equals 2. This is calculated as $(1 + 2 + 3) \div 3$ or $6 \div 3$.

- **Median:** The median is the middle value in a sorted list of values. If there is an odd number of items in the list, then the median is the actual middle value. In lists with an even number of items there is no actual middle value. In this case, the median is the mean of the two values in the middle. For example, the median of 1, 2, 3, 4, 5 = 3, because the middle value is 3. The median of 1, 2, 3, 4, 5, 6 = 3.5. There is no middle value, so the mean of 3 and 4 is used as the median. The values 3 and 4 straddle the middle in this example.

- **Mode:** The mode is the value that has the highest occurrence in a list of values. It may not exist! In the list of values: 1, 2, 3, 4 there is no mode, because each number is used the same number of times. In the list of values 1, 2, 2, 3, 4 the mode is 2, because 2 is used twice, and the other numbers are used once.

Let's get you started! These steps will create three results in your worksheet, using the AVERAGE, MEDIAN, and MODE functions. Try this:

1. **Enter a list of numerical values.**

   Any mix of numbers will do.

2. **Position the cursor in the cell where you want the *mean* to appear.**

3. **Enter =AVERAGE(to start the function.**

4. **Drag the mouse over the list, or enter the address of the range.**

5. **Enter a closing parenthesis to end the AVERAGE function.**

6. **Position the cursor in the cell where you want the *median* to appear.**

7. **Enter =MEDIAN(to start the function.**

8. **Drag the mouse over the list, or enter the address of the range.**

9. **Enter a closing parenthesis to end the MEDIAN function.**

10. **Position the cursor in the cell where you want the *mode* to appear.**

11. **Enter =MODE(to start the function.**

12. **Drag the mouse over the list, or enter the address of the range.**

13. **Enter a closing parenthesis to end the MODE function.**

Depending on the numbers you entered, the three results may be the same, or about the same, or fairly different. The MODE function will have returned #N/A if there were no repeating values.

The mean is calculated using the AVERAGE function.

Imagine this: Three people use a new toothpaste for six months, then all go to the dentist. Two have no cavities. Hey, this toothpaste is great! The third person has three cavities. Uh oh!:

Person	*Cavities*
A	0
B	0
C	3

The average number of cavities for this group is 1. That is, if you're using the *mean* as the average. This doesn't sound like a good toothpaste if, on average, each person who used it got a cavity! On the other hand, both the median and the mode equal 0. The median equals 0 because that's the middle value in the sorted list. The mode equals 0 because that's the highest occurring value. As you can see, statistics prove that the new toothpaste gives 0 cavities, on average — sort of.

Let's look at another example. Figure 9-1 shows the results of a midterm tests for a hypothetical class. The mean, median, and mode are shown for the distribution of grades.

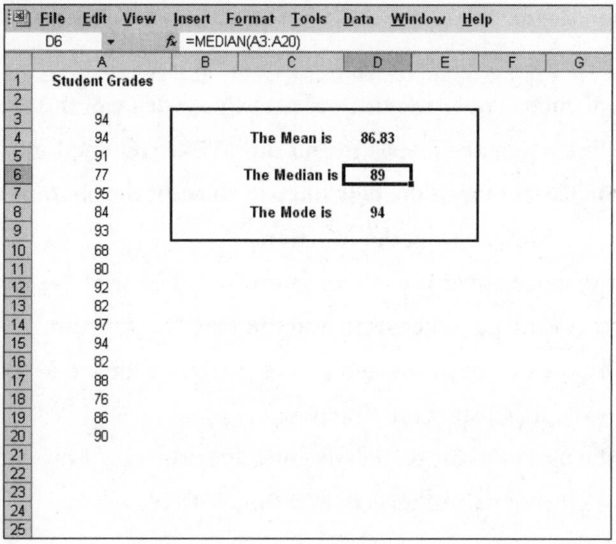

Figure 9-1:
Defining
central
tendencies
in a list of
grades.

As often happens, the mean, the median, and the mode all return a different number. In the fairest sense, we can say the average grade is 86.83, or the mean value. But if the teacher or the school had the notion to make their impact on students look better, they could point out that the highest occurring score is 94. This is the mode and, sure enough, three students did receive a 94. But is this the best representation of the overall results?

Working with the functions that return these central tendencies — AVERAGE, MEDIAN, and MODE — makes for interesting scrutiny. Here is one more example of how extreme these different averaging functions are, here are the statistics of six customers and what they spent with a company last year:

Customer	Total amount spent last year
A	$300
B	$90
C	$2,600
D	$850
E	$28,400
F	$1,000

The mean (using the AVERAGE function) is $5,540. The median is $925. These two amounts aren't even close! Which one best represents the "average" of how much a customer spent last year? Note there is no mode for this set of numbers because there is no value that repeats.

The issue with this set of data is that one value — $28,400 — is so much larger than the other values that it skews the mean. You may be led to believe that each customer spent about $5,540. But looking at the real values, only one single customer spent a lot of money, relatively speaking. Customers A, B, C, D, and F spent nowhere near $5,540, so how can that "average" apply to them?

Figure 9-2 shows this situation in which one value is way out of league with the rest and makes the average not too useful. Figure 9-2 also shows how much the mean changes if the one oddball customer is left out.

File Edit View Insert Format Tools Data Window Help

G15 =AVERAGE(G7:G11)

Scenario 1		*Scenario 2*	
All Customers		Customer E is left out	
Customer	**Amount Spent Last Year**	**Customer**	**Amount Spent Last Year**
A	$ 300	A	$ 300
B	$ 90	B	$ 90
C	$ 2,600	C	$ 2,600
D	$ 850	D	$ 850
E	$ 28,400	F	$ 1,000
F	$ 1,000		
Mean	**$ 5,540**	**Mean**	**$ 968**
Median	**$ 925**	**Median**	**$ 850**

Figure 9-2: Deciding what to do with an unusual value.

In Scenario 2, Customer E is left out. The mean and the median are much closer together — $968 and $850, respectively. Either amount reasonably represents the mid value of what customers spent last year.

But can you just drop a customer like that (not to mention the biggest customer)? Yikes! Instead, you can consider a couple of creative averaging solutions. Either use the median or use a weighted average (a calculation of the mean, but in which the relevance of each value is taken into account). Figure 9-3 shows the result of each approach.

Scenario 1 shows the mean and the median for the set of customer amounts. Here, using the median is a better representation of the central tendency of the group.

File Edit View Insert Format Tools Data Window Help
F18 ▼ ƒ =SUMPRODUCT(F9:F14,G9:G14)/SUM(G9:G14)

	A	B	C	D	E	F	G	H	I
1									
2		*Scenario 1*				*Scenario 2*			
3		Just the facts!			Customer E is treated with a dampening weight factor				
4									
5									
6		Customer	Amount Spent		Customer	Amount Spent	Weight		
7			Last Year			Last Year	Factor		
8									
9		A	$ 300		A	$ 300	18		
10		B	$ 90		B	$ 90	18		
11		C	$ 2,600		C	$ 2,600	18		
12		D	$ 850		D	$ 850	18		
13		E	$ 28,400		E	$ 28,400	10		
14		F	$ 1,000		F	$ 1,000	18		
15									
16		Total	$ 33,240						
17									
18		Mean	$ 5,540		Mean	$ 3,711			
19		Median	$ 925		Median	$ 925			
20									
21									
22									
23									
24									
25									

Figure 9-3:
Calculating
a creative
mean.

When results that are based on a non-typical calculation are reported, it's good practice to add a footnote that explains how the answer was determined. If you were to report that the "average" expenditure was $925, a note should explain this is the median, not the mean.

Scenario 2 in Figure 9-3 is a little more complex. This involves making a weighted average, which is used to let individual values be more or less influential in the calculation of a mean. This is just what we need! Customer E needs to be less influential.

Weighted averages are the result of applying a weight factor to each value used in the mean. In our example, all the customers are given a weight factor of 18, except Customer E has a weight factor of 10. Essentially, all customers except Customer E have been given increased weight, or Customer E has been given less weight. Both of these viewpoints are valid because, effectively, all the customers have been moved away of having an equal weight of 16.667 (calculated as 100 ÷ Number of Customers). When weights are applied in an average, the sum of the weights must equal 100. Without applying any new weights, each customer effectively has a weight of 16.667. This is calculated as 100 ÷ 6. Applying a weight of 10 to Customer E, and 18 to all the other customers, keeps the sum of the weights at 100: 18 × 5 + 10. The values of 18 and 10 have been subjectively chosen.

The mean in Scenario 2 is $3,711. This figure is still way above the median or even the mean of just the five customers without Customer E (refer to Figure 9-2). Even so, it's less than the plain mean shown in Scenario 1.

By the way, the mean in Scenario 2 is not calculated with the AVERAGE function. Instead, the SUMPRODUCT function is used. The actual formula in cell F18 looks like this:

```
=SUMPRODUCT(F9:F14,G9:G14)/SUM(G9:G14)
```

The amount that each customer spent last year is multiplied by its weight, and a sum of those products is attained with SUMPRODUCT. Then the sum of the products is divided by the sum of the weights.

Deviating from the Middle

Life is full of variety! And Excel gives you the functions to see just how much variety there is. Take an average apple, whatever that might be. Assume an ideal apple of a deep red color, perfectly round, and 3 inches in diameter. How many apples exactly match this description? Some are lighter in color, some are deeper in color. Some are bigger, some smaller. There are green and yellow apples. You get the picture.

A very useful handful of Excel functions let you measure how items deviate from the mean, and even let you compare how two sets of data deviate from each other.

Measuring variance

Variance is a measure of how spread out a set of data is, in relation to the mean. Variance is calculated by summing the squared deviations. In particular, variance does the following:

1. **Calculates the mean of the set of values.**
2. **Calculates the difference from the mean for each value.**
3. **Squares each difference.**
4. **Sums up the squares.**
5. **Divides by the number of items in the sample, minus 1.**

A sample is a selected set of values taken from the population. A sample is easier to work with. For example, any statistical results found on 1,000 sales transactions probably would return the same, or close to the same results if run on the entire population of 10,000 transactions.

Note that the last step differs whether the VAR or VARP function is used. VAR uses the number of items, minus 1, as the denominator. VARP uses the number of items.

Figure 9-4 shows these steps in calculating a variance. Column B has a handful of values. Column C shows the deviation of each figure from the *mean* of the values. The mean, which equals 7.8, is never actually shown. Instead, the mean is calculated within the formula that computes the difference. For example, cell C8 has this formula:

```
=B8-AVERAGE($B$4:$B$8)
```

Column D squares the values in column C. This is an easy calculation. Here are the contents of cell D8: =C8^2. Finally, the sum of the squared deviations is divided by the number of items, less one item. The formula in cell D12 is =SUM(D4:D8)/(COUNT(B4:B8)-1).

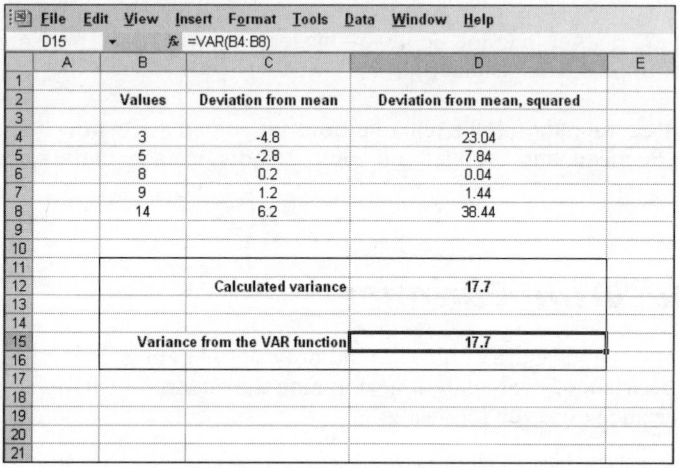

Figure 9-4: Calculating variance from the mean.

Now that you know how to create a variance the textbook way, you can forget it all! We showed the mathematical steps so you could understand what happens, but Excel provides the VAR and VARP functions to do all the grunge work for you.

In Figure 9-4, cell D15 shows the variance calculated directly with the VAR function: =VAR(B4:B8).

Try it yourself. Here's how:

1. **Enter a list of numerical values.**

   Any mix of numbers will do.

2. **Position the cursor in the cell where you want the *variance* to appear.**

3. **Enter =VAR(to start the function.**

4. **Drag the mouse over the list, or enter the address of the range.**

5. **Enter a closing parenthesis to end the function.**

Variance is calculated on either a population of data or a sample of the population:

- ✔ The VAR function is used to calculate variance on a sample of a population's data.

- ✔ The VARP function is used to calculate variance on the full population.

The calculation is slightly different in that the denominator for variance of a population is the number of items. The denominator for variance of a sample is the number of items minus 1. Figure 9-5 shows how VAR and VARP are used on a sample and the full population. Cells A4:A43 contain the number of hours of television watched daily by 40 individuals.

	A	B	C	D
1				
2	# Of Daily TV Viewing Hours			
3				Formula Used
4	2			
5	3	Variance for A4:A23	1.796710526	=VAR(A4:A23)
6	2.5			
7	1			
8	0.5	Variance for A4:A43	1.43734375	=VARP(A4:A43)
9	0.5			
10	1			
11	0			
12	3			
13	3			
14	4			
15	2			
16	0			
17	2.5			
18	1.5			
19	0.5			
20	1			
21	5			
22	2			
23	1.5			
24	2			
25	2.5			
26	0			
27	0			
28	2			
29	1			
30	1			
31	3			

Figure 9-5: Calculating variance from the mean.

The VAR function is used to calculate the variance of a sample of 20 values. The VARP function is used to calculate the variance of the full population of 40 values. VARP is entered in the same fashion as VAR. Here's how:

1. **Enter a list of numerical values.**

    Any mix of numbers will do.

2. **Position the cursor in the cell where you want the *variance* to appear.**

3. Enter =VARP(to start the function.

4. Drag the mouse over the list, or enter the address of the range.

5. Enter a closing parenthesis to end the function.

Analyzing deviations

Often, finding the mean is an adequate measure of a sample of data. Another useful measure though is the average *deviation* from the mean. That is, finding the average of how far individual values differ from the mean of the sample. For example, you may not need to know the average score on a test, but you want to find out how far a score can differ from the average. In other words, it's only the relative difference that's needed, not any actual hard numbers.

Here's an example:

Score	Deviation from mean (mean is 83.17)
78	5.17
92	8.83
97	3.83
80	3.17
72	11.17
90	6.83

The mean of this sample of values is 83.17. Use the AVERAGE function, if you want to double-check. Each individual value deviates somewhat from the mean. For example, 92 has a deviation value of 8.83 from the mean. A simple equation proves this: 92 – 83.17 = 8.83.

If we were to use the AVERAGE function to get the mean of the deviations, we would have the average deviation. It's even easier than that, though. Excel provides the AVEDEV function for this very purpose!

Here's how to use the AVEDEV function:

1. Enter a list of numerical values.

2. Position the cursor in the cell where you want the *average deviation* to appear.

3. Enter =AVEDEV(to start the function.

4. Drag the pointer over the list, or enter the address of the range.

5. Enter a closing parenthesis to end the function.

The AVEDEV function averages the *absolute* deviations. For example, a value of 10 has a deviation of –40 from a mean of 50: 10 – 50 = –40. However AVEDEV will use the absolute value of the deviation, 40, instead of –40.

The variance, explained earlier in the chapter, serves as the basis for a common statistical value called the *standard deviation.* Technically speaking, the standard deviation is the square root of the variance. Variance is calculated by *squaring* deviations from the mean.

The variance and the standard deviation are both valid measurements of deviation. However, the variance can be a confusing number to work with. In Figure 9-4, the variance was calculated to be 17.7 for a group of values whose range is just 12 (14 – 2). How can a range that is only a size of 12 show a variance of 17.7? Well, it does, as shown earlier in Figure 9-4.

This oddity is removed when using the standard deviation. The reversing of the squaring brings the result back to the range of the data. The standard deviation value fits inside the range of the sample values. Excel has a standard deviation formula — STDEV. This is how you use it:

1. **Enter a list of numerical values.**

2. **Position the cursor in the cell where you want the *standard deviation* to appear.**

3. **Enter =STDEV(to start the function.**

4. **Drag the mouse over the list, or enter the address of the range.**

5. **Enter a closing parenthesis to end the function.**

Figure 9-6 takes the data sample and variance shown in Figure 9-4 and adds the standard deviation to the picture. The standard deviation is 4.207136794. This number fits inside the range of the sample data.

The standard deviation is one of the most widely used measures in statistical work. It's often used to analyze deviation in a normal distribution. A distribution is the frequency of occurrences of values in a population or sample. A *normal* distribution often occurs in large sets of data that have a natural or random attribute. For example, taking a measurement of the height of 1,000 10-year-old children will produce a normal distribution. Most of the measured heights will center around and deviate somewhat from the mean. A few measured heights will be extreme — both considerably larger than the mean, and considerably smaller than the mean.

A normal distribution is often visually represented as a graph in the shape of a bell. Hence the popular name, the *bell curve.* Figure 9-7 shows a normal distribution.

	File	Edit	View	Insert	Format	Tools	Data	Window	Help	

D15   ▼   *fx* =STDEV(C4:C8)

	A	B	C	D	E
1					
2			**Values**		
3					
4			3		
5			5		
6			8		
7			9		
8			14		
9					
10					
11					
12			Variance	17.7	
13					
14					
15			Standard Deviation	4.207136794	
16					
17					
18					
19					
20					
21					

Figure 9-6:
Calculating
the standard
deviation.

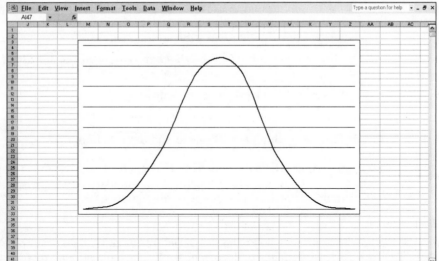

Figure 9-7:
Displaying a
normal
distribution
in a graph.

A normal distribution has a few key characteristics:

✔ The curve is symmetrical around the mean — half the measurements are
greater than the mean and half are less than the mean.

✔ The mean, median, and mode are all the same.

✔ The highest point of the curve is the mean.

✔ The width and height are determined by the standard deviation. The larger the standard deviation, the wider and flatter the curve. You can have two normal distributions with the same mean and different standard deviations.

✔ 68.2 percent of the area under the curve is within one standard deviation of the mean (both to the left and the right); 95.44 percent of the area under the curve is within two standard deviations, and 99.72 percent of the area under the curve is within three standard deviations.

✔ The extreme left and right ends of the curve are called the tails. Extreme values are found in the tails. For example, in a distribution of height, very short heights would be found in the left tail, and very large heights would be found in the right tail.

Different sets of data will likely produce a different mean and standard deviation and, therefore, a different shaped bell curve. Figure 9-8 shows two superimposed normal distributions. Each is a valid normal distribution, however the width of each is a function of its own data. The wider curve has a larger standard deviation.

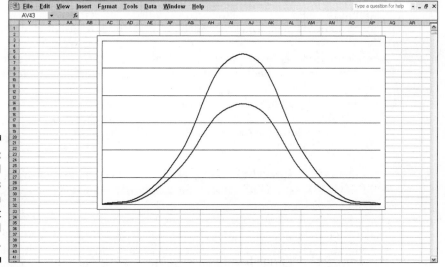

Figure 9-8:
Normal
distributions
come in
different
heights and
widths.

Analysis is often done with normal distributions to determine probabilities. For example, what is the probability that a 10-year-old child's height is 54 inches? Somewhere along the curve is a discrete point that represents this height. Then further computation (outside the scope of this discussion) returns the probability. What about finding the probability that a 10-year-old is 54 inches *or greater?* Then the *area* under the curve is considered. These are the type of questions and answers that are determined with normal distributions.

A good amount of analysis of normal distributions involves the values in the *tails* — the areas to the extreme left and right of the normal distribution curve.

All normal distributions have a mean and a standard deviation. However there is a special normal distribution, the *standard normal distribution,* that is characterized by having the mean equal 0 and the standard deviation equal 1.

There is a table of values that serves as a lookup in determining probabilities for areas under the standard normal curve. This table is useful when working with data that has been coerced to be "standard." This table is often found in the appendix section of statistics books and on the Internet as well. Try http://goldwing.Kennesaw.edu/csis3400/normaltable.htm or www.statsoft.com/textbook/sttable.html.

In order to use this table of standard normal curve probabilities, the data being analyzed must be standardized. Excel provides the STANDARDIZE function for just this purpose. STANDARDIZE takes three arguments: the data point, the mean, and the standard deviation. The returned value is what the data point value is, when the mean is 0 and the standard deviation is 1.

An individual value from a nonstandard normal distribution is referred to as x. An individual value from a standard normal distribution is referred to as z.

Figure 9-9 shows how the STANDARDIZE function changes raw values to standard values. The standard deviation of the raw data is 9.357842337, but the standard deviation of the standardized values is 1. The mean of the standardized values is 0.

Column B in Figure 9-9 has a long list of 1,200 random values. The mean is 18.74111235, as seen in cell C2. The standard deviation is 9.357842337, as seen in cell C3.

For each data point in Column B, the standardized value is displayed in Column E. The list of values in Column E are those returned with the STANDARDIZE function. The function takes three arguments: the data point, the mean of the distribution, and the standard deviation of the distribution. So for example, this is the formula in cell E7: =STANDARDIZE(B7,C$2,C$3).

Note how a few key properties of the distribution have changed after the values are standardized:

 ✔ The standard deviation is 1.

 ✔ The mean is 0.

 ✔ The standardized values fall within the range –3.9 to 3.9.

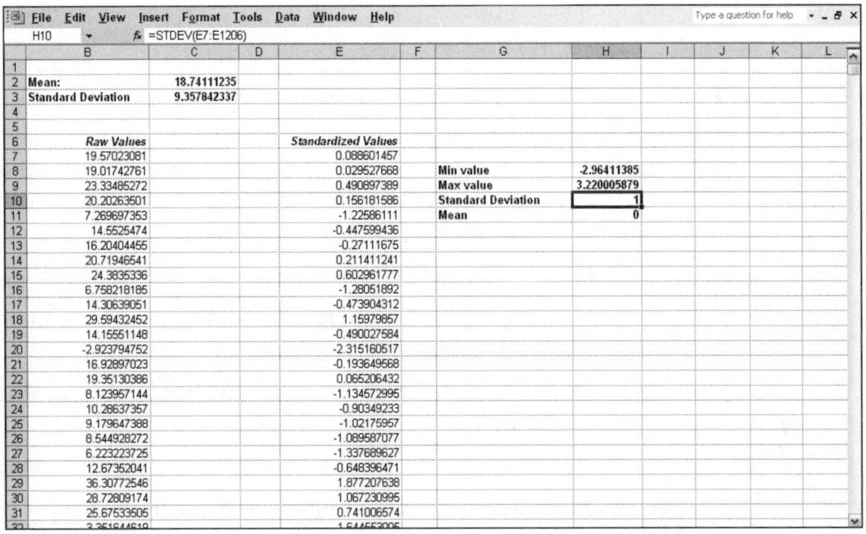

	B	C	E	G	H
1					
2	Mean:	18.74111235			
3	Standard Deviation	9.357842337			
4					
5					
6	*Raw Values*		*Standardized Values*		
7	19.57023081		0.088601457		
8	19.01742761		0.029527668	Min value	-2.96411385
9	23.33485272		0.490897389	Max value	3.220005879
10	20.20263501		0.156181586	Standard Deviation	1
11	7.269697353		-1.22586111	Mean	0
12	14.5525474		-0.447599436		
13	16.20404455		-0.27111675		
14	20.71946541		0.211411241		
15	24.3835336		0.602961777		
16	6.758218185		-1.28051892		
17	14.30639051		-0.473904312		
18	29.59432452		1.15979857		
19	14.15551148		-0.490027584		
20	-2.923794752		-2.315160517		
21	16.92897023		-0.193649568		
22	19.35130386		0.065206432		
23	8.123957144		-1.134572995		
24	10.28637357		-0.90349233		
25	9.179647388		-1.02175957		
26	8.544928272		-1.089587077		
27	6.223223725		-1.337689627		
28	12.67352041		-0.648396471		
29	36.30772546		1.877207638		
30	28.72809174		1.067230995		
31	25.67533505		0.741006574		

Figure 9-9: Standardizing a distribution of data.

This third point is concluded by using the MIN and MAX functions, respectively, in cells H8 and H9. Having values fall in the range –3.9 to 3.9 allows the values to be analyzed with the Areas Under the Standard Normal Curve table mentioned earlier. That is, it's a property of standard normal curves to have all values fit into this range.

Here's how to use the STANDARDIZE function:

1. **Enter a list of numerical values into a column.**

   It makes sense if this list is a set of random observable data, such as heights, weights, or amounts of monthly rainfall.

2. **Calculate the mean and standard deviation.**

   See the section "Deciding Where the Middle Is with AVERAGE, MEDIAN, and MODE" to learn about the mean.

   These values will be referenced by the STANDARDIZE function. Remember the mean is calculated with the AVERAGE function and the standard deviation is calculated with the STDEV function.

3. **Place the cursor in the adjacent cell to the first data point entered in Step 1.**

4. **Enter** =STANDARDIZE(**to start the function.**

5. **Click on the cell that has the first data point.**

6. **Enter a comma (,).**

7. **Click on the cell that has the mean.**

8. **Enter a comma (,).**

9. **Click on the cell that has the standard deviation.**

10. **Enter a closing parenthesis to end the function.**

    The formula with the STANDARDIZE function is now complete However, it needs to be edited to fix the references to the mean and standard deviation. The references need to be made absolute so they won't change when the formula is dragged down to other cells.

11. **Double-click on the cell with the formula to enter the edit mode.**

12. **Precede the row part of the reference to the cell that contains the mean with a dollar ($) sign.**

13. **Precede the row part of the reference to the cell that contains the standard deviation with a dollar ($) sign.**

14. **Press the Enter key, the Tab key, or the Esc key to end the editing.**

15. **Use the fill handle to drag the formula down to the rest of the cells that are adjacent to the source data points.**

It's important that the references to the mean and standard deviation are treated as absolute references so they won't change when the formula is dragged to the other cells. Therefore, the formula should end up looking like this (note the $ signs): `=STANDARDIZE(B7,C$2,C$3)`.

There is deviation in a distribution. But who says the deviation is uniform? Not all distributions are normal. This type of distribution, therefore, is *skewed,* with more values clustered either below the mean or above it:

✔ When more values fall below the mean, the distribution is *positively* skewed.

✔ When more values fall above the mean, the distribution is *negatively* skewed.

Here are a few examples:

Values	*Mean*	*Comment*
1, 2, 3, 4, 5	3	No skew, an even number of values fall above and below the mean.
1, 2, 3, 6, 8	4	The distribution is positively skewed. More values fall below the mean.
1, 2, 8, 9, 10	6	The distribution is negatively skewed. More values fall above the mean.

Figure 9-10 shows a plot of a distribution. One thousand values are in the distribution, ranging between 1 and 100. The values are summarized in a table of frequencies (discussed later in this chapter). The table of frequencies is the source of the chart.

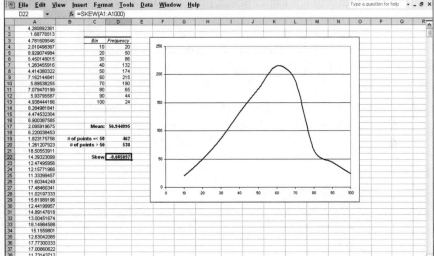

Figure 9-10:
Working with skewed data.

The mean of the distribution is 50.945, shown in cell D17. Cells D19 and D20 show the number of values that fall above and below the mean. There are more values above the mean, than below. The distribution, therefore, is negatively skewed.

The actual skew factor is –0.0850969. The formula in cell D22 is =SKEW(A1:A1000). The chart makes it easy to see the amount of skew. The plot is leaning to the right.

Finding out the amount of skew of a distribution helps identify any bias in the data. If for example, the data is meant to be a random sampling of height for a given population segment (such as 10-year-old children), and the data is skewed, then you have to wonder how there can be a bias in the data. Perhaps a number of 12-year-old children were measured and those heights were mixed in with the data.

Here's how to use the SKEW function:

1. **Enter a list of numerical values.**

2. **Position the cursor in the cell where you want amount of skew to appear.**

3. Enter =SKEW(to start the function.

4. Drag the mouse over the list, or enter the address of the range.

5. Enter a closing parenthesis to end the function.

The KURT function measures the *kurtosis* of a distribution. This is a measure of the peakedness or flatness of a distribution, compared with the normal distribution. This is also a measure of the size of the tails of the curves. The KURT function returns a positive value if the distribution is relatively peaked compared with the normal distribution. A negative result means the distribution is relatively flat.

Figure 9-11 shows the curves of two distributions. The one on the left has a negative kurtosis of –0.2204 indicating a relatively flat distribution. The distribution on the right is just about 0, which means the distribution is just about normal. The value of -0.0102 is very close to 0. The uniformity of the curve's shape confirms this.

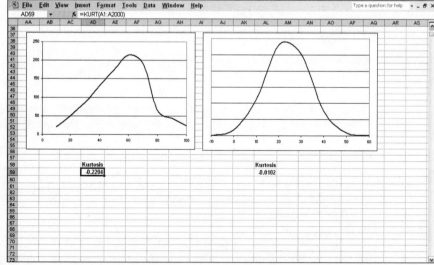

Figure 9-11:
Measuring the kurtosis of two distributions.

This is how to use the KURT function:

1. Enter a list of numerical values.

2. Position the cursor in the cell where you want *kurtosis* to appear.

3. Enter =KURT(to start the function.

4. Drag the mouse over the list, or enter the address of the range.

5. Enter a closing parenthesis to end the function.

Comparing sets of data for similarity

At times you need to compare two sets of data to see how they relate to one another. For example, how does the amount of snowfall affect the number of customers entering a store? Or, as another example, does the money spent on advertising have any affect on reaching customers?

Excel provides two functions that answer these questions: COVAR and CORREL. These return the *covariance* and *correlation* coefficient results from comparing two sets of data.

The COVAR function takes two arrays as its arguments and returns a single value. The value can be positive or negative. A positive value means generally that the two arrays of data move in the same direction. A negative value means that overall the direction of the values in the second array does not follow the direction of the values in the first array.

If COVAR returns 0, then there is no discernable relationship between the two sets of values. Also, the size of the answer, whether positive or negative, is based on the actual units of the data (the CORREL function handles this differently, demonstrated further in this section).

When COVAR returns 0, there is no relation between the two sets of data.

Sales of bread will likely create sales of butter; they're somewhat related. In other words, the amount of butter a store sells is likely to follow the amount of bread it sells:

Day	*Loaves of bread sold*	*Tubs of butter sold*
Monday	62	12
Tuesday	77	15
Wednesday	95	26

As bread sales increase, so does sales of butter. Therefore, sales of butter have a positive relation to sales of bread. These items complement each other. In contrast, bread and muffins compete against each other. As bread is purchased, the sales of muffins likely suffer, because people will eat one or the other. Without even using any function, we can conclude that bread sales and butter sales move in the same direction, and that bread sales and muffin sales move in differing directions. But by how much?

Figure 9-12 shows an example that measures snowfall and the number of customers coming into a store. Two covariance calculations are given — one for snowfall between 0 and 3 inches, and one for snowfall between 0 and 8 inches.

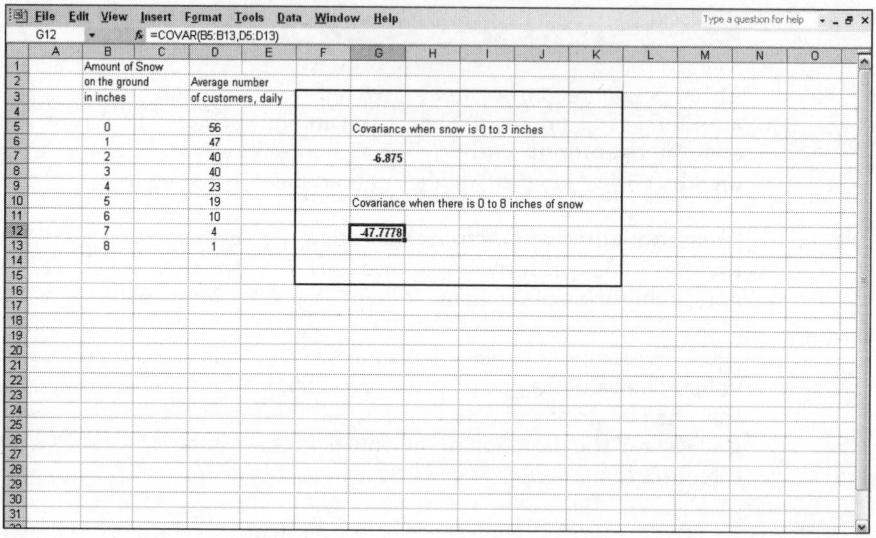

	A	B	C	D	E	F	G	H	I	J	K	L	M	N	O
1		Amount of Snow													
2		on the ground		Average number											
3		in inches		of customers, daily											
4															
5		0		56			Covariance when snow is 0 to 3 inches								
6		1		47											
7		2		40			-6.875								
8		3		40											
9		4		23											
10		5		19			Covariance when there is 0 to 8 inches of snow								
11		6		10											
12		7		4			-47.7778								
13		8		1											

Figure 9-12:
Using
COVAR to
look for a
relationship.

In Figure 9-12, the first COVAR measures the similarity of the amount of snow-fall with the number of customers, but just for 0 to 3 inches of snow. The formula in cell G7 is =COVAR(B5:B8,D5:D8). The answer is –6.875. This means that, as snowfall increases, the number of customers decreases. The two sets of data go in opposite directions. As one goes up, the other goes down. This is confirmed by the result being negative.

The formula in cell G12 is =COVAR(B5:B13,D5:D13). This examines all the values of the data sets, inclusive of 0 to 8 inches of snow. The covariance is -47.7778. This, too, confirms that as snowfall increases the number of customers decreases.

However, note that the covariance of the first calculation, for 0 to 3 inches of snow, is not as severe as the second calculation for 0 to 8 inches. When there is just up to 3 inches of snow on the ground, some customers stay away — but not that many. On the other hand when there is 8 inches of snow, there are no customers. The first covariance is comparably less than the second: –6.875 versus –47.7778. The former number is closer to 0 — and tells that there is not that a few inches of snow don't have much effect. The latter number is significantly distanced from 0 — and, sure enough, when up to 8 inches of snow is considered, customers stay home.

Here's how to use the COVAR function:

1. **Enter two lists of numbers.**

   The lists must be the same size.

2. **Position the cursor in the cell where you want *covariance* to appear.**

3. **Enter =COVAR(to start the function.**

4. **Drag the mouse over the first list, or enter the address of the range.**

5. **Enter a comma (,).**

6. **Drag the mouse over the second list, or enter the address of the range.**

7. **Enter a closing parenthesis to end the function.**

A problem with covariance is that, although it does produce a result, that result is dependent on the actual units of the data sets. The snowfall/customer example returned a covariance figure of –47.7778. As you can see, this number is somewhat based on the actual units, such as the customer counts.

The CORREL function works in the manner as COVAR, but the result is always between –1 and 1. The result is, in effect, set to a standard. Then the result of one correlation can be compared to another.

A negative result means there is an inverse correlation. As one set of data goes up, the other goes down. The actual negative value tells to what degree the inverse correlation is. A value of –1 means the two sets of data move perfectly in opposite directions. A value of –0.5, for example, means the two sets move in somewhat opposite directions.

A positive result means the two data sets move in the same direction. A value of 1 means the two sets move perfectly in the same direction.

A value of zero means there is no correlation.

Figure 9-13 shows three correlation results. The correlations display how customers reacted (as a percentage increase in sales) with regard to three types of advertising.

The CORREL function returns a value between –1 and 0. A positive value means the two sets of data move in the same direction. A negative value means the two sets of data move in opposite directions. A value of 0 means there is no relation between the sets of data.

All three advertising campaigns show a positive correlation. As more money is spent, customer responsiveness increases, or at least doesn't reverse its direction.

| File | Edit | View | Insert | Format | Tools | Data | Window | Help | | | | | | Type a question for help | | | |

I14 =CORREL(B13:B17,F13:F17)

	A	B	C	D	E	F	G	H	I	J	K	L	M	N	O
1															
2		Amount spent on magazine advertising				Customer Responsiveness Percentage									
3															
4		$ 10,000				2									
5		$ 20,000				4		Correlation:	0.96896279						
6		$ 30,000				5									
7		$ 40,000				7									
8		$ 50,000				7									
9															
10															
11		Amount spent on radio advertising													
12															
13		$ 4,000				3									
14		$ 5,000				6		Correlation:	0.932095302						
15		$ 6,000				8									
16		$ 7,000				8.5									
17		$ 8,000				9									
18															
19															
20		Amount spent on direct mail													
21															
22		$ 20,000				4									
23		$ 24,000				4		Correlation:	0.447213595						
24		$ 28,000				3.5									
25		$ 32,000				4									
26		$ 36,000				4.5									
27															
28															
29															
30															
31															

Figure 9-13: Comparing the results of advertising campaigns.

All three returned correlation values fall within the range of 0 to 1 and, therefore, are easy to compare. The evidence is clear — direct mail is not as efficient as magazine or radio advertising. Both the magazine and radio advertising score high; the returned values are close to 1. However, direct mail returns a correlation of 0.4472. A positive correlation does exist — that is, direct-mail expenditures create an increase in customer responsiveness. But the correlation is not as strong as magazine or radio advertising. The money spent on direct mail would be better spent elsewhere.

Here's how to use the CORREL function:

1. **Enter two lists of numbers.**

   The lists must be the same size.

2. **Position the cursor in the cell where you want *correlation* to appear.**

3. **Enter =CORREL(to start the function.**

4. **Drag the mouse over the first list, or enter the address of the range.**

5. **Enter a comma (,).**

6. **Drag the mouse over the second list, or enter the address of the range.**

7. **Enter a closing parenthesis to end the function.**

Putting Numbers Where They Belong

At times, analyzing data in groups or at least knowing where certain data is positioned in a distribution makes sense. For example, the charts shown earlier in Figures 9-7, 9-8, 9-10, and 9-11 are all based on the raw data being represented in groups. These groups may be referred to as bins, buckets, frequencies, and so forth.

Some analysis requires knowing where in a distribution certain data is positioned. Is it near the beginning? Is it near the middle or the end? The functions that answer these questions don't segregate the data but do tell you how to work with chunks of data.

And finally some functions just tell you about values in the sample. What is the largest value? What is the smallest?

Let's get started. Imagine this, a pharmaceutical company is testing a new drug to lower cholesterol. From the population of people taking the drug, 500 cholesterol readings are used for a sample.

In Figure 9-14, the 500 cholesterol readings are in Column A. Of interest is where in these results are the 25 percent, the 50 percent, and the 75 percent mark. That is, what cholesterol reading is found 25 percent into the data. What value is at the 50 percent position? These measures are called *quartiles,* because they divide the sample into four quarters.

The QUARTILE function is designed specifically for this kind of analysis. The function takes two arguments: One is the range of the sample data, and the other indicates which quartile to return. The second argument can be a 0, 1, 2, 3, or 4:

Formula	*Result*
=QUARTILE(A4:A503,0)	Returns the minimum value in the data
=QUARTILE(A4:A503,1)	Returns the value at the 25th percentile
=QUARTILE(A4:A503,2)	Returns the value at the 50th percentile
=QUARTILE(A4:A503,3)	Returns the value at the 75th percentile
=QUARTILE(A4:A503,4)	Returns the maximum value in the data

QUARTILE works on ordered data, but you don't have to do the sorting, the function takes care of that. In Figure 9-14, the quartiles have been calculated. The minimum and maximum values have been returned by using a 0 and a 5, respectively, as the second argument.

	File	Edit	View	Insert	Format	Tools	Data	Window	Help				Type a question for help		- 日 ×

	A	B	C	D	E	F	G	H	I	J	K	L	M
1	Total Cholesterol												
2													
3													
4	208		Minimum Value	165									
5	176		25th Percentile	183									
6	233		50th Percentile	211									
7	268		75th Percentile	248									
8	266		Maximum Value	279									
9	275												
10	166												
11	211												
12	264												
13	180												
14	193												
15	170												
16	168												
17	183												
18	190												
19	166												
20	197												
21	204												
22	228												
23	206												
24	207												
25	205												
26	269												
27	218												
28	214												
29	199												
30	277												
31	257												
32	278												

D6 ▾ 𝑓ₓ =QUARTILE(A4:A503,2)

Figure 9-14:
Finding out values at quarter percentiles.

Here's how to use the QUARTILE function:

1. **Enter a list of numerical values.**

2. **Position the cursor in the cell where you want a particular quartile to appear.**

3. **Enter =QUARTILE(to start the function.**

4. **Drag the mouse over the list, or enter the address of the range.**

5. **Enter a comma (,).**

6. **Enter a value between 0 and 5 for the second argument.**

7. **Enter a closing parenthesis to end the function.**

The PERCENTILE function is similar to QUARTILE, except you can specify which percentile to use when returning a value. You aren't locked into fixed percentiles such as 25, 50, or 75.

PERCENTILE takes two arguments. The first is the range of the sample. The second argument is a value between 0 and 1. This tells the function which percentile to use. For example 0.1 is the 10th percentile, 0.2 is the 20th percentile, and so on.

Use the QUARTILE function to analyze data at the fixed 25th , 50th, and 75th percentiles. Use the PERCENTILE function to analyze data at any percentile.

Figure 9-15 shows a sample of test scores. Who scored at or above the 90th percentile? The winners deserve some recognition. Bear in mind that scoring at the 90th percentile is not the same as getting a score of 90. Values at or above the 90th percentile are those that are in the top 10 percent of whatever scores are in the sample.

	A	B	C	D	E	F	G	H	I	J	K	L
1		Score on the Trivia Test										
2												
3	Wendy	59			Score found at the 90th percentile							
4	Alex	54				80						
5	Daniel	82	A winner!									
6	Rob	16										
7	Andrea	53										
8	Matthew	78										
9	Michele	58										
10	Les	58										
11	Micheal	62										
12	Louise	61										
13	Mark	37										
14	Steven	25										
15	Lisa	23										
16	Ilse	80	A winner!									
17	Warren	70										
18	Werner	38										
19	Hanni	37										
20	Dill	59										
21	Kirk	54										
22	Geoffrey	72										
23	Nichola	72										
24	Manny	46										
25	Annette	62										
26	Glen	80	A winner!									
27	Crystale	80	A winner!									

Figure 9-15:
Using
PERCENTILE
to find high
scorers.

It so happens that the score that is positioned at the 90th percentile, is 80. Cell F4 has the formula =PERCENTILE(B3:B27,0.9), which uses 0.9 as the second argument.

The cells in C3:C27 all have a formula that tests whether the cell to the left, in column B, is at or greater than the 90th percentile. For example, cell C3 has this formula: =IF(B3>=PERCENTILE(B$3:B$27,0.9),"A winner!","").

If the value in cell B3 is equal to or greater than the value at the 90th percentile, then cell C3 displays the text "A winner!" The value in cell B3 is 59, which doesn't make for a winner. On the other hand, the value in cell B5 is greater than 80, so cell C5 displays the message.

Here's how to use the PERCENTILE function:

1. **Enter a list of numerical values.**

2. **Position the cursor in the cell where you want the result to appear.**

3. **Enter =PERCENTILE(to start the function.**

4. **Drag the mouse over the list, or enter the address of the range.**

5. **Enter a comma (,).**

6. **Enter a value between 0 and 1 for the second argument.**

   This tells the function what percentile to seek.

7. **Enter a closing parenthesis to end the function.**

The RANK function tells you where a particular number is positioned within a distribution. The function takes three arguments:

- ✔ **The number being tested for rank:** If this number isn't found in the data, an error is returned.

- ✔ **The range to look in:** A reference to a range of cells goes here.

- ✔ **A 0 or a 1, telling the function how to sort the distribution:** A 0 (or if the argument is omitted) tells the function to sort the values in descending order. A 1 tells the function to sort in ascending order. The order of the sort makes a difference in how the result in interpreted. Is the value in question being compared to the top value of the data, or the bottom value?

Figure 9-16 displays a list of employees and the bonuses they earned. Let's say you're the employee who earned $4,800. You want to know where you rank in the range of bonus payouts. Cell F4 contains a formula with the RANK function: =RANK(C9,C3:C20). The function returns an answer of 4. Note that the function was entered without the third argument. This tells the function to sort the distribution descending in determining where the value is positioned. This makes sense for determining how close to the *top* of the range a value is.

Figure 9-16: Determining the rank of a value.

	File Edit View Insert Format Tools Data Window Help							
	F4		ƒx =RANK(C9,C3:C20)					
	A	B	C	D	E	F	G	H
1								
2		Employee	Bonus		Where does $4800 rank?			
3		RT	$ 4,000					
4		GB	$ 3,500		Rank:	4		
5		RN	$ 6,200					
6		SP	$ 1,200					
7		HM	$ 1,000					
8		JJ	$ 5,000		Percent Rank:	0.823		
9		FS	$ 4,800					
10		AB	$ 3,200					
11		RO	$ 3,500					
12		WM	$ 7,400					
13		DA	$ 4,600					
14		DT	$ 3,000					
15		EV	$ 3,100					
16		BH	$ 4,400					
17		TK	$ 1,000					
18		MN	$ 1,700					
19		CF	$ 2,000					
20		GW	$ 2,500					
21								
22								
23								
24								
25								

Follow these steps to use the RANK function:

1. **Enter a list of numerical values.**

2. **Position the cursor in the cell where you want the result to appear.**

3. **Enter =RANK(to start the function.**

4. **Click on the cell that has the value you want to find the rank for, or enter its address.**

   You can also just enter the actual value.

5. **Enter a comma (,).**

6. **Drag the mouse over the list of values, or enter the address of the range.**

7. **If you want to have the number evaluated against the list in *ascending* order, enter a comma (,), and then enter a 1.**

   Descending order is the default and doesn't require an argument to be entered.

8. **Enter a closing parenthesis to end the function.**

The PERCENTRANK formula also returns the rank of a value but tells you where the value is as a percentage. In other words, PERCENTRANK may tell you that a value is positioned 20 percent into the ordered distribution. PERCENTRANK takes three arguments:

- ✔ The range of the sample.
- ✔ The number being evaluated against the sample.
- ✔ An indicator of how many decimal points to use in the returned answer. (This is an optional argument. If left out, 3 decimal points are used.)

In Figure 9-16, the percent rank of the $4,800 value is calculated to be 82.3 percent (0.823). Therefore, $4,800 ranks at the 82.3 percent position in the sample. The formula in cell F8 is =PERCENTRANK(C3:C20,C9).

In the RANK function, the value being evaluated is the first argument and the range of the values is the second argument. In the PERCENTRANK function, the order of these arguments is reversed.

Follow these steps to use the PERCENTRANK function:

1. **Enter a list of numerical values.**

2. **Position the cursor in the cell where you want the result to appear.**

3. **Enter =PERCENTRANK(to start the function.**

4. **Drag the mouse over the list of values, or enter the address of the range.**

5. **Enter a comma (,).**

6. **Click on the cell that has the value you want to find the rank for, or enter its address.**

   You can also just enter the actual value.

7. **If you want to have more or less than three decimal points returned in the result, enter a comma (,), and then enter the number of desired decimal points.**

8. **Enter a closing parenthesis to end the function.**

The FREQUENCY function places the count of values in a sample into *bins*. A bin is established for certain numeric ranges (not to be confused with cell ranges). Typically, a number of bins are established that cover the full range of values in the sample. Each bin covers a piece of the overall range.

For example, if the sample data has values between 1 and 100, you might establish 10 bins, each covering a range of 10 values. The first bin would be for values of 1 to 10, the second bin would be for values of 11 to 20, and so forth.

Figure 9-17 illustrates this. There are 300 values in the range B3:B304. The values are random, between 1 and 100. Cells D3 through D12 have been set as bins that each cover a range of ten values. Note that, for each bin, its number is the top of the range it's used for. For example, the 30 bin is used for holding the count of how many values fall between 21 and 30.

A bin holds the count of values within a numeric range. The bin's number is the top of *its* range.

	A	B	C	D	E	F	G	H
					E3	▼	ƒx {=FREQUENCY(B3:B304,D3:D12)}	
1		Raw Values		Bins	Count of values, per bin			
2								
3		29		10	5			
4		49		20	12			
5		58		30	34			
6		47		40	43			
7		61		50	54			
8		69		60	55			
9		76		70	49			
10		42		80	30			
11		67		90	11			
12		33		100	7			
13		72						
14		48						
15		64						
16		49						
17		43						
18		46						
19		84						
20		39						
21		18						
22		43						
23		40						
24		38						
25		20						

Figure 9-17: Setting up bins to use with the FREQUENCY function.

FREQUENCY is an array function and requires specific steps to be used correctly. Here is how it's done:

1. **Enter a list of values.**

   This can be a lengthy list and likely represents some observed data, such as the age of people using the library, or the number of miles driven on the job. Obviously, there are many types of observable data that you can use.

2. **Determine the high and low values of the data.**

   You can use the MAX and MIN functions for this.

3. **Determine what your bins should be.**

   This is subjective. For example, if the data has values from 1 to 100, you can use 10 bins that each cover a range of 10 values. Or you can use 20 bins that each cover a range of 5 values. Or you can use 5 bins that each cover a range of 20 values.

4. **Enter a list of the bins by entering the high number of each bin's range, as shown in Figure 9-17.**

5. **Click on the first cell where FREQUENCY should be.**

6. **Drag the mouse down to select the rest of the cells.**

   There should now be a range of selected cells. The size of this range should match the number of bins. Figure 9-18 shows what the worksheet should look like at this step.

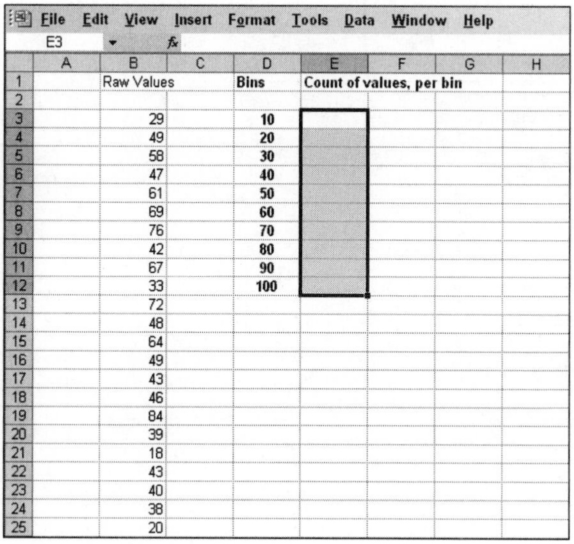

Figure 9-18: Preparing to enter the FREQUENCY function.

7. **Enter =FREQUENCY(to start the function.**

8. **Drag the cursor over the sample data, or enter the address of the range.**

9. **Enter a comma (,).**

10. **Drag the cursor over the list of bins, or enter the address of that range.**

Figure 9-19 shows what the worksheet should look like at this point.

11. **Enter a closing parenthesis.**

Do *not* press Enter.

12. **Press Ctrl+ Shift+Enter at the same time to end the function entry.**

Hurray, you did it! You have entered an array function. All the cells in the range where FREQUENCY was entered have the same exact formula. The returned values in these cells are the count of values from the raw data that fall within the bins. This is called a *frequency distribution*.

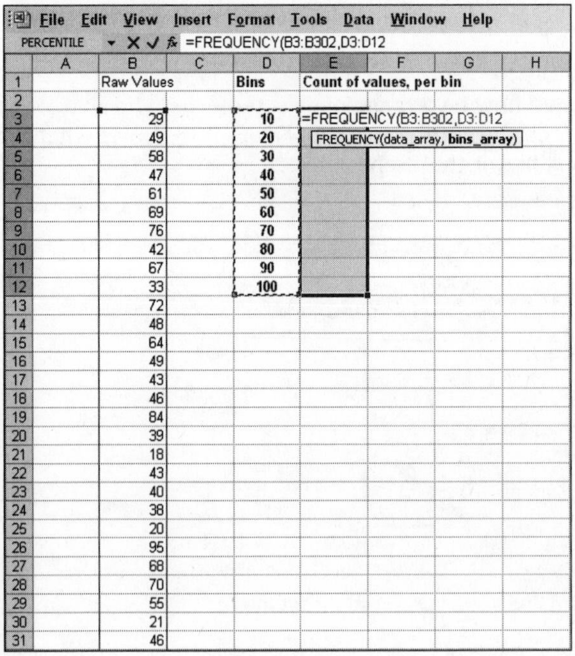

Figure 9-19: Completing the entry of the FREQUENCY function.

Next, let's take this distribution and plot a curve from it:

1. **Select the Count of Values, Per Bin range, E5:E12 in this example.**

2. **Click the Chart Wizard button, or select the Insert ⇨ Chart menu.**

3. **Select XY (Scatter) as the chart type.**

4. **Select the chart sub type that is described as Scatter with Data Points Connected by Smoothed Lines without Markers.**

   See Figure 9-20 for the Chart Wizard selections.

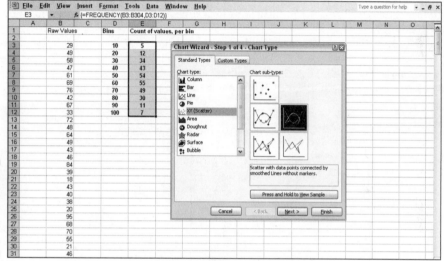

Figure 9-20: Preparing to plot the frequency distribution.

5. **Click Finish.**

   A chart with a distribution curve based on the bins is now displayed, as shown in Figure 9-21.

A frequency distribution is also known as a *histogram*.

Excel has two functions — MIN and MAX — that return the lowest and highest values in a set of data. These functions are simple to use. The functions take up to 30 arguments, which can be cells, ranges, or values.

Figure 9-22 shows a list of home sales. What are the highest and lowest values? Cell F4 displays the lowest price in the list of sales, with this formula: =MIN(C4:C1000). Cell F6 displays the highest price with this formula: =MAX(C4:C1000).

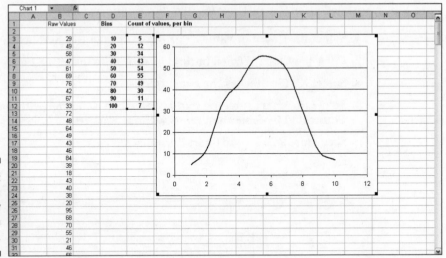

Figure 9-21: Displaying a frequency distribution as a curve.

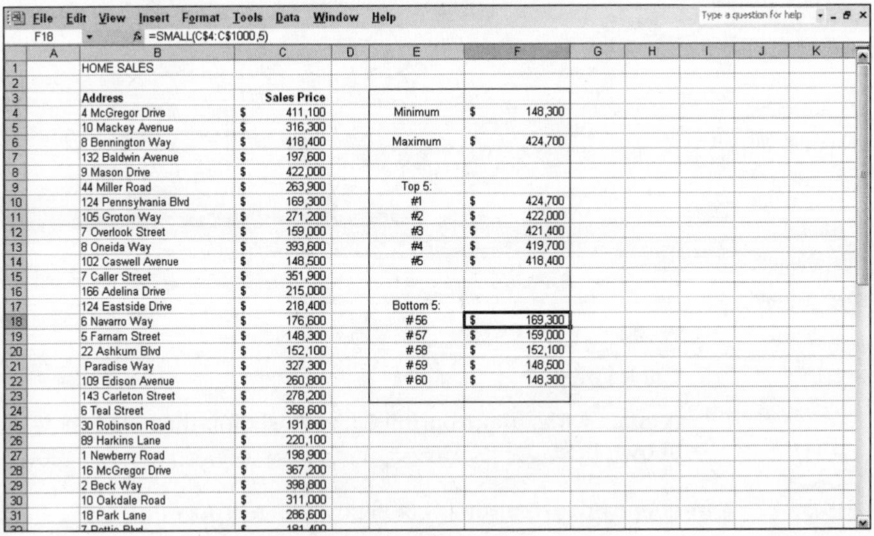

Figure 9-22: Finding high and low values.

Here's how to use the MIN or MAX function:

1. **Enter a list of numerical values.**

2. **Position the cursor in the cell where you want the result to appear.**

3. **Enter either =MIN(or =MAX(to start the function.**

4. **Drag the mouse over the list, or enter the address of the range.**

5. **Enter a closing parenthesis to end the function.**

MIN and MAX return the upper and lower values of the data. What if you need to know the value of the second highest price? Or the third?

The LARGE and SMALL functions let you find out a value that is positioned at a certain point in the data. LARGE is used to find the value at a position that is offset from the highest value. SMALL is used to find the value at a position that is offset from the lowest value.

Figure 9-22 displays the top five home sales, as well as the bottom five. Both the LARGE and SMALL functions take two arguments: the range of the data in which to find the value, and the position relative to the top or bottom.

The top five home sales are found by using LARGE. The highest sale, in cell F10, is returned with this formula: =LARGE(C$4:C$1000,1). Because the function used here is LARGE, and the second argument is 1, the function returns the value at the first position. By no coincidence, this value is also returned by the MAX function.

To find the second highest home sales, a 2 is entered as the second argument to LARGE. Cell F11 has this formula: =LARGE(C$4:C$1000,2). The third, fourth, and fifth largest home sales are returned in the same fashion, respectively, using 3, 4, and 5 as the second argument.

The bottom 5 sales are returned in the same fashion, but by using the SMALL function. For example, cell F22 has this formula: =SMALL(C$4:C$1000,1). The returned value, $148,300, matches the value returned with the MIN function. The cell just above it, F21, has this formula: =SMALL(C$4:C$1000,2).

Hey, wait! You may have noticed that the functions are looking down to row 1000 for values, but the bottom listing is numbered as 60. An interesting thing to note in this example is that all the functions use row 1000 as the bottom row to look in, but this doesn't mean there are that many listings. This in intentional. There are only 60 listings, for now. What happens when new sales are added to the bottom of the list? By giving the functions a considerably larger than expected range, we've built in the ability to handle a growing list. It's interesting to see how the labels were created with regard to this.

The labels in cells E10:E14 (#1, #2, and so on) are just entered as is. Clearly any ranking that starts from the top would start with #1, then #2, and so on.

However the labels in cells E18:E22 (#56, #57, and so on) were created with formulas. The COUNT function is used to count the total number of listings.

Even though the function looks down to row 1000, it only finds 60 listings, so that is the returned count. The #60 label is based on this count. The other labels (#59, #58, #57, and #56) are created by reducing the count by 1, 2, 3, and 4, respectively:

- The formula in cell E22 is `="# " & COUNT(C$4:C$1000)`.
- The formula in cell E21 is `="# " & COUNT(C$4:C$1000)-1`.
- The formula in cell E20 is `="# " & COUNT(C$4:C$1000)-2`.
- The formula in cell E19 is `="# " & COUNT(C$4:C$1000)-3`.
- The formula in cell E18 is `="# " & COUNT(C$4:C$1000)-4`.

Here's how to use the LARGE or SMALL function:

1. **Enter a list of numerical values.**

2. **Position the cursor in the cell where you want the result to appear.**

3. **Enter either =LARGE(or =SMALL(to start the function.**

4. **Drag the pointer over the list, or enter the address of the range.**

5. **Enter a closing parenthesis to end the function.**

Use LARGE to find a value's position relative to the highest value. Use SMALL to find a value's position relative to the smallest value.

Going for the Count

The COUNT and COUNTIF functions return, well, a count. What else could it be with a name like that?

COUNT is straightforward. It counts how many items are in a range of values. There is a catch, though: Only numeric values and dates are counted. Text values are not counted, nor are blank cells.

To use the COUNT function:

1. **Enter a list of numerical values.**

2. **Position the cursor in the cell where you want the result to appear.**

3. **Enter =COUNT(to start the function.**

4. Drag the mouse over the list, or enter the address of the range.

5. Enter a closing parenthesis to end the function.

Figure 9-23 shows a list of popular movies along with the sales figure and the year for each movie. Cell F4 displays the count of movies, returned with the COUNT function. The formula in cell F4 is =COUNT(C4:C460).

Note that the range entered in the function looks at the years the movie were made. This is intentional. A year is a numeric value. If count used the range of movie titles, in Column A, the count would be 0 because this column contains text data.

	A	B	C	D	E	F	G	H	I	J	K
1											
2											
3	Movie	Gross	Year								
4	101 Dalmatians	$ 152,551,111	1961		Count of Movies	306					
5	101 Dalmatians	$ 136,200,000	1996								
6	2 Fast 2 Furious	$ 127,083,765	2003		Movies in 1998	18					
7	50 First Dates	$ 120,776,832	2004								
8	8 Mile	$ 116,724,075	2002	Movies over $200,000,000		56					
9	9 to 5	$ 103,290,500	1980								
10	A Beautiful Mind	$ 170,708,996	2001								
11	A Bug's Life	$ 162,698,584	1998	Movies over $200,000,000							
12	A Few Good Men	$ 141,340,178	1992		in 1998	2					
13	A League of Their Own	$ 107,439,000	1992								
14	A Time to Kill	$ 108,700,000	1996								
15	Ace Ventura: When Nature Calls	$ 108,344,348	1995								
16	Air Force One	$ 172,600,000	1997								
17	Aladdin	$ 217,350,219	1992								
18	American Beauty	$ 130,058,047	1999								
19	American Graffiti	$ 115,000,000	1973								
20	American Pie	$ 101,736,215	1999								
21	American Pie 2	$ 145,096,820	2001								
22	American Wedding	$ 104,354,205	2003								
23	An Officer and a Gentleman	$ 129,795,549	1982								
24	Analyze This	$ 106,823,373	1999								
25	Anger Management	$ 133,756,285	2003								
26	Apollo 13	$ 173,772,641	1995								
27	Armageddon	$ 201,551,346	1998								
28	As Good as It Gets	$ 147,637,474	1997								
29	Attack of the Clones	$ 310,675,583	2002								
30	Austin Powers in Goldmember	$ 213,079,163	2002								
31	Austin Powers: The Spy Who Shag	$ 205,957,794	1999								

Figure 9-23: Counting with and without criteria.

The COUNTIF function is handy when you need to count how many items are in a list but that meet a certain condition. In Figure 9-23, cell F6 shows the count of movies made in 1998. The formula in cell F6 is =COUNTIF(C4:C309,1998).

The COUNTIF function takes two arguments. The first argument is the address of the list to count from. The second argument is the criteria.

Table 9-1 lists some treatments of the second argument.

Table 9-1	Using Criteria with the COUNTIF Function
Example	**Comment**
`=COUNTIF(C4:C309,"=1998")`	Returns the count of movies made in 1998.
`=COUNTIF(C4:C309,1998)`	Returns the count of movies made in 1998. Note that this is a unique in that the criteria do not need to be in double quotes. This is because the criterion is a simple equality.
`=COUNTIF(C4:C309,"<1998")`	Returns the count of movies made before 1998.
`=COUNTIF(C4:C309,">=1998")`	Returns the count of movies made in or after 1998.
`=COUNTIF(C4:C309,"<>1998")`	Returns the count of movies not made in 1998.

The criteria can also be based on text. For example COUNTIF can count all occurrences of "Detroit" in a list of business trips. You can use wildcards with COUNTIF. The asterisk (*) is used to represent any number of characters, and the question mark (?) is used to represent a single character.

As an example, using an asterisk after "Batman" returns the number of Batman movies found in Column A in Figure 9-23. A formula to do this looks like this: `=COUNTIF(A4:A309,"Batman*")`. Notice the asterisk after Batman. This lets the function count "Batman and Robin," "Batman Returns," and "Batman Forever," along with just "Batman."

Cell F8 in Figure 9-23 returns the count of movies that have earned over $200,000,000. The formula is `=COUNTIF(B4:B309,">200000000")`. What if you need to determine the count of data items that match two conditions?

The formula in Cell F12 returns the count of movies that were made in 1998 *and* earned $200,000,000 or more. However, COUNTIF is not useful for this type of multiple condition count. Instead, the SUMPRODUCT function is used. The formula in cell F12 is

```
=SUMPRODUCT((B4:B309>200000000)*(C4:C309=1998))
```

Believe it or not, this works. Although this formula looks like it's multiplying the number of movies that earned at least $200,000,000 by the number of movies made in 1998, it's really returning the count of movies that meet the two conditions. Quick trivia — which two 1998 movies earned at least $200,000,000? The answer (drum roll, please): *Armageddon* and *Saving Private Ryan.*

To use the COUNTIF function:

1. **Enter a list of numerical values.**

2. **Position the cursor in the cell where you want the result to appear.**

3. **Enter =COUNTIF(to start the function.**

4. **Drag the mouse over the list, or enter the address of the range.**

5. **Enter a comma (,).**

6. **Enter a condition, and enclose the condition in double quotes.**

   Use an equal sign (=), a greater-than sign (>), a less-than sign (<), and/or wildcards as needed. Use a greater-than sign and a less-than sign together (<>) to indicate a not-equal-to condition.

7. **Enter a closing parenthesis to end the function.**

   The result is a count of cells that match the condition.

Chapter 10

Using Significance Tests

*W*hen you have data from a population, you can draw a sample and run your statistical analysis on the sample. You can also run the analysis on the population itself. Is the mean of the sample data the same as the mean of the whole population? You can calculate the mean of both the sample and the population and then know precisely how well the sample represents the population. Are the two means exact? Off a little bit? How much different?

The problem with this though is that getting the data of the population in the first place isn't always feasible. On average, how many miles per gallon does a Toyota Camry get after five years on the road? You cannot answer this question to an exact degree because it's impossible to test every Camry out there.

So instead we infer the answer. Testing a handful, or sample, of Camrys is certainly possible. Then the mean gas mileage of the sample is used to represent the mean gas mileage of all 5-year-old Camrys. The mean of the sample group will not necessarily match the mean of the population, but it is the best value that can be attained.

This type of statistical work is known as estimation (it's sometimes also called *inferential statistics*). In this chapter, we show you the functions that work with the Student t distribution, useful for gaining insight into the unknown population properties. This is the method of choice when using a small sample, say 30 data points or less.

The tests presented in this chapter deal with probabilities. If the result of a test — a t-test, for example — falls within a certain probability range, then the result is said to be significant. Outside that range, the result is considered non-significant. A common rule of thumb is to consider probabilities less than 5 percent, or 0.05, to be significant, but exceptions to this rule exist.

The Student t distribution has nothing to do with students. The originator of the method was not allowed to use his real name due to his employer's rules. So instead he used the name Student.

Testing to the T

The TTEST function returns the probability that two samples come from populations that have the same mean. For example, a comparison of the salaries of accountants and professors in New York City is under way. Are the salaries, overall (on average), the same for these two groups? Each group is a separate population, but if the means are the same, then the average salaries are the same.

Polling all the accountants and professors isn't possible, so a sample of each is taken. Twenty-five random members of each group divulge their salary in the interest of the comparison. Figure 10-1 shows the salaries of the two groups, as well as the results of the TTEST function.

Student t testing is generally used when the sample size is 30 items or fewer.

	File	Edit	View	Insert	Format	Tools	Data	Window	Help		
	E8	▼		*fx* =TTEST(A3:A27,B3:B27,2,2)							
	A		B		C	D	E	F	G
1									
2	Accountants		Professors						
3	$	75,172	$	88,655			TTEST Arguments		
4	$	76,761	$	82,203			2-tailed test		
5	$	85,329	$	60,401			Not a paired test		
6	$	72,421	$	77,893					
7	$	54,129	$	80,727			TTEST		
8	$	88,233	$	77,152			0.732954		
9	$	73,102	$	73,092					
10	$	82,714	$	86,726					
11	$	76,084	$	88,745					
12	$	58,810	$	64,700					
13	$	79,072	$	85,952					
14	$	65,972	$	70,997					
15	$	56,465	$	78,002					
16	$	83,861	$	89,023					
17	$	81,898	$	57,464					
18	$	83,360	$	75,366					
19	$	88,856	$	73,093					
20	$	85,584	$	91,540					
21	$	69,243	$	56,852					
22	$	58,572	$	86,642					
23	$	65,127	$	81,478					
24	$	80,350	$	58,917					
25	$	87,796	$	76,012					
26	$	76,051	$	89,150					
27	$	79,354	$	59,775					
28									
29									
30									

Figure 10-1: Comparing salaries.

The TTEST function returns 73.3 percent (0.732954) based on how the arguments to the function were entered. This percentage says there is a 73.3 percent probability that the mean of the underlying populations are the same. Said another way, this is the likelihood that the mean of all accountant salaries in New York City matches the mean of all professor salaries in New York City. The formula in cell E8 is:

```
=TTEST(A3:A27,B3:B27,2,2)
```

The arguments of the TTEST function are listed in Table 10-1.

Table 10-1	Arguments of the TTEST Function
Argument	*Comment*
Array 1	This is the reference to the range of the first array of data.
Array 2	This is the reference to the range of the second array of data.
Tails	Either a 1 or 2. For a one-tailed test, enter a 1. For a 2-tailed test, enter a 2.
Type	Type of t test to perform. The choices are a 1, 2, or 3. A number 1 indicates a paired test. A number 2 indicates a two-sample test with equal variance. A number 3 indicates a two-sample test with unequal variance.

The third argument of TTEST tells whether to conduct a one-tailed or two-tailed test. A one-tailed test is used when there is a question of whether one set of data is larger or smaller than the other. A two-tailed test is used to tell whether the two sets are just different from each other.

The first two arguments are the ranges of two respective sets of values. A pertinent consideration here is how the two sets of data are related. The sets could be comprised of elements that have a corresponding member in each set. For example there could be a set of "before" data and a set of "after" data. For example:

Seedling	*Height at Week 1*	*Height at Week 2*
#1	4 inches	5 inches
#2	3¾ inches	5 inches
#3	4½ inches	5½ inches
#4	5 inches	5 inches

This type of data is entered into the function as *paired*. In other words, each data value in the first sample is linked to a data value in the second sample. In this case, the link is due to the fact that the data values are "before" and "after" measurements from the same seedlings. Data can be paired in other ways. In the salary survey, for example, each accountant may be paired with a professor of the same age to ensure that length of time on the job does not affect the results — in this case, you would also use a paired t-test.

When you're using TTEST for paired samples, the two ranges entered in the first and second arguments must be the same size. When you're comparing two independent (nonpaired) samples, the two samples don't have to be the same size, although they happen to be the same size in the figure.

Use TTEST to determine the probability that two samples come from the same population.

Here's how to use the TTEST function:

1. **Enter two sets of data.**

2. **Position the cursor in the cell where you want the result to appear.**

3. **Enter =TTEST(to start the function.**

4. **Drag the mouse over the first list, or enter the address of its range.**

5. **Enter a comma (,).**

6. **Drag the mouse over the second list, or enter the address of its range.**

7. **Enter a comma (,).**

8. **Enter a 1 for a one-tailed test, or enter a 2 for a two-tailed test.**

9. **Enter a comma (,).**

10. **Enter a 1 for a for a paired test, a 2 for a test of two samples with equal variance, or a 3 for a test of two samples with unequal variance.**

11. **Enter a closing parenthesis to end the function.**

If you ever took a statistics course, you may recall that a t-test returns a *t-value,* which you then had to look up in a table to determine the associated probability. Excel's TTEST function combines these two steps. It calculates the t-value internally and determines the probability. You never see the actual t-value, just the probability — which is what you're interested in anyway!

The TDIST function returns the probability for a given t-value and degrees of freedom. You would use this function if you had a calculated t-value and wanted to determine the associated probability. Note that the TTEST function doesn't return a t-value, but rather a probability, so you wouldn't use TDIST with the result that is returned by TTEST. Instead, you would use TDIST if you had one or more t-values calculated elsewhere and needed to determine the associated probabilities.

TDIST takes three arguments:

✔ The t value

✔ The degrees of freedom

✔ The number of tails (1 or 2)

A t-distribution is similar to a normal distribution. The plotted shape is a bell curve. However a t-distribution differs particularly in the thickness of the tails. How much so is dependent on the degrees of freedom. The degrees of freedom roughly relate to the number of elements in the sample, less one. All t-distributions are symmetrical around 0, as is the normal distribution. In practice, however, you always work with the right half of the curve — positive t values.

To use the TDIST function:

1. **Position the cursor in the cell where you want the result to appear.**

2. **Enter =TDIST(to start the function.**

3. **Enter a value for t (or click on a cell that has the value).**

4. **Enter a comma (,).**

5. **Enter the degrees of freedom.**

6. **Enter a comma (,).**

7. **Enter a 1 for a one-tailed test, or enter a 2 for a two-tailed test.**

8. **Enter a closing parenthesis to end the function.**

If the t value is based on a paired test, then the degrees of freedom is equal to the count of items in either sample (the samples are the same size), less 1. When the t value is based on two independent samples, then the degrees of freedom = (count of sample-1 items – 1) + (count of sample-2 items – 1).

The TINV function produces the inverse of TDIST. That is, TINV takes two arguments — the probability and the degrees of freedom, and returns the value of t. To use TINV:

1. **Position the cursor in the cell where you want the result to appear.**

2. **Enter =TINV(to start the function.**

3. **Enter the probability value (or click on a cell that has the value).**

4. **Enter a comma (,).**

5. **Enter the degrees of freedom.**

6. **Enter a closing parenthesis to end the function.**

Comparing Results to an Estimate

The Chi Square test is a statistical method for determining whether observed results are within an acceptable range compared with what the results were expected to be. In other words, the Chi Square is a test of how well a before and after compare. Did the observed results come close enough to the expected results that we can safely assume there is no real difference? Or were the observed and expected results far enough apart that we must conclude there is a real difference?

A good example is the flipping of a coin, done 100 times. The expected outcome is 50 times heads, 50 times tails. Figure 10-2 shows how a Chi Square test statistic is calculated in a worksheet without using any functions.

Figure 10-2: Calculating a Chi Square.

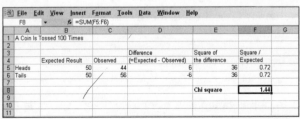

Cells B5:B6 are the expected results — that heads and tails will each show up 50 times. Cells C5:C6 show the observed results. Heads appeared 44 times, and tails appeared 56 times. With this information, here is how the Chi Square test statistic is calculated:

1. **For each expected and observed pair, calculate the difference as (Expected – Observed).**

2. **Calculate the square of each difference as (Expected – Observed)^2.**

3. **Divide the squares from the previous step by their respective expected values.**

4. **Sum up the results of the previous step.**

Of course, a comprehensive equation can be used for the first three steps, such as =(expected - observed)^2/expected.

The result in this example is 1.44. This number — the Chi Square value — is then looked up in a table of Chi Square distribution values. This table is a matrix of degrees of freedom and confidence levels. Seeing where the calculated value is positioned in the table for the appropriate degrees of freedom (one less than the number of data points) will show you the probability that the difference between the expected and observed values is significant. That is, is the difference within a reasonable error of estimation or is it real (for example, caused by an unbalanced coin)?

The table of degrees of freedom and confidence levels is often found in the appendix of a statistics book or can be found on the Internet.

The CHITEST function returns the probability value (p) derived from the expected and observed ranges. There are two arguments to the function: the range of observed (or actual) values, and the range of expected values. These ranges must, of course, contain the same number of values, and they must be matched (first item in the *expected* list is associated with the first item in the *observed* list, and so on). Internally, the function takes the degrees of freedom into account, calculates the Chi Square statistic value, and computes the probability.

To use the CHITEST function:

1. **Enter two ranges of values as expected and observed results.**

2. **Position the cursor in the cell where you want the result to appear.**

3. **Enter =CHITEST(to start the function.**

4. **Drag the cursor over the range of observed (actual) values, or enter the address of the range.**

5. **Enter a comma (,).**

6. **Drag the cursor over the range of expected values, or enter the address of the range.**

7. **Enter a closing parenthesis to end the function.**

Figure 10-3 shows a data set of expected and actual values. The Chi Square test statistic is calculated as before, delivering a value of 1.594017, seen in cell F12. The CHITEST function, in cell D16, returns a value of 0.953006566, the associated probability. Remember that CHITEST doesn't return the Chi Square statistic but rather the associated probability.

D16 =CHITEST(C4:C10,B4:B10)

	A	B	C	D	E	F
1		Expected Completed	Actual Completed	Difference	Square of	Square /
2		Print Runs	Print Runs	(=Expected - Observed)	the difference	Expected
3						
4	Monday	15	18	-3	9	0.6
5	Tuesday	18	20	-2	4	0.222222222
6	Wednesday	19	19	0	0	0
7	Thursday	24	20	4	16	0.666666667
8	Friday	26	25	1	1	0.038461538
9	Saturday	24	24	0	0	0
10	Sunday	15	16	-1	1	0.066666667
11						
12						**1.594017094**
13						
14						
15						
16			**CHIITEST**	**0.953006566**	this is known as the p value	
17						
18			**CHIDIST**	**0.953006566**	this is known as the p value	
19						
20			**CHIINV**	**1.594017094**	gives the test statistic value for a given p value	

Figure 10-3: Determining probability.

Let's tie in a relationship between the manually calculated Chi Square and the value returned with CHITEST. If you looked up our manually calculated Chi Square value (1.59) in a Chi Square table for degrees of freedom of 6 (one less than the number of observations), you would find it associated with a probability value of 0.95. Of course, the CHITEST function does this for you, returning the probability value, which is what you're after. But suppose you've manually calculated Chi Square values and want to know the associated probabilities. Do you have to use a table? Nope — the CHIDIST function comes to the rescue. And furthermore, if you have a probability and want to know the associated Chi Square value, you can use the CHIINV function.

Figure 10-3 demonstrates the CHIDIST and CHIINV functions as well. CHIDIST takes two arguments: a value to be evaluated for a distribution (the Chi Square value, 1.59 in our example), and the degrees of freedom (6 in the example). Cell D18 displays 0.953006566, which is the same probability value returned by the CHITEST function — just as it should be! The formula in cell D18 is `=CHIDIST(F12,6)`.

CHITEST and CHIDIST both return the same probability value but calculate the result with different arguments. CHITEST uses the actual expected and observed values and internally calculates the test statistic to return the probability. This is done behind the scenes — just the probability is returned. CHIDIST needs the test statistic fed in as an argument.

To use the CHIDIST function:

1. **Position the cursor in the cell where you want the result to appear.**
2. **Enter** =CHIDIST(**to start the function.**
3. **Click on the cell that has the Chi Square test statistic, or just enter it.**
4. **Enter a comma (,).**
5. **Enter the degrees of freedom.**
6. **Enter a closing parenthesis to end the function.**

The CHIINV function rounds out the list of Chi Square functions in Excel. CHIINV in the inverse of CHIDIST. That is, with a given probability and degrees of freedom number, CHINV returns the Chi Square test statistic.

Cell D20 in Figure 10-3 has the formula =CHIINV(D16,6). This returns the value of the Chi Square: 1.594017094. CHIINV is useful then when you know the probability and degrees of freedom and need to determine the Chi Square test statistic value.

To use the CHIINV function:

1. **Position the cursor in the cell where you want the result to appear.**
2. **Enter** =CHIINV(**to start the function.**
3. **Click on the cell that has the probability, or just enter it.**
4. **Enter a comma (,).**
5. **Enter the degrees of freedom.**
6. **Enter a closing parenthesis to end the function.**

Working with inferential statistics is difficult! We suggest further reading to help with the functions and statistical examples discussed in this chapter. A great book to read is *Statistics For Dummies* by Deborah Rumsey (Wiley).

Chapter 11

Using Prediction and Probability Functions

In This Chapter

▶ Understanding linear and exponential trends

▶ Predicting future data from existing data

▶ Working with normal and Poisson distributions

*W*hen analyzing data, one of the most important steps is usually to determine what model fits the data. No, we aren't talking about a model car or model plane! This is a mathematical model or, put another way, a formula that describes the data. The question of a model is applicable for all data that comes in X-Y pairs, such as:

- ✔ Comparisons of weight and height measurements
- ✔ Data on salary versus educational level
- ✔ Number of fish feeding in a river by time of day
- ✔ Number of employees calling in sick as related to day of the week

Suppose now that you plot all the data points on a chart — a *scatter chart* in Excel terminology. What does the pattern look like? If the data are linear, they'll fall more or less along a straight line. If they fall along a curve rather than a straight line, they aren't linear and are likely to be exponential. These two models — linear and exponential — are the two most commonly used models, and Excel provides you with functions to work with them.

In a linear model, the mathematical formula that models the data is as follows:

```
Y = mX + b
```

This tells us that for any X value, you calculate the Y value by multiplying X by a constant *m* and then adding another constant *b*. The value *m* is called the slope of the line and *b* is the Y intercept (the value of Y when X = 0). This formula gives a perfectly straight line, and real-world data won't fall right on such a line. The point is that the line, called the linear regression line, is the best fit for the data. Of course, the constants *m* and *b* will be different for each data set.

In an exponential model, the following formula is used to model the data:

```
Y = bmX
```

The values *b* and *m* are again constants. Many natural processes are modeled by exponential curves including bacterial growth and change in temperature. Figure 11-1 shows an example of an exponential curve. This curve is the result of the above formula when *b* = 2 and *m* = 1.03.

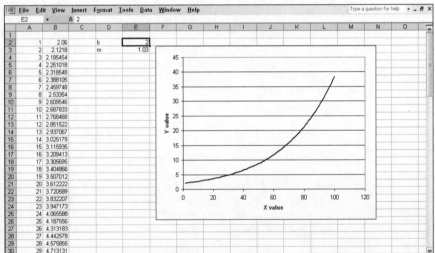

Figure 11-1:
An exponential curve.

Again, *b* and *m* are constants that will be different for each data set.

In the following section, we look at the functions that Excel provides for working with linear and exponential data.

Getting It Straight: Using SLOPE and INTERCEPT to Describe Linear Data

As we discuss earlier, many data sets can be modeled by a straight line — in other words, the data are linear. The line that models the data, known as the *linear regression line,* is characterized by its slope and its Y intercept. Excel provides the SLOPE and INTERCEPT functions to calculate the slope and Y intercept of the linear regression line for a set of data pairs.

The SLOPE and INTERCEPT functions both take the same two arguments:

✔ The first argument is a range or array containing the Y values of the data set.

✔ The second argument is a range or array containing the X values of the data set.

The two ranges must contain the same number of values; otherwise, an error occurs. To use either of these functions:

1. **In a blank worksheet cell, enter** =SLOPE(**or** =INTERCEPT(**to start the function entry.**

2. **Drag the mouse over the range containing the Y data values, or enter the range address.**

3. **Enter a comma (,).**

4. **Drag the mouse over the range containing the X data values, or enter the range address.**

5. **Enter a closing parenthesis.**

6. **Press Enter to complete the formula.**

When you know the slope and Y intercept of a linear regression line, you can calculate predicted values of Y for any X using the formula $Y = mX + b$ where m is the slope and b is the Y intercept. But Excel's FORECAST and TREND functions can do this for you.

Knowing the slope and intercept of a linear regression line is one thing, but what can you do with this information? One very useful thing is to actually draw the regression line along with the data points. This method of graphical presentation is commonly used — it lets the viewer see how well the data fit the model.

To see how this is done, look at the worksheet in Figure 11-2. Columns A and B contain the X and Y data, and the chart shows a scatter plot of this data. It seems clear that the data are linear and that you can validly use SLOPE and INTERCEPT with them. The first step is to put these functions in the worksheet as follows. You can use any worksheet that has linear X-Y data in it.

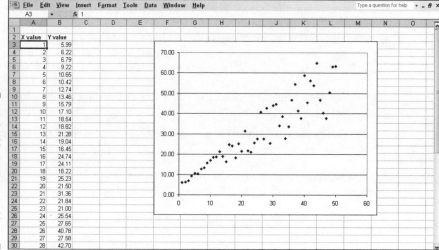

Figure 11-2:
The scatter plot indicates that the X and Y data in this worksheet are linear.

1. **Enter the label** Slope **in an empty cell.**

2. **In the cell to the right, enter** =SLOPE(**to start the function entry.**

3. **Drag the mouse over the range containing the Y data values, or enter the range address.**

4. **Enter a comma (,).**

5. **Drag the mouse over the range containing the X data values, or enter the range address.**

6. **Enter a closing parenthesis.**

7. **Press Enter to complete the formula.**

8. **In the cell below the slope label, enter the label** Intercept.

9. **In the cell to the right, enter** =Intercept(.

10. **Drag the mouse over the range containing the Y data values, or enter the range address.**

11. **Enter a comma (,).**

12. **Drag the mouse over the range containing the X data values, or enter the range address.**

13. **Enter a closing parenthesis.**

14. **Press Enter to complete the formula.**

At this point, the worksheet will display the slope and intercept of the linear regression line for your data. The next task is to display this line on the chart:

1. **If necessary, add a new, empty column to the worksheet to the right of the Y value column.**

2. **Place the cursor in this column in the same row as the first X value.**

3. **Enter an equal sign (=) to start a formula.**

4. **Click the cell where the SLOPE function is located to enter its address in the formula.**

5. **Press F4 to convert the address to an absolute reference — it will display with dollar signs.**

6. **Enter the multiplication symbol (*).**

7. **Click the cell containing the X value for that row.**

8. **Enter the addition symbol (+).**

9. **Click the cell containing the INTERCEPT function to enter its address in the formula.**

10. **Press F4 to convert the address to an absolute reference.**

    It will display with dollar signs.

11. **Press Enter to complete the formula.**

12. **Make sure the cursor is on the cell where you just entered the formula.**

13. **Press Ctrl+C to copy the formula to the clipboard.**

14. **Hold down the Shift key and press the down-arrow key until the entire column is highlighted down to the row containing the last X value.**

15. **Press Enter to copy the formula to all selected cells.**

At this point, the column of data you just created contains the Y values for the linear regression line. The final step is to create a chart that displays both the actual data as well as the computed regression line.

1. **Highlight all three columns of data — the X values, the actual Y values, and the computed Y values.**

2. **Click the Chart Wizard button on the toolbar to display the Chart Wizard dialog box (shown in Figure 11-3).**

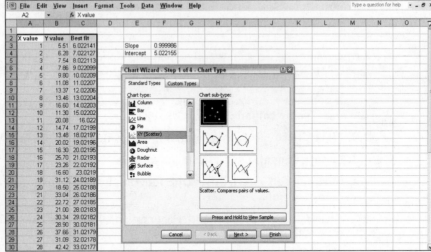

Figure 11-3:
Creating a
chart with
the Chart
Wizard.

3. **In the Chart Type list, select XY (scatter).**

4. **Under Chart Subtype select the option that has symbols but no lines.**

5. **Click the Finish button.**

The chart will display as shown in Figure 11-4. You can see there are two sets of points — the scattered ones are the actual data while the straight line is the linear-regression line.

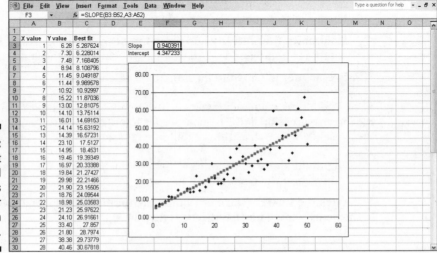

Figure 11-4:
A data set
displayed
with its
linear
regression
line.

What's in the Future: Using FORECAST, TREND, and GROWTH to Make Predictions

The FORECAST function does just what its name suggests — it forecasts an unknown data value based on existing, known data values. The function is based on a single important assumption — that the data are linear. What exactly does this mean?

The data that FORECAST works with are in pairs — there's an X value and a corresponding Y value in each pair. For example, perhaps you're investigating the relationship between people's heights and their weight. Each data pair would be one person's height, the X value, and their weight, the Y value. Many kinds of data are in this form — sales by month, for example, or income as a function of educational level.

You can use the CORREL function to determine the degree of linear relationship between two sets of data. See Chapter 9 to find out about the CORREL function.

To use the FORECAST function, you must have a set of X-Y data pairs. You then provide a new X value, and the function returns the Y value that would be associated with that X value based on the known data. The function takes three arguments:

- ✔ The first argument is the X value that you want a forecast for.

- ✔ The second argument is a range containing the known Y values.

- ✔ The third argument is a range containing the known X values.

Note that the X and Y ranges must have the same number of values or an error is returned by the function. The X and Y values in these ranges are assumed to be paired in order.

Don't use FORECAST with data that isn't linear — it will produce inaccurate results.

Now we can work through an example of using FORECAST to make a prediction. Imagine that you're the sales manager at a large corporation. You've noticed that the yearly sales results for each of your salespeople is related to the number of years of experience they have. You've hired a new salesman with 16 years of experience. How much in sales can you expect this person to make?

Figure 11-5 shows the existing data for salespeople — their years of experience and annual sales last year. This worksheet also contains a scatter chart of these data to show that they're linear — it's clear that the data points fall fairly well along a straight line. To create the prediction:

1. **In a blank cell (cell C24 in the figure), enter =FORECAST(to start the function entry.**

2. **Enter 16, the X value that you want a prediction for.**

3. **Enter a comma (,).**

4. **Drag the mouse over the Y range, or enter the cell range (C3:C17 in the example).**

5. **Enter a comma (,).**

6. **Drag the mouse over the X range, or enter the cell range (B3:B17 in the example).**

7. **Enter a closing parenthesis, and press Enter to complete the formula.**

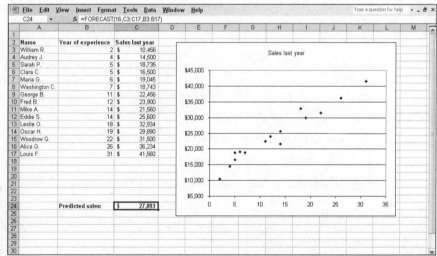

Figure 11-5:
Forecasting
sales.

After formatting the cell as Currency, the result shown in Figure 11-5 displays the prediction that your new salesman will make $27,093 in sales his first year. But remember: This is just a prediction and not a guarantee!

You just saw how the FORECAST function can predict a Y value for a known X based on an existing set of linear X,Y data. What if you have more than one X value to predict? Have no fear, TREND is here! What FORECAST does for a single X value, TREND does for a whole array of X values.

Like FORECAST, the TREND function is intended for working with linear data. If you try to use it with nonlinear data, the results will be incorrect.

The TREND function takes up to four arguments:

- ✔ The first argument is a range containing the known Y values.
- ✔ The second argument is a range containing the known X values.
- ✔ The third argument is a range containing the X values that you want predictions for.
- ✔ The fourth argument is a logical value. It tells the function whether to force the constant *b* to 0. If the fourth argument is TRUE or omitted, the linear regression line (used to predict Y values) is calculated normally. If this argument is FALSE the linear regression line is calculated to go through the origin (where both X and Y are 0).

Note that the ranges of known X and Y values must be the same size (contain the same number of values).

TREND returns an array of values, one predicted Y for each X value. In other words, it's an array function and must be treated as such. (See Chapter 3 for help with array functions.) Specifically, this means selecting the range where you want the array formula results, typing in the formula, and pressing Ctrl+Shift+Enter rather than pressing Enter alone to complete the formula.

When would you use the TREND function? Here's an example: You've started a part-time business and your income has grown steadily over the past 12 months. The growth seems to be linear, and you want to predict how much you will earn in the coming six months. The TREND function is ideal for this situation. Here's how to do it:

1. **In a new worksheet, insert numbers 1 through 12 representing the past 12 months, in a column.**

2. **In the adjacent cells, place the income figure for each of these months.**

3. **Label this area** Actual Data.

4. **In another section of the worksheet, enter the numbers 13 through 18 in a column to represent the upcoming six months.**

5. **In the column adjacent to the projected month numbers, select the six adjacent cells (empty at present) by dragging over them.**

6. **Type** =TREND(**to start the function entry.**

7. **Drag the mouse over the range of known Y values, or enter the range address. The known Y values are the income figures entered in Step 2.**

8. **Enter a comma (,).**

9. **Drag the mouse over the range of known X values, or enter the range address. The known X values are the numbers 1 through 12 entered in Step 1.**

10. **Enter a comma (,).**

11. **Drag the mouse over the list of month numbers for which you want projections (the numbers 13 through 18). These are the new X values.**

12. **Enter a closing parenthesis.**

13. **Press Ctrl+Shift+Enter to complete the formula.**

When you've completed these steps, you'll see the projected income figures, calculated by the TREND function, displayed in the worksheet. An example is shown in Figure 11-6. There's no assurance you'll have this income — but it may be even higher! You can always hope for the best.

	File	Edit	View	Insert	Format	Tools	Data	Window	Help
	B16	▼		*fx* {=TREND(B3:B14,A3:A14,A16:A21)}					
	A	B	C	D	E	F			
1	Actual Data								
2	Month	Income							
3	1	$11,245.12							
4	2	$12,272.73							
5	3	$12,344.55							
6	4	$12,481.82							
7	5	$12,557.27							
8	6	$12,645.45							
9	7	$12,134.12							
10	8	$12,829.09							
11	9	$12,899.09							
12	10	$13,020.91							
13	11	$13,090.91							
14	12	$13,208.18							
15	Projected data								
16	13	$ 13,380.82							
17	14	$ 13,506.99							
18	15	$ 13,633.15							
19	16	$ 13,759.31							
20	17	$ 13,885.47							
21	18	$ 14,011.63							
22									
23									
24									
25									
26									
27									
28									
29									
30									

Figure 11-6: Using the TREND function to calculate predictions for an array.

The GROWTH function is like TREND in that it uses existing data to predict Y values for a set of X values. It's different in that it's designed for use with data that fits an exponential model. The function takes four arguments:

✔ The first argument is a range or array containing the known Y values.

✔ The second argument is a range or array containing the known X values.

✔ The third argument is a range or array containing the X values for which you want to calculate predicted Y values.

✔ The fourth value is omitted or TRUE if you want the constant *b* calculated normally. If this argument is FALSE, *b* is forced to 1. You won't use FALSE except in special situations.

The number of known X and known Y values must be the same or an error will occur. As you'd expect, GROWTH is an array formula and must be entered accordingly.

To use the GROWTH function, follow these steps. *Note:* This assumes that you have a worksheet that already contains known X and Y values that fit the exponential model.

1. **Enter the X values for which you want to predict Y values in a column of the worksheet.**

2. **Select a range of cells in a column that has the same number of rows as the X values you entered in Step 1.**

   Often this range will be in the column next to the X values, but it doesn't have to be.

3. **Enter** =Growth(**to start the function entry.**

4. **Drag the mouse over the range containing the known Y values, or enter the range address.**

5. **Enter a comma (,).**

6. **Drag the mouse over the range containing the known X values, or enter the range address.**

7. **Enter a comma (,).**

8. **Drag the mouse over the range containing the X values for which you want to predict Y values, or enter the range address.**

9. **Enter a closing parenthesis.**

10. **Press Ctrl+Shift+Enter to complete the formula.**

Figure 11-7 shows an example of using the GROWTH function to forecast exponential data. Columns A and B contain the known data and the range D10:D19 contains the X values for which predictions are desired. The GROWTH array formula was entered in E10:E19. The chart shows a scatter plot of the actual data, up to X = 40, and the projected data, for X values above 40. You can see how the projected data continues the exponential curves that are fit by the actual data.

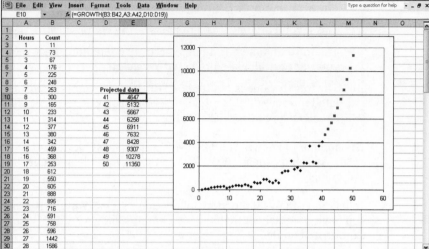

	A	B	C	D	E	F
2	Hours	Count				
3	1	11				
4	2	73				
5	3	67				
6	4	176				
7	5	225				
8	6	248				
9	7	253			Projected data	
10	8	300		41	4647	
11	9	165		42	5132	
12	10	233		43	5667	
13	11	314		44	6258	
14	12	377		45	6911	
15	13	380		46	7632	
16	14	342		47	8428	
17	15	459		48	9307	
18	16	368		49	10278	
19	17	253		50	11350	
20	18	612				
21	19	550				
22	20	605				
23	21	888				
24	22	895				
25	23	716				
26	24	591				
27	25	758				
28	26	596				
29	27	1442				
30	28	1586				

Figure 11-7: Demonstrating use of the GROWTH function to project exponential data.

Using NORMDIST and POISSON to Determine Probabilities

You can get a good introduction to the normal distribution in Chapter 9. To recap briefly, a normal distribution is characterized by its *mean* (the value in the middle of the distribution) and by its *standard deviation* (the extent to which values spread out on either side of the mean). The normal distribution is a continuous distribution, which means that X values can be fractional and aren't restricted to integers. The normal distribution has a lot of uses because so many processes, both natural and human, follow it.

The word *normal* in this context doesn't mean "good" or "okay," and a distribution that is not normal is not flawed in some way. Normal is used simply to mean "typical" or "common."

Excel provides you with the NORMDIST function for calculating probabilities from a normal distribution. The function takes four arguments:

✔ The first argument is the value for which you want to calculate a probability.

✔ The second argument is the mean of the normal distribution.

✔ The third argument is the standard deviation of the normal distribution.

✔ The fourth argument is TRUE if you want the cumulative probability and FALSE if you want the non-cumulative probability.

A cumulative probability is the chance of getting any value between 0 and the specified value. A non-cumulative probability is the chance of getting exactly the specified value.

Normal distributions come into play for a wide variety of measurements. Examples include blood pressure, atmospheric carbon dioxide levels, wave height, leaf size, and oven temperature. If you know the mean and standard deviation of a distribution, you can use NORMDIST to calculate related probabilities.

Here's an example: Your firm manufactures hardware, and a customer wants to buy a large quantity of 50mm bolts. Due to the manufacturing process, the length of bolts varies slightly. The customer will place the order only if at least 95 percent of the bolts are between 49.9mm and 50.1mm. Measuring each one isn't practical, but previous data shows that the distribution of bolt lengths is a normal distribution with a mean of 50 and a standard deviation of 0.05. You can use Excel and the NORMDIST function to answer the question. Here's the plan:

1. **Use the NORMDIST function to determine the cumulative probability of a bolt being at least 50.1mm long.**

2. **Use the NORMDIST function to determine the cumulative probability of a bolt being at least 49.9mm long.**

3. **Subtract the second value from the first to get the probability that a bolt is between 49.9mm and 50.1mm long.**

Here are the steps to follow:

1. **In a new worksheet, enter the values for the mean, standard deviation, upper limit, and lower limit in separate cells.**

   Optionally, add adjoining labels to identify the cells.

2. **In another cell, enter =NORMDIST(to start the function entry.**

3. **Click the cell containing the lower limit value (49.9) or enter the cell address.**

4. **Enter a comma (,).**

5. **Click the cell containing the mean, or enter the cell address.**

6. **Enter a comma (,).**

7. **Click the cell containing the standard deviation, or enter the cell address.**

8. **Enter a comma (,).**

9. **Enter** TRUE **and a closing parenthesis.**

10. **Press Enter to complete the function.**

    This cell now displays the probability of a bolt being less than or equal to the lower limit.

11. **In another cell, enter** =NORMDIST(**to start the function entry.**

12. **Click the cell containing the upper-limit value (50.1), or enter the cell address.**

13. **Repeat Steps 4 through 10.**

    This cell now displays the probability of a bolt being less than or equal to the upper limit.

14. **In another cell, enter a formula that subtracts the lower-limit probability from the upper-limit probability.**

    This cell now displays the probability that a bolt will be within the specified limits.

Figure 11-8 shows a worksheet that was created to solve this problem. You can see from cell B8 that the answer is 0.9545 — in other words, 95.45 percent of your bolts fall in the prescribed limits, and you can accept the customer's order. Note in this worksheet that the formulas in cells B6:B8 are presented in the adjacent cells so you can see what they look like.

Figure 11-8:
Using the
NORMDIST
function to
calculate
probabilities.

	A	B	C	D
		B8	▼	*fx* =B7-B6
1				
2	Mean	50		
3	Standard deviation	0.05		
4	Upper limit	50.1		
5	Lower limit	49.9		
6	Probability <= lower limit	0.02275	=NORMDIST(B5, B2, B3, TRUE)	
7	Probability <= upper limit	0.97725	=NORMDIST(B4, B2, B3, TRUE)	
8	Probability between limits	0.9545	=B7-B6	
9				
10				
11				

File   Edit   View   Insert   Format   Tools   Data   Window   Help

The Poisson distribution is another kind of distribution that is used in many areas of statistics. Its most common use is to model the number of events taking place in a specified time period. Suppose you were modeling the number of employees calling in sick each day, or the number of defective items produced at your factory each week — in these cases, the Poisson distribution would be appropriate.

The Poisson distribution is useful for analyzing rare events. What exactly does *rare* mean? People calling in sick at work is hardly rare, but a specific number calling in sick is rare, at least statistically speaking. Situations where Poisson is applicable would include numbers of car accidents, counts of customers arriving, manufacturing defects, and the like. One way to express it is that the events are individually rare, but there are many opportunities for them to happen.

The Poisson distribution is a discrete distribution. This means that the X values in the distribution can only take on specified, discrete values such as X = 1, 2, 3, 4, 5 and so on. This is different from the normal distribution, which is a continuous distribution in which X values can take any value (X = 0.034, 1.2365, and so on). The discrete nature of the Poisson distribution is suited to the kinds of data you use it with. For example, with employees calling in sick, you may have 1, 5, or 8 on a given day but certainly not 1.45, 7.2, or 9.15!

Figure 11-9 shows a Poisson distribution that has a mean of 20. Values on the X axis are number of occurrences (of whatever you're studying) and values on the Y axis are probabilities. You can use this distribution to determine the probability of a specific number of occurrences happening. For example, this chart tells us that the probability of having exactly 15 occurrences is approximately 0.05 (5 percent).

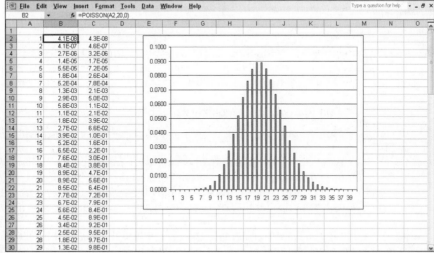

Figure 11-9: A Poisson distribution with a mean of 20.

The Poisson distribution is a discrete distribution and is used only with data that takes on discrete (integer) values, such as counting items.

A Poisson distribution is not always symmetrical as the one shown in Figure 11-9 is. Negative X values make no sense in a Poisson distribution — after all, you can't have fewer than zero people calling in sick! If the mean is a small value, the distribution will be skewed, as shown in Figure 11-10 for a Poisson distribution with a mean of 4.

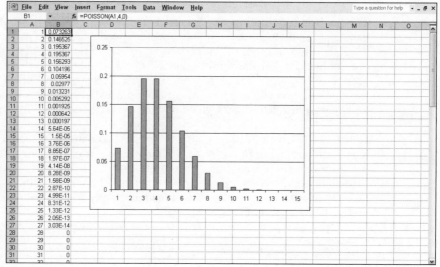

Figure 11-10:
A Poisson distribution with a mean of 4.

Excel's POISSON function lets you calculate the probability that a specified number of events will occur. All you need to know is the mean of the distribution. There are two ways that this function can calculate the probability:

✔ **Cumulative:** The probability that between 0 and X events will occur.

✔ **Non-cumulative:** The probability that exactly X events will occur.

The two Poisson graphs shown earlier were for non-cumulative probabilities. Figure 11-11 shows the cumulative Poisson distribution corresponding to Figure 11-9. You can see from this chart that the cumulative probability of 15 events — the probability of 15 or fewer events occurring — is about 0.15.

TIP

What if you want to calculate the probability that more than X events will occur? Simple! Just calculate the cumulative probability for X and subtract the result from 1.

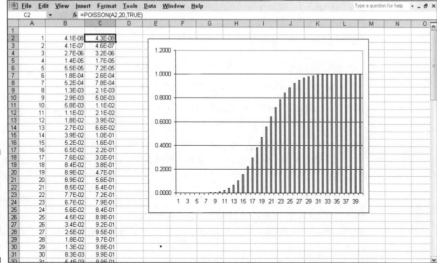

Figure 11-11: A cumulative Poisson distribution with a mean of 20.

The POISSON function takes three arguments:

- The first argument is the number of events that you want to calculate the probability for. This must be an integer value greater than 0.

- The second argument is the mean of the Poisson distribution to use. This too must be an integer value greater than 0.

- The third argument is TRUE if you want the cumulative probability and FALSE if you want the non-cumulative probability.

For example, suppose that you're the manager of a factory that makes brake shoes. Your district manager has announced an incentive — you'll receive a bonus for each day that the number of defective shoes is less than 20. How many days a month will you meet this goal, knowing that the average number of defective brake shoes is 25 per day? Here are the steps to follow:

1. **In a new worksheet, enter the average number of defects per day (25) in a cell.**

   If desired, enter an adjacent label to identify the cell.

2. **In the cell below, start typing** =POISSON(**to start the function entry.**

3. **Enter the value 20.**

4. **Enter a comma (,).**

5. **Click the cell where you entered the average defects per day, or enter its cell address.**

6. **Enter a comma (,).**

7. **Enter TRUE followed by a closing parenthesis.**

8. **Press Enter to complete the formula.**

9. **If desired, enter a label in an adjacent cell to identify this as the probability of 20 or fewer defects.**

10. **In the cell below, enter a formula that multiplies the number of working days per month (22) by the result just calculated with the POISSON function.**

    In our worksheet, this formula is =22*B3, entered in cell B4.

11. **If desired, enter a label in an adjacent cell to identify this as the number of days per month you can expect to have 20 or fewer defects.**

The finished worksheet is shown in Figure 11-12. In this example, we have formatted cells B3:B4 with two decimal places. You can see that with an average of 25 defects per day you can expect to earn a bonus 4 days a month.

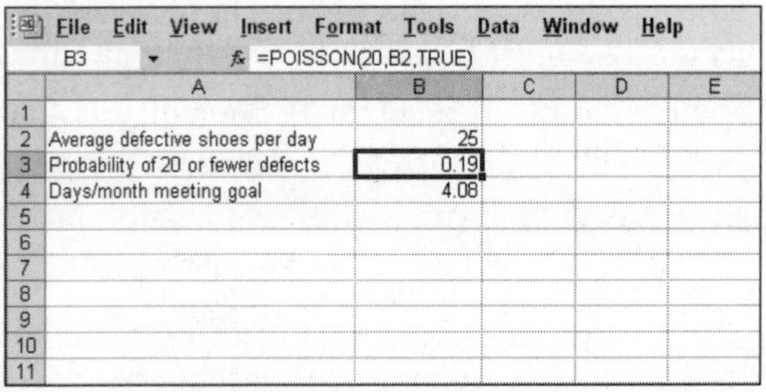

Figure 11-12:
Using the
POISSON
function to
calculate a
cumulative
probability.

Part IV
Working with Data

In this part . . .

We show you a variety of functions that work with dates and time, looking up values, getting information about your information, and manipulating text. We show you how to calculate how long something will take. Excel even has a function that counts elapsed days but knows not to count the weekends. How cool is that!? We show you how to determine what day of the week a date is. In this Part is the notable IF function — one of the workhorses of Excel. Got a lot of data on a worksheet? The Excel lookup and database functions make it easy to find a needle in that haystack! Finally, there are several functions to work with text. What for, you ask? Plenty! Ever need to reverse people's names, from last name, first name, to first name, last name? We show you how. How about finding a piece of text inside a larger one? Another no-brainer with Excel on your side.

Chapter 12

Working with Date Functions

*O*ften when working with Excel, you need to manage dates. Perhaps you have list of dates when you visited a client and you need to count how many times you were there in September. On the other hand, maybe you are tracking a project over a few months, and want to know how many days are in between the milestones.

Excel has a number of useful Date functions to make your work easier! This chapter explains how to work with parts of a date, such as the month or year, and even how to count the number of days between two dates. You can always reference the current data from your computer's clock and use it in a calculation.

Understanding How Excel Handles Dates

Imagine if, on January 1, 1900, you starting counting by ones, each day adding one more to the total. This is just how Excel thinks of dates. January 1, 1900, is one; January 2, 1900, is two; and so on. We'll always remember 25,404 as the day man first walked on the moon, and 36,892 as the start of the new millennium!

The millennium actually started on January 1, 2001. The year 2000 is the last year of the 20th century.

Excel represents dates as a serial number — specifically, the number of days between January 1, 1900, and the date in question. Excel can handle dates from January 1, 1900 to December 31, 9999. Using the serial numbering system, that's 1 through 2,958,465!

Because Excel represents dates in this way, it can work with dates in the same manner as numbers. For example, you can subtract one date from another to find out how many days are between them. Likewise, you can add 14 to today's date to get a date two weeks in the future. This trick is very useful but people are used to seeing dates represented in traditional formats, not as numbers. Fortunately, Excel has the tools for date formatting as well.

In Excel for the Mac, the serial numbering system begins on January 1, 1904.

The way years are handled requires special mention. When a year is fully displayed in four digits, such as 2005, there is no ambiguity. However, when a date is written in a shorthand style, such as in 3/1/02, it isn't clear what the year is. It could be 2002, or it could be 1902. Let's say 3/1/02 is a shorthand entry for someone's birthday. Then on March 1, 2005, he is either 3 years old or 103 years old. In some countries this would be January 3, 1902 or January 3, 2002.

Excel and the Windows operating system have a default way of interpreting shorthand years. Windows 2000 and later has a setting in the Customize Regional Options dialog box found in the Control Panel. Here's how to open and set it:

1. **Click on your computer's Start button.**

2. **Select Control Panel.**

3. **Select Regional and Language Options.**

4. **In the Regional and Language Options dialog box, select the Regional Options tab if it is not selected by default.**

5. **Click the Customize button.**

   The Customize Regional Options dialog box appears.

6. **Select the Date tab in the Customize Regional Options dialog box.**

7. **Enter a four-digit ending year (such as 2029) to indicate the latest year that will be used when interpreting a two-digit year.**

8. **Click OK to close each dialog box.**

This setting guides how Excel will interpret years. So if the setting is 1930 through 2029, then 3/1/02 indicates the year 2002, but 3/1/45 indicates the year 1945, not 2045. Figure 12-1 shows this setting.

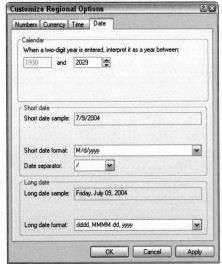

Figure 12-1:
Setting how
years are
interpreted.

To ensure full accuracy when working with dates, always enter the full four
digits for the year.

Formatting Dates

When you work with dates, you'll probably need to format cells in your worksheet. It's great that Excel tells you that June 1, 2005, is serially represented
as 38504, but we don't think that's what you want on a report. To format
dates, you use the Format Cells dialog box, shown in Figure 12-2. To format
dates, follow these steps:

1. **Choose Format ⇨ Cells.**

   The Format Cells dialog box appears.

2. **Select the Number tab in the Format Cells dialog box if it is not
   already selected.**

3. **Select Date in the Category List.**

4. **Select an appropriate format in the Type List.**

Now you can turn the useful but pesky serial dates into a user-friendly format.

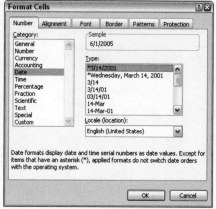

Figure 12-2:
Using the
Format Cells
dialog box
to control
how dates
are
displayed.

Assembling a Date with the DATE Function

You can use the DATE function to create a complete date when you have separate year, month, and day information. The DATE function can be useful because dates don't always appear as, well, dates, in a worksheet. You may have a column of values between 1 and 12 that represents the month, and another column of values between 1 and 31 for the day of the month. A third column may hold years — in either the two-digit shorthand or the full four digits.

The DATE function combines individual day, month, and year components into a single usable date. This makes using and referencing dates in your worksheet easy. To use the DATE function:

1. **Select the cell where you want the results displayed.**

2. **Enter =DATE(to begin the function entry.**

3. **Click the cell that has the year.**

4. **Enter a comma (,).**

5. **Click the cell that has the number (1–12) that represents the month.**

6. **Enter a comma (,).**

7. **Click the cell that has the number (1–31) that represents the day of the month.**

8. **Enter a closing parenthesis to end the function, and press Enter.**

Figure 12-3 displays a fourth column of dates that are created using DATE and the values from the first three columns. The fourth column of dates has been formatted so the dates are displayed in a standard format, not as a raw date serial number.

	File	Edit	View	Insert	Format	Tools	Data	Window	Help
	D3	▼		f_x =DATE(C3,A3,B3)					

	A	B	C	D	E
1	MONTH	DAY	YEAR	DATE	
2					
3	4	19	2005	4/19/2005	
4	2	22	2004	2/22/2004	
5	2	22	2005	2/22/2005	
6	8	24	2004	8/24/2004	
7	12	20	2005	12/20/2005	
8	7	6	2005	7/6/2005	
9	5	7	2005	5/7/2005	
10	1	12	2004	1/12/2004	
11	9	8	2005	9/8/2005	
12	9	2	2005	9/2/2005	
13	4	4	2004	4/4/2004	
14	3	21	2004	3/21/2004	
15	10	9	2005	10/9/2005	
16	12	1	2005	12/1/2005	
17	4	16	2005	4/16/2005	
18	8	16	2004	8/16/2004	
19	7	18	2005	7/18/2005	
20					
21					

Figure 12-3: Using the DATE function to assemble a date from separate month, day, and year values.

Breaking Apart a Date with the DAY, MONTH, and YEAR Functions

That which can be put together can also be taken apart. In the preceding section, we show you how to use the DATE function to create a date from separate year, month, and day data. In this section, you find out how to do the reverse — split a date into individual year, month, and day components using the DAY, MONTH, and YEAR functions. In Figure 12-4, the dates in column A are split apart by day, month, and year, respectively, in columns B, C, and D.

Isolating the day with the DAY function

Isolating the day part of a date is useful in applications where just the day, but not the month or year, is relevant. For example, say you own a store and want to figure out if more customers come to shop in the first half or the second half of the month. You're interested in this trend over several months. So the task may be to average the number of sales by the day of the month only.

	File	Edit	View	Insert	Format	Tools	Data	Window	Help		

A2 ▾ ƒ 1/1/2005

	A	B	C	D	
1	Date	DAY	MONTH	YEAR	
2	1/1/2005	1	1	2005	
3	3/31/2005	31	3	2005	
4	8/12/2005	12	8	2005	
5	9/13/2005	13	9	2005	
6	2/13/2005	13	2	2005	
7	4/5/2005	5	4	2005	
8	4/27/2005	27	4	2005	
9	11/30/2005	30	11	2005	
10	1/12/2005	12	1	2005	
11	4/9/2005	9	4	2005	
12	6/8/2005	8	6	2005	
13	9/22/2005	22	9	2005	
14	12/9/2005	9	12	2005	
15	4/14/2005	14	4	2005	
16	7/20/2005	20	7	2005	
17	12/10/2005	10	12	2005	
18	11/7/2005	7	11	2005	
19	4/18/2005	18	4	2005	
20	8/30/2005	30	8	2005	
21	10/1/2005	1	10	2005	
22	3/3/2005	3	3	2005	
23	12/17/2005	17	12	2005	
24	1/10/2005	10	1	2005	
25	3/20/2005	20	3	2005	

Figure 12-4:
Splitting
apart a
date with
the DAY,
MONTH,
and YEAR
functions.

The DAY function is useful for this because you can use it to return just the day for a lengthy list of dates. Then you can examine results by the day only.

Here's how you use the DAY function:

1. **Position the mouse in the cell where you want the results displayed.**

2. **Enter =DAY(to begin the function entry.**

3. **Click the cell that has the date.**

4. **Enter a closing parenthesis to end the function, and press Enter.**

   Excel returns a number between 1 and 31.

Figure 12-5 shows how the DAY function can be used to analyze customer activity. Column A contains a full year's sequential dates. In Column B, the day part of each date has been isolated. Column C shows the customer traffic for each day.

This is all the information that is needed to analyze whether there is a difference in the amount of customer traffic between the first half and second half of the month.

Cells E4 and E10 show the average daily customer traffic for the first half and second half of the month, respectively. The value for the first half of the month was obtained by adding all the customer values for those day values in the range 1 to 15, and then dividing by the total number of days. The value for the second half of the month was done the same way, but using day values in the range 16 to 31.

	File Edit View Insert Format Tools Data Window Help					
	E4 ▼	*fx* =SUMIF(B2:B367,"<16",C2:C367)/COUNTIF(B2:B367,"<16")				
	A	B	C	D	E	F
1	Date	DAY	Customers			
2	1/1/2004	1	8		Average Daily Customers	
3	1/2/2004	2	61		for the 1st though 15th of the month	
4	1/3/2004	3	48		48.56	
5	1/4/2004	4	41			
6	1/5/2004	5	36			
7	1/6/2004	6	69			
8	1/7/2004	7	34		Average Daily Customers	
9	1/8/2004	8	37		for the 16th though end of the month	
10	1/9/2004	9	55		54.46	
11	1/10/2004	10	56			
12	1/11/2004	11	34			
13	1/12/2004	12	64			
14	1/13/2004	13	59			
15	1/14/2004	14	33			
16	1/15/2004	15	26			
17	1/16/2004	16	78			
18	1/17/2004	17	64			
19	1/18/2004	18	68			
20	1/19/2004	19	52			
21	1/20/2004	20	65			
22	1/21/2004	21	51			
23	1/22/2004	22	65			
24	1/23/2004	23	67			
25	1/24/2004	24	25			
26	1/25/2004	25	38			
27	1/26/2004	26	48			
28	1/27/2004	27	68			
29	1/28/2004	28	51			
30	1/29/2004	29	32			
31	1/30/2004	30	70			

Figure 12-5:
Using
the DAY
function to
analyze
customer
activity.

The day parts of the dates, in Column B, were key to these calculations:

✔ In cell E4 the calculation is =SUMIF(B2:B367,"<16",C2:C367)/COUNT
   IF(B2:B367"<16").

✔ In cell E10 the calculation is =SUMIF(B2:B367,">15",C2:C367)/COUNT
   IF(B2:B367,">15").

The SUMIF function is discussed in Chapter 7. The COUNTIF function is discussed in Chapter 11.

The DAY function has been instrumental in showing that more customers visit the fictitious store in the second half of the month. This type of information is great for a store owner to plan staff assignments, sales specials, and so on.

Isolating the month with the MONTH function

Isolating the month part of a date is useful in applications where just the month, but not the day or year, is relevant. For example, you may have a list of random dates and need to determine the number of dates that fall in each of the 12 months.

You could sort the dates and then count the number for each month. That would be easy enough, but sorting may not be an option based on other requirements. Besides, why manually count when you have right in front of you one of the all-time greatest counting software programs ever made!

Figure 12-6 shows a worksheet in which the MONTH function has been used to extract the numeric month value (1–12) into Column B from the dates in Column A. Cell B2 contains the formula =MONTH(A2) and so on down the column. Columns C and D contain a summary of dates per month. The formula used in cell D3 is:

```
=COUNTIF($B$2:$B$201,1)
```

This counts the number of dates where the month value is 1. Cells D4 through D14 contain similar formulas for month values 2 through 12.

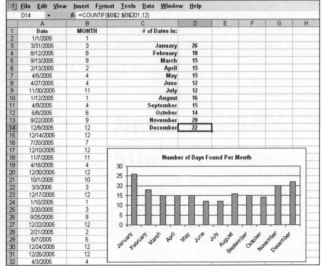

Figure 12-6:
Using the MONTH function to count the number of dates falling in each month.

See Chapter 14 for information on the COUNTIF function.

In Figure 12-6, the dates in Column A are random, so discerning much about the dates is difficult. However, the summary, as well as the chart based on the summary, show that more dates appear in the winter months (assuming you're in the Northern Hemisphere).

To use the MONTH function:

1. **Select the cell where you want the results displayed.**

2. **Enter** =MONTH(**to begin the function entry.**

3. **Click the cell that has the date.**

4. **Enter a closing parenthesis to end the function, and press Enter.**

   Excel returns a number between 1 and 12.

Isolating the year with the YEAR function

Isolating the year part of a date is useful in applications where just the year, but not the day or month, is relevant. In practice, this is less used than the DAY or MONTH functions because date data is often — though not always — from the same year.

To use the YEAR function:

1. **Select the cell where you want the results displayed.**

2. **Enter =YEAR(to begin the function entry.**

3. **Click the cell that has the date.**

4. **Enter a closing parenthesis to end the function, and press Enter.**

   Excel returns the four-digit year.

Using DATEVALUE to Convert a Text Date into a Numerical Date

You may have data in your worksheet that looks like a date but is not represented as an Excel date value. For example, you could enter the text "01-14-04" in a cell, and Excel would have no way of knowing whether this is January 14, 2004, or the code for your combination lock. Don't tell anyone! But if it looks like a date, you can use the DATEVALUE function to convert it into an Excel date value.

Why not enter dates as text data? Because although they may look fine, you can't use them for any of Excel's powerful date calculations without first converting them to date values.

The DATEVALUE function recognizes almost all commonly used ways that dates are written. Here are some ways that people may enter August 5, 2005:

- 8/5/05
- 5-Aug-2005
- 2005/08/05

DATEVALUE can convert these and several other date representations to a date serial number.

After you've converted the dates to a date serial number, the dates can be used in other date formulas or to perform calculations as described in other parts of this chapter.

To use the DATEVALUE function, follow these steps:

1. **Select the cell where you want the date serial number located.**

2. **Enter =DATEVALUE(to begin the function entry.**

3. **Click the cell that has the text format date.**

4. **Enter a closing parenthesis to end the function, and press Enter.**

   The result will be a date serial number, unless the cell where the result is displayed has already been set to a date format.

Figure 12-7 shows how some nonstandard dates in Column A have been converted with the DATEVALUE function.

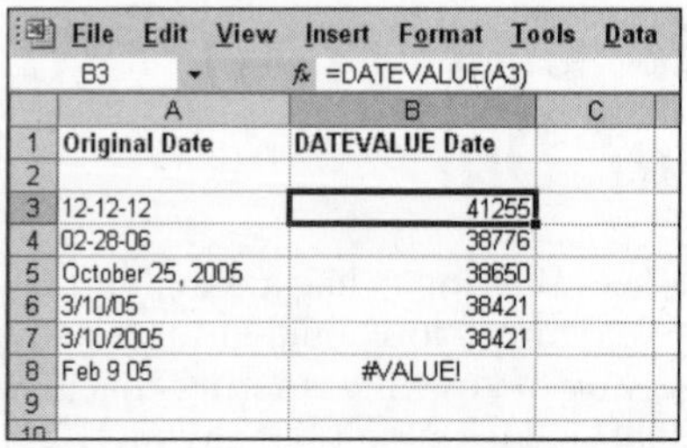

Figure 12-7:
Converting
dates into
their serial
equivalents
with the
DATEVALUE
function.

Did you notice something funny in Figure 12-7? Normally, you won't be able to enter a value such as the one in cell A4 — 02-28-06 — without losing the leading zero. The cells in Column A had been changed to the Text format. This format tells Excel to leave your entry as it is. The Text format is one of the choices in the Category list in the Format Cells dialog box (refer to Figure 12-2).

In reality, you won't need DATEVALUE too often because Excel is pretty good at recognizing dates that you enter in the standard formats. If, for example, you enter "12/5/04" in a cell, Excel recognizes that this is meant as a date and not as text. It's automatically converted to a date serial number and displayed using the default date format. DATEVALUE is used most often when you're importing text data from another application and Excel fails to perform the automatic conversion.

Please look back at Figure 12-7, specifically at cell B8. Excel could not figure out how to interpret the Feb 9 05 value in cell A8. Therefore, cell B8 shows an error. We did say Excel is great at recognizing dates, but we did not say it is perfect! In cases such as this, you'll have to edit the date to put it into a format that DATEVALUE can recognize.

Using the TODAY Function to Find Out the Current Date

Often, when working in Excel, you need to use the current date. Each time a worksheet is printed, for example, you may want it to show the date it was printed. The TODAY function fills the bill perfectly for this. TODAY simply get the date from your computer's internal clock. To use the TODAY function, follow these steps:

1. **Position the mouse to the cell where you want the result.**

2. **Type** =TODAY( ).

3. **Press Enter to end the function.**

That's it! You now have the date from your computer. If your computer's clock is not set correctly, don't blame Excel. Like all dates in Excel, what you really end up with is a serial number, but the Date formatting displays the date in a readable fashion.

As with all functions in Excel, you can embed functions in other functions. So, for example, if you need to know just the month of the current date, you can combine the TODAY function with the MONTH function, like this:

```
=MONTH(TODAY())
```

Counting the number of days until Christmas

Have a bit of shopping left to do for the holidays? Excel can help keep track of how many days are left. Remember that Excel is able to perform mathematical operations on dates. So let Excel do the counting. This formula, entered in a cell, tells you how many days are left until Christmas 2005:

```
=DATE(2005,12,25) - TODAY()
```

The formula assumes you're counting days in the year 2005. Change the year reference as needed.

The DATE function is used to enter the day, month, and year of Christmas. This avoids having a shorthand entry, such as 12/25/2005 be interpreted as a mathematical operation on its own.

If the entry was `=12/25/2005 - TODAY()`, an incorrect answer would be calculated; because this effectively says, "Divide 12 by 25, then divide that result by 2005, then subtract the serial number of today's date." The answer would be incorrect.

Using the DATE function to represent dates in which a mathematical operation is performed is a good idea.

Counting your age, in days

Sometimes you're asked how old you are. Maybe you'd rather not say. Here's a way to tell but in a way that will still leave the person who asked you unsure of the answer. Answer by saying how old you are in days!

Excel can help figure this out. All you have to do is count the number of days between your birth date and the current date. A simple formula tells you this:

```
=TODAY() - DATE(birth year, birth month, birth day)
```

Just substitute your real birth year, month, and day into the formula.

Determining the Day of the Week with the WEEKDAY Function

The Beatles wrote a song called "Eight Days a Week," but for the rest of us seven days is the norm. The WEEKDAY function helps you figure out which day of the week a date falls on. Using this function, you can find out what day of the week an upcoming event will occur on, such as what day your birthday will fall on next year.

Here is how you use the WEEKDAY function:

1. **Select the cell where you want the results displayed.**

2. **Enter** =WEEKDAY(**to begin the function entry.**

3. **Select the cell that has the date you want to find out the weekday for.**

4. **Enter a closing parenthesis to end the function, and press Enter.**

   WEEKDAY returns a number between 1 and 7. Table 12-1 shows what the returned number means.

Table 12-1	WEEKDAY Returned Values
Returned Value	*Weekday*
1	Sunday
2	Monday
3	Tuesday
4	Wednesday
5	Thursday
6	Friday
7	Saturday

Don't confuse the returned numbers with actual dates! Just because, in Table 12-1, a value of 4 indicates a Wednesday doesn't mean the fourth of a month is a Wednesday. The values of the returned numbers are also a bit confusing because most people consider Monday, not Sunday, to be the first day of the week. You can go argue the point with Microsoft if you like!

The numbers 1 through 7 that are returned from the WEEKDAY function are not the same as the first through seventh of the month.

The WEEKDAY function lets you extract interesting information from date-related data. For example, maybe you're on a diet and you're keeping a tally of how many calories you consume each day for a month. Then you start wondering — are you eating more on weekends than on weekdays? Figure 12-8 shows a worksheet that calculates the average calories consumed on each day of the week over a month's time. A quick glance at the results shows that Saturdays and Sundays are high calorie-consumption days. Well, at least you can hope they're also outdoor activity days!

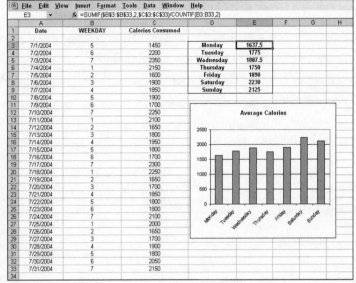

E3   ▼   *fx* =SUMIF($B$3:$B$33,2,$C$3:$C$33)/COUNTIF(B3:B33,2)

	A	B	C	D	E	F	G	H
1	Date	WEEKDAY	Calories Consumed					
2								
3	7/1/2004	5	1450	Monday	1637.5			
4	7/2/2004	6	2200	Tuesday	1775			
5	7/3/2004	7	2350	Wednesday	1887.5			
6	7/4/2004	1	2150	Thursday	1750			
7	7/5/2004	2	1600	Friday	1890			
8	7/6/2004	3	1900	Saturday	2230			
9	7/7/2004	4	1850	Sunday	2125			
10	7/8/2004	5	1900					
11	7/9/2004	6	1700					
12	7/10/2004	7	2250					
13	7/11/2004	1	2100					
14	7/12/2004	2	1650					
15	7/13/2004	3	1800					
16	7/14/2004	4	1950					
17	7/15/2004	5	1800					
18	7/16/2004	6	1700					
19	7/17/2004	7	2300					
20	7/18/2004	1	2250					
21	7/19/2004	2	1650					
22	7/20/2004	3	1700					
23	7/21/2004	4	1850					
24	7/22/2004	5	1800					
25	7/23/2004	6	1800					
26	7/24/2004	7	2100					
27	7/25/2004	1	2000					
28	7/26/2004	2	1650					
29	7/27/2004	3	1700					
30	7/28/2004	4	1900					
31	7/29/2004	5	1800					
32	7/30/2004	6	2050					
33	7/31/2004	7	2150					
34								

Figure 12-8:
Using
WEEKDAY
tells you
which day
of the week
a date
falls on.

Determining How Many Workdays Are in a Range of Dates with NETWORKDAYS

The NETWORKDAYS function tells you how many working days are in a range of dates. As an example, you can use this function to figure out how many days of work are left in the year. Ever sit at your desk and stare at the calendar trying to count how many working days are left? Excel can answer this vital question for you!

The NETWORKDAYS function is available when the Analysis ToolPak add-in is loaded. See Chapter 20 for more information on the Analysis ToolPak.

NETWORKDAYS counts the number of days in a range that you supply. The function purposely does not count Saturdays and Sundays. You can add an additional list of dates that should not be counted, if you want. This optional list is where you can put holidays, vacation time, and so on.

Figure 12-9 shows an example using NETWORKDAYS. Cells C3 and C4 show the start and end dates, respectively. In this example, the start date is provided with the TODAY function. Therefore, the result will always reflect a count that starts from the current date. The end date is the last day of the year.

	File	Edit	View	Insert	Format	Tools	Data	Window	Help		

	C6	▼	*fx*	=NETWORKDAYS(C3,C4,C10:C24)			

	A	B	C	D	E	F
1						
2						
3		Today's Date	7/11/2004			
4		End of Year	12/31/2004			
5						
6		**Remaining Work Days:**	115			
7						
8						
9						
10		New Year's Day	1/1/2004			
11		Martin Luther King Jr. Day	1/19/2004			
12		President's Day	2/16/2004			
13		Memorial Day	5/31/2004			
14		Independence Day (work day off)	7/5/2004			
15		Vacation	8/2/2004			
16		Vacation	8/3/2004			
17		Vacation	8/4/2004			
18		Vacation	8/5/2004			
19		Vacation	8/6/2004			
20		Labor Day	9/6/2004			
21		Columbus Day	10/11/2004			
22		Election Day	11/2/2004			
23		Thanksgiving	11/25/2004			
24		Christmas Eve	12/24/2004			
25						
26						

Figure 12-9:
Counting
workdays
with
NETWORK
DAYS.

The function in cell C6 is:

```
=NETWORKDAYS(C3,C4,C10:C24)
```

The function includes the cells that have the start and end dates. Then there is a range of cells — C10 through C24. In these cells are dates that should not be counted in the total of workdays. In the list of dates are holidays and vacation days. You can put anything in here — Excel doesn't care.

To use NETWORKDAYS, follow these steps:

1. **Select the cell where you want the results displayed.**

2. **Enter =NETWORKDAYS(to begin the function entry.**

3. **Click the cell that has the start date for the range of dates to be counted.**

4. **Enter a comma (,).**

5. **Click the cell that has the number end date for the range of dates to be counted.**

   If you want to add a list of dates to exclude in the count, continue to Steps 6 and 7; otherwise, skip these and go to Step 8.

6. **Enter a comma (,).**

7. **Click and drag the mouse over the cells that have the dates to be excluded in the workdays count.**

8. **Enter a closing parenthesis to end the function, and press Enter.**

   The result is a count of days, between the start and end dates, that do not fall on Saturday or Sunday and are not in an optional list of exclusion dates.

Calculating Time between Two Dates with the DATEDIF Function

Excel provides the DATEDIF function to calculate the number of days, months, or years between two dates. This is an undocumented function, that is, you will not see it in the Insert Function dialog box, and you cannot find it in the Excel Help system. But how cool this is! Impress your friends and co-workers. The only thing you have to do is remember how to enter it. Of course, we don't mind if you keep this book around to look it up.

DATEDIF takes three arguments: the start date, the end date, and the interval. The interval argument tells the function what type of result to return, summarized in Table 12-2.

Table 12-2	Settings for the Interval Argument of DATEDIF	
Value	*What it means*	*Comment*
"d"	Days	The count of inclusive days from the start date through the end date.
"m"	Months	The count of complete months between the dates. Only those months that fully occur between the dates are counted. For example, if the first date starts after the first of the month then that first month is not included in the count. For the end date, even when it is the last day of the month, that month is not counted. See Figure 12-10 for an example.

Value	What it means	Comment
"y"	Years	The count of complete years between the dates. Only those years that fully occur between the dates are counted. For example, if the first date starts later than January 1 then that first year is not included in the count. For the end date, even when it is December 31, that year is not counted. See Figure 12-10 for an example.
"yd"	Days excluding Years	The count of inclusive days from the start date through then end date, but as if the two dates are in the same year. The year is ignored.
"ym"	Months excluding Years	The count of complete months between the dates, but as if the two dates are in the same year. The year is ignored.
"md"	Days excluding Months and Years	The count of inclusive days from the start date through the end date, but as if the two dates are in the same month and year. The month and year are ignored.

Figure 12-10 shows some examples of using DATEDIF. Column A has start dates. Column B has end dates. Columns C through H contain formulas with DATEDIF. The DATEDIF function uses the start and end dates on each given row, and the interval is labeled at the top of the each column, C through H.

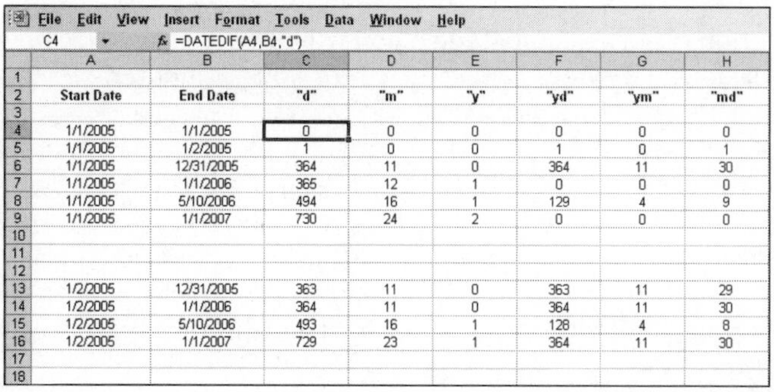

Figure 12-10: Counting with DATEDIF.

The spreadsheet contents:

	A	B	C	D	E	F	G	H
			=DATEDIF(A4,B4,"d")					
2	Start Date	End Date	"d"	"m"	"y"	"yd"	"ym"	"md"
4	1/1/2005	1/1/2005	0	0	0	0	0	0
5	1/1/2005	1/2/2005	1	0	0	1	0	1
6	1/1/2005	12/31/2005	364	11	0	364	11	30
7	1/1/2005	1/1/2006	365	12	1	0	0	0
8	1/1/2005	5/10/2006	494	16	1	129	4	9
9	1/1/2005	1/1/2007	730	24	2	0	0	0
13	1/2/2005	12/31/2005	363	11	0	363	11	29
14	1/2/2005	1/1/2006	364	11	0	364	11	30
15	1/2/2005	5/10/2006	493	16	1	128	4	8
16	1/2/2005	1/1/2007	729	23	1	364	11	30

Here are some highlights from the DATEDIF example in Figure 12-10:

✔ When the start date and end date are the same, the count of days is zero. The formula in cell C4 is =DATEDIF(A4,B4,"d").

✔ With a start date of 1/1/2005 and an end date of 12/31/2005, only 11 months are counted. The month of the end date is not counted. The formula in cell D6 is =DATEDIF(A6,B6,"m").

✔ With a start date of 1/1/2005 and an end date of 5/10/2006, DATEDIF used with the "md" interval returns 9 as the count of days between the dates even though the real count is 494. The formula in cell H8 is =DATEDIF(A8,B8,"md").

Here's how to use DATEDIF:

1. **Select the cell where you want the results to appear.**

2. **Enter** =DATEDIF(**to begin the function entry.**

3. **Click on a cell where you have a date, or enter its address.**

4. **Enter a comma (,).**

5. **Click on a cell where you another date.**

   This date must be the same or greater than the first date from Step 3 or an error will be returned.

6. **Enter a comma (,).**

7. **Enter an interval.**

   See Table 12-2 for the list of intervals that you can use with the function. Make sure that the interval is enclosed in double quotes.

8. **Enter a closing parenthesis to end the function and press Enter.**

This function is not documented so you will have to memorize how to use it, or else jot down its syntax and keep it near your computer.

Chapter 13

Keeping Track with Time Functions

*E*xcel has a superb handful of functions for working with time calculations. You can analyze data to the hour, minute, or second. And Excel helps you get this done in a New York minute!

Understanding How Excel Handles Time

In the previous chapter, we explained how Excel uses a serial number system to work with dates. Well, guess what? The same system is used to work with time. The key difference is that, although dates are represented by the integer portion of a serial number, time is represented by the decimal portion.

What does this mean? Consider this serial number: 38353. That is the serial number representation for January 1, 2005. Notice, though, that there is no concern for the time of that given day. The assumed time then is 12:00 a.m. (midnight), the start of the day. You can, however, represent specific times if needed.

Excel uses the decimal side of the serial number to represent time as a fraction of the 24-hour day. Thus, 12 p.m. (noon) is 0.5 and 6 p.m. is 0.75 Table 13-1 shows some more examples and also shows how dates and time information are combined in a single serial number.

Table 13-1	How Excel Represents Time
Date and Time	*Serial Format*
January 1, 2005 12:00 a.m.	38353
January 1, 2005 12:01 a.m.	38353.00069
January 1, 2005 10:00 a.m.	38353.41667
January 1, 2005 12:00 p.m.	38353.5
January 1, 2005 4:30 p.m.	38353.6875
January 1, 2005 10:00 p.m.	38353.91667
January 1, 2005 11:59 p.m.	38353.99931

Time is represented in a string of decimal values — up to five decimal digits. A decimal value of 0 is the equivalent of 12:00 a.m. A decimal value of .5 is the equivalent of 12:00 p.m. — the midpoint of the day. The value of .99931 is the same as the 23rd hour and *start* of the 59th minute. A value of .99999 is the same as the 23rd hour, the 59th minute, and the 59th second — in other words, one second before the start of the next day.

Formatting Time

When you work with time values, you'll probably need to format cells in your worksheet so the times display in a standard format that people will understand. The decimal numbers don't make sense to us human folk. To format time, you use the Format Cells dialog box, shown in Figure 13-1. To format time, follow these steps:

1. **Choose Format ⇨ Cells.**

   The Format Cells dialog box appears.

2. **Select the Number tab in the Format Cells dialog box, if it is not already selected.**

3. **Select Time in the Category List.**

4. **Select an appropriate format in the Type List.**

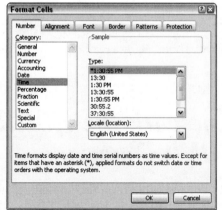

Figure 13-1:
Using the
Format Cells
dialog to
control how
time is
displayed.

Time can be displayed a number of ways. Excel can format time so that an hour can be between 1 and 12, as either a.m. or p.m. Alternatively, an hour can be between 0 and 23. The latter system, known to some as *military time,* is commonly used in computer systems.

Excel can display time in both regular (12-hour) and military (24-hour) format.

Note that Excel stores a date and time together in a single serial number. Therefore, some of the formatting options in both the time and date categories will display a complete date and time.

Assembling Time with the TIME Function

You can use the TIME function to combine hours, minutes, and seconds into a single usable value. Figuring out the serial number representation of a particular moment in time isn't easy. Luckily, the TIME function does this for you. You provide an hour, minute, and second, and TIME tells you the serial value. To do this, follow these steps:

1. **Select the cell where you want the results displayed.**

2. **Enter =TIME(to begin the function entry.**

3. **Click the cell that has the hour (0–23), or enter such a value.**

4. **Enter a comma (,).**

5. **Click the cell that has the minute (0–59), or enter such a value.**

6. **Enter a comma (,).**

7. **Click the cell that has the second (0–59), or enter such a value.**

8. **Enter a closing parenthesis to end the function, and press Enter.**

   The result is a decimal serial number, or a readable time if the cell is formatted properly.

Breaking Apart Time with the HOUR, MINUTE, and SECOND Functions

Any moment in time really is a combination of an hour, a minute, and a second. In the preceding section, we show you how the TIME function puts these three components together. In this section, we show you how to break them apart using the HOUR, MINUTE, and SECOND functions. The worksheet in Figure 13-2 shows a date and time in several rows going down Column A. The same dates and times are shown in Column B, with a different format. Columns C, D, and E show the hour, minute, and second, respectively, from the values in Column A.

Figure 13-2:
Splitting time apart with the HOUR, MINUTE, and SECOND functions.

	A	B	C	D	E	F
	Date and Time in General Format	Date and Time in Date and Time Format	Hour	Minute	Second	
1						
2						
3						
4						
5	38579.89993	8/15/05 9:35 PM	21	35	54	
6	38632.55213	6/29/05 1:15 PM	13	15	4	
7	38636.23043	10/11/05 5:31 AM	5	31	49	
8	38389.34513	2/6/05 8:17 AM	8	17	0	
9	38390.33813	2/7/05 8:06 AM	8	6	55	
10	38486.64845	5/14/05 3:33 PM	15	33	46	
11	38700.36713	12/14/05 8:48 AM	8	48	40	
12	38605.83913	9/10/05 8:08 PM	20	8	21	
13	38563.13843	7/30/05 3:19 AM	3	19	21	
14	38468.04363	4/26/05 1:02 AM	1	2	50	
15						
16						
17						

C5 = HOUR(A5)

Isolating the hour with the HOUR function

Extracting the hour from a time is useful in applications that tally hourly events. A common use of this occurs in call centers. If you've ever responded to an infomercial or a pledge drive, you may realize that a group of workers wait for incoming phone calls such as the one you made (we hope you got a good bargain). A common metric in this type of business is the number of calls per hour.

Figure 13-3 shows a worksheet that summarizes calls per hour. Calls have been tracked for October 2004. The incoming call dates and times are listed in Column A. In Column B, the hour of each call has been isolated with the HOUR function. Column D is a summary of calls per hour, over the course of the month.

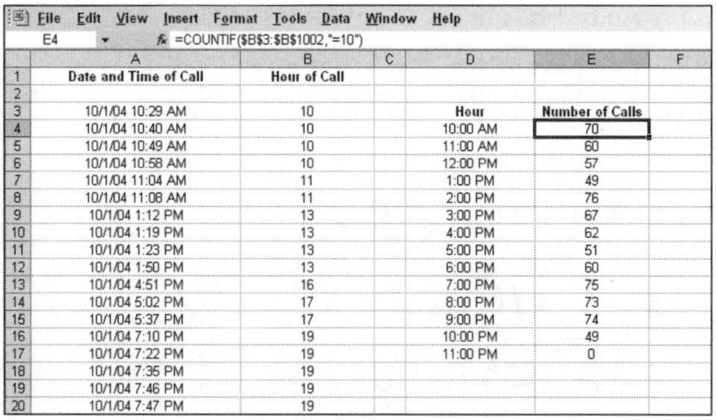

File Edit View Insert Format Tools Data Window Help

E4 =COUNTIF($B$3:$B$1002,"=10")

	A	B	C	D	E	F
1	Date and Time of Call	Hour of Call				
2						
3	10/1/04 10:29 AM	10		Hour	Number of Calls	
4	10/1/04 10:40 AM	10		10:00 AM	70	
5	10/1/04 10:49 AM	10		11:00 AM	60	
6	10/1/04 10:58 AM	10		12:00 PM	57	
7	10/1/04 11:04 AM	11		1:00 PM	49	
8	10/1/04 11:08 AM	11		2:00 PM	76	
9	10/1/04 1:12 PM	13		3:00 PM	67	
10	10/1/04 1:19 PM	13		4:00 PM	62	
11	10/1/04 1:23 PM	13		5:00 PM	51	
12	10/1/04 1:50 PM	13		6:00 PM	60	
13	10/1/04 4:51 PM	16		7:00 PM	75	
14	10/1/04 5:02 PM	17		8:00 PM	73	
15	10/1/04 5:37 PM	17		9:00 PM	74	
16	10/1/04 7:10 PM	19		10:00 PM	49	
17	10/1/04 7:22 PM	19		11:00 PM	0	
18	10/1/04 7:35 PM	19				
19	10/1/04 7:46 PM	19				
20	10/1/04 7:47 PM	19				

Figure 13-3: Using the HOUR function to summarize results.

In Figure 13-3 the values in Column D are calculated using the COUNTIF function. There is a COUNTIF for each hour from 10:00 a.m. through 11:00 p.m. Each COUNTIF looks at the range of numbers in Column B (the hours) and counts the values that match the criteria. Each COUNTIF uses a different hour value for its criteria. For example:

```
=COUNTIF($B$3:$B$1002,"=16")
```

Here is how you use the HOUR function:

1. **Select the cell where you want the results displayed.**
2. **Enter** =HOUR(**to begin the function entry.**
3. **Click the cell that has the full-time entry.**
4. **Enter a closing parenthesis to end the function, and press Enter.**

   Excel returns a number between 0 and 23.

Isolating the minute with the MINUTE function

Isolating the minute part of a time is necessary in applications that track activity down to the minute. A timed test is a perfect example. Remember in school when the teacher would yell, "Pencils down"? It didn't matter if you answered five questions out of ten correctly — you still didn't finish.

Excel can easily calculate how long something takes by subtracting one time from another. In the case of a test, the MINUTE function helps with the calculation, because how long something took in minutes is being figured out.

Figure 13-4 shows a list of times it took for students to take a test. All students started the test at 10:00 a.m. Then, when each student finished, the time was noted. The test should have taken a student no more than 15 minutes.

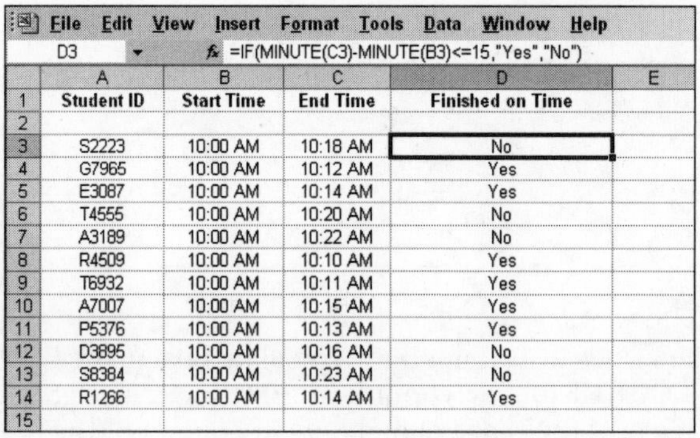

	A	B	C	D	E
1	Student ID	Start Time	End Time	Finished on Time	
2					
3	S2223	10:00 AM	10:18 AM	No	
4	G7965	10:00 AM	10:12 AM	Yes	
5	E3087	10:00 AM	10:14 AM	Yes	
6	T4555	10:00 AM	10:20 AM	No	
7	A3189	10:00 AM	10:22 AM	No	
8	R4509	10:00 AM	10:10 AM	Yes	
9	T6932	10:00 AM	10:11 AM	Yes	
10	A7007	10:00 AM	10:15 AM	Yes	
11	P5376	10:00 AM	10:13 AM	Yes	
12	D3895	10:00 AM	10:16 AM	No	
13	S8384	10:00 AM	10:23 AM	No	
14	R1266	10:00 AM	10:14 AM	Yes	
15					

Figure 13-4: Calculating minutes elapsed with the MINUTE function.

For each data row, Column D contains a formula that subtracts the minute in the end time, in Column C, from the start time, in Column B. This math operation is embedded in an IF statement. If the result is 15 or less than Yes appears in column D; otherwise a No appears:

```
=IF(MINUTE(C3)-MINUTE(B3)<=15,"Yes","No")
```

Like the HOUR function, the MINUTE function takes a single time reference as its argument.

Isolating the second with the SECOND function

Isolating the second from a date value is useful in situations where highly accurate time calculations are needed. In practice, this isn't a common requirement in Excel applications.

To use the SECOND function:

1. **Position the cursor in the cell where you want the results displayed.**
2. **Enter** =SECOND(**to begin the function entry.**
3. **Click the cell that has the time value, or enter a time value.**
4. **Enter a closing parenthesis to end the function, and press Enter.**

Using the NOW Function to Find Out the Current Time

Sometimes when working in Excel you may need to access the current time. For example, you may be working on a client project and need to know how much time you've spent on it. A great way for doing this is to use the NOW function to get the time when you first open the workbook, and then again use NOW when finished. Subtracting one value from the other provides the elapsed time.

Here's how to use the NOW function:

1. **Select the cell where you want the result.**

2. **Type in** =NOW().

3. **Press Enter to end the function.**

Note that one additional step need be done to make the preceding time calculation work. When you get the current time at the start, copy the value and then use Paste Special to paste it back as a value. This strategy prevents it from updating all the time to the current time.

NOW provides not just the current time, but also the current date. This is similar to the TODAY function. TODAY returns the current date — without the current time. NOW returns the full current date and time. See Chapter 12 for more information on the TODAY function.

Calculating Elapsed Time over Days

Each day has 24 hours. Multiplying 24 by 7 tells us there are 168 hours in a week. How many hours are in a month? This is not as easy to tell. A month may have 28, 29, 30, or 31 days.

Counting elapsed time, in hours, could require a complex algorithm. Luckily, a couple of functions in Excel make this a breeze. By leveraging Excel's ability to treat dates as numbers, you can easily calculate the number of hours that have passed between two dates and times.

Figure 13-5 shows a worksheet with start and end dates and times in two columns. A third column shows the calculated number of elapsed hours.

File	Edit	View	Insert	Format	Tools	Data	Window	Help

C3 ▾ *fx* =(INT(B3)-INT(A3))*24 + HOUR(B3) - HOUR(A3)

	A	B	C
1	**Start Date and Time**	**End Date and Time**	**Number of Elapsed Hours**
2			
3	10/1/04 9:00 AM	10/1/04 9:30 AM	0
4	10/1/04 9:00 AM	10/1/04 9:00 PM	12
5	10/1/04 9:00 AM	10/1/04 11:59 PM	14
6	10/1/04 9:00 AM	10/2/04 12:00 AM	15
7	10/1/04 9:00 AM	10/2/04 2:00 AM	17
8	10/1/04 9:00 AM	10/2/04 9:00 AM	24
9	10/1/04 9:00 AM	10/31/04 9:05 AM	720
10	10/1/04 9:00 AM	10/31/04 9:05 AM	732
11	10/1/04 9:00 AM	11/1/04 8:55 AM	743
12	10/1/04 9:00 AM	12/15/04 2:15 PM	1805
13	10/1/04 9:00 AM	1/1/05 12:00 AM	2199
14	10/1/04 9:00 AM	1/1/05 1:00 AM	2200
15	10/1/04 9:00 AM	3/31/05 4:30 PM	4351
16	10/1/04 9:00 AM	10/1/05 9:00 AM	8760
17			
18			

Figure 13-5:
Calculating
elapsed
time.

In Column A and Column B are dates and times. These dates and times are
really just serial numbers with a decimal portion. Using the INT function,
Excel counts the difference in days, even if the span pops over to a new year.
Then the HOUR function is used to calculate the difference of the decimal
portion. The formula for the first row is:

```
=(INT(B3)-INT(A3))*24 + HOUR(B3) - HOUR(A3)
```

Each successive row has the same formula in Column C, but with the cell references pointed to the values on the row.

The first part of the formula calculates the difference in days, and multiplies
this by 24 for the total number of hours in the number of days.

The trick is to correctly calculate the time between the start and end values.
The hour portion of both the start and end values is determined with the
HOUR function, and then one value is subtracted from the other. The result
of this subtraction is added to the precalculated number of hours from the
count of days.

Chapter 14

Using Lookup, Logical, and Reference Functions

Decisions, decisions! If one of our students gets an 88 on the test, is that a B+ or is it an A? If our company's new product earns at least $15,000 in revenue, how much bonus should we give out to the team? Or do we have to get to $20,000 before we do that? How does this affect the financial statements?

Excel cannot make decisions for you but it can help you make better decisions. Using functions, such as IF and CHOOSE, you can set up your worksheet to chart a course through the possibilities. Hey, things could be worse! Were it not for Excel, you might have to try the old Ouija board technique.

Have a busy worksheet? Data all over the place? It's okay to admit it. That's what we're here for! In this chapter, we are going to show you a slew of functions that make it easy to look up information that's spread around the rows and columns.

Speaking of data, did you ever mistakenly organize your information along a row or rows and then realize that you are going to run out of room! Yes, us too. Been there, done that. What started out as a project to track some stocks became a problem when the number of stocks grew past 256. In case you are not aware, there are only 256 columns available in Excel! The project got so big we were going to run out of room. Help!

The answer was of course to reorient the information to go down a column. Whew, lucky us! Excel provides the TRANSPOSE function to take care of this!

It's a good thing an Excel worksheet has 65,536 columns. That gives plenty of wiggle room!

By the way this was paper trading, otherwise there would not have been 256 stocks in the portfolio. Did pretty well though!

Testing on One Condition

The IF function is like the Swiss Army knife of Excel functions. Really, it is used in many situations. Often it is used with other functions. You see quite a bit of that in this chapter.

IF, structurally, is easy to understand. The function takes three arguments, but with a caveat. The second argument or the third argument is used, *but never both*. The three arguments are:

1. **A test that gives a true or false answer.**

   For example, the test "is A5=A8" is either true or false. We are not looking for a result of a calculation here. Adding A5 with A8 (A5 + A8) would produce an error.

2. **What to do if the test if true.**

3. **What to do if the test is false.**

Sounds easy enough. Here are some examples:

Function	*Comment*
`=IF(D10>D20, D10, D20)`	If the value in D10 is greater than the value in D20 then the value in D10 is returned because the test is true. If the value in D10 is not greater than D20 than the value in D20 is returned. If the values in D10 and D20 are equal, the test returns false and the value in D20 is returned.
`=IF(D10>D20, "Good news!", "Bad news!")`	If the value in D10 is greater than the value in D20, then "Good News!" is returned. Otherwise "Bad News!" is returned.
`=IF(D10>D20, "", "Bad news!")`	If the value in D10 is greater than the value in D20, then *nothing* is returned. Otherwise "Bad News!" is returned. Note that the second argument is empty.
`=IF(D10>D20, "Good news!", "")`	If the value in D10 is greater than the value in D20, then "Good News!" is returned. Otherwise *nothing* is returned. Not that the third argument is empty.

An important aspect to note about using IF is the option of letting the second or third argument return nothing. Actually what is returned is an empty string, and the best way to do this is to place two double quote marks together with nothing in the middle.

IF therefore lets you set up two specific actions to take — one for when the test is true and another for when the test is false. Or, you can specify one test to take for either the true or false result, and do nothing for the opposite result.

As seen in the previous example, a common use of IF is to see how two values compare to each other, and return either one value or the other, depending of course on how you set up the test in the first argument.

IF is often used as a validation check to avoid errors. The probable best use of this is to avoid a division by 0 error. Simply put, wherever you have a division operation in you worksheet, you can instead use an IF to avoid an error if the denominator is 0. For example, this formula:

```
=G2/G4
```

is replaced with this one:

```
=IF(G4<>0, G2/G4, 0)
```

Think of what would happen if G4 was ever 0. You would get the dreaded #DIV/0! error! But this can never happen if you put the division operation in the IF statement. If G4 is ever 0, then 0 is the result. The test is to see if G4 is not equal to 0. If G4 is not equal to 0 then the division operation occurs because the test is true. If G4 is 0, then the third argument (the action to take when the test is false) says to instead just return 0. You can write the function to take a different action, such as to return a statement such as Cannot complete calculation.

Note too that in this example, the true action is taken even if G4 is less than 0. That's mathematically okay, but may not be what you need. Perhaps you need to make sure G4 is greater than 0, such as this:

```
=IF(G4>0, G2/G4, "Cannot complete calculation")
```

One of the all time favorite uses of the IF function is to test for 0 in the denominator of a division operation. Then an action can be taken to avoid a division by 0 error.

Figure 14-1 shows how IF can be put to good use in a business application. A fictitious guitar shop — "Ken's Guitars" (kinda snappy, don't you think!) — keeps tabs on inventory in an Excel worksheet.

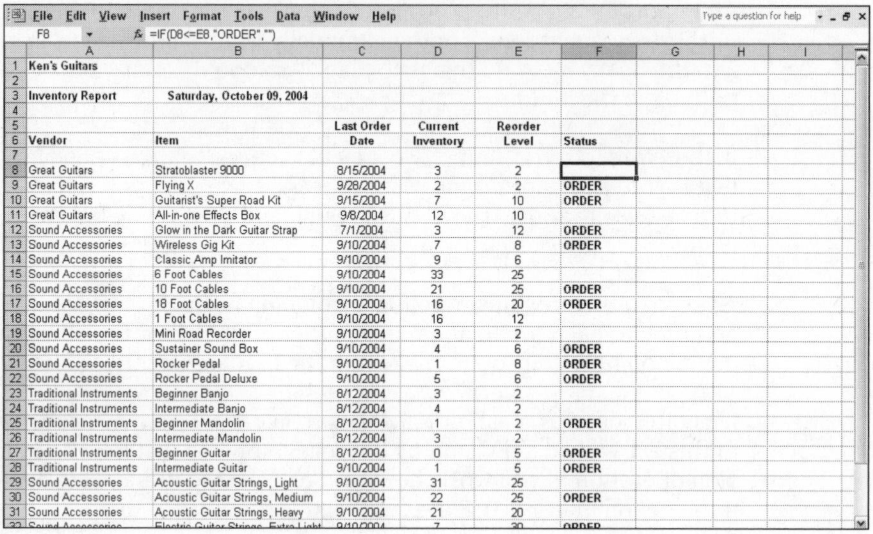

Figure 14-1:
Keeping an
eye on
inventory at
the guitar
shop.

Column D shows the inventory levels, and column E shows the reorder levels. The way this works is when a products' inventory level is the same or less than the reorder level than it is time to order more of the product. (We don't know about you but we love the thought of being surrounded by a bunch of stratoblasters!)

The cells in column F contain a formula. Here is the formula in cell F8:

```
=IF(D8<=E8,"ORDER","")
```

What this says is that if the number of Stratoblaster 9000 guitars in stock is the same or less than the reorder level, then return Order. If the number in stock is greater than the reorder level, then nothing is returned. There are three in stock and the reorder level is two, therefore nothing is returned.

In the next row, the number of Flying X's is equal to the reorder level, therefore cell F9 displays Order.

Using IF is easy. Just remember there are three arguments: The test, the action to take when the test is true, and the action to take when the test is false. Try it out:

1. **Enter two values in a worksheet.**

   These values should have some meaning to you, such as the inventory levels example in Figure 14-1.

2. **Click the cell where you want the result to appear.**

3. **Enter =IF(to start the function.**

4. **Decide on what test you want to perform.**

   You can test to see if the two values equal each other; if one is larger than the other; if subtracting one from the other is greater than, equal to, or less than 0; and so on. For example, to test if the first value equals the second value, click the first cell (or enter its address), enter an equal sign (=), and then finally click the second cell (or enter its address).

5. **Enter a comma (,).**

6. **Enter the result that should appear if the test is *true*.**

   For example, enter The values are equal.

7. **Enter a comma (,).**

8. **Enter the result that should appear if the test is *false*.**

   For example, enter The values are not equal.

9. **Enter a closing parenthesis to end the function and press Enter.**

The IF function can do a whole lot more, as you see next. Nested IF functions offer a bunch of possibilities on what value to return. A bit of perseverance is necessary to get through this.

You can place an IF function inside another IF function. That is, the inner IF is placed where the true or false argument in the outer IF goes (or even use internal IFs for both of the arguments). Why would you do this?

The other night we were deciding where to go out for dinner. Our thought was if the restaurant is Italian, then if they serve manicotti, then we will have manicotti, otherwise we will just eat pizza.

Logically this decision looks like this:

```
If the restaurant is Italian, then
If the restaurant serves manicotti, then
we will have manicotti
else
we will have pizza
```

This looks a lot like programming code. we have left out the End If statements on purpose to avoid confusion because the IF function has no equivalent value.

That's it! Make note that the inner IF statement has a result for both the true and false possibilities. The outer IF does not. Here is the structure of this as nested Excel IF statements:

```
=IF(Restaurant=Italian, IF(Restaurant serves manicotti, "mani-
cotti", "pizza"), "")
```

TIP

Wow, if the restaurant was not Italian, then it didn't matter what we ate. Literally this is true according to how this is structured. The third argument of the outer IF is empty.

You can nest up to seven IF statements.

Apply a nested IF statement to the inventory worksheet from Figure 14-1. Figure 14-2 has an additional column — Hot Item. A Hot Item takes two forms:

✔ If the inventory level is half or less of the reorder level, and the last order date is within the last 30 days, then this is a *Hot Item*. The point of view is that in 30 days or less the stock sold down to half or less than the reorder level. This means the inventory is turning over at a fast pace.

✔ If the inventory level is half or less of the reorder level, and the last order date is within the last 31-60 days, then this is a *Warm Item*. The point of view is that in 31-60 days the stock sold down to half or less than the reorder level. This means the inventory is turning over at a medium pace.

	File Edit View Insert Format Tools Data Window Help					Type a question for help ▾ _ ✕
	G21 ▾ *fx* =IF(D21<=(E21*0.5),IF(NOW()-C21<=30,"HOT!",IF(NOW()-C21<=60,"Warm!","")),"")					

	A	B	C	D	E	F	G	H	I
1	Ken's Guitars								
2									
3	Inventory Report	Saturday, October 09, 2004							
4									
5			Last Order	Current	Reorder				
6	Vendor	Item	Date	Inventory	Level	Status	Hot Item		
7									
8	Great Guitars	Stratoblaster 9000	8/15/2004	3	2				
9	Great Guitars	Flying X	9/28/2004	2	2	ORDER			
10	Great Guitars	Guitarist's Super Road Kit	9/15/2004	7	10	ORDER			
11	Great Guitars	All-in-one Effects Box	9/8/2004	12	10				
12	Sound Accessories	Glow in the Dark Guitar Strap	7/1/2004	3	12	ORDER			
13	Sound Accessories	Wireless Gig Kit	9/10/2004	7	8	ORDER			
14	Sound Accessories	Classic Amp Imitator	9/10/2004	9	6				
15	Sound Accessories	6 Foot Cables	9/10/2004	33	25				
16	Sound Accessories	10 Foot Cables	9/10/2004	21	25	ORDER			
17	Sound Accessories	18 Foot Cables	9/10/2004	16	20	ORDER			
18	Sound Accessories	1 Foot Cables	9/10/2004	16	12				
19	Sound Accessories	Mini Road Recorder	9/10/2004	3	2				
20	Sound Accessories	Sustainer Sound Box	9/10/2004	4	6	ORDER			
21	Sound Accessories	Rocker Pedal	9/10/2004	1	8	ORDER	HOT!		
22	Sound Accessories	Rocker Pedal Deluxe	9/10/2004	5	6	ORDER			
23	Traditional Instruments	Beginner Banjo	8/12/2004	3	2				
24	Traditional Instruments	Intermediate Banjo	8/12/2004	4	2				
25	Traditional Instruments	Beginner Mandolin	8/12/2004	1	2	ORDER	Warm!		
26	Traditional Instruments	Intermediate Mandolin	8/12/2004	3	2				
27	Traditional Instruments	Beginner Guitar	8/12/2004	0	5	ORDER	Warm!		
28	Traditional Instruments	Intermediate Guitar	9/10/2004	1	5	ORDER	HOT!		
29	Sound Accessories	Acoustic Guitar Strings, Light	9/10/2004	31	25				
30	Sound Accessories	Acoustic Guitar Strings, Medium	9/10/2004	22	25	ORDER			
31	Sound Accessories	Acoustic Guitar Strings, Heavy	9/10/2004	21	20				
32	Sound Accessories	Electric Guitar Strings, Extra Light	9/10/2004	7	20	ORDER	HOT!		

Figure 14-2: Looking for hot inventory items.

There are Hot Items and there are Warm Items. They both share a common attribute that the inventory is 50 percent or less of the reorder level. Only after that first condition is met is the amount of days since the last order considered. Sounds like a nested IF to me! Here is the formula in cell G9:

```
=IF(D9<=(E9×0.5),IF(NOW()-C9<=30,"HOT!",IF(NOW()-
        C9<=60,"Warm!","")),"")
```

Okay, take a breath. We will explain. No Excel user will be left behind.

The outer IF tests if the inventory in column D is equal to or less than half (50 percent) of the reorder level. The piece of the formula that does that is =IF(D9<=(E9×0.5). This test, of course, produces a true or false answer. If it is false, then the false part of the outer IF is taken, which is just an empty string, found at the end of the formula: ,""").

That leaves the whole middle part to wade through. Stay with it!

If the first test is true, then the true part of the outer IF is taken. It just so happens that this true part is another IF function:

```
IF(NOW()-C9<=30,"HOT!",IF(NOW()-C9<=60,"Warm!",""))
```

The first argument of the inner IF tests whether the number of days since the last order date (in column C) is less than or equal to 30. You do this by subtracting the last order date from "today." The NOW function returns the current date and time.

If the test is true, and the last order date is within the last 30 days, then "HOT!" is returned. A hot seller indeed! If the test is false then . . . wait, what's this? Another IF function! Yes, an If inside an IF, inside an IF.

If the number of days since the last order date is greater than 30, then the next nested IF tests if the number of days is within the last 60 days: IF (NOW()-C9<=60.

If this test is true, then Warm! is returned. If the test is false, then nothing is returned.

A few key points about this triple level IF statement:

- ✔ The IF that tests if the number of elapsed days is 30 or less has a value to return if true (HOT!), and an action to take for false (the next nested IF).

- ✔ The outer IF and the most inner IF return nothing when either of their tests in false.

- ✔ On the surface of it, the test for 60 or less days, *also would catch a date that is 30 days or less since the last order date!* This is not really what is meant to be. The test should be whether the number of elapsed days is 60 or less, *but more than 30!* The reason we do not have to actually spell it out this way is because the only way the formula got to the point of testing for the 60 day threshold is because the 30 day threshold already failed. Gotta watch out for these things!

Choosing the Right Value

The CHOOSE function is ideal for converting a value into a *literal*. In plain speak, this means turning a number, such as 4, into a word, such as "April." CHOOSE takes up to 30 arguments. The first argument acts as key to the rest of the arguments. In fact the other arguments do not get processed per se by the function. Instead the function takes the value of the first argument and returns the value of a corresponding argument.

The first argument must be, or evaluate to, a number. This number in turn indicates which of the following arguments to return. For example, following returns "Two":

```
=CHOOSE(2 ,"One", "Two", "Three")
```

The first argument is the number 2. This means return the second of the list of arguments following the first argument. But watch out — this is not the same as returning the second argument! It is meant to return the second argument in the list of arguments *following* the first argument.

Figure 14-3 shows a useful example of CHOOSE. Say you have a column of months that are in the numerical form (1 through 12). You need to have these displayed as the month names (January through December). CHOOSE to the rescue!

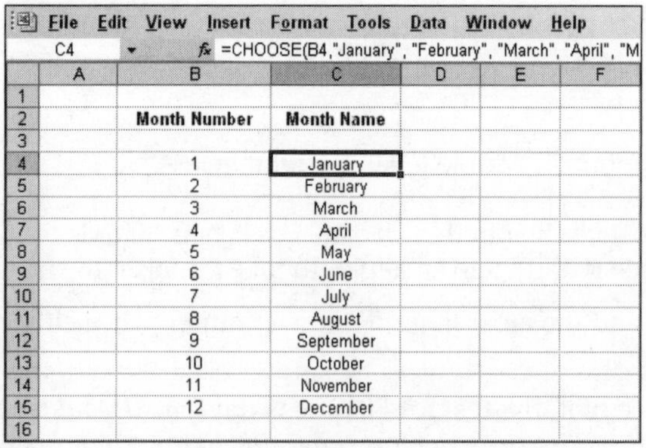

Figure 14-3:
Choosing
what
to see.

Cells C4:C15 contain formulas with the CHOOSE function. The formula in cell C4 is:

```
=CHOOSE(B4,"January", "February", "March", "April", "May",
        "June", "July", "August", "September", "October",
        "November", "December")
```

Cell B4 has 1 for the value, so the first argument starting in the list of possible returned strings is "January".

CHOOSE is most often used to return meaningful text that relates to a number, such as returning the name of a month from its numeric value. But CHOOSE is not restricted to returning text strings. You can use it to return numbers.

Try it yourself! Here's how:

1. **Enter a list of numeric values into a worksheet column.**

   These values should all be small, such as 1, 2, 3, and so on.

2. **Click the cell to the right of the first value.**

3. **Enter** =CHOOSE(**to start the function.**

4. **Click the cell to the left, the one that has the first value.**

   Or you can enter its address.

5. **Enter a comma (,).**

6. **Enter a list of text strings that each have an association with the numbers entered in Step 1.**

   Each text string should be in double quotes and the text strings must be separated with commas. For example: "January", "February", "March".

7. **Enter a closing parenthesis and press Enter.**

8. **The cell to the right of the first item in the list now displays the returned text.**

   You need to enter the formula into the rest of the cells adjacent to the list items. To do this use the fill handle from the first cell with the formula and drag the formula down to all the other cells adjacent to list entries.

Being Logical About It All

I once worked on a grammar problem that provided a paragraph with no punctuation and asked that the punctuation be added. The paragraph was:

That that is is not that that is not is not that it it is

The answer is:

That that is, is not that that is not. Is not that it? It is.

So true! That that is, such as an apple, is not that that is not, such as an orange. (Is your head spinning yet?)

Not is a logical operator. It is used to reverse a truth or falsehood. In terms of Excel the NOT function reverses the a logical value, turning True to False or False to True.

Try this out. Enter this formula into a cell: `= 5 + 5 = 10`. The result is the word `TRUE`. Makes sense. The math checks out. Now try this:

```
=NOT(5 + 5 = 10)
```

What happens? The word FALSE is returned.

The NOT function gives you another way to facilitate the logical test in the IF function. A useful application of NOT is to exclude items from being a part of a calculation. Figure 14-4 shows how this works. The task is to sum up all orders, except those in June. Column A lists the months and column C lists the amounts.

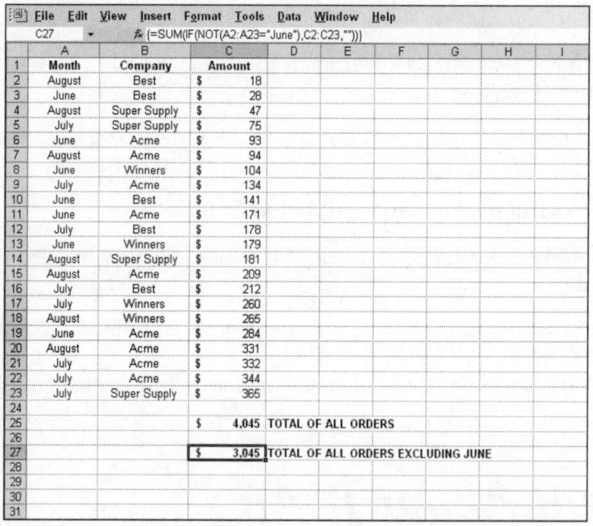

	A	B	C	D
1	Month	Company	Amount	
2	August	Best	$ 18	
3	June	Best	$ 28	
4	August	Super Supply	$ 47	
5	July	Super Supply	$ 75	
6	June	Acme	$ 93	
7	August	Acme	$ 94	
8	June	Winners	$ 104	
9	July	Acme	$ 134	
10	June	Best	$ 141	
11	June	Acme	$ 171	
12	July	Best	$ 178	
13	June	Winners	$ 179	
14	August	Super Supply	$ 181	
15	August	Acme	$ 209	
16	July	Best	$ 212	
17	July	Winners	$ 260	
18	August	Winners	$ 265	
19	June	Acme	$ 284	
20	August	Acme	$ 331	
21	July	Acme	$ 332	
22	July	Acme	$ 344	
23	July	Super Supply	$ 365	
24				
25			$ 4,045	TOTAL OF ALL ORDERS
26				
27			$ 3,045	TOTAL OF ALL ORDERS EXCLUDING JUNE
28				
29				
30				
31				

Figure 14-4: Being selective with summing.

Cell C25 calculates the full sum with this formula: `=SUM(C2:C23)`. The total is $4,045.

On the other hand, the formula in cell C27 is:

```
{=SUM(IF(NOT(A2:A23="June"),C2:C23,""))}
```

This says to sum up values in the range C2:C23 only for where the associated month in column A is not June.

Note that this formula is an array. When entered, the entry was completed with CTRL + Shift + Enter, instead of just plain Enter.

See Chapter 3 for more information on array formulas.

Next are the AND & OR functions. AND & OR both return a logical answer — either True or False, based on one or more logical tests (such as the way IF works):

- ✔ The AND function returns True if *all* the tests are true. Otherwise False is returned.
- ✔ The OR function returns True if *any* of the tests is true. Otherwise False is returned.

The syntax of both AND & OR is to place the tests inside the function's parentheses, and the tests themselves are separated by commas. Here is an example that returns True if the value in cell D10 equals 20 *or* 30 *or* 40:

```
=OR(D10=20,D10=30,D10=40)
```

Check out how this works. In Figure 14-3, you see how the CHOOSE function can be used to return the name of a month derived from the number of the month. Well, that works okay, but what if a wrong number or even a non-numerical value is used as the first argument in CHOOSE?

As is, the CHOOSE function shown in Figure 14-3 returns the #VALUE! error if the first argument is a number greater or less than the number of arguments (not counting the first argument). So as is, the function only works when the first argument evaluates to a number between 1 and 12. If only life were that perfect!

The next best thing then is to include a little validation in the function. Think this through, both statements must be true:

- ✔ The first argument must be greater than 0.
- ✔ The first argument must be less than 13.

The formula that uses CHOOSE needs a overhaul, and here it is:

```
=IF(AND(B4>0,B4<13),CHOOSE(B4,"January", "February", "March",
        "April", "May", "June", "July", "August",
        "September", "October", "November",
        "December"),"That is not a month!")
```

Wow, that's a mouthful, or rather, a cell-full. The CHOOSE function is still there, but it is nested inside an IF. The IF has a test (which is explained shortly). If the test returns true, then the CHOOSE function is used to return the name of the month. If the IF test returns false, then a simple That is not a month! message is returned. Figure 14-5 shows this in action.

	File Edit View Insert Format Tools Data Window Help	Type a question for help _ 8 ×

C4 ▼ *fx* =IF(AND(B4>0,B4<13),CHOOSE(B4,"January", "February", "March", "April", "May", "June", "July", "August", "September", "October",
"November", "December"),"That is not a month!")

	A	B	
1			
2	Month Number	Month Name	
3			
4	1	January	
5	2	February	
6	3	March	
7	4	April	
8	5	May	
9	16	That is not a month!	
10	7	July	
11	8	August	
12	9	September	
13	10	October	
14	11	November	
15	Twelve	That is not a month!	
16			
17			
18			

Figure 14-5:
Being
logical
about what
to choose.

The test part of the IF function is this:

```
AND(B4>0,B4<13)
```

The AND returns True if the value in Cell B4 is both greater than 0 *and* less than 13. When that happens the True part of the IF statement is taken — which uses the CHOOSE statement. Otherwise the "That is not a month!" statement is displayed. In Figure 14-5 this is just what happens in cells C9 and C15, which respectively look at the problem values in cells B9 and B15.

AND returns True when every condition is true. OR returns True when any condition is true.

Here's how to use AND or OR:

1. **Click a cell where you want the result to appear.**

2. **Enter either** =AND(, **or** =OR(**to start the function.**

3. **Enter one or more logical tests.**

    A test typically is a comparison of values in two cells or an equation, such as A1=B1 or A1 + B1 = C1. Separate the tests with commas.

4. **Enter a closing parenthesis to end the function and press Enter.**

    If you enter the AND function, the result is True if all the tests are true. If you enter the OR function, the result is True if at least one of the tests is true.

Finding Where It Is

The ADDRESS function takes a relative cell reference and turns it into one that is absolute, partially absolute, or still relative. Also it lets you toggle the reference style, explained in the next section.

What is a *relative reference* and what is an *absolute reference*? Glad you asked. A relative address is expressed as the column letter and row number, for example M290. Using a dollar sign ($) in front of either the column letter, or the row number tells Excel not to change that column or row even as you use the fill handle to copy a formula into multiple cells, or copy and paste the formula and so forth.

And of course you can put the dollar sign in front of both the column *and* row to make sure neither the column or row changes. Figure 14-6 shows a worksheet in which entering a formula with a completely relative cell reference causes a problem. Totals are the result of adding the tax to the amount. The tax is a percentage (0.075) for a 7.5 percent tax rate. This percentage is in cell C1 and is referenced by the formulas. The first formula that was entered is in cell C7 and looks like this: =B7×(1 + C1).

That first formula is correct. It references cell C1 to calculate the total. From cell C7, you use the fill handle to enter the formula into cells C8 and C9. Uh-oh, look what happened. The reference to cell C1 changed respectively to cell C2 and C3. That's why the totals in cells C8 and C9 are the same as the amounts to the left (no tax is added).

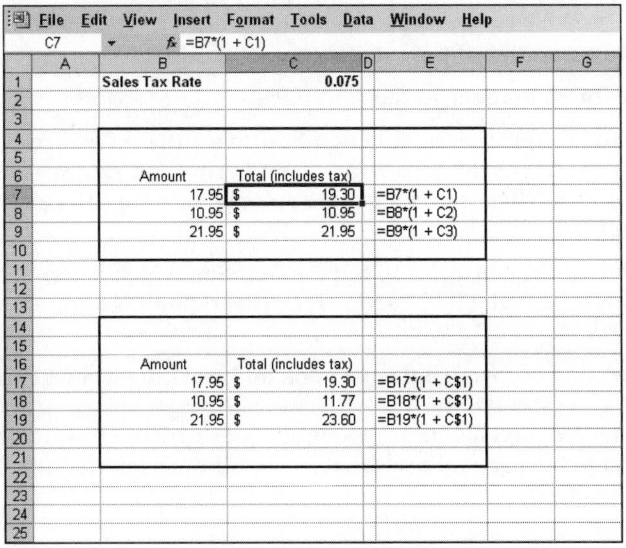

Figure 14-6:
Changing a reference from relative to absolute.

To better understand, column D displays the formulas in column C. When the formula in cell C7 was dragged down the C1 reference changed to C2 in cell C8, and to C3 in cell C9.

The information in B16:D19 is a duplicate to the previous information, but shows how the formulas stayed corrected by turning the reference to C1into a partially absolute one. The dollar sign was put in front of the 1 in C1. The formula in cell C17 looks like this: =B17×(1 + C$1). When this formula was dragged down into C18 and C19, the reference stayed to C1.

Note that in this example only the row part of the reference is made absolute. That's all that is necessary. You can make he reference completely absolute by doing this: =B17×(1 + $C$1)

A dollar sign precedes the column letter of a reference to turn the column part of the reference into an absolute column reference. A dollar sign precedes the row number of a reference to turn the row part of the reference into an absolute row reference.

You have two reference styles: the good old A1 style and the R1C1 style. You see the A1 style throughout the book, such as D4 or B2:B10. Note that it is a column letter followed by a row number. The R1C1 style uses a numerical system for both the row and the column, such as this: R4C10 — literally Row 4 Column 10 in this example.

The ADDRESS function takes up to five arguments:

1. **The row number of the reference.**

2. **The column number of the reference.**

3. **A number that tells the function how to set the reference. This can be a 1 for full absolute; a 2 for absolute row and relative column; a 3 for relative row and absolute column; or 4 for full relative. The default is 1.**

4. **A value of True or False to tell the function which reference style to use. False uses the R1C1 style. True (the default if omitted) uses the A1 style.**

5. **A worksheet or external workbook and worksheet reference.**

Only the first two arguments are required. These are the row number and column number being addressed. Table 14-1 shows a few settings using the ADDRESS function.

Table 14-1	Using the ADDRESS Function	
Syntax	*Result*	*Comment*
=ADDRESS(5,2)	$B$5	Only the column and row are used as arguments. The function returns a full absolute address.

Syntax	Result	Comment
=ADDRESS(5,2,1)	$B$5	When a 1 is used for the third argument, a full absolute address is returned. This is the same as leaving out the third argument.
=ADDRESS(5,2,2)	B$5	When a 2 is used for the third argument a mixed reference is returned. The column is relative and the row is absolute.
=ADDRESS(5,2,3)	$B5	When a 3 is used for the third argument a mixed reference is returned. The column is absolute and the row is relative.
=ADDRESS(5,2,4)	B5	When a 4 is used for the third argument a full relative reference is returned.
=ADDRESS (5,2,1,FALSE)	R5C2	When the fourth argument is False, a R1C1 style is used to return the reference.
=ADDRESS (5,2,3,FALSE)	R[5]C2	This example tells the function to return a mixed reference in the R1C1 style.
=ADDRESS (5,2,1,, "Sheet4")	Sheet4!$B$5	The fifth argument is used to return a reference to a worksheet or external workbook. This returns an A1 style reference to B5 on Sheet 4.
=ADDRESS (5,2,1,FALSE, "Sheet4")	Sheet4!R5C2	This returns an R1C1 style reference to B5 on Sheet 4.

How you use ADDRESS is:

1. **Click a cell where you want the result to appear.**
2. **Enter** =ADDRESS(**to start the function.**
3. **Enter a row number, a comma, and a column number.**
4. **If you want the result to be returned in a mixed or full reference, then enter a comma and the appropriate number: 2, 3, or 4.**
5. **If you want the result to be returned in R1C1 style, then enter a comma and enter False.**

6. **If you want the result to be a reference to another worksheet, then enter a comma and put the name of the worksheet in double quote marks.**

    Or if you want the result to be a reference to an external workbook, then enter a comma and enter the workbook name and worksheet name together. The workbook name goes in brackets, and the entire reference goes in double quote marks, such as this: `"[Book1]Sheet2"`.

7. **Enter a closing parenthesis to end the function and press Enter.**

Instead of directly entering a row number and column number into ADDRESS, you can enter cell references. However, the values you find in those cells must evaluate to numbers that can be used as a row number and column number.

A useful example of ADDRESS follows the discussion of ROW, ROWS, COLUMN, and COLUMNS.

ROW and COLUMN respectively return a row number or a column number. Sounds simple enough. These functions take a single optional argument. The argument is a reference to a cell or range. Then the function returns the associated row number or column number. When the reference is a range it is the first cell of the range (the upper-left) that is used by the function.

ROW and COLUMN are particularly useful when the argument is a name (for a named area). When ROW or COLUMN are used without an argument they return the row number or column number of the cell they are in. What the point of that is we don't know. Here are examples of ROW and COLUMN:

Formula	Result
`=ROW(D3)`	3
`=ROW(D3:G15)`	3
`=COLUMN(D3)`	4
`=COLUMN(D3:G15)`	4
`=ROW(Team_Scores)`	The first row of the Team_Scores area
`=COLUMN(Team_Scores)`	The first column of the Team_Scores area

The ROWS and COLUMNS functions (notice these are now plural), respectively return the number of rows or the number of columns in a reference. For example:

- `=ROWS(Team_Scores)` returns the number of rows in the Team_Scores area.

- `=COLUMNS(Team_Scores)` returns the number of columns in the Team_Scores area.

Now we are getting somewhere. Use these functions along with ADDRESS to make something useful out of all this. Here's the scenario. You have a named area in which the bottom row has summary information, such as averages. You need to get at the bottom row, but don't know the actual row number.

Figure 14-7 shows this situation. The Team_Scores area is in B3:C9. Row 9 contains the average score. You need that value in a calculation.

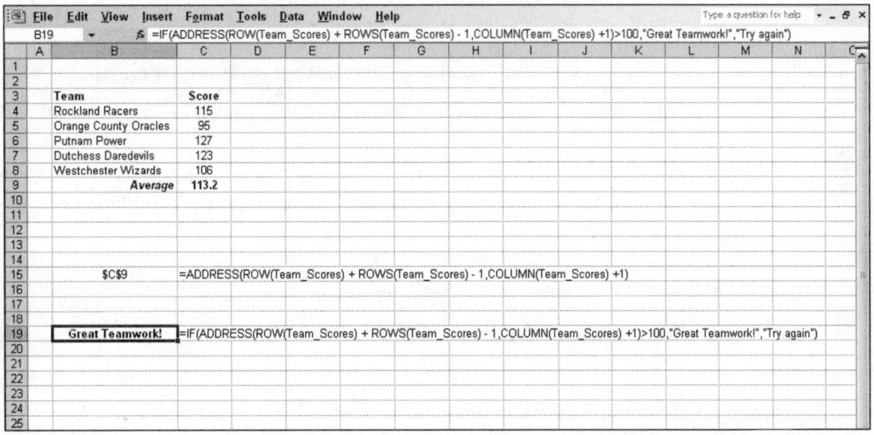

Figure 14-7:
Using
reference
functions
to find
a value.

Cell B15 uses a combination of ADDRESS, ROW, ROWS, and COLUMN to determine the cell address where the average score is calculated. That formula is:

```
=ADDRESS(ROW(Team_Scores) + ROWS(Team_Scores) -
          1,COLUMN(Team_Scores) +1)
```

ROW and ROWS are both used. ROW returns the row number of the first cell of Team_Scores. That row number is 3. ROWS returns the number of rows in the named area. That count is 7. Adding these two numbers is not quite right. A one is subtracted from that total to give the true last row, number 9.

Only COLUMN is needed here because it understood that the second column is the column of scores. In other words, we have no idea how many rows there are in the range, so ROW and ROWS are both used, but we do know the scores are in the second column.

Okay, so this tells us that cell C9 contains the average score. Now what? CellB19 contains an IF that uses the address:

```
=IF(ADDRESS(ROW(Team_Scores) + ROWS(Team_Scores) -
          1,COLUMN(Team_Scores) +1)>100,"Great
          Teamwork!","Try again")
```

The IF tests if the average score is greater than 100. If it is then the "Great Teamwork!" message is displayed. This test is possible because the ADDRESS, ROW, ROWS, and COLUMN functions all helped to give the IF function the address of the average score.

Using ROW, ROWS, COLUMN, or COLUMNS is easy. Here's how:

1. **Click the cell where you want the results to appear.**

2. **Enter** =ROW(**or** =ROWS(**or** =COLUMN(**or** =COLUMNS(**to start the function.**

3. **Enter a reference or drag the mouse over an area of the worksheet.**

4. **Enter a closing parenthesis and press Enter.**

The OFFSET function also provides a way to get to the value in a cell that is offset from another reference. OFFSET takes up to five arguments. The first three are required:

1. **A cell address or a range address:** Names areas are not allowed here.

2. **The number of rows to offset:** This can be a positive or negative number.

3. **The number of columns to offset:** This can be a positive or negative number.

4. **Optionally, the number of rows to return:** Use this in conjunction with another formula.

5. **Optionally, the number of columns to return:** Use this in conjunction with another formula.

Figure 14-8 shows some examples of using OFFSET. Columns A through C contain a ranking of the states in the U.S by size in square miles. Column E shows how OFFSET has been used to return different values from cells that are offset from cell A3. Some highlights:

- Cell E4 returns the value of cell A3 because both the row and column offset is set to 0: =OFFSET(A3,0,0).

- Cell E7 returns the value you find in cell A1 (the value also is "A1"). This is because the row offset is -2. From the perspective of A3, minus two rows is row number 1: =OFFSET(A3,-2,0).

- Cell E8 displays an error because the OFFSET is attempting to reference a column that is less than the first column: =OFFSET(A3,0,-2).

- Cell E10 makes use of the two optional OFFSET arguments to tell the SUM function to calculate the sum of the range C4:C53: =SUM(OFFSET(A3,1,2,50,1)).

	A	B	C	D	E	F	G	H
	File Edit View Insert Format Tools Data Window Help							
	E10	▼	fx =SUM(OFFSET(A3,1,2,50,1))					
1	A1	B1	C1					
2								
3	State	Area Ranking	Square Miles					
4	Alaska	1	656,425		State	=OFFSET(A3,0,0)		
5	Texas	2	268,601		656425	=OFFSET(A3,1,2)		
6	California	3	163,707		New Mexico	=OFFSET(A3,5,0)		
7	Montana	4	147,046		A1	=OFFSET(A3,-2,0)		
8	New Mexico	5	121,593		#REF!	=OFFSET(A3,0,-2)		
9	Arizona	6	114,006					
10	Nevada	7	110,567		3,786,816	=SUM(OFFSET(A3,1,2,50,1))		
11	Colorado	8	104,100					
12	Oregon	9	98,386					
13	Wyoming	10	97,818					
14	Michigan	11	96,810					
15	Minnesota	12	86,943					
16	Utah	13	84,904					
17	Idaho	14	83,574					
18	Kansas	15	82,282					
19	Nebraska	16	77,358					
20	South Dakota	17	77,121					
21	Washington	18	71,303					
22	North Dakota	19	70,704					
23	Oklahoma	20	69,903					
24	Missouri	21	69,709					
25	Florida	22	65,758					
26	Wisconsin	23	65,503					
27	Georgia	24	59,441					
28	Illinois	25	57,918					
29	Iowa	26	56,276					
30	New York	27	54,475					

Figure 14-8:
Finding values using the OFFSET function.

Here's how to use the OFFSET function:

1. **Click a cell where you want the result to appear.**

2. **Enter =OFFSET(to start the function.**

3. **Enter a cell address or a range of cells.**

4. **Enter a comma (,).**

5. **Enter the number of rows you want to offset where the function looks for a value.** This number can be a positive number, a negative number, or just 0 for no offset.

6. **Enter a comma (,).**

7. **Enter the number of columns you want to offset where the function looks for a value.** This can be a positive number, a negative number, or just 0 for no offset.

8. **Enter a closing parenthesis to end the function and press Enter.**

Looking It Up

Excel has a neat group of functions that let you get values out of lists and tables. What is a table? A table is a dedicated matrix of rows and columns that collectively form a cohesive group of data.

The HLOOKUP and VLOOKUP functions in particular return a value you find in a table that is based on another value in the table. The HLOOKUP function first searches across the top row of a table for a supplied argument value, *horizontally* in other words, and then returns a value from that column, from a specified row underneath.

The VLOOKUP function first searches down the leftmost column of a table for a supplied argument value, *vertically* in other words, and then returns a value from that row, from a specified column to the right.

HLOOKUP takes four arguments, of which the first three are required:

1. **The value to find in the top row of the table.**

2. **The address of the table itself. This is either a range or a named area.**

3. **The row offset from the top row. This is not a fixed row number but rather the number of rows relative from the top row.**

4. **Optionally, a True or False value. If True (or omitted) a partial match is acceptable. If False only, an exact match is allowed.**

Figure 14-9 shows how HLOOKUP is used to pull values from a table and present them elsewhere in the worksheet. This function is quite useful if you need to print a report and set a dedicated print area. The HLOOKUP function is used to have the report area point to the actual data in the table.

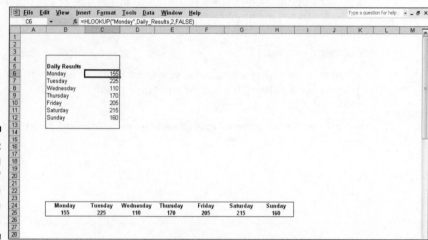

Figure 14-9:
Using
HLOOKUP
to locate
data in
a table.

In Figure 14-9 the table is the range B24:H25. This range has been named `Daily_Results`. Each cell in the range C6:C12 uses HLOOKUP to locate a value in the table. For example cell C6 has this formula:

```
HLOOKUP("Monday",Daily_Results,2,FALSE)
```

The first argument tells the function to search for Monday in the first row of the table. The table itself, as a named area, is entered in the second argument. The third argument tell the function to return the data in the second row where the column starts with Monday. Note that this table has just two rows. Finally the fourth argument is given the False setting to make sure each day name is found (otherwise they are similar because they all have "day" in them.

The VLOOKUP function finds a value in a table by first searching for a key value in the first column. The arguments are:

1. **The value to find in the leftmost column of the table.**

2. **The address of the table itself. This is either a range or a named area.**

3. **The column offset from the left-most column. This is not a fixed column number but rather the number of columns relative from the left most column.**

4. **Optionally, a True or False value. If True (or omitted) a partial match is acceptable. If False only, an exact match is allowed.**

Figure 14-10 shows products and annual revenue for the fictitious guitar shop presented earlier in the chapter. The range A11:D42 has been named `Sales`.

Figure 14-10: Using VLOOKUP to locate data in a table.

	A	B	C	D
	B6	=VLOOKUP("Wireless Gig Kit",OFFSET(Sales,0,1),3, FALSE)		
1	SALES FOR 2004			
2				
3				
4	Revenue for Stratoblaster 9000	$ 129,000		
5				
6	Total for the Wireless Gig Kit	$ 75,000		
7				
8				
9				
10				
11	Vendor	Product	Category	Amount
12	Great Guitars	Stratoblaster 9000	Instrument	$ 129,000
13	Great Guitars	Flying X	Instrument	$ 87,000
14	Great Guitars	Guitarist's Super Road Kit	Accessory	$ 32,000
15	Great Guitars	All-in-one Effects Box	Accessory	$ 6,750
16	Sound Accessories	Glow in the Dark Guitar Strap	Accessory	$ 4,360
17	Sound Accessories	Wireless Gig Kit	Accessory	$ 75,000
18	Sound Accessories	Classic Amp Imitator	Accessory	$ 16,700
19	Sound Accessories	6 Foot Cables	Accessory	$ 4,000
20	Sound Accessories	10 Foot Cables	Accessory	$ 8,500
21	Sound Accessories	18 Foot Cables	Accessory	$ 6,250
22	Sound Accessories	1 Foot Cables	Accessory	$ 2,250
23	Sound Accessories	Mini Road Recorder	Accessory	$ 40,000
24	Sound Accessories	Sustainer Sound Box	Accessory	$ 7,000
25	Sound Accessories	Rocker Pedal	Accessory	$ 7,250
26	Sound Accessories	Rocker Pedal Deluxe	Accessory	$ 5,250
27	Traditional Instruments	Beginner Banjo	Instrument	$ 27,000
28	Traditional Instruments	Intermediate Banjo	Instrument	$ 14,750
29	Traditional Instruments	Beginner Mandolin	Instrument	$ 1,450
30	Traditional Instruments	Intermediate Mandolin	Instrument	$ 6,500
31	Traditional Instruments	Beginner Guitar	Instrument	$ 45,000
32	Traditional Instruments	Intermediate Guitar	Instrument	$ 32,000

Cell A4 identifies the Stratoblaster 9000 guitar, and cell B4 returns the amount of revenue. Cells A4 and B4 both use VLOOKUP:

- ✔ The formula in cell A4 is = "Revenue for " & VLOOKUP("Great Guitars",Sales,2, FALSE).
- ✔ The formula is cell B4 is =VLOOKUP("Great Guitars",Sales,4,FALSE).

The formula in cell A4 does not strictly look for the Stratoblaster 9000, instead the first argument specifies a search for Great Guitars. When the first occurrence of Great Guitars is found, the function then looks in the second column (the third argument is the number 2) relative to the range defined by the second argument. Using the False value in the fourth argument ensures that the first occurrence of Great Guitars is used.

Likewise the formula in cell B4 finds the first occurrence of Great Guitars but instead returns the value found in the fourth column relative to the Sales area.

Cell B6 uses OFFSET to force VLOOKUP to search for the key value in the second column of the Sales area (instead of the left most column). OFFSET defines an offset of 1 column to the right, and also note that the value that is returned is from the fourth column of Sales, yet is the third column relative to the defined area in the VLOOKUP's second column:

```
=VLOOKUP("Wireless Gig Kit",OFFSET(Sales,0,1),3, FALSE)
```

Here's how to use either HLOOKUP or VLOOKUP:

1. **Click a cell where you want the result to appear.**

2. **Enter either =HLOOKUP(or =VLOOKUP(to start the function.**

3. **Enter a value that matches a value in the top row of the table if using HLOOKUP or in the first column if using VLOOKUP.**

4. **Enter a comma(,).**

5. **Enter the range that defines the table of data or enter its name if it is given one.**

6. **Enter a comma(,).**

7. **Enter a number to indicate the row of the value to return if using HLOOKUP or enter a number to indicate the column of the value to return if using VLOOKUP.**

   Remember that the number entered here is relative to the range or area defined in the second argument.

8. **Optionally, enter a comma and False to force the function to find an exact match for the value entered in the first argument.**

9. **Enter a closing parenthesis and press Enter to end the function.**

Excel also provides the LOOKUP function that can be used to return the value from the last row or column of a single row or column range. See Excel Help for more information on this function.

The MATCH function returns the relative row number or column number of a value in a table. The key point here is that it returns where a value is, but does not return any actual value.

This function is useful when you need the position of an item. This fact in turn is typically used in one of the functions that uses a row number of column number as an argument. We show you how shortly.

MATCH takes three arguments:

1. **The value to search for:** This can be a number, text, or a logic value; or a value supplied with a cell reference.

2. **Where to look:** This is a range spanning a single row or column, or a named area of a single row or column.

3. **How the match is to be applied:** This argument is optional.

The third argument can be one of three values: -1, 0, or 1. A -1 tells the function to make an exact match or use the next possible value larger than the value in first argument. A value of 1 tells the function to make an exact match or use the next possible value smaller than the value in first argument. Using values of -1 requires that the range being searched is in descending order. Using values of 1 requires that the range being searched is in ascending order.

A value of 0 for the third argument tells the function to accept only an exact match. When the argument is left out the default is 1.

Figure 14-11 shows the products and revenue for the guitar shop. The formula in cell B2 — `=MATCH("Beginner Banjo",Products,0)` — returns the relative row number of the match from the start of the range defined in the second argument. In particular the term `Beginner Banjo` is being searched for in a named area `Products`. The range of `Products` is B7:B38. Note that this range is within a single column. The MATCH function requires that the range specified in the second column is either within a single column or a single row.

You find the Beginner Banjo in row 17 relative to the start of the Products area. The first row of Products is 7. The absolute row for Beginner Banjo is 23. If it seems that this should be row 24 (17 + 7), remember that row 7 is part of the count of 17 rows.

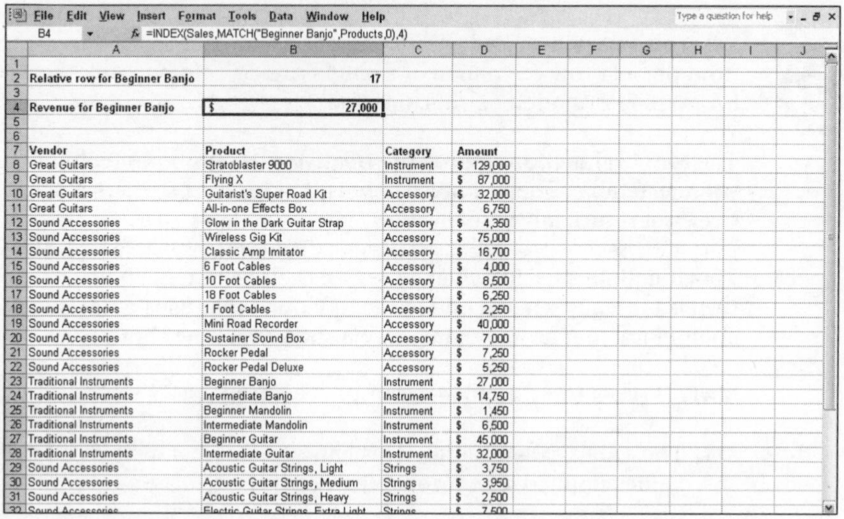
B4 =INDEX(Sales,MATCH("Beginner Banjo",Products,0),4)

	A	B	C	D
1				
2	Relative row for Beginner Banjo	17		
3				
4	Revenue for Beginner Banjo	$ 27,000		
5				
6				
7	Vendor	Product	Category	Amount
8	Great Guitars	Stratoblaster 9000	Instrument	$ 129,000
9	Great Guitars	Flying X	Instrument	$ 87,000
10	Great Guitars	Guitarist's Super Road Kit	Accessory	$ 32,000
11	Great Guitars	All-in-one Effects Box	Accessory	$ 6,750
12	Sound Accessories	Glow in the Dark Guitar Strap	Accessory	$ 4,350
13	Sound Accessories	Wireless Gig Kit	Accessory	$ 75,000
14	Sound Accessories	Classic Amp Imitator	Accessory	$ 16,700
15	Sound Accessories	6 Foot Cables	Accessory	$ 4,000
16	Sound Accessories	10 Foot Cables	Accessory	$ 8,500
17	Sound Accessories	18 Foot Cables	Accessory	$ 6,250
18	Sound Accessories	1 Foot Cables	Accessory	$ 2,250
19	Sound Accessories	Mini Road Recorder	Accessory	$ 40,000
20	Sound Accessories	Sustainer Sound Box	Accessory	$ 7,000
21	Sound Accessories	Rocker Pedal	Accessory	$ 7,250
22	Sound Accessories	Rocker Pedal Deluxe	Accessory	$ 5,250
23	Traditional Instruments	Beginner Banjo	Instrument	$ 27,000
24	Traditional Instruments	Intermediate Banjo	Instrument	$ 14,750
25	Traditional Instruments	Beginner Mandolin	Instrument	$ 1,450
26	Traditional Instruments	Intermediate Mandolin	Instrument	$ 6,500
27	Traditional Instruments	Beginner Guitar	Instrument	$ 45,000
28	Traditional Instruments	Intermediate Guitar	Instrument	$ 32,000
29	Sound Accessories	Acoustic Guitar Strings, Light	Strings	$ 3,750
30	Sound Accessories	Acoustic Guitar Strings, Medium	Strings	$ 3,950
31	Sound Accessories	Acoustic Guitar Strings, Heavy	Strings	$ 2,500

Figure 14-11: Making a match.

Here's how to use the MATCH function:

1. **Click a cell where you want the result to appear.**
2. **Enter** =MATCH(**to start the function.**
3. **Enter a value to match.**

   This can be a numeric, text, or logic value. You can enter a cell address provided the referenced cell has a usable value.

4. **Enter a comma (,).**
5. **Enter the range in which to look for a match.**

   This can be a range reference or a named area.

6. **Optionally enter a comma and enter a -1, 0, or 1 to tell the function how to make a match.**

   The default is 1 if not supplied. A 0 forces an exact match.

7. **Enter a closing parenthesis to end the function and press Enter.**

Knowing that Beginner Banjo is in row 17 is not very useful. Use this value in the INDEX function to get a useful value instead.

INDEX returns the value found in a relative row and cell intersection within a table. There are three arguments: the table area to look in; the row number; relative to the first row of the table; and the column number relative to the left-most column of the table.

INDEX requires knowing the row and column numbers. The MATCH function in this example has returned the row number. Neat!

In Figure 14-11, cell B4 uses INDEX with MATCH to return a value from the Sales table. The formula in cell B4 is

```
=INDEX(Sales, MATCH("Beginner Banjo",Products,0),4)
```

The requirement is to find the revenue for the Beginner Banjo. We know the product name, and we know that revenue figures are in the fourth column of the Sales area (defined as A7:D38). What we don't know is which row is the data for the Beginner Banjo. The MATCH function provides the relative row number, and the revenue value is found.

Here's how to use the INDEX function:

1. **Click a cell where you want the result to appear.**

2. **Enter =INDEX(to start the function.**

3. **Enter a reference to the table.**

   You can drag the mouse over the range or enter its address. If the table has been named, you can enter the name.

4. **Enter a comma (,).**

5. **Enter the row number relative to the first row of the table.**

   This number can be the result of a calculation or the value returned from a function.

6. **Enter a comma (,).**

7. **Enter the column number relative to the leftmost column of the table.**

   This number can be the result of a calculation or the value returned from a function.

8. **Enter a closing parenthesis to end the function and press Enter.**

Using TRANSPOSE To Turn Data on Its Ear

Here's the situation. You have a table of data on you worksheet, only the orientation is wrong. The rows should be columns and the columns should be rows. Reentering all the data would be a nightmare!

TRANSPOSE to the rescue. This function swaps rows and columns for an indicated area of information. That is, TRANSPOSE shifts the horizontal and vertical orientations.

A transpose feature is in the Paste Special dialog box. Using this you can copy and paste transposed data quite easily. The difference with TRANSPOSE is that the function references the original data area. This is great because any changes to the data are made in the original area and the transposed data gets updated.

TRANSPOSE is entered as an array function. So, an area is first selected for the function entry (instead of a single cell). After the function has been entered the last step is to press CTRL + Shift + Enter.

The TRANSPOSE function is entered into a selected area that is the same dimension as the data area, but with the height and width reversed. A data area of three rows and ten columns would be transposed into an area of ten rows and three columns.

The area where TRANSPOSE is being entered must be the same size as the area of data being transposed. For example, for a data area of three columns and six rows, TRANSPOSE enters into a selected area of six columns and three rows.

TRANSPOSE takes a single argument — the area of the data. Here's how to use the TRANSPOSE function:

1. **Select an area to receive the transposed data.**

   Make sure this is the same size as the data, but with the dimensions reversed. Figure 14-12 shows a worksheet with a data in the range B14:C20. This is 7 rows by 2 columns. Above this area, B4:H5 is selected. The selected area is 2 rows by 7 columns.

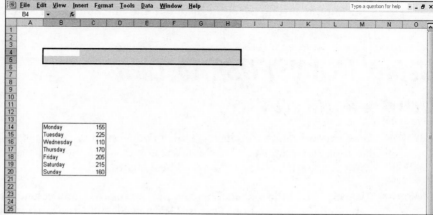

Figure 14-12:
Selecting an area for the TRANPOSE function.

2. **Enter =TRANSPOSE(to start the function.**

3. **Drag the cursor over the data area or enter its address.**

   In our example, the data is in B14:C20, as seen in Figure 14-13.

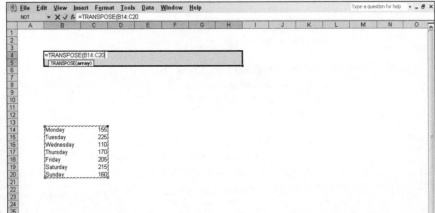

Figure 14-13:
Entering
the
TRANPOSE
function.

4. **Enter a closing parenthesis and then press CTRL + Shift + Enter to end the function entry.**

Figure 14-14 shows the results. The data area is reoriented. Any changes made to the original data are reflected in the transposed data area.

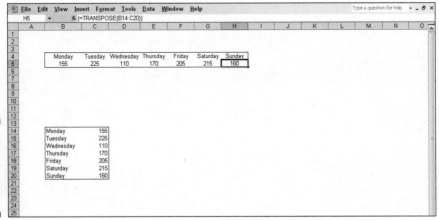

Figure 14-14:
A successful
data
reorien-
tation.

Chapter 15

Working with Information Functions

⬤ ⬤

In This Chapter

▶ Getting information about a cell or range

▶ Finding out about Excel or your computer system

▶ Testing for numbers, text, and errors

⬤ ⬤

*I*n this chapter, we show you how to use Excel's information functions, which you use to obtain information about cells, ranges, and the workbook you're working in. You can even get information about the computer you're using. What will they think of next!?

The information functions are great for getting formulas to focus on just the data that matters. Some functions even help shield you from Excel's confusing error messages. The first time we saw the #NAME? error we thought Excel was asking for a name to be entered. Just another of the more exciting Excel moments. Now at least we know to use the ISERROR or ERROR.TYPE functions to make error messages more meaningful. And after reading this chapter, so will you!

Getting Informed with the CELL Function

The CELL function provides feedback about cells and ranges in a worksheet. You can find out what row and column a cell is in, what type of formatting it has, whether it's protected, and so on.

CELL takes two arguments. The first argument, which is enclosed in double quotes, tells the function what kind of information to return. The second argument tells the function which cell or range to evaluate. If you specify a range that contains more than one cell, the function returns information about the top-left cell in the range. The second argument is optional; when it isn't provided, Excel reports back on the most recently changed cell.

Table 15-1 shows the list of possible entries for the first argument of the CELL function.

Table 15-1	Selecting the First Argument for the CELL Function	
Argument	*Example*	*Comment*
address	=CELL ("address")	Returns the address of the last changed cell.
col	=CELL ("col",Sales)	Returns the column number of the first cell in the Sales range.
color	=CELL ("color",B3)	Tells whether a particular cell (in this case, cell B3) is formatted in such a way that negative numbers are represented in color. The number, currency, and custom formats have selections for displaying negative numbers in red. If the cell is formatted for color-negative numbers, a 1 is returned; otherwise, a 0 is returned.
contents	=CELL ("contents",B3)	Returns the contents of a particular cell (in this case, cell B3). If the cell contains a formula, returns the result of the formula and not the formula itself.
filename	=CELL ("filename")	Returns the path, filename, and worksheet name of the workbook and worksheet that has the Cell function in it (for example, C:\Customers\[Acme Company]Sheet1). Trying this out in a new workbook that has not yet been saved returns a blank answer.
format	=CELL ("format",D12)	Returns the number format of a cell (in this case, cell D12). See Table 15-2 for a list of possible returned values.
parentheses	=CELL ("parentheses", D12)	Returns 1 if a cell (in this case, cell D12) is formatted to have positive values, or all values, to have parentheses. Otherwise, 0 is returned. A custom format is needed to make parentheses appear with positive values in the first place.

Argument	Example	Comment
prefix	=CELL ("prefix",R25)	Returns the type of text alignment in a cell (in this case, cell R25). There are a few possibilities: a single quotation mark (') if the cell is left-aligned; a double quotation mark (") if the cell is right-aligned; a carat (^) if the cell is set to centered; or a backslash(\) if the cell is fill-aligned. If the cell being evaluated is blank or has a number, then the function returns nothing.
protect	=CELL ("protect",D12)	Returns 1 if the protection of a cell (in this case, cell D12) is set to locked; otherwise, a 0 is returned. The returned value is not affected by whether the worksheet is currently protected.
row	=CELL ("row",Sales)	Returns the row number of the first cell in the Sales range.
type	=CELL ("row",Sales)	Returns a value corresponding to the type of information in a cell (in this case, cell D12). There are three possible values: b if the cell is blank; 1 if the cell has alphanumeric data; and v for all other possible values including numbers and errors.
width	=CELL ("width")	Returns the width of the last changed cell, rounded to an integer. For example a width of 18.3 is returned as 18.

The second argument, whether it's there or not, plays a key role in how the CELL function works. When included, the second argument is either a cell address, such as B12, or a range name, such as Sales. Of course, you could have a range that is only one cell but let's not confuse the issue!

If you enter a nonexistent range name for the second argument Excel returns the #NAME? error. Excel can't return information about something that doesn't exist!

An interesting way to use CELL is to keep track of what the last entry was on a worksheet. Let's say you're updating a list of values. The phone rings and you're tied up for a while on the call. When you get back to your list, you've forgotten where you left off. Yikes! What a time to think "If only I had used the CELL function!"

Figure 15-1 shows such a worksheet. Cell B18 displays the address of the last cell that was changed.

	File	Edit	View	Insert	Format	Tools	Data	Window	H
B18				fx	=CELL("address")				

	A	B	C
1	Office	Contracts	
2	Baltimore	15	
3	Birmingham	16	
4	Bismark	12	
5	Chicago	16	
6	Cleveland	14	
7	Denver	15	
8	Detroit	22	
9	Houston	24	
10	Lexington	20	
11	Norfolk	15	
12	Phoenix	16	
13	Raleigh	18	
14	St. Louis	24	
15	St. Paul	15	
16			
17			
18	Last Cell Changed:	$B$10	
19			
20			
21			
22			
23			
24			

Figure 15-1: Keeping track of which cell had the latest entry.

Using CELL with the filename argument is great for displaying the workbook's path. This technique is common for printed worksheet reports. Being able to find the workbook file that a report was printed from six months ago is a real timesaver. Don't you just love it when the boss gives you an hour to create a report, doesn't look at it for six months, and *then* wants to make a change? Here's how the CELL function is entered to return the filename:

```
=CELL("filename")
```

You can format cells in many different ways. When the first argument to CELL is "format", a code is returned that corresponds to the formatting. The possible formats are those found in the Format Cells dialog box. Table15-2 shows the formats and the code that CELL returns.

Table 15-2	Returned Values for the "Format" Argument
Format	*Returned Value from CELL Function*
General	G
0	F0

Format	Returned Value from CELL Function
#,##0	,0
0.00	F2
#,##0.00	,2
$#,##0_);($#,##0)	C0
$#,##0_);[Red]($#,##0)	C0-
$#,##0.00_);($#,##0.00)	C2
$#,##0.00_);[Red]($#,##0.00)	C2-
0%	P0
0.00%	P2
0.00E+00	S2
# ?/? or ??/??	G
m/d/yy or m/d/yy h:mm or mm/dd/yy	D4
d-mmm-yy or dd-mmmm-yy	D1
d-mmm or dd-mmm	D2
mmm-yy	D3
mm/dd	D5
h:mm AM/PM	D7
h:mm:ss AM/PM	D6
h:mm	D9
h:mm:ss	D8

Using CELL with the "format" argument lets you add a bit of smarts to your worksheet. Figure 15-2 shows an example where CELL makes sure information is correctly understood. The dates in Column A are of the d-mmm format. The downside of this format is that the year is not known. So, cell A1 has been given a formula that uses CELL to test the format of the dates. If the d-mmm format is found in the first date (in cell A4) then cell A1 displays a message that includes the year from cell A4. After all, cell A4 *has* a year — it's just formatted not to show it. This way the year is always present — either in the dates themselves, or at the top of the worksheet.

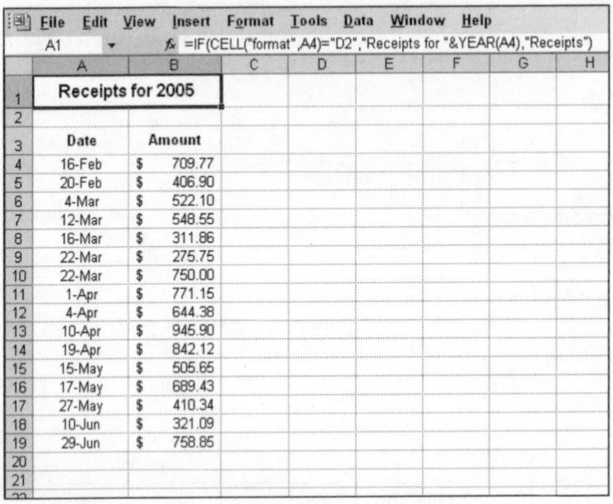

Figure 15-2:
Using CELL
and the
"format"
argument to
display a
useful
message.

This formula is in Cell A1:

```
=IF(CELL("format",A4)="D2","Receipts for
          "&YEAR(A4),"Receipts")
```

This formula says that, if the formatting in A4 is d-mmm (according to the values in Table 15-2), then display the message with the year; otherwise, just display Receipts.

Here's how to use the CELL function:

1. **Position the cursor in the cell where you want the results to appear.**
2. **Enter =CELL(to begin the function entry.**
3. **Enter one of the first argument choices listed in Table 15-1.**

   Make sure to surround it with double quotes (" ").
4. **If you want to tell the function which cell or range to use, enter a comma (,).**
5. **If you want, enter a cell address or the name of a range.**
6. **Enter a closing parenthesis to end the function, and press Enter.**

Getting Information about Excel and Your Computer System

Excel provides the INFO function to get information about your computer and about Excel. INFO takes a single argument that tells the function what type of information to return. Table 15-3 shows how to use the INFO function.

Table 15-3   Using INFO to Find Out about Your Computer or Excel

Argument	*Example*	*Comment*
directory	=INFO ("directory")	Returns the path of the current directory. Note that this is not necessarily the same path of the open workbook.
memavail	=INFO ("memavail")	Returns the amount of available memory in bytes.
memused	=INFO ("memused")	Returns the amount of memory, in bytes, being used at the time the function is run. The more applications and/or files that are open, the higher the number will be.
numfile	=INFO ("numfile")	Returns the number of work sheets in all open workbooks. This number includes worksheets of add-ins, so the number could be misleading.
origin	=INFO ("origin")	Returns the address of the cell that is at the top and left of the scrollable area. An A$ prefix is put in front of the cell address for compatibility with Lotus 1-2-3.
osversion	=INFO ("osversion")	Returns the name of the current operating system.
recalc	=INFO ("recalc")	Returns the status of the recalculation mode: either Automatic or Manual.
release	=INFO ("release")	Returns the version number of Excel being run.
system	=INFO ("system")	Returns the name of the operating environment: either mac or pcdos.
totmem	=INFO ("totmem")	Returns the sum of the available memory and the used memory.

One useful application of the INFO function is to use the returned Excel version number to determine whether the workbook can use a newer feature. For example the ability to work with XML data has only been available in

Excel 2002 and later. By testing the version number, a user can be notified whether he can work with XML data. This formula uses the "release" choice as the argument:

```
=IF(INFO("release")>9,"This version can import XML", "This
          version cannot import XML")
```

Figure 15-3 shows values returned with the INFO function. The information shows facts about Ken's computer. Please, no comments on how much memory he has!

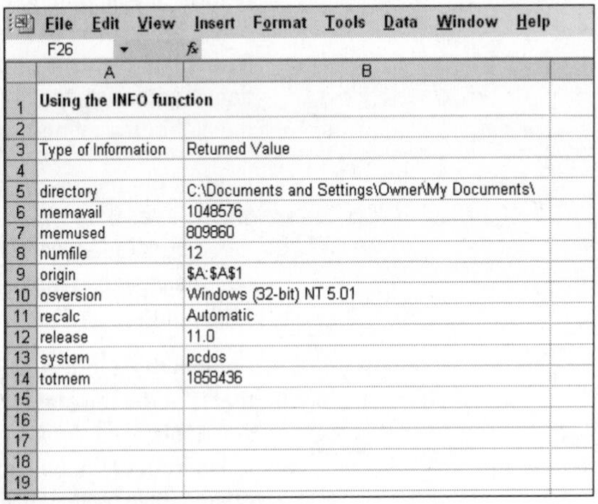

	A	B
1	**Using the INFO function**	
2		
3	Type of Information	Returned Value
4		
5	directory	C:\Documents and Settings\Owner\My Documents\
6	memavail	1048576
7	memused	809860
8	numfile	12
9	origin	$A:$A$1
10	osversion	Windows (32-bit) NT 5.01
11	recalc	Automatic
12	release	11.0
13	system	pcdos
14	totmem	1858436
15		
16		
17		
18		
19		

Figure 15-3: Getting facts about the computer with the INFO function.

Here's how to use the INFO function:

1. **Position the cursor in the cell where you want the results to appear.**
2. **Enter** =INFO(**to begin the function entry.**
3. **Enter one of argument choices listed in Table 15-3.**

   Make sure to surround it with double quotes (" ").
4. **Enter a closing parenthesis to end the function, and press Enter.**

Finding Out What Is and What Is Not

A handful of IS functions report back a True or False answer about certain cell characteristics — for example, is a cell blank or does it contain text. These functions are often used in combination with other functions, typically the IF function, to handle errors or other unexpected or undesirable results.

The errors Excel reports are not very friendly. What on earth does "#N/A" really tell you? Well, the functions we describe in this section won't make the error any clearer, but they give you a way to instead display a message that's friendly, like, "Something is wrong, but I don't know what it is."

Table 15-4 shows the IS functions and how they're used. They all return either True or False, so the table just lists them.

Table 15-4	Using the IS Functions to See What Really Is
Function	*Comment*
=ISBLANK(value)	Tells whether a cell is blank.
=ISERR(value)	Tells whether a cell contains any error, other than the #N/A error.
=ISERROR(value)	Tells whether a cell contains any error.
=ISLOGICAL(value)	Tells whether value is logical.
=ISNA(value)	Tells whether a cell contains the #N/A error.
=ISNONTEXT(value)	Tells whether a cell contains a number or error.
=ISNUMBER(value)	Tells whether a cell contains a number.
=ISREF(value)	Tells whether value is a reference.
=ISTEXT(value)	Tells whether a cell contains text.

Let's look at some of these functions. First, three of the IS functions tell you about an error: ISERR, ISERROR, and ISNA.

Error Function	*Comments*
ISERR	Returns True if the error is anything except the #N/A error. For example the #DIV/0! Error returns True.
ISNA	This function is the opposite of the ISERR function. It only returns True if the error is #N/A.
ISERROR	Returns True for any type of error. This includes #N/A, #VALUE!, #REF!, DIV/0!, #NUM!, #NAME?, and #NULL!

Why is #N/A treated separately? It is excluded from being handled with ISERR, and has its own ISNA function. Actually #N/A can be used to your advantage to avoid errors. How so? Figure 15-4 shows an example that calculates the percentage of surveys returned for some of Florida's larger cities. The calculation is simple — just divide the returned number by the number sent.

However, errors do creep in (creepy errors, yuck!). For example, no surveys were sent to Gainesville, yet 99 came back. Interesting! The calculation becomes a division by zero error, which makes sense.

On the other hand, Tallahassee had no surveys sent, but here the returned value is the #N/A error, purposely entered. Next look at Column E. In this column, `True` or `False` is returned to indicate whether the calculation, per city, should be considered an error — Gainesville true, Tallahassee false.

TRUE or FALSE appears in Column E because all the cells in Column E use the ISERR function. The formula in cell E13, which tests the calculation for Tallahassee is this:

```
=ISERR(D13)
```

Simply put, D13 displays the #N/A error because its calculation (`=C13/B13`) uses a cell with an entered #N/A. The ISERR does not consider #N/A to be an error; therefore, E13 returns False. The upshot to all this is that eyeballing Column E makes distinguishing entry and math errors from purposeful flagging of certain rows as having incomplete data easy.

	File Edit View Insert Format Tools Data Window Help			
	H28 ▼ *fx*			
	A	B	C	D	E
1		Number of	Number of	Response	
2	Location	Surveys Sent	Surveys Returned	Rate	Error?
3					
4	Daytona Beach	300	120	40.00%	FALSE
5	Gainesville	0	99	#DIV/0!	TRUE
6	Jacksonville	300	0	0.00%	FALSE
7	Key West	300	58	19.33%	FALSE
8	Melbourne	300	111	37.00%	FALSE
9	Miami	300	0	0.00%	FALSE
10	Orlando	300	168	56.00%	FALSE
11	Sarasota	300	4	1.33%	FALSE
12	St. Petersburg	300	#N/A	#N/A	FALSE
13	Tallahassee	0	#N/A	#N/A	FALSE
14	Tampa	300	Unknown	#VALUE!	TRUE
15					
16					
17					
18					
19					

Figure 15-4:
Putting an error to your advantage.

The ISBLANK, ISNONTEXT, ISTEXT, and ISNUMBER functions tell you what type of data is in a cell. Actually ISBLANK returns True when nothing is in a cell. Using ISBLANK is useful to count how many cells in a range are blank. Perhaps you're responsible for making sure that 200 employees get their timesheets in every week. You can use a formula that lets you know how many employees have not yet handed in their hours.

Such a formula uses ISBLANK along with the IF and SUM functions, like this:

```
{=SUM(IF(ISBLANK(B5:B204),1,0))}
```

This formula makes use of an array. See Chapter 3 for more information on using array formulas. Figure 15-5 shows how this formula works. In columns A and B are long lists of employees and their hours. The formula in cell A1 reports how many employees are missing their hours.

ISTEXT returns True when a cell contains any type of text. ISNONTEXT returns True when a cell contains anything that is not text, including numbers, dates, and times. The ISNONTEXT function also returns True if the cell contains an error.

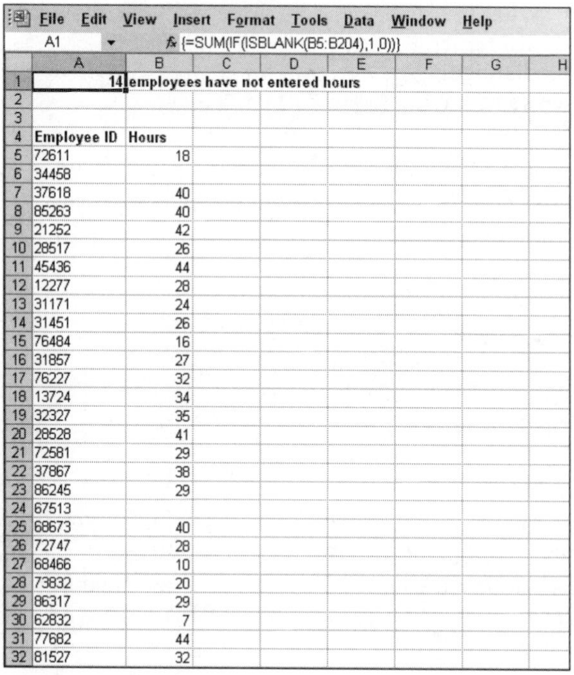

Figure 15-5:
Calculating
how many
employees
are missing
an entry.

	A	B	C
1	14	employees have not entered hours	
4	Employee ID	Hours	
5	72611	18	
6	34458		
7	37618	40	
8	85263	40	
9	21252	42	
10	28517	26	
11	45436	44	
12	12277	28	
13	31171	24	
14	31451	26	
15	76484	16	
16	31857	27	
17	76227	32	
18	13724	34	
19	32327	35	
20	28528	41	
21	72581	29	
22	37867	38	
23	86245	29	
24	67513		
25	68673	40	
26	72747	28	
27	68466	10	
28	73832	20	
29	86317	29	
30	62832	7	
31	77682	44	
32	81527	32	

The ISNUMBER function returns True when a cell contains a number, which can be an actual number or a number resulting from evaluation of a formula in the cell. You can use ISNUMBER as an aid to help data entry. Let's say you designed a worksheet that people use to fill out. One of the questions is their age. Most people would enter a numeric value such as 18, 25, 70, and so on. But someone could type in the age as text, such as "eighteen" or "thirty-two" or maybe even "none of your business." An adjacent cell could use ISNUMBER to return a message about entering the numeric age. The formula would look something like this:

```
=IF(ISNUMBER(B3),"","Please enter your age as a number")
```

Here's how to use any of the IS functions:

1. **Position the cursor in the cell where you want the results to appear.**

2. **Enter one of the IS functions, for example, enter** =ISTEXT(**to begin the function entry.**

3. **Enter a cell address.**

4. **Enter a closing parenthesis to end the function, and press Enter.**

   The result is always either True or False.

Getting to Know Your Type

The TYPE function tells you what the type of the information is. Possible types are a number, text, a logical value, an error, or an array. In all cases TYPE returns a number:

- ✔ 1 is returned for numbers.
- ✔ 2 is returned for text.
- ✔ 4 is returned for logical values.
- ✔ 16 is returned for errors.
- ✔ 64 is returned for arrays.

Figure 15-6 shows each of these values returned by the TYPE function. Cells B3:B7 contain the TYPE function, with each row looking at the adjacent cell in Column A. The returned value of 64 in cell B7 is a little different. This indicates an array as the type. The formula in cell B7 is =TYPE(A7:A9). This is an array of values from cells A7:A9.

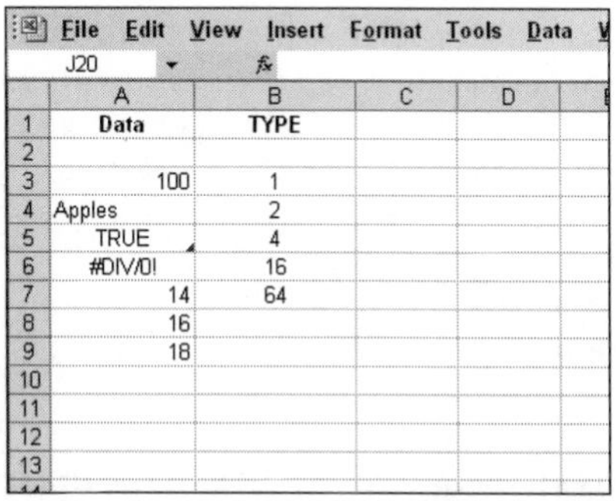

Figure 15-6:
Getting the
type of
the data.

Here's how to use the TYPE function:

1. **Position the cursor in the cell where you want the results to appear.**

2. **Enter =TYPE(to begin the function entry.**

3. **Enter a cell address, or click on a cell.**

4. **Enter a closing parenthesis to end the function, and press Enter.**

The ERROR.TYPE function returns a number that corresponds to the particular error in a cell. Table 15-5 shows the error types and the returned numbers.

Table 15-5	Getting a Number of an Error
Error Type	*Returned Number*
#NULL!	1
#DIV/0!	2
#VALUE!	3
#REF!	4
#NAME?	5
#NUM!	6
#N/A	7

The best thing about the ERROR.TYPE function is that you can use it to change those pesky errors into something readable! To do this, use the CHOOSE function along with ERROR.TYPE, like this:

```
=CHOOSE(ERROR.TYPE(H14),"Nothing here!","You can't divide by
       0","A bad number has been entered", "The formula
       is referencing a bad cell or range","There is a
       problem with the entry","There is a problem with
       the entered value","Something is seriously
       wrong!")
```

See Chapter 14 for assistance on using the CHOOSE function. This is how you use the ERROR.TYPE function:

1. **Position the cursor in the cell where you want the results to appear.**

2. **Enter =ERROR.TYPE(to begin the function entry.**

3. **Enter a cell address, or click on a cell.**

4. **Enter a closing parenthesis to end the function, and press Enter.**

Chapter 16

Working with Text Functions

A rose is still a rose by any other name. Or maybe not when you use Excel's sophisticated text-manipulation functions to change it into something else. Case in point: You can use the REPLACE function to change a rose into a tulip or a daisy, literally!

Did you ever have to work on a list where people's full names are in one column but you need to use only their last names? You could extract the last names to another column manually, but that strategy only works for a few names at best. What if the list contains hundreds or thousands of names? This is just one example of text manipulations that you can easily and quickly do with Excel's text functions.

Excel has a great set of text functions. Often, you'll use a combination of them to get your task completed. This chapter is fun. Fasten your seat belts. Here we go!

Breaking Apart Text

Excel has three functions that are handy to extract part of a text value (often referred to as a *string*). The LEFT, RIGHT, and MID functions let you get to the parts of a text value that their name implies, extracting part of a text value from the left, the middle, or the right. Mastering these functions gives you the power to literally break text apart.

How about this: You have a list of codes of inventory items. The first three characters are the vendor ID. You need just the vendor IDs. How do you do this? How do you get the rest of the codes, but not including the first three characters? Excel functions to the rescue!

Bearing to the left

The LEFT function lets you grab a specified number of characters from the left side of a larger string. All you do is tell the function what or where the string is and how many characters you need to extract.

Figure 16-1 demonstrates how the LEFT function is used to isolate the Vendor ID in a hypothetical product code list (Column A). The Vendor ID is the first three characters in each product code. You want to extract the first three characters of each product code and put them in column B. You'll put the LEFT function in Column B with the first argument specifying where the larger string is (Column A) and the second argument specifying how many characters to extract (three). See Figure 16-1 for an illustration of the formula bar.

	File	Edit	View	Insert	Format	Tools	Data	Window	Help
	B4	▼		*fx*	=LEFT(A4,3)				

	A	B	C	D	E
1	INVENTORY CONTROL				
2					
3	Product Code	Vendor	Internal Tracking Number		
4	WES7164	WES	7164		
5	NER6574	NER	6574		
6	NER8090	NER	8090		
7	APP2341	APP	2341		
8	BOT1466	BOT	1466		
9	POW1251	POW	1251		
10	APP5343	APP	5343		
11	POW7622	POW	7622		
12	WES1111	WES	1111		
13	APP7235	APP	7235		
14	POW1524	POW	1524		
15	WES3113	WES	3113		
16	BOT5482	BOT	5482		
17	NER4526	NER	4526		
18	WES5968	WES	5968		
19	BOT8374	BOT	8374		
20	TRE2762	TRE	2762		
21	APP4251	APP	4251		
22	APP2376	APP	2376		
23	POW4664	POW	4664		
24	APP6143	APP	6143		
25	NER8532	NER	8532		
26	POW7666	POW	7666		
27	WES1145	WES	1145		

Figure 16-1: Getting the three left characters from a larger string.

Try it yourself! The LEFT function is really handy and yet so easy to use!

1. **Position the cursor in the cell where you want the extracted string displayed.**

2. **Enter =LEFT(to start the function.**

3. **Click on the cell containing the original string, or enter its address.**

4. **Enter a comma (,).**

5. **Enter a number.**

   This number tells the function how many characters to extract from the left of the larger string. If you enter a number that is equal to or larger than the number of characters in the string, then the whole string is returned.

6. **Enter a closing parenthesis to end the function, and press Enter.**

Swinging to the right

Excel does not favor sides. Because there is a LEFT function, there also is RIGHT function. RIGHT is used to extract a certain number of characters from the right of a larger string. It works pretty much the same way as the LEFT function.

Column C of Figure 16-1 uses the RIGHT function to extract the rightmost four characters from the product codes. Cell C4, for example, has this formula: `=RIGHT(A4,4)`.

Here's how to use the RIGHT function:

1. **Position the cursor in the cell where you want the extracted string displayed.**

2. **Enter =RIGHT(to start the function.**

3. **Click on the cell containing the original string, or enter its address.**

4. **Enter a comma (,).**

5. **Enter a number.**

   This number tells the function how many characters to extract from the right of the larger string. If you enter a number that is equal to or larger than the number of characters in the string, then the whole string is returned.

6. **Enter a closing parenthesis to end the function and press Enter.**

Use LEFT and RIGHT to extract characters from the start or end of a text string. Use MID to extract characters from the middle.

Staying in the middle

MID is a powerful text extraction function. It lets you pull out a portion of a larger string— from anywhere within the larger string. The LEFT and RIGHT functions allow you to extract from the start or end of a string, but not the middle.

That's where MID comes in. MID takes three arguments: the larger string (or a reference to one); the character position to start at; and how many characters to extract. Here's how to use MID:

1. **Position the cursor in the cell where you want the extracted string displayed.**

2. **Enter =MID(to start the function.**

3. **Click on the cell that has the full text entry, or enter its address.**

4. **Enter a comma (,).**

5. **Enter a number to tell the function which character to start the extraction from.**

   This number can be anything from 1 to the full count of characters of the string. Typically the starting character position used with MID is greater than 1. Why? If you need to start at the first position, you may as well use the simpler LEFT function. If you enter a number for the starting character position that is greater than the length of the string, then nothing is returned.

6. **Enter a comma (,).**

7. **Enter a number to tell the function how many characters to extract.**

   If you enter a number that is greater than the remaining length of the string, then the full remainder of the string is returned. For example, if you tell MID to extract characters 2 through 8 of a six-character string, then MID returns characters 2 through 6.

8. **Enter a closing parenthesis to end the function, and press Enter.**

Here are some examples of how MID works:

Example	*Result*
=MID("APPLE",4,2)	LE
=MID("APPLE",4,1)	L
=MID("APPLE",2,3)	PPL
=MID("APPLE",5,1)	E

Figure 16-2 shows how the MID function helps to isolate the fourth and fifth characters in the hypothetical inventory shown in Figure 16-1. These characters could represent a storage-bin number for the inventory. The MID function makes it easy to get this piece of the larger text.

	File	Edit	View	Insert	Format	Tools	Data	Window	Help	

	D4	▼		*fx* =MID(A4,4,2)			

	A	B	C	D	E
1	INVENTORY CONTROL				
2					
3	Product Code	Vendor	Internal Tracking Number	Bin Number	
4	WES7164	WES	7164	71	
5	NER6574	NER	6574	65	
6	NER8090	NER	8090	80	
7	APP2341	APP	2341	23	
8	BOT1466	BOT	1466	14	
9	POW1251	POW	1251	12	
10	APP5343	APP	5343	53	
11	POW7622	POW	7622	76	
12	WES1111	WES	1111	11	
13	APP7235	APP	7235	72	
14	POW1524	POW	1524	15	
15	WES3113	WES	3113	31	
16	BOT5482	BOT	5482	54	
17	NER4526	NER	4526	45	
18	WES5968	WES	5968	59	
19	BOT8374	BOT	8374	83	
20	TRE2762	TRE	2762	27	
21	APP4251	APP	4251	42	
22	APP2376	APP	2376	23	
23	POW4664	POW	4664	46	
24	APP6143	APP	6143	61	
25	NER8532	NER	8532	85	
26	POW7666	POW	7666	76	
27	WES1145	WES	1145	11	
28	BOT3434	BOT	3434	34	

Figure 16-2:
Using MID to pull out characters from any position in a string.

Putting Text Together

The CONCATENATE function pulls multiple strings together into one larger string. A good use of this is when you have a column of first names and a column of last names and need to put the two together to use as full names.

CONCATENATE takes up to 30 arguments. Each argument is a string or a cell reference, and the arguments are separated by commas. The function does not insert anything, such as a space, between the strings. If you need to separate the substrings, as you would with the first name and last name example, you must explicitly insert the separator. Figure 16-3 makes this clear — you can see that the second argument to the CONCATENATE function is a space.

In Figure 16-3, the full names that are displayed in Column C are concatenated from the first and last names in columns A and B respectively. In the arguments of the function, a space is entered between the references to cells in columns A and B. A space is entered by enclosing a space between double quotation marks, like this: " ".

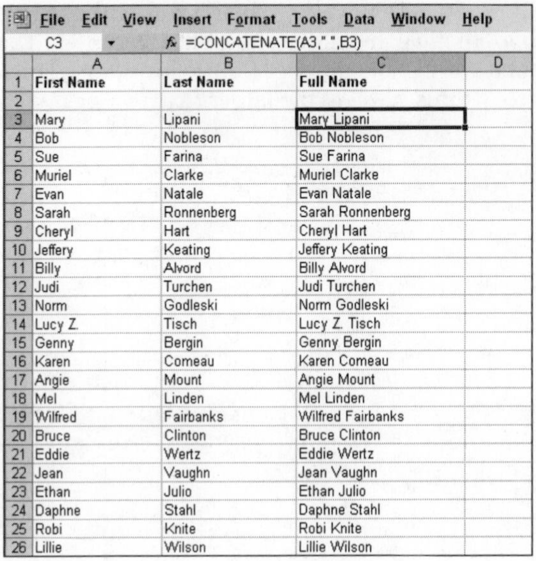

	A	B	C	D
1	First Name	Last Name	Full Name	
2				
3	Mary	Lipani	Mary Lipani	
4	Bob	Nobleson	Bob Nobleson	
5	Sue	Farina	Sue Farina	
6	Muriel	Clarke	Muriel Clarke	
7	Evan	Natale	Evan Natale	
8	Sarah	Ronnenberg	Sarah Ronnenberg	
9	Cheryl	Hart	Cheryl Hart	
10	Jeffery	Keating	Jeffery Keating	
11	Billy	Alvord	Billy Alvord	
12	Judi	Turchen	Judi Turchen	
13	Norm	Godleski	Norm Godleski	
14	Lucy Z.	Tisch	Lucy Z. Tisch	
15	Genny	Bergin	Genny Bergin	
16	Karen	Comeau	Karen Comeau	
17	Angie	Mount	Angie Mount	
18	Mel	Linden	Mel Linden	
19	Wilfred	Fairbanks	Wilfred Fairbanks	
20	Bruce	Clinton	Bruce Clinton	
21	Eddie	Wertz	Eddie Wertz	
22	Jean	Vaughn	Jean Vaughn	
23	Ethan	Julio	Ethan Julio	
24	Daphne	Stahl	Daphne Stahl	
25	Robi	Knite	Robi Knite	
26	Lillie	Wilson	Lillie Wilson	

Figure 16-3: Pulling strings together with CONCATENATE.

There is another way to concatenate strings. You can use the ampersand (&) character instead, and skip using CONCATENATE altogether. For example, another way to create the full names seen in Figure 16-3 is by entering the following formula in the target cell: `=A3 & " " & B3`. Either method gets the job done of concatenating strings. There really is no compelling reason to use one over the other — it's up to you, empowered user!

You can give this a whirl on your own. Surely, you must have a list of names somewhere in an Excel workbook. Well, open that workbook, or at least enter first names and last names on your own, and then do the following:

1. **Position the cursor in an empty column, in the same row as the first text entry, and enter** =CONCATENATE(**to start the function.**
2. **Click on the cell that has the *first* name, or enter its address.**
3. **Enter a comma (,).**
4. **Enter a space inside double quotation marks.**

   It should look like this: " ".
5. **Enter a comma (,).**
6. **Click on the cell that has the *last* name, or enter its address.**
7. **Enter a closing parenthesis to end the function, and press Enter.**

8. **Use the fill handle to drag the function into the rows below, as many rows as there are text entries in the first column.**

You can combine text strings in two different ways. You can use the CONCATENATE function, or you can use the ampersand (&) to combine separate strings together.

Changing Text

There must be a whole lot of issues around text. We say that because there are a whole lot of functions that let you work with text. There are functions that format text, replace text with other text, and clean text (yes, text needs a good scrubbing at times). There are functions for just making lowercase letters into capitals and capitals into lowercase.

Making money

Formatting numbers as currency is a common need in Excel. The Format Cells dialog box or the Currency Style button on the Formatting toolbar are the usual places to go to format cells as currency. Excel also has the DOLLAR function. On the surface, DOLLAR seems to do the same thing as the similar currency formatting options, but there are some key differences:

- ✓ **DOLLAR converts a number to text.** The DOLLAR function takes a number, and changes it to text. This means you cannot perform math on a DOLLAR value. For example, a series of DOLLAR amounts cannot be summed into a total.

- ✓ **DOLLAR displays a value from another cell.** As its first argument DOLLAR takes a cell address or a number entered directly into the function. DOLLAR is handy when you want to preserve the formatting of the original cell. In other words, you may need to present a value as currency but also need to let a number stay in its original format. Using DOLLAR lets you take the original number and present it as currency in another cell — the one you place the DOLLAR function in.

- ✓ **DOLLAR includes a rounding feature.** DOLLAR has a bit more muscle than the currency style. DOLLAR takes a second argument that specifies how many decimal places to display. When negative values are entered for the second argument, this serves to apply rounding to the digits on the left side of the decimal.

Figure 16-4 shows how the DOLLAR function can be applied to present and alter various numeric values. In the worksheet is an area of detailed revenues near the bottom. At the top is a summary.

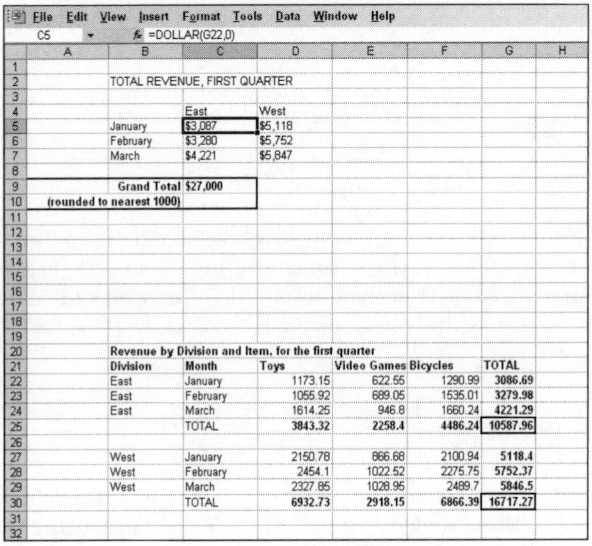

Figure 16-4: Using DOLLAR to round numbers and format them as currency.

Specifically, the cells in the range C5:D7 use the DOLLAR function to present values from the detail area, and also rounds them down to no decimals. For example, cell C5 contains =DOLLAR(G22,0). The grand total in cell C9 takes advantage of DOLLAR to round to the nearest 1,000. In this case the second argument is set to –3, like this: =DOLLAR(G25+G30,-3). Here are examples of how the rounding feature works:

Example	Result
=DOLLAR(1234.56,2)	$1,234.56
=DOLLAR(1234.56,1)	$1,234.6
=DOLLAR(1234.56,0)	$1,235
=DOLLAR(1234.56,-1)	$1,230
=DOLLAR(1234.56,-2)	$1,200
=DOLLAR(1234.56,-3)	$1,000

Using DOLLAR is easy. Here's how:

1. **Position the cursor in the cell where you want the results to appear.**

2. **Enter** =DOLLAR(**to begin the function entry.**

3. **Either click on a cell that contains a number or just enter a number.**

4. **Enter a comma (,).**

5. **Enter a number to indicate the number of decimal points to display.**

   If the number is 0, then no decimal points are displayed. Numbers less than 0 force rounding to occur to the left of the decimal point.

6. **Enter a closing parenthesis to end the function, and press Enter.**

The DOLLAR function is named DOLLAR in countries that use dollars, such as the United States and Canada. In countries that use a different currency, the name of the function should match the name of the currency.

Making numbers look like text

The TEXT function is a bit like the DOLLAR function in that it converts a number value to text data, but it gives you more options on how to format the result. The first argument is a number or reference to a cell that contains a number. The second argument is a formatting pattern that tells the function how to format the number. You can see some formatting patterns in the Custom category, on the Number tab, in the Format Cells dialog box (shown in Figure 16-5).

Figure 16-5:
Formatting
options in
the Format
Cells dialog
box.

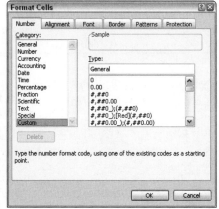

Excel lets you create custom formatting patterns. Then you can present your data in just the way you need to. For example, you can specify whether numbers use a thousands separator, whether decimal values are always displayed to the third decimal point, and so on.

These patterns are created with the use of a few key symbols. A pound sign (#) is a placeholder for a number. Interspersing pound signs with fixed literal characters, such as $, %, a comma, or a period, establishes a pattern. For example this pattern — $#,###.# — says to display a dollar sign in front of the number, and that the number uses a comma for a thousands separator, and displays one decimal point. Some formatting options used with the TEXT function are shown in Table 16-1. Look up custom number formatting in the Excel Help system for more information on custom format patterns.

Table 16-1	Formatting Options for the TEXT Function
Format	**Displays**
=TEXT(1234.56,"#.##")	1234.56
=TEXT(1234.56,"#.#")	1234.6
=TEXT(1234.56,"#")	1235
=TEXT(1234.56,"$#")	$1235
=TEXT(1234.56,"$#,#")	$1,235
=TEXT(1234.56,"$#,#.##")	$1,234.56
=TEXT(0.4,"#%")	40%
=TEXT("3/15/2005","mm/dd/yy")	03/15/05
=TEXT("3/15/2005","mm/dd/yyyy")	03/15/2005
=TEXT("3/15/2005","mmm-dd")	Mar-15

Figure 16-6 shows how the TEXT function is used to format values that are incorporated into sentences. Column C contains the formulas that use TEXT. For example, C4 has this formula: ="We spent " & TEXT(B4,"$#,#.#0") & " on " & A4. Cell C8 has this formula: ="We opened the office on " & TEXT(B8,"mmm-dd-yyyy").

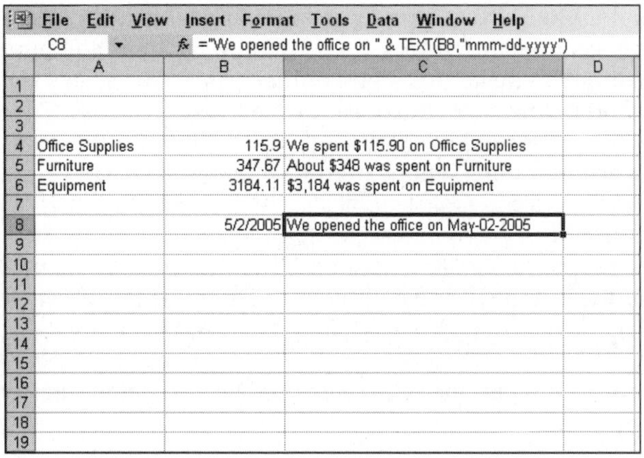

Figure 16-6:
Using TEXT
to report in
a well-
formatted
manner.

Here's how to use TEXT:

1. **Position the cursor in the cell where you want the results to appear.**

2. **Enter** =TEXT(**to begin the function entry.**

3. **Click on a cell that contains a number or a date; or enter its address.**

4. **Enter a comma (,).**

5. **Enter a double quote mark, and then a formatting pattern.**

   See the Format Cells dialog box (Custom category on the Number tab) for guidance.

6. **Enter another double-quote mark after the pattern is entered.**

7. **Enter a closing parenthesis to end the function, and press Enter.**

The VALUE function does the opposite of TEXT — it converts strings to numbers. Excel does this by default anyway so we don't cover the VALUE function here. You can look it up in Excel's Help system if you're curious about it.

Repeating text

REPT is a nifty function that does nothing other than repeat a string of text. There are two arguments for REPT. The first argument is the string or a reference to a cell that contains text. The second argument is the number of times to repeat the text.

REPT makes it a breeze to enter a large number of repeating characters.
Figure 16-7 shows how this works. Cells B14 and B15 contain important summary information. To make this stand out, a string of asterisks (*) has been
place above and below, respectively, in B13 and B16. The REPT function was
used here, with this formula: =REPT("*",120). This simple function has
removed the drudgery of having to enter 120 asterisks.

Try it out. Here's how:

1. **Position the cursor in the cell where you want the results to appear.**

2. **Enter =REPT(to begin the function entry.**

3. **Either click on a cell that contains text, or enter text enclosed in
   double quotes.**

   Typically, a character, such as a period or an asterisk, is entered but any
   text will work.

4. **Enter a comma (,).**

5. **Enter a number to tell the function how many times to repeat the text.**

6. **Enter a closing parenthesis to end the function, and press Enter.**

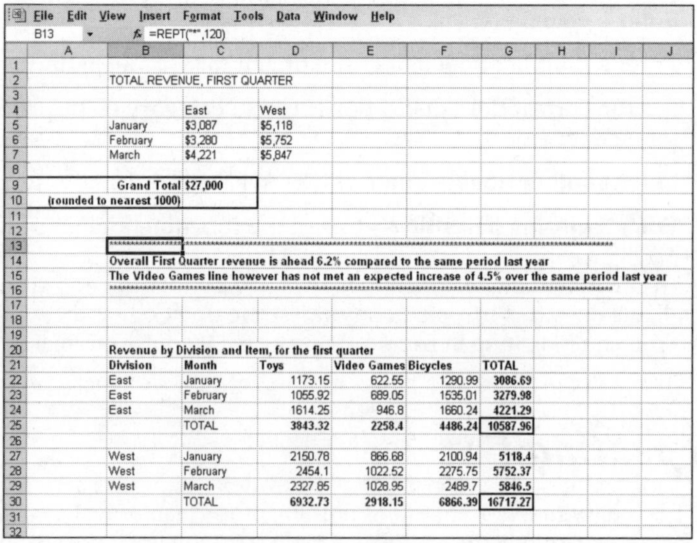

Figure 16-7:
Repeating
text with
the REPT
function.

File Edit View Insert Format Tools Data Window Help									
B13 ▼ ƒx =REPT("*",120)									
A	B	C	D	E	F	G	H	I	J
1									
2	TOTAL REVENUE, FIRST QUARTER								
3									
4		East	West						
5	January	$3,087	$5,118						
6	February	$3,280	$5,752						
7	March	$4,221	$5,847						
8									
9	Grand Total	$27,000							
10	(rounded to nearest 1000)								
11									
12									
13	*****************								
14	Overall First Quarter revenue is ahead 6.2% compared to the same period last year								
15	The Video Games line however has not met an expected increase of 4.5% over the same period last year								
16	*****************								
17									
18									
19									
20	Revenue by Division and Item, for the first quarter								
21	Division	Month	Toys	Video Games	Bicycles	TOTAL			
22	East	January	1173.15	622.55	1290.99	3086.69			
23	East	February	1055.92	689.05	1535.01	3279.98			
24	East	March	1614.25	946.8	1660.24	4221.29			
25		TOTAL	3843.32	2258.4	4486.24	10587.96			
26									
27	West	January	2150.78	866.68	2100.94	5118.4			
28	West	February	2454.1	1022.52	2275.75	5752.37			
29	West	March	2327.85	1028.95	2489.7	5846.5			
30		TOTAL	6932.73	2918.15	6866.39	16717.27			
31									
32									

Replacing text

Two functions — REPLACE and SUBSTITUTE — replace a portion of a string
with other text. The functions are nearly identical in concept but are used in
different situations.

Both REPLACE and SUBSTITUTE replace text within a text string. Use REPLACE when you know the position of the text you want to replace. Use SUBSTITUTE when you don't know the position of the text you want to replace.

REPLACE is used when you know the location in the target string where the text to be replaced is located. You won't always know where it is, but when you do, REPLACE is the function to use. The function takes four arguments:

- The target string as a cell reference.
- The character position in the target string at which to start replacing.
- The number of characters to replace.
- The string to replace with.

For example, if cell A1 contains the string "Our Chicago office has closed" then the formula =REPLACE(A1,5,7,"Dallas") will return the string "Our Dallas office has closed."

Let's see how REPLACE may be used with the Inventory Control data from earlier in the chapter, shown in Figure 16-8. A new task is at hand. To be compatible with a new computer system, the Product codes have to be modified to have a dash in between the Vendor ID and the Internal Tracking Number. The original codes are in Column A. A combination of REPLACE and LEFT functions are used to get the job done, like this:

```
=REPLACE(A4, 1, 3, LEFT(A4,3) & "-")
```

These arguments tell REPLACE to replace the original three characters in each product code with the same three characters followed by a dash. Figure 16-8 shows how REPLACE is used to alter the Product codes.

In Figure 16-8, the first three characters of the product codes are replaced with themselves and a dash. The LEFT function and the dash serve as the fourth argument of REPLACE. A couple of points about REPLACE:

- **You need to know where the text being replaced is in the larger text.** Specifically, you have to tell the function what position the text starts in, and how many positions it occupies.
- **The text being replaced and the new text taking its place don't have to be the same size.**

	File	Edit	View	Insert	Format	Tools	Data	Window	Help		
D4	▼	*fx* =REPLACE(A4, 1, 3, LEFT(A4,3) & "-")									
	A		B		C			D		E	
1	INVENTORY CONTROL										
2											
3	Product Code		Vendor		Internal Tracking Number			New Product Code			
4	WES7164		WES		7164			WES-7164			
5	NER6574		NER		6574			NER-6574			
6	NER8090		NER		8090			NER-8090			
7	APP2341		APP		2341			APP-2341			
8	BOT1466		BOT		1466			BOT-1466			
9	POW1251		POW		1251			POW-1251			
10	APP5343		APP		5343			APP-5343			
11	POW7622		POW		7622			POW-7622			
12	WES1111		WES		1111			WES-1111			
13	APP7235		APP		7235			APP-7235			
14	POW1524		POW		1524			POW-1524			
15	WES3113		WES		3113			WES-3113			
16	BOT5482		BOT		5482			BOT-5482			
17	NER4526		NER		4526			NER-4526			
18	WES5968		WES		5968			WES-5968			
19	BOT8374		BOT		8374			BOT-8374			
20	TRE2762		TRE		2762			TRE-2762			
21	APP4251		APP		4251			APP-4251			
22	APP2376		APP		2376			APP-2376			
23	POW4664		POW		4664			POW-4664			
24	APP6143		APP		6143			APP-6143			
25	NER8532		NER		8532			NER-8532			
26	POW7666		POW		7666			POW-7666			
27	WES1145		WES		1145			WES-1145			
28	BOT3434		BOT		3434			BOT-3434			
29	TRE5723		TRE		5723			TRE-5723			

Figure 16-8:
Using
REPLACE to
change text.

Here's how to use the REPLACE function:

1. **Position the cursor in the cell where you want the result to appear.**

2. **Enter =REPLACE(to begin the function entry.**

3. **Click on a cell that contains the full string of which a portion is to be replaced.**

4. **Enter a comma (,).**

5. **Enter a number to tell the function the starting position of the text to be replaced.**

6. **Enter a comma (,).**

7. **Enter a number to tell the function how many characters are to be replaced.**

8. **Enter a comma (,).**

9. **Either click on a cell that contains text, or enter text enclosed in double quotes.**

   This is the replacement text.

10. **Enter a closing parenthesis to end the function, and press Enter.**

The SUBSTITUTE function is used when you don't know the position in the target string of the text to be replaced. Instead of telling the function the starting position and number of characters (as you do with REPLACE), you just tell it what string to look for and replace.

SUBSTITUTE takes three required arguments and an optional fourth argument:

- ✔ A reference to the cell that contains the target text string.
- ✔ The string within the target string that is to be replaced.
- ✔ The replacement text.
- ✔ An optional number to tell the function which occurrence of the string to replace.

The fourth argument tells SUBSTITUTE which occurrence of the text to be changed (the second argument) and actually replaced with the new text (the third argument). The text to be replaced may appear more than once in the target string. If the fourth argument is omitted, then all occurrences are replaced. The examples in Table 16-2 make this clear.

Table 16-2	Applying the SUBSTITUTE Function	
Example	*Returned String*	*Comment*
=SUBSTITUTE("apple banana cherry fig", " ",",")	apple,banana, cherry,fig	All spaces are replaced with commas.
=SUBSTITUTE("apple banana cherry fig", " ",",",1)	apple,banana cherry fig	The first space is replaced with a comma. The other spaces remain as they are.
=SUBSTITUTE("apple banana cherry fig", " ",",",3)	apple banana cherry,fig	The third space is replaced with a comma. The other spaces remain as they are.
=SUBSTITUTE("There are two cats and two birds.","two", "three")	There are three cats and three birds.	Both occurrences of "two" are replaced with "three."
=SUBSTITUTE("There are two cats and two birds.","two", "three",2)	There are two cats and three birds.	Only the second occurrence of "two" is replaced with "three."

If you don't use the fourth argument, then the substitution is applied to all occurrences of the text. This is the case in the first example in Table 16-2 — all spaces are replaced with commas.

In the last example in Table 16-2, only the second occurrence of the word *two* is changed to the word *three*.

Try it yourself! Here is what you do:

1. **Position the cursor in the cell where you want the result to appear.**
2. **Enter** =SUBSTITUTE(**to begin the function entry.**
3. **Either click on a cell that contains text, or enter its address.**

   This is the full string of which a portion is to be replaced.
4. **Enter a comma (,).**
5. **Either click on a cell that contains text, or enter text enclosed in double quotes.**

   This is the portion of text that is to be replaced.
6. **Enter a comma (,).**
7. **Either click on a cell that contains text, or enter text enclosed in double quotes.**

   This is the replacement text. If you want to specify which occurrence of text to change, then continue with Steps 8 and 9; otherwise, go to Step 10.
8. **Enter a comma (,).**
9. **Enter a number that tells the function which occurrence to apply the substitution to.**
10. **Enter a closing parenthesis to end the function, and press Enter.**

You can use SUBSTITUTE to remove spaces from text. In the second argument (what to replace), enter a space enclosed in double quote marks. In the third argument, enter two double-quote marks, *with nothing in between them.* This is known as an *empty string.*

Giving text a trim

Spaces have a way of sneaking in and ruining your work. The worst thing is you often can't even see them! The SUBSTITUTE function can be used to remove spaces, but it can mistakenly remove too many spaces.

Often, the space or spaces you need to remove are at the beginning or end of a string. The TRIM function is used for this — it simply trims any leading and/or trailing spaces from a string. Figure 16-9 shows how this works. In Column A is a list of names. Looking closely at cells A5 and A10 you can see that spaces precede the names. Column B shows the correction using TRIM. Here is the formula in cell A5: =TRIM(A5).

	File Edit View Insert Format Tools Data Window Help			
	B5	*fx* =TRIM(A5)		
	A	B	C	D
1				
2				
3	Kevin C. Zamore	Kevin C. Zamore		
4	Wayne Danna	Wayne Danna		
5	Arthur Gasco	Arthur Gasco		
6	Jose Campbell	Jose Campbell		
7	Connor G. Douglas	Connor G. Douglas		
8	Herbie Lampert	Herbie Lampert		
9	Joyce Lord	Joyce Lord		
10	Laura Irwin	Laura Irwin		
11	Tamera MacDonald	Tamera MacDonald		
12	Daniella W. Eitts	Daniella W. Eitts		
13	Fred C. Rossel	Fred C. Rossel		
14	Walt M. Glonsrad	Walt M. Glonsrad		
15	Garry Heacox	Garry Heacox		
16	Doris Avakian	Doris Avakian		
17	Nina O. Bereal	Nina O. Bereal		
18	Patrica Escalante	Patrica Escalante		
19				
20				
21				

Figure 16-9: Removing spaces with the TRIM function.

Trim takes just one argument — the text to be cleaned of leading and trailing spaces. Here's how it works:

1. **Position the cursor in the cell where you want the result to appear.**

2. **Enter =TRIM(to begin the function entry.**

3. **Click on a cell that contains the text that has leading and/or trailing spaces; or enter the cell address.**

4. **Enter a closing parenthesis to end the function, and press Enter.**

Be on the lookout for one thing with TRIM. Although generally used to remove leading and trailing spaces, TRIM will remove extra spaces in the middle of a string. That is, if there are two or more spaces next to each other, TRIM removes the extra spaces and leaves one space in place.

This is usually a good thing. Most times you don't want extra spaces in the middle of your text, but what if you do? Here are a couple of alternatives to remove a leading space, if it is there, without affecting the middle of the string:

Formula to Remove Leading Space	Comment
=IF(LEFT(E10,1)=" ",SUBSTITUTE (E10," ","",1), E10)	If a space is found in the first position, then substitute it with an empty string; otherwise, just return the original string.
=IF(LEFT(E10,1)=" ",RIGHT (E10,LEN(E10)-1), E10)	If a space is found in the first position, return the right side of the string, less the first position. (See LEN, later in this chapter.)

Making a case with the case functions

In school we were taught to use uppercase at the start of a sentence, as well as for proper nouns and names. But that was a while ago and now the brain cells are a bit fuzzy. Lucky thing Excel has a way to help fix case, er Case, um CASE — well, you know what we mean.

Three functions alter the case of text: UPPER, LOWER, and PROPER. All three functions take a single argument — the text that will have its case altered. Here are a few examples:

Formula	Result
=LOWER("The Cow Jumped Over The Moon")	the cow jumped over the moon
=UPPER("the cow jumped over the moon")	THE COW JUMPED OVER THE MOON
=PROPER("the cow jumped over the moon")	The Cow Jumped Over The Moon

Perhaps you noticed there is another possibility that needs to be addressed. What about when just the first word needs to start with an uppercase letter, and the rest of the string is all lowercase? Some people refer to this as *sentence case.* You can create sentence case by using the UPPER, LEFT, RIGHT, and LEN functions. (LEN is explained further later in this chapter.) With the assumption that the text is in cell B10, here is how the formula looks:

```
=UPPER(LEFT(B10,1)) & RIGHT(B10,LEN(B10)-1)
```

In a nutshell, the UPPER function is applied to the first letter, which is isolated with the help of the LEFT function. Then this is concatenated with the remainder of the string. You know how much is left by using LEN to get the length of the string, and using the RIGHT function to get all the characters from the right, less one. Easy? Not quite? This type of multiuse function work takes a bit of getting used to.

Try this out:

1. **Enter a sentence in a cell.**

   Any old sentence will do but don't make any letters uppercase — for example, "excel is great" or "computers give me a headache."

2. **Position the cursor in an empty cell.**

3. **Enter =UPPER(to start the function.**

4. **Click on the cell that has the sentence, or enter its address.**

5. **Enter a closing parenthesis to end the function and press the Enter key.**

6. **In another empty cell, enter =PROPER(to start the function.**

7. **Click on the cell that has the sentence, or enter its address.**

8. **Enter a closing parenthesis to end the function and press the Enter key.**

   You should now have two cells that show the sentence with a case change. One cell has the sentence in uppercase, the other cell in proper case.

Finding Out about Text

Excel has many functions that manipulate text, but sometimes you just need to find out about the text before you do anything else! A handful of functions check if text matches other text, let you find text inside other text, and tell you how long a string is. The functions are passive — that is, they do not alter text.

Going for perfection with the EXACT function

The EXACT function lets you compare two strings of text to see if they're the same. The function takes two arguments — the two strings of text, and returns a True or False value. EXACT is case-sensitive, so two strings that contain the same letters but with differing case ("Apple" and "APPLE" for example) will produce a result of False (they are not identical).

EXACT is great for finding changes in data. Figure 16-10 shows two lists of employees, one for each year, in columns A and B. Are they identical? You could spend a number of minutes staring at the two lists. This would give us a headache! Or you can use EXACT. The cells in Column C contain the EXACT function, used to check Column A with Column B. The returned values are True for the most part. This means there is no change.

A few names are different in the second year. Marriage, divorce, misspellings — it could be any of these. EXACT returns False for these names, which means they aren't identical in the two lists and should be checked manually.

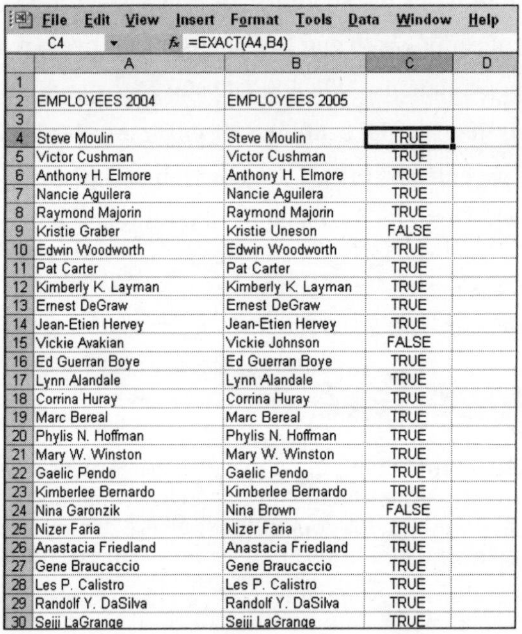

	A	B	C	D
1				
2	EMPLOYEES 2004	EMPLOYEES 2005		
3				
4	Steve Moulin	Steve Moulin	TRUE	
5	Victor Cushman	Victor Cushman	TRUE	
6	Anthony H. Elmore	Anthony H. Elmore	TRUE	
7	Nancie Aguilera	Nancie Aguilera	TRUE	
8	Raymond Majorin	Raymond Majorin	TRUE	
9	Kristie Graber	Kristie Uneson	FALSE	
10	Edwin Woodworth	Edwin Woodworth	TRUE	
11	Pat Carter	Pat Carter	TRUE	
12	Kimberly K. Layman	Kimberly K. Layman	TRUE	
13	Ernest DeGraw	Ernest DeGraw	TRUE	
14	Jean-Etien Hervey	Jean-Etien Hervey	TRUE	
15	Vickie Avakian	Vickie Johnson	FALSE	
16	Ed Guerran Boye	Ed Guerran Boye	TRUE	
17	Lynn Alandale	Lynn Alandale	TRUE	
18	Corrina Huray	Corrina Huray	TRUE	
19	Marc Bereal	Marc Bereal	TRUE	
20	Phylis N. Hoffman	Phylis N. Hoffman	TRUE	
21	Mary W. Winston	Mary W. Winston	TRUE	
22	Gaelic Pendo	Gaelic Pendo	TRUE	
23	Kimberlee Bernardo	Kimberlee Bernardo	TRUE	
24	Nina Garonzik	Nina Brown	FALSE	
25	Nizer Faria	Nizer Faria	TRUE	
26	Anastacia Friedland	Anastacia Friedland	TRUE	
27	Gene Braucaccio	Gene Braucaccio	TRUE	
28	Les P. Calistro	Les P. Calistro	TRUE	
29	Randolf Y. DaSilva	Randolf Y. DaSilva	TRUE	
30	Seiji LaGrange	Seiji LaGrange	TRUE	

Figure 16-10: Comparing strings with the EXACT function.

Here's how you use EXACT:

1. **Position the cursor in the cell where you want the results to appear.**
2. **Enter** =EXACT(**to begin the function entry.**
3. **Click on a cell that contains text, or enter its address.**
4. **Enter a comma (,).**

5. **Click on another cell that has text, or enter its address.**

6. **Enter a closing parenthesis to end the function, and press Enter.**

If you get a True result, the strings are identical. A False result means they're different.

Finding and searching

Two functions, FIND and SEARCH, work in a quite similar fashion. A couple of differences are key to figuring out which to use.

FIND finds one string inside a larger string, and tells you at what position in the larger string it begins. FIND is case-sensitive. It will not, for example, find "At" inside "heat."

FIND takes three arguments: the string to find; the larger string to search in; and the position in the larger string to start looking at. The third argument is optional. If left out, the function starts looking at the beginning of the larger string. Here are some examples:

Value in cell A1	Function	Result
Happy birthday to you	=FIND("Birthday",A1)	#VALUE!
Happy birthday to you	=FIND("birthday",A1)	7
Happy birthday to you	=FIND("y",A1)	5
Happy birthday to you	=FIND("y",A1,10)	14

In the first example using FIND, an error is returned. The #VALUE! error is what FIND returns if the text cannot be found. Birthday is not the same as birthday, at least to the case-sensitive FIND function.

The SEARCH function takes the same arguments as FIND. SEARCH differs from FIND in two key ways:

- ✔ SEARCH is not case-sensitive, FIND is case-sensitive.
- ✔ SEARCH can use wildcards in the first argument.

SEARCH recognizes two common wildcards: the asterisk (*) and the question mark (?). An asterisk tells the function to accept any number of characters (including zero characters). A question mark tells the function to accept any single character. It is not uncommon to see more than one question mark together as a wildcard pattern. Table 16-3 shows several examples.

Table 16-3	Using the SEARCH Function		
Value in Cell A1	**Function**	**Result**	**Comment**
Happy birthday to you	=SEARCH ("Birthday",A1)	7	Birthday starts in position 7.
Happy birthday to you	=SEARCH("y??",A1)	5	The first place where a *y* is followed by any two characters is at position 5. This is the last letter in *Happy,* a space, and the first letter in *birthday.*
Happy birthday to you	=SEARCH("yo?",A1)	19	The first place where *yo* is followed by any single character is the word *you.*
Happy birthday to you	=SEARCH("b*d",A1)	7	The search pattern is the letter *b,* followed by any number of characters, followed by the letter *d.* This starts in position 7. The best way to use an asterisk is between two fixed characters, as shown in this example.
Happy birthday to you	=SEARCH("*b",A1)	1	The asterisk says search for any number of characters before the letter *b.* The start of characters before the letter *b* is at position *1.* Using an asterisk at the start is not useful. It will either return a *1,* or an error if the fixed character or characters (the letter *b* in this example) is not in the larger text.
Happy birthday to you	=SEARCH("t*",A1)	10	The asterisk says search for any number of characters after the letter *t.* Because the search starts with a fixed character, its position is the result. The asterisk serves no purpose here.

Value in Cell A1	Function	Result	Comment
Happy birthday to you	=SEARCH("t", A,1,12)	16	Finds the position of the first letter *t,* starting after position 12. The result is the position of the first letter in the word *to.* The letter *t* in birthday is ignored.

Way, way back, in Figure 16-3, we showed you how to concatenate first and last names together. What if you have full names to separate into first names and last names? SEARCH to the rescue! (Does that make this a search-and-rescue mission?)

Figure 16-11 shows how the SEARCH, LEFT, RIGHT, and ISERROR functions work together to turn names into individual first and last names.

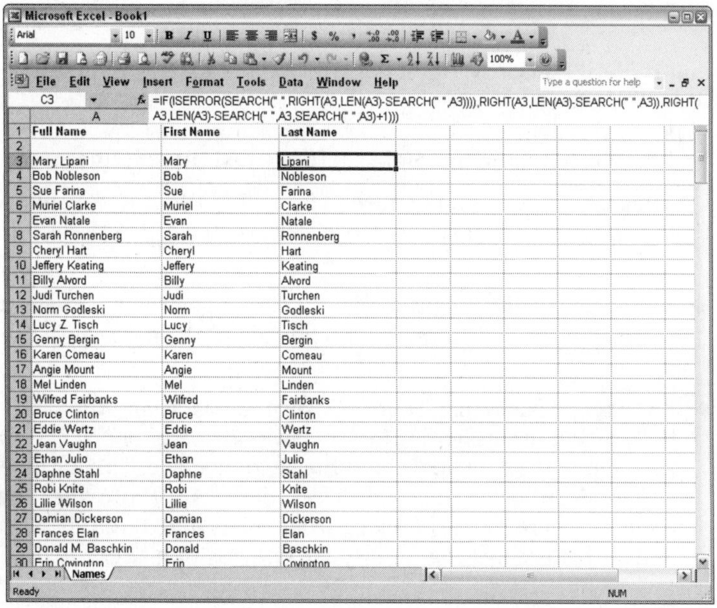

Figure 16-11: Splitting names apart.

Isolating the first name from a full name is straightforward. You just use LEFT to get characters up to the first space. The position of the first space is returned from the SEARCH function. Here is how this looks:

```
=LEFT(A3,SEARCH(" ",A3)-1)
```

Getting the last names is just as simple — *not!* When the full name has only first and last names (no middle name or initials), you need the SEARCH, RIGHT, and LEN, like this:

```
=RIGHT(A3,LEN(A3)-SEARCH(" ",A3))
```

However, this does not work for middle names or initials. Think of a name with a middle initial. How about Franklin D. Roosevelt. If you rely on the last name being after the first space, then the last name becomes D. Roosevelt. An honest mistake, but we can do better.

What you need is a way to test for the second space, and then return everything to the right of that space. There are likely a number of ways to do this. Here is the one we used in Column C, in Figure 16-11:

```
=IF(ISERROR(SEARCH(" ",RIGHT(A3,LEN(A3)-SEARCH("
          ",A3)))),RIGHT(A3,LEN(A3)-SEARCH("
          ",A3)),RIGHT(A3,LEN(A3)-SEARCH(" ",A3,SEARCH("
          ",A3)+1)))
```

Admittedly, it's a doozy. But it gets the job done. Here is an overview of what this formula does:

- ✔ It's an IF function, therefore there is a test that is either true or false.

- ✔ The test is if an error is returned from SEARCH for trying to find a space to the right of the first space: `ISERROR(SEARCH(" ",RIGHT(A3,LEN(A3) -SEARCH(" ",A3))))`.

- ✔ If the test is true, then there is no other space, which means there is no middle initial, so just return the portion of the name after the first space: `RIGHT(A3,LEN(A3)-SEARCH(" ",A3))`.

- ✔ If the test if false, then there is a second space, and the task is to return the portion of the string after the second space. SEARCH tells both the position of the first space and the second space. This is done by nesting one SEARCH inside the other. The inner SEARCH provides the third argument — where to start looking from. A 1 is added to this so the outer SEARCH starts looking for a space one position after the first space: `RIGHT(A3,LEN(A3)-SEARCH(" ",A3,SEARCH(" ",A3)+1))`.

We can only imagine the glazed-over eyes, but we're done! That's it!

Here's how to use FIND or SEARCH:

1. Position the cursor in the cell where you want the results to appear.

2. Enter either =FIND(**or** =SEARCH(**to begin the function entry.**

3. **Enter a string of text that you want to locate in a larger string, enclosed with double quotes; or click on a cell that contains the text.**

4. **Enter a comma (,).**

5. **Either click on a cell that contains the larger text, or enter its address.**

   If you want the function to begin searching at the start of the larger string then go to Step 7.

6. **If you want to have the function begin the search in the larger string at a position other than 1, enter a comma (,), and then the position number.**

7. **Enter a closing parenthesis to end the function, and press Enter.**

Finding out the long and short of it with the LEN function

The LEN function returns the length of a string. It takes a single argument — the string being evaluated. LEN is often used with other functions such as LEFT or RIGHT.

Manipulating text sometimes requires a little math. For example, you may need to calculate how many characters to isolate with the RIGHT function. A common configuration of functions to do this is RIGHT, SEARCH, and LEN, like this:

```
=RIGHT(A1,LEN(A1)- SEARCH(" ",A1))
```

This calculates the number of characters to return as the full count of characters less the position where the space is. Used with the RIGHT function, this then returns the characters to the right of the space.

The LEN function is often used with other functions, notably LEFT, RIGHT, and MID. In this manner, LEN helps determine the value of an argument to the other function.

Here's how to use LEN:

1. **Position the cursor in the cell where you want the results to appear.**

2. **Enter =LEN(to begin the function entry.**

3. **Click on a cell that contains text or enter its address, or just enter a string, enclosed with double quotes.**

4. **Enter a closing parenthesis to end the function, and press Enter.**

Chapter 17

Summarizing Data with Database Functions

*B*elieve it or not, an Excel worksheet has the same structure as a database table. A database table has fields and records; an Excel worksheet has columns and rows. Same thing. Given this fact, why not ask questions of, or query, your information in much the same way as is done with a database?

In this chapter, we tell you how to use Excel's database functions to get quick answers from sizeable lists of information. Let's say for example, you had a client list on a worksheet — name, address, that sort of thing. You want to know how many clients are in New York. You may think about sorting your list by state and then counting the number of rows. Forget it — that's the old way! In this chapter, we show you how to do this sort of thing with a single function.

Putting Your Data into a Database Structure

In order to use the database functions, you need to put your data into a structured format. Excel is very flexible. Usually, you put data wherever you want.

But to make the best of the database functions, you need to get your data into a contiguous area of rows and columns.

Figure 17-1 shows a database on a worksheet. This example is a list of students (by ID number), and the class, teacher, and grade for each student. Each student occupies a row in the database. There are four fields: Student ID, Class, Teacher, and Final Grade. Each field is in one column.

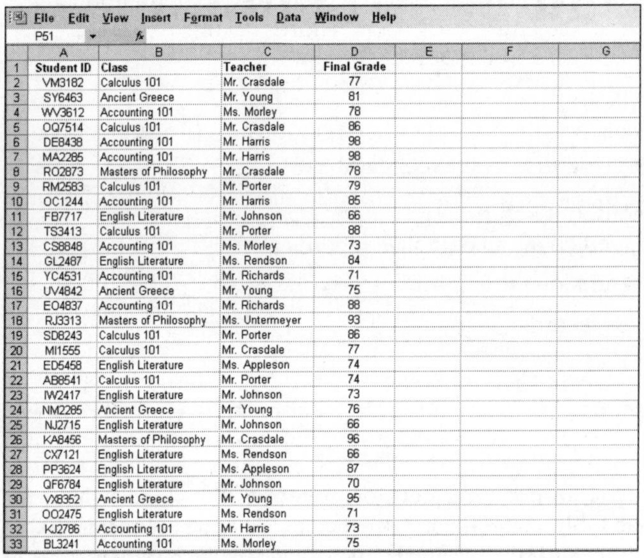

	A	B	C	D	E	F	G
1	Student ID	Class	Teacher	Final Grade			
2	VM3182	Calculus 101	Mr. Crasdale	77			
3	SY6463	Ancient Greece	Mr. Young	81			
4	WV3612	Accounting 101	Ms. Morley	78			
5	OQ7514	Calculus 101	Mr. Crasdale	86			
6	DE8438	Accounting 101	Mr. Harris	98			
7	MA2285	Accounting 101	Mr. Harris	98			
8	RO2873	Masters of Philosophy	Mr. Crasdale	78			
9	RM2583	Calculus 101	Mr. Porter	79			
10	OC1244	Accounting 101	Mr. Harris	85			
11	FB7717	English Literature	Mr. Johnson	66			
12	TS3413	Calculus 101	Mr. Porter	88			
13	CS8848	Accounting 101	Ms. Morley	73			
14	GL2487	English Literature	Ms. Rendson	84			
15	YC4531	Accounting 101	Mr. Richards	71			
16	UV4842	Ancient Greece	Mr. Young	75			
17	EO4837	Accounting 101	Mr. Richards	88			
18	RJ3313	Masters of Philosophy	Ms. Untermeyer	93			
19	SD8243	Calculus 101	Mr. Porter	86			
20	MI1555	Calculus 101	Mr. Crasdale	77			
21	ED5458	English Literature	Ms. Appleson	74			
22	AB8541	Calculus 101	Mr. Porter	74			
23	IW2417	English Literature	Mr. Johnson	73			
24	NM2285	Ancient Greece	Mr. Young	76			
25	NJ2715	English Literature	Mr. Johnson	66			
26	KA8456	Masters of Philosophy	Mr. Crasdale	96			
27	CX7121	English Literature	Ms. Rendson	66			
28	PP3624	English Literature	Ms. Appleson	87			
29	QF6784	English Literature	Mr. Johnson	70			
30	VX8352	Ancient Greece	Mr. Young	95			
31	OO2475	English Literature	Ms. Rendson	71			
32	KJ2786	Accounting 101	Mr. Harris	73			
33	BL3241	Accounting 101	Ms. Morley	75			

Figure 17-1: Using a database to store student information.

The data on the worksheet in Figure 17-1 is really just normal data. There is nothing special about it. However, the data sits in organized rows and columns, making it ready for working with Excel's database functions:

- Each column is a field that holds one particular item of data, such as Student ID or Class. It must contain no other data.
- Each row is a field that contains one record. In this example, a record is the data for one student.
- The top row of the database contains labels that identify the fields.

This sample data is used to describe the database functions.

Understanding How the Database Functions Work

The database functions all follow the same format. These functions all use the following three arguments:

- ✔ **The database range:** This argument tells the function where the database is. You enter it using cell addresses (for example, A1:D200) or a named range (for example, Students).

- ✔ **The field:** You must tell a database function which field to operate on. You can't expect it to figure this out by itself! You can enter either the column number or the field heading. A column number, if used, is the number of the column offset from the first column of the database area. In other words, if a database starts in Column C, and the field is in Column E, the column number is 3, not 5.If a heading is used, put it inside a set of double quotation marks. Database functions calculate a result based on the values in this field. Just how many values are used depends on the third argument — the criteria.

- ✔ **The criteria:** This tells the function where the criteria are located. The criteria tell the function which records to use. The criteria are set up in a separate part of the worksheet that is not part of the database area, and you include the criteria range for this argument. Criteria use a heading and a value. The heading is the same as a field name, and a particular value goes underneath the heading. You can use an empty value to get a database function to operate on all the records in the database. We show you in more detail how criteria work throughout the chapter.

Establishing your database

All database functions take a database reference as the first argument. The database area must include headers (field names) in the first row. In Figure 17-1, the first row uses Student ID, Class, Teacher, and Final Grade as headers to the information in each respective column.

A great way to work with the database functions is to give the database area a name. Then you enter the name into the function instead of the range address. To set up a name, follow these steps:

1. **Select the database area.**

   Make sure the top row has headers and is included in the selection.

2. **Choose Insert ➪ Name ➪ Define.**

   The Define Name dialog box appears. The dialog box will already have the range set in the Refers To box.

3. **Type a name in the top box (or use the suggested name).**

4. **Click OK to close the dialog box.**

Later, if records are added to the bottom of the database, the range of the named area will have to be redefined. You can do this by going back into the Define Name dialog box and adjusting the reference. Here's how:

1. **Choose Insert ➪ Name ➪ Define to open the Define Name dialog box.**

2. **Click the named area in the Names in Workbook list.**

   Figure 17-2 shows an example of the Database_Area named area selected.

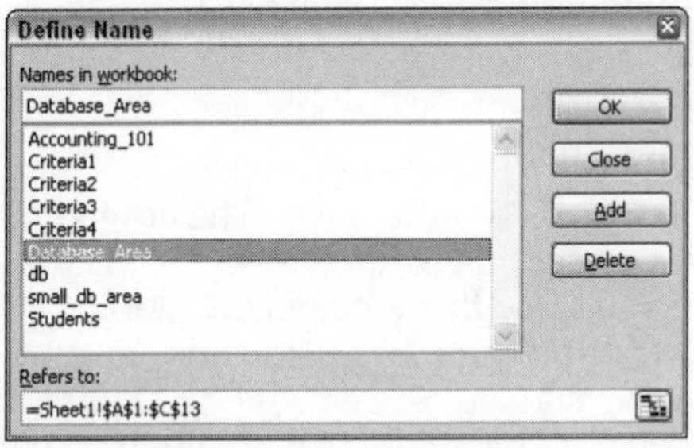

Figure 17-2:
Updating the reference to a named area.

```
Define Name                                       ×
Names in workbook:
Database_Area
Accounting_101                              OK
Criteria1
Criteria2                                   Close
Criteria3
Criteria4                                   Add
Database_Area
db                                          Delete
small_db_area
Students
Refers to:
=Sheet1!$A$1:$C$13
```

3. **Change the reference in the Refers To box.**

   You can use the small square button to the right of the Refers to box to define the new reference by dragging the mouse pointer over it. Clicking the small square button reduces the size of the Define Name dialog box and allows you access to the worksheet. When you are done dragging the mouse over the new worksheet area, press Enter to get back to the Define Name dialog box.

4. **Click the OK button to save the reference change and close the dialog box.**

Establishing the criteria area

The database functions look to an area of the worksheet that you specify to be the criteria. The criteria area can contain one or more individual criterion; each individual criterion is structured as follows:

✔ In one cell, enter the field name (header) of the database column that the criterion will be for.

✔ In the cell below, enter the value that the field data must meet.

Figure 17-3 shows the student database with a criteria area to the right of the database. There are places to put criterion for the Class, Teacher, and Final Grade. In the example, criterion has been set for the Class. The criterion will force the database function to only process records (rows) where the Class is Accounting 101. Note, though, that a criterion can be set for more than one field. In this example, the Teacher and Final Grade criteria have been left blank so they don't affect the results.

The DAVERAGE function has been entered into cell F8. The three arguments are in place: The name Students is used to tell the function where the database is; the Final Grade field (column) is where the function finds values to calculate; and the criteria are set to the worksheet range that contains the criteria that tell the function to use only records where the Class is Accounting 101. The entry in cell F8 looks like this:

```
=DAVERAGE(Students,"Final Grade",F2:F3)
```

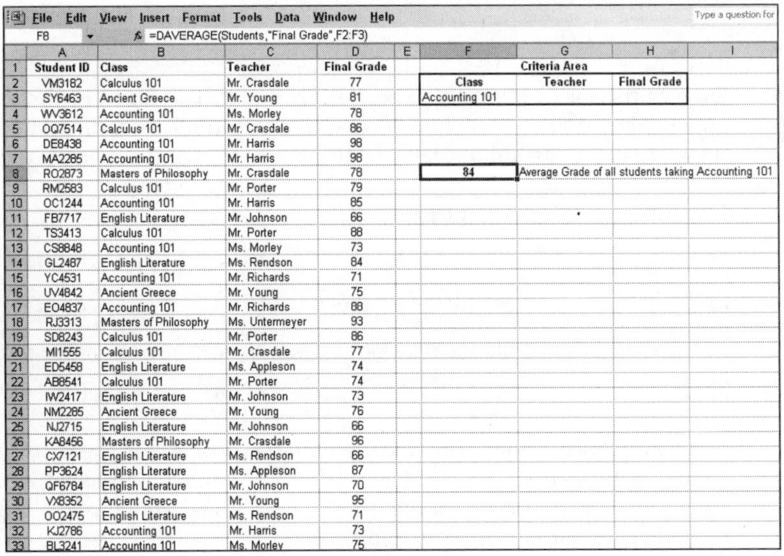

Figure 17-3: Selecting criteria to use with a database function.

You may notice that the DAVERAGE formula in Figure 17-3 does *not* make use of a named criteria area. It usually makes sense to name the database area itself, because this information is usually static. Even if rows are added or deleted, the name updates to reflect the correct range.

Using a named area for the criteria is not so simple. Figure 17-4 shows the Student database with four different criteria areas. These areas have all been named as Criteria1, Criteria2, Criteria3, and Criteria4. (How's that for original?)

	B	C	D	E	F	G	H	I	J
1	Class	Teacher	Final Grade		Criteria1				
2	Calculus 101	Mr. Crasdale	77		Class	Teacher			
3	Ancient Greece	Mr. Young	81		Accounting 101	Ms. Morley			
4	Accounting 101	Ms. Morley	78		28				
5	Calculus 101	Mr. Crasdale	86						
6	Accounting 101	Mr. Harris	98						
7	Accounting 101	Mr. Harris	98		Criteria 2				
8	Masters of Philosophy	Mr. Crasdale	78		Class	Teacher			
9	Calculus 101	Mr. Porter	79		Accounting 101	Ms. Morley			
10	Accounting 101	Mr. Harris	85		Accounting 101	Mr. Harris			
11	English Literature	Mr. Johnson	66		54				
12	Calculus 101	Mr. Porter	88						
13	Accounting 101	Ms. Morley	73						
14	English Literature	Ms. Rendson	84						
15	Accounting 101	Mr. Richards	71		Criteria 3				
16	Ancient Greece	Mr. Young	75		Class	Teacher			
17	Accounting 101	Mr. Richards	88		Accounting 101	Ms. Morley			
18	Masters of Philosophy	Ms. Untermeyer	93						
19	Calculus 101	Mr. Porter	86		203				
20	Calculus 101	Mr. Crasdale	77						
21	English Literature	Ms. Appleson	74						
22	Calculus 101	Mr. Porter	74						
23	English Literature	Mr. Johnson	73		Criteria4				
24	Ancient Greece	Mr. Young	76		Class	Teacher			
25	English Literature	Mr. Johnson	66		Accounting 101	Ms. Morley			
26	Masters of Philosophy	Mr. Crasdale	96		Accounting 101	Mr. Harris			
27	English Literature	Ms. Rendson	66		28				
28	English Literature	Ms. Appleson	87						
29	English Literature	Mr. Johnson	70						
30	Ancient Greece	Mr. Young	95						
31	English Literature	Ms. Rendson	71						
32	Accounting 101	Mr. Harris	73						
33	Accounting 101	Ms. Morley	75						

F4 ▼ =DCOUNT(Students,"Final Grade",Criteria1)

Figure 17-4: Using named criteria areas.

Each criteria area has a thick border around it. The name is above each one, and a calculated value is below each one. Although all four calculations are trying to calculate similar answers, only the first and second are correct.

Cell	Formula
F4	=DCOUNT(Students,"Final Grade",Criteria1)
F11	=DCOUNT(Students,"Final Grade",Criteria2)
F19	=DCOUNT(Students,"Final Grade",Criteria3)
F27	=DCOUNT(Students,"Final Grade",Criteria4)

The problem isn't the formulas; instead, the problem is the result of how the named criteria areas are used. Essentially, the named areas are prone to providing too much or not enough criteria. Table 17-1 summarizes how the named criteria areas are returning correct or incorrect results.

Table 17-1		Why Named Criteria Areas Are a Problem
Criteria Area Name	*Criteria Range*	*What Happens*
Criteria1	F2:G3	The criteria say to use the records where the class is Accounting 101 and the teacher is Ms. Morley. The size of the named criteria matches the criteria itself and the correct answer is calculated.
Criteria2	F8:G10	The criteria say to use the records where the class is Accounting 101 and the teacher is either Ms. Morley or Mr. Harris. The size of the named criteria matches the criteria itself and the correct answer is calculated.
Criteria3	F16:G18	The criteria, unintentionally, say to use the records where the class is Accounting 101 and the teacher is Ms. Morley, or where the class and teacher don't matter. Because the named criteria area is larger than the supplied criterions and contains a couple of blank cells, the function returns a result based on incorrect criteria. The result is that all the database records are used in the calculation.
Criteria4	F24:G25	The intention is for the criteria to say to use the records where the class is Accounting 101 and the teacher is either Ms. Morley or Mr. Harris. However the named criteria area is too small and, therefore, the calculation does not take Mr. Harris into account.

Giving the criteria area a name may not make sense. If the amount of criteria used changes from time to time, then using a fixed area may give incorrect results. In this case, you're better off just typing in the range address where the criteria are located. If the size of the criteria and the amount of criteria stay constant, then a named area makes sense.

Here's how you enter any of the database functions. This example uses the DSUM function but the instructions are the same for all the database functions:

1. **Import or create a database of information on a worksheet.**

   The information should be in contiguous rows and columns. Be sure to use field headers.

2. **Optionally, use the Define Name dialog box to give the database a name.**

   To name your database, see the section on "Establishing your database."

3. **Select a portion of the worksheet to be the criteria area, then provide headers in this area that match database headers.**

   You only have to provide criteria headers for database fields that criteria are applied to. For example, your database area may have 10 columns, but you only apply criteria on 3 columns. Therefore the criteria area can be 3 columns wide.

4. **Position the cursor in the cell where you want the results to appear.**

   This cell must not be in the database area or the criteria area.

5. **Enter =DSUM(to begin the function entry.**

6. **Enter the range of the database, or a name if one is set.**

7. **Enter a comma (,).**

8. **Either enter the header name, in quotes, of the database field that the function should process, or just enter the column number.**

9. **Enter a comma (,).**

10. **Enter the range of the criteria area.**

11. **Enter a closing parenthesis to end the function, and press Enter.**

Adding Up Only What Matters with DSUM

The DSUM function lets you sum up numbers in a database column for just those rows that match the criteria you specify. Figure 17-5 shows an example using DSUM. The hypothetical students in Accounting 101 decided that the class that scored the highest cumulative grade would throw the end-of-the-school-year party (there are three different teachers). Because the class sizes are close, the students didn't worry whether any single class would have an advantage. After all, a smaller class filled with bright students can beat a larger class with a few students that get a low grade.

To calculate this, three criteria areas are created. All three set Accounting 101 as the class, but then each criteria area uses a different teacher to filter records. Thus, there are three different answers, in cells F12:F14. Each of the cells holds an identical formula, except for where the DSUM function looks for criteria. For example, here is the formula in cell F14:

```
=DSUM(Students,"Final Grade",F8:G9)
```

Figure 17-5 shows how the worksheet is set up to calculate this problem. Ms. Morley's class has the highest overall grade. We hear there will be pizza, ice cream cake, and a stand-up comedian. See you there!

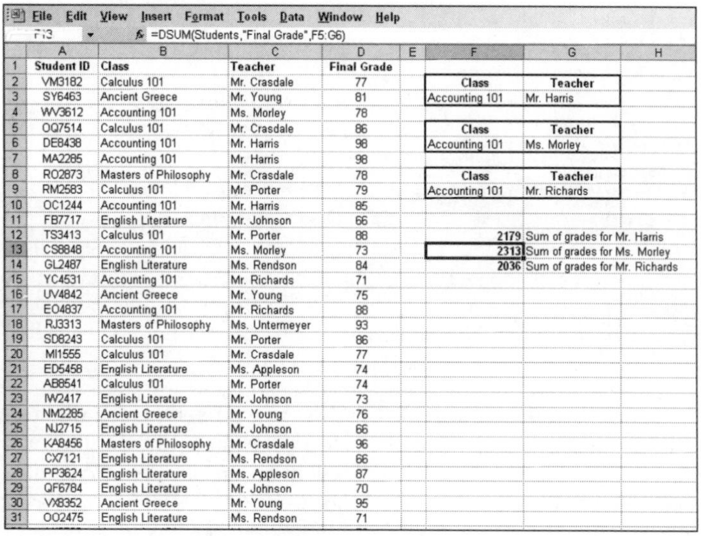

	A	B	C	D	E	F	G	H
1	Student ID	Class	Teacher	Final Grade				
2	VM3182	Calculus 101	Mr. Crasdale	77		Class	Teacher	
3	SY6463	Ancient Greece	Mr. Young	81		Accounting 101	Mr. Harris	
4	WV3612	Accounting 101	Ms. Morley	78				
5	OQ7514	Calculus 101	Mr. Crasdale	86		Class	Teacher	
6	DE8438	Accounting 101	Mr. Harris	98		Accounting 101	Ms. Morley	
7	MA2285	Accounting 101	Mr. Harris	98				
8	RO2873	Masters of Philosophy	Mr. Crasdale	78		Class	Teacher	
9	RM2583	Calculus 101	Mr. Porter	79		Accounting 101	Mr. Richards	
10	OC1244	Accounting 101	Mr. Harris	85				
11	FB7717	English Literature	Mr. Johnson	66				
12	TS3413	Calculus 101	Mr. Porter	88		2179	Sum of grades for Mr. Harris	
13	CS8848	Accounting 101	Ms. Morley	73		2313	Sum of grades for Ms. Morley	
14	GL2487	English Literature	Ms. Rendson	84		2036	Sum of grades for Mr. Richards	
15	YC4531	Accounting 101	Mr. Richards	71				
16	UV4842	Ancient Greece	Mr. Young	75				
17	EO4837	Accounting 101	Mr. Richards	88				
18	RJ3313	Masters of Philosophy	Ms. Untermeyer	93				
19	SD8243	Calculus 101	Mr. Porter	86				
20	MI1555	Calculus 101	Mr. Crasdale	77				
21	ED5458	English Literature	Ms. Appleson	74				
22	AB8541	Calculus 101	Mr. Porter	74				
23	IW2417	English Literature	Mr. Johnson	73				
24	NM2285	Ancient Greece	Mr. Young	76				
25	NJ2715	English Literature	Mr. Johnson	66				
26	KA8456	Masters of Philosophy	Mr. Crasdale	96				
27	CX7121	English Literature	Ms. Rendson	66				
28	PP3624	English Literature	Ms. Appleson	87				
29	QF6784	English Literature	Mr. Johnson	70				
30	VX8352	Ancient Greece	Mr. Young	95				
31	OO2475	English Literature	Ms. Rendson	71				

Figure 17-5: Calculating the sum of grades with the DSUM function.

Going For the Middle with DAVERAGE

The DAVERAGE function lets you find an average for a group of numbers in a database column, for just the rows that match the criteria.

Figure 17-6 shows a worksheet in which the average grade for each course has been calculated. For example, cell G22 shows the average grade for English Literature. Here is the formula:

```
=DAVERAGE(Students,"Final Grade",F11:G12)
```

Each calculated average uses a different criteria area. Each area filters the result by a particular course. In all cases, the criteria area for the Teacher is left blank. Therefore, the results are based on all students taking the course, regardless of who teaches the course.

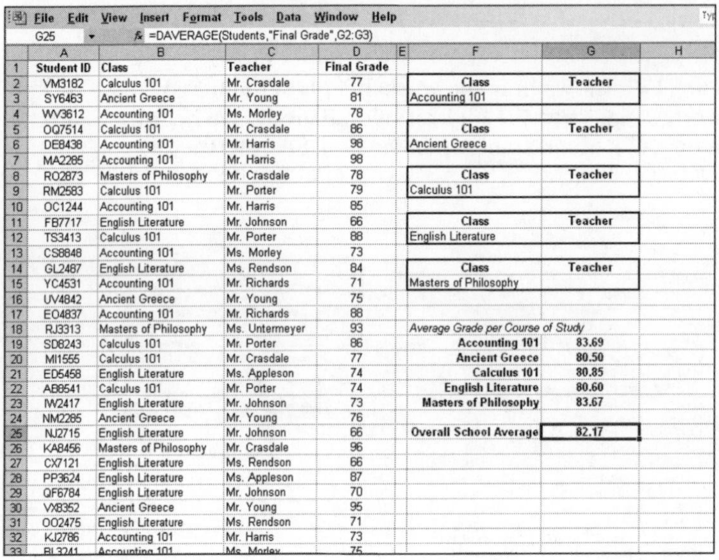

Figure 17-6:
Calculating the average grade per course of study.

For the sake of comparison, DAVERAGE is also used in cell G25 to show the overall school average. Because a criterion is a required function argument, the calculation in cell G25 is set to look at an empty cell. None of the Class criteria cells are free, so the function looks to the Teacher criterion in cell G3. Because this cell has no particular teacher entered as a criterion, the entire database is used to create the result. Here is the formula in cell G25:

```
=DAVERAGE(Students,"Final Grade",G2:G3)
```

It doesn't matter which field header is used in the criterion when getting a result based on all records in a database. What does matter is that there is no actual criterion underneath the header.

Counting Only What Counts with DCOUNT

The DCOUNT function lets you calculate a count of records, or rows, that match the criteria.

Figure 17-7 shows how DCOUNT is used to count how many students are in each course. Cells G19:G23 contain formulas that count records based on the criterion (the CLASS) in the associated criteria sections. Here is the formula used in cell G21, which counts the number of students in Calculus 101:

```
=DCOUNT(Students,"Final Grade",F8:G9)
```

Note that DCOUNT requires a column of numbers to count on. Therefore, the Final Grade heading is put in the function. Using Class or Teacher to count on would result in zero. Having to use a column that specifically has numbers may seem a little odd. The function is not summing the numbers, it just counts the number of records. But what the heck? It works.

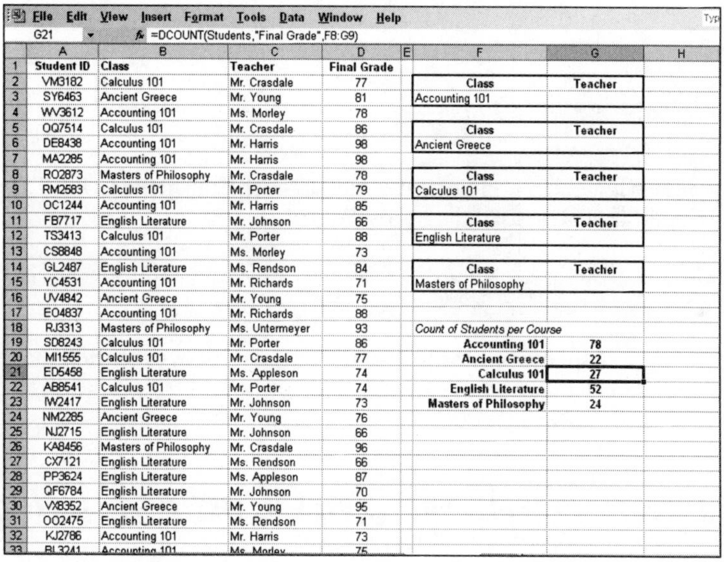

Figure 17-7: Calculating the number of students per course of study.

Let's take this a step further. How about counting the number of students who got a grade of 90 or better? How can this be done?

This calculation requires a change in the criterion. You're no longer looking to segregate answers by Class. So, one criteria section will do, only now you're filtering on the actual grade. Figure 17-8 shows a worksheet with this type of criterion.

| | File | Edit | View | Insert | Format | Tools | Data | Window | Help | | |

| F6 | | | | =DCOUNT(Students,"Final Grade",F2:F3) &" students received a 90 or better." | | | |

	A	B	C	D	E	F
1	Student ID	Class	Teacher	Final Grade		
2	VM3182	Calculus 101	Mr. Crasdale	77		Final Grade
3	SY6463	Ancient Greece	Mr. Young	81		>89
4	WV3612	Accounting 101	Ms. Morley	78		
5	OQ7514	Calculus 101	Mr. Crasdale	86		
6	DE8438	Accounting 101	Mr. Harris	98		52 students received a 90 or better.
7	MA2285	Accounting 101	Mr. Harris	98		
8	RO2873	Masters of Philosophy	Mr. Crasdale	78		
9	RM2583	Calculus 101	Mr. Porter	79		
10	OC1244	Accounting 101	Mr. Harris	85		
11	FB7717	English Literature	Mr. Johnson	66		
12	TS3413	Calculus 101	Mr. Porter	88		
13	CS8848	Accounting 101	Ms. Morley	73		
14	GL2487	English Literature	Ms. Rendson	84		
15	YC4531	Accounting 101	Mr. Richards	71		
16	UV4842	Ancient Greece	Mr. Young	75		
17	EO4837	Accounting 101	Mr. Richards	88		
18	RJ3313	Masters of Philosophy	Ms. Untermeyer	93		
19	SD8243	Calculus 101	Mr. Porter	86		
20	MI1555	Calculus 101	Mr. Crasdale	77		
21	ED5458	English Literature	Ms. Appleson	74		
22	AB9541	Calculus 101	Mr. Porter	74		
23	IW2417	English Literature	Mr. Johnson	73		
24	NM2285	Ancient Greece	Mr. Young	76		
25	NJ2715	English Literature	Mr. Johnson	66		
26	KA8456	Masters of Philosophy	Mr. Crasdale	96		
27	CX7121	English Literature	Ms. Rendson	66		
28	PP3624	English Literature	Ms. Appleson	87		
29	QF6784	English Literature	Mr. Johnson	70		
30	VX8352	Ancient Greece	Mr. Young	95		
31	OO2475	English Literature	Ms. Rendson	71		

Figure 17-8:
Calculating
the number
of students
that earned
a certain
grade.

The result in cell F6 concatenates the answer from the DCOUNT function with a string of text. The formula looks like this:

```
=DCOUNT(Students,"Final Grade",F2:F3) & " students received a
           90 or better."
```

The criterion specifically states to use all records where the Final Grade is greater than 89.

Finding the Highest and Lowest Values

The DMIN and DMAX functions find the minimum or maximum value, respectively, in a database column, for just the rows that match the criteria. Figure 17-9 shows how these two functions have been used to find the highest and lowest grade for English Literature.

The formulas in cells F8 and F10 are practically identical. Here is the formula in cell F8:

```
="The highest grade in " & $F$3 & " is " &
           DMAX(Students,"Final Grade",$F$2:$F$3)
```

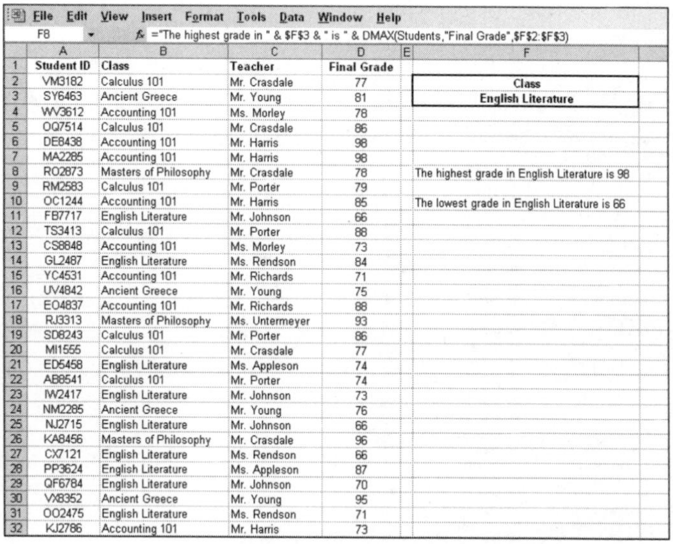

Figure 17-9: Calculating the highest and lowest grades.

Using DGET to Find Duplicate Values

DGET is a unique database function. It returns three possible values:

- ✔ If one record matches based on the criteria, DGET returns the criteria.
- ✔ If no records match based on the criteria, DGET returns the #VALUE! error.
- ✔ If more than one record matches based on the criteria, DGET returns the #NUM! error.

By building in a test to see if DGET returns an error, you can discover problems with your data. Imagine this: A teacher alerts you that a student is registered twice for his course. Therefore, in the database there probably are two records that have the same Student ID and Class.

Figure 17-10 shows this on a worksheet. The RM2583 Student ID is being tested for duplicate entry in the Calculus 101 course. If there is more than one record, sure enough, an error will appear.

Cell F5 contains a formula that nests the DGET function inside the ISERROR function, and then all of that is inside the IF function. So, if DGET returns an error, return such a message; otherwise, return a different message. Here is the formula:

```
=IF(ISERROR(DGET(Students,"Student ID",F2:G3)),F3 & " has
            duplicate records", F3 & " has one record")
```

	A	B	C	D	E	F	G	H
1	Student ID	Class	Teacher	Final Grade				
2	VM3182	Calculus 101	Mr. Crasdale	77		Student ID	Class	
3	SY6463	Ancient Greece	Mr. Young	81		RM2583	Calculus 101	
4	WV3612	Accounting 101	Ms. Morley	78				
5	OQ7514	Calculus 101	Mr. Crasdale	86		RM2583 has duplicate records		
6	DE8436	Accounting 101	Mr. Harris	98				
7	MA2285	Accounting 101	Mr. Harris	98				
8	RO2873	Masters of Philosophy	Mr. Crasdale	78				
9	RM2583	Calculus 101	Mr. Porter	79				
10	OC1244	Accounting 101	Mr. Harris	85				
11	FB7717	English Literature	Mr. Johnson	66				
12	TS3413	Calculus 101	Mr. Porter	88				
13	CS8848	Accounting 101	Ms. Morley	73				
14	GL2487	English Literature	Ms. Rendson	84				
15	YC4531	Accounting 101	Mr. Richards	71				
16	UV4842	Ancient Greece	Mr. Young	75				
17	EO4837	Accounting 101	Mr. Richards	88				
18	RJ3313	Masters of Philosophy	Ms. Untermeyer	93				
19	SD8243	Calculus 101	Mr. Porter	86				
20	MI1555	Calculus 101	Mr. Crasdale	77				
21	ED5458	English Literature	Ms. Appleson	74				
22	AB8541	Calculus 101	Mr. Porter	74				
23	IW2417	English Literature	Mr. Johnson	73				
24	NM2285	Ancient Greece	Mr. Young	76				
25	NJ2715	English Literature	Mr. Johnson	66				
26	KA8456	Masters of Philosophy	Mr. Crasdale	96				
27	CX7121	English Literature	Ms. Rendson	66				
28	PP3624	English Literature	Ms. Appleson	87				
29	QF6784	English Literature	Mr. Johnson	70				
30	VX8352	Ancient Greece	Mr. Young	95				
31	OO2475	English Literature	Ms. Rendson	71				
32	KJ2786	Accounting 101	Mr. Harris	73				
33	RL3241	Accounting 101	Ms. Morley	75				

Figure 17-10: Using DGET to test for duplicate records.

Getting Criteria to Work the Way You Want

Excel's database functions would not be of much use if you could not create sophisticated queries. A few common query uses include the following:

- Find out a result based on criteria that fall between two values (such as a low and high number)

- Find out a result based on criteria that have to match all conditions (uses AND logic)

- Find out a result based on criteria that have to match any conditions (uses OR logic)

- Find out a result based on criteria that match a pattern

Figure 17-11 shows a rather busy worksheet that shows how all these types of queries are assembled. There are several criteria areas and several calculations.

| | File | Edit | View | Insert | Format | Tools | Data | Window | Help | | | Type a questic |
| | F29 | | | ƒx | =DCOUNT(Students,"Final Grade",F27:F28) | | | | | | | |

	A	B	C	D	E	F	G	H	I
1	Student ID	Class	Teacher	Final Grade		BETWEEN			
2	VM3182	Calculus 201	Mr. Crasdale	77		Final Grade	Final Grade		
3	SY6463	Ancient Greece	Mr. Young	81		>=80	<=90		
4	WV3612	Accounting 101	Ms. Morley	78		63	Students with grade between 80 and 90		
5	OQ7514	Calculus 201	Mr. Crasdale	86					
6	DE8438	Accounting 101	Mr. Harris	98		AND			
7	MA2285	Accounting 101	Mr. Harris	98		Class	Teacher		
8	RO2873	Masters of Philosophy	Mr. Crasdale	78		Accounting 101	Mr. Harris		
9	RM2583	Calculus 101	Mr. Porter	79		26	Students in Accounting 101 with Harris		
10	OC1244	Accounting 101	Mr. Harris	85					
11	FB7717	English Literature	Mr. Johnson	66					
12	TS3413	Calculus 101	Mr. Porter	88		AND with OR			
13	CS8848	Accounting 101	Ms. Morley	73		Class	Teacher		
14	GL2487	English Literature	Ms. Rendson	84		Accounting 101	Mr. Harris		
15	YC4531	Accounting 101	Mr. Richards	71		Accounting 101	Mr. Richards		
16	UV4842	Ancient Greece	Mr. Young	75		50	Students in Accounting 101		
17	EO4837	Accounting 101	Mr. Richards	88			with Harris or Richards		
18	RJ3313	Masters of Philosophy	Ms. Untermeyer	93					
19	SD8243	Calculus 101	Mr. Porter	86		OR			
20	MI1555	Calculus 201	Mr. Crasdale	77		Class	Teacher		
21	ED5458	English Literature	Ms. Appleson	74		Ancient Greece			
22	AB8541	Calculus 101	Mr. Porter	74			Ms. Rendson		
23	IW2417	English Literature	Mr. Johnson	73		40	Student who are in Ancient Greece OR		
24	NM2285	Ancient Greece	Mr. Young	76			have Ms. Rendson		
25	NJ2715	English Literature	Mr. Johnson	66					
26	KA8456	Masters of Philosophy	Mr. Crasdale	96		PATTERN			
27	CX7121	English Literature	Ms. Rendson	66		Class			
28	PP3624	English Literature	Ms. Appleson	87		Calc			
29	QF6784	English Literature	Mr. Johnson	70		27	Students in any Calculus class		
30	VX8352	Ancient Greece	Mr. Young	95					
31	OO2475	English Literature	Ms. Rendson	71					
32	KJ2786	Accounting 101	Mr. Harris	73					

Figure 17-11: Creating sophisticated queries.

Let's take each type of query one-by-one. In all these examples, the DCOUNT function is used to count records that meet the criteria.

Finding records that have values in a range

To create criteria that look for records that match a range of values, set up two columns in the criteria area that filter on the *same* field. Then enter conditions that filter in opposing directions.

Cell F4 reports the count of how many students received a grade *between* 80 and 90. The criteria used here is in F2:G3. The criteria area has two headers, but they are both for the same field! One of the criterions says to look for records that have a Final Grade of 80 or greater. The other criterion says to look for records that have a Final Grade of 90 or less.

Normally, either one of these criterion conditions would return a greater number when used by itself. For example, if the only criterion was to find records where the Final Grade was 90 or less, then the count would be higher (unless maybe this is M.I.T or Harvard). But taken together, only records that match both of the conditions are counted.

Finding records that must match more than one condition

To create criteria that look for records that must match on more than one field, set up a column in the criteria area for each of the fields. Enter the criteria in the same row.

Cell F9 reports the count of students who are in Accounting 101 *and* have Mr. Harris for the teacher. The criteria used here is in F7:G8. Both conditions must be met because the criteria conditions are in the same row.

A common query is where one condition is fixed on one value, but the second condition can be based on more than one value. Cell F16 reports the count of students in Accounting 101 that have Mr. Harris or Mr. Roberts. Two conditions must still be met. However, the second criterion can now be more than one value — Mr. Harris *or* Mr. Roberts. The criteria used here is in F13:G15.

Finding records that match one or more conditions

To create criteria that look for records that can match on one field *or* another, set up a column in the criteria area for each of the fields. However, do not enter the actual criteria in the same row. Instead, enter the criteria in different rows. The criteria area must be sized to accommodate this.

Cell F23 reports the count of students that are in the Ancient Greece class *or* have Ms. Rendson. The criteria used here is in F20:G22.

Finding records that match a pattern

By default, the Excel database functions use partial criteria to find records. To demonstrate this, some of the records have been changed from Calculus 101 to Calculus 201. Now there are students in both classes but they are all in Calc, which serves as a pattern to finding records for both Calculus 101 and Calculus 102.

Cell F29 reports the count of students taking one or the other class, because the criteria (in F27:F28) tells the function to use the partial spelling.

Part V
The Part of Tens

The 5th Wave
By Rich Tennant

"WHAT EXACTLY ARE WE SAYING HERE?"

In this part . . .

*J*ust when you think you discovered it all, we show you more! This part includes the top ten tips for working with formulas. Some real gemstones are here that will make your work easier than ever. Did you know that you can even write your own functions? Yes, you can! Part V also has our list of the top ten functions. Well actually fifteen of them. They're all so good we had to include them all. Last in this part is an introduction to the Analysis ToolPak. This add-in utility gives you even more functions and functionality. Advanced math, finance, and statistical goodies abound. The hits just keep on coming!

Chapter 18

Ten + One Great Tips for Working with Formulas

Several elements can help you be as productive as possible when writing and correcting formulas. You can view all your formulas at once and correct errors one by one. You can use add-in wizards to help write functions. You can even create functions all on your own!

Operator Precedence

One of the most important factors when writing formulas is to get the operators correct. We do not mean the telephone company operators. This has to do with mathematical operators. You know, little details such as plus signs, and multiplication signs, and where the parentheses go. Operator precedence — the order in which operations are performed — can make a big difference in the result. You have an easy way to keep your operator precedence in order. All you have to remember is "Please excuse my dear Aunt Sally."

No, we have not lost our minds! This phrase is a mnemonic for:

1. Parentheses

2. Exponents

3. Multiplication

4. Division

5. Addition

6. Subtraction

Thus, parentheses have the first (highest) precedence and subtraction has the last precedence. Well, to be honest, multiplication has the same precedence as division, and addition has the same precedence as subtraction, but you get the idea!

For example, the formula =1 + 2 × 15 equals 31. If you think it should equal 45 then you better go visit our aunt! The answer will equal 45 if you include parenthesis, such as this: =(1 + 2) × 15.

Getting the order of the operators correct is critical to the well-being of your worksheet. Excel generates an error when the number of open and closed parentheses does not match, but if you meant to add two numbers before the multiplication, Excel will not know that you simply left the parentheses out!

A few minutes of refreshing your memory on operator order can save you a lot of headaches down the road.

Display Formulas

In case you haven't noticed, it's kind of hard to view your formulas without accidentally editing them. That's because any time you are in "edit" mode and the active cell has a formula, the formula might incorporate the address of any other cell you click. This totally messes things up.

Wouldn't it be easy if you could just *look* at all your formulas? Well there is a way! It's simple. Go to the Options dialog (choose Tools ⇨ Options). Then click the View Tab. Figure 18-1 shows the dialog box with the View tab on top.

Figure 18-1:
Setting
Options.

Notice under Window options is a check box for Formulas. This box tells Excel that for any cells that have formulas, to display the formula itself instead of the calculated result. Figure 18-2 shows a worksheet that displays the formulas. To return to normal view, repeat these steps and uncheck the Formulas option.

	F	G	H	I	J	
22	=D22/E22	=D22-F22	0	=G22+H22	=IF(B22=0,"NA",I22/B22)	=
23	=D23/E23	=D23-F23	0	=G23+H23	=IF(B23=0,"NA",I23/B23)	=
24	=D24/E24	=D24-F24	0	=G24+H24	=IF(B24=0,"NA",I24/B24)	=
25	=D25/E25	=D25-F25	168516.91	=G25+H25	=IF(B25=0,"NA",I25/B25)	=
26	=D26/E26	=D26-F26	914628.68	=G26+H26	=IF(B26=0,"NA",I26/B26)	=
27	=D27/E27	=D27-F27	2750063.59	=G27+H27	=IF(B27=0,"NA",I27/B27)	=
28	=D28/E28	=D28-F28	3828284.98	=G28+H28	=IF(B28=0,"NA",I28/B28)	=
29	=D29/E29	=D29-F29	3584543.01	=G29+H29	=IF(B29=0,"NA",I29/B29)	=
30	=D30/E30	=D30-F30	2662323.89	=G30+H30	=IF(B30=0,"NA",I30/B30)	=
31	=D31/E31	=D31-F31	768516.91	=G31+H31	=IF(B31=0,"NA",I31/B31)	=
32	=D32/E32	=D32-F32	1319064.76	=G32+H32	=IF(B32=0,"NA",I32/B32)	=
33	=D33/E33	=D33-F33	396610.39	=G33+H33	=IF(B33=0,"NA",I33/B33)	=
34	=D34/E34	=D34-F34	682974.96	=G34+H34	=IF(B34=0,"NA",I34/B34)	=
35	=D35/E35	=D35-F35	691125.76	=G35+H35	=IF(B35=0,"NA",I35/B35)	=
36	=SUM(F22:F35)	=SUM(G22:G35)	=SUM(H22:H35)	=SUM(I22:I35)	=IF(B36=0,"NA",I36/B36)	
37	=SUMIF(M22:M35,"x",F22)	=SUMIF(M22:M35,"x",G22:G35)	=SUMIF(M22:M35,"x",H22:H35)	=SUMIF(M22:M35,"x",I22:I35)	=IF(B37=0,"NA",I37/B37)	
38						
39						
40						
41						
42						

Figure 18-2:
Viewing
formulas the
easy way.

This option sure makes it easy to see what all the formulas are!

Functions can still be accidentally edited even when the View Formulas option is selected. So be careful clicking around the worksheet.

Fixing Formulas

Suppose your worksheet has some errors — don't panic! It happens to even the savviest users, and Excel can help figure out what's going wrong. Under the Tools menu is a nifty item called Error Checking. Clicking the menu item displays the Error Checking dialog box shown in Figure 18-3. That is, the dialog box appears if there are any errors on your worksheet. Otherwise it just pops up a message that the error check is complete. It's that smart!

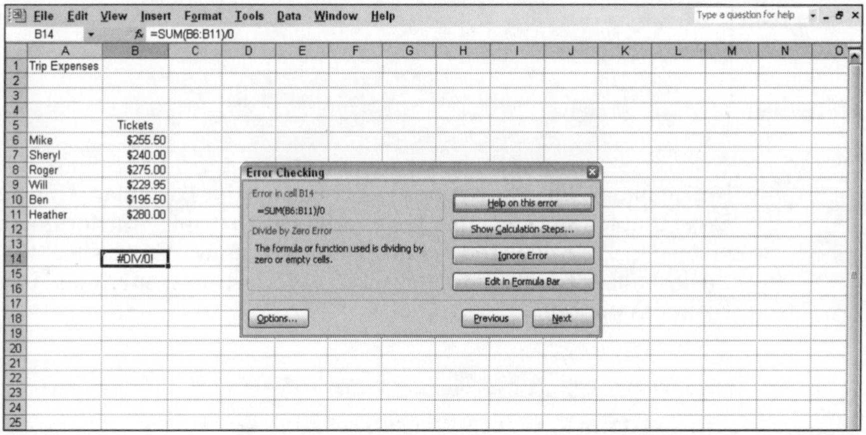

Figure 18-3: Checking for errors.

When there *are* errors, the dialog box appears and sticks around while you work on each error. The Next and Previous buttons let you cycle through all the errors before the dialog box closes. For each error it finds, you choose what action to take:

- **Help On This Error:** This leads to the Help system and displays the help topic for the particular type of error.

- **Show Calculation Steps:** Opens the Evaluate Formula dialog box where you can watch step-by-step how the formula is calculated. This lets you identify the particular step that caused the error.

- **Ignore Error:** Maybe Excel is wrong? So ignore the error.

- **Edit in Formula Bar:** A quick way to just fix the formula yourself if you don't need any other help.

The Error Checking dialog box also has an Options button. Clicking the button opens the Error Checking tab from the Options dialog box. In the Error Checking tab, you can select settings and rules for how errors are recognized and triggered.

Use Absolute References

If you are going to use the same formula for a bunch of cells, such as those going down a column, the best method is to write the formula once, and then drag it down to the other cells by using the fill handle. The problem is that when you drag the formula to new locations, any relative references change.

Often this *is* the intention. When there is one column of data and an adjacent column of formulas, typically each cell in the formula column refers to its neighbor in the data column. But if the formulas all reference a cell that is not adjacent, usually the intention is for all the formula cells to reference an unchanging cell reference.

The way to get this to work correctly is to use an absolute reference to the cell. To do this, use the dollar sign ($) before the row or column number (or before both). Do this when you write the first formula, before dragging it to other cells, or else you will have to update all the formulas. So for example, instead of this:

```
=A4 × (B4 + A2)
```

Write it this way:

```
=A4 × (B4 + $A$2)
```

This way all the formulas will reference A2 no matter where you copy them to, instead of that reference turning into A3, and A4, and so on.

Here's another timesaver — when you are entering or editing a formula, you can cycle a cell reference between relative, row absolute, column absolute, and fully absolute by placing the editing cursor on the reference and pressing F4.

Turn Calc On/Turn Calc Off

The Excel default is to calculate your formulas automatically as they are entered or when any change is made in the worksheet. In some situations you may want to set the calculation to manual. Leaving the setting on automatic is usually not an issue, but if you are working on a hefty workbook with lots of calculations, you may need to rethink this one.

Imagine this: You have a cell that innocently does nothing but display the date. But then there are dozens of calculations throughout the workbook that reference that cell. Then there are dozens more calculations that reference the first batch of cells that reference the cell with the data. Get the picture? In a complex workbook there could be a lot of calculating going on. And the time this takes can be noticeable.

Turning the calculation setting to manual lets you decide when to calculate. The place to do this is in the Options dialog box (choose Tools ⇨ Options). In the dialog box is a Calculation tab, shown in Figure 18-4. You can check for one of the automatic calculations settings or for manual calculation.

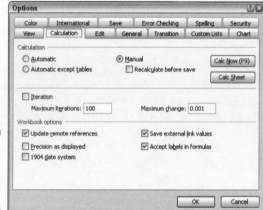

Figure 18-4:
Setting the
calculation
method.

Pressing F9 calculates the workbook. Use it when the calculation is set to manual. Here are some further options.

What you press	*What you get*
F9	Calculates formulas that have changed since the last calculation, in all open workbooks.
Shift + F9	Calculates formulas that have changed since the last calculation, just in the active worksheet.
CTRL + ALT + F9	Calculates all formulas in all open workbooks, regardless of when they were last calculated.

The calculation setting has no effect on whether a function can be entered. Even with calculation set to Manual, you can still enter functions and get an initial returned value. The only catch is that the value won't update without pressing F9.

Use Named Areas

Heck, maybe it's us, but we think it is easier to remember a word such as Customers or Inventory or December than it is to remember B14:E26 or AF220:AR680. So what we do is create names for the ranges we know we will be referencing in our formulas and functions.

Naming areas is easy to do, and in fact, you have two ways to do this. The first is to use the Define Name dialog box. You can get to this dialog box by choosing the Insert ⇨ Name ⇨ Define menu. In the dialog box, you set a range, give it a name, and press the Add button. See this in Figure 18-5.

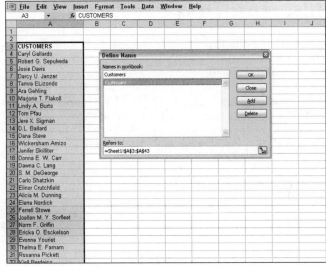

Figure 18-5: Defining a named area

This dialog box lets you add, update, and delete named areas. A real quick way to just add them (but not update or delete), is to:

1. **Select an area on the worksheet.**

2. **Click in the Name Box and enter the name.** The Name Box is part of the Formula Bar and sits to the left of where formulas are entered.

3. **Press Enter.**

Done! Now you can use the name as you please. Figure 18-6 shows a name being entered by using the Name Box. Of course you can use a particular name only once in a workbook.

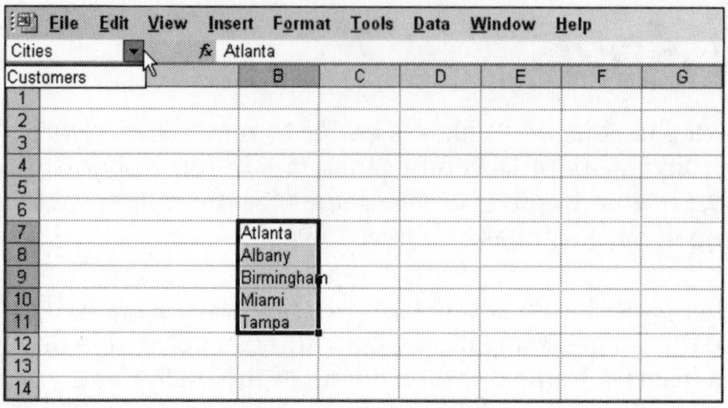

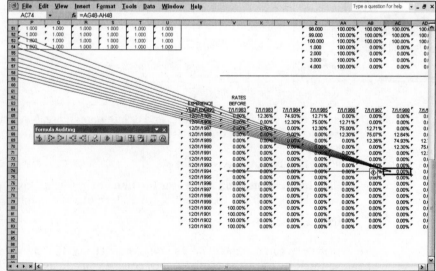

Figure 18-6:
Defining
a named
area the
easy way.

Use Formula Auditing

There are precedents and dependents. There are external references. There is interaction everywhere. How can you track where the formula references are coming from and going to?

Use the Formula Auditing toolbar, that's how! First, make it visible by choosing the View ➪ Toolbars menu. Then use it to find the references that go into a formula, and where cells are referenced. Figure 18-7 shows the toolbar and the tracing arrows that match formulas with references.

Figure 18-7:
Auditing
your
formulas.

The auditing toolbar has a number of features for wading through your formulas. Besides showing tracing arrows it also can also check errors, evaluate formulas, check for invalid data, and add comments to worksheets.

Use Conditional Formatting

Just like the IF function returns a certain value when the first argument condition is true and another value when it's false, Conditional Formatting lets you apply a certain format when a condition is true. This feature is implemented in the Conditional Formatting dialog box under the Format ⇨ Conditional Formatting menu.

The dialog box, shown in Figure 18-8, lets you set the condition and select the format for when the condition is met.

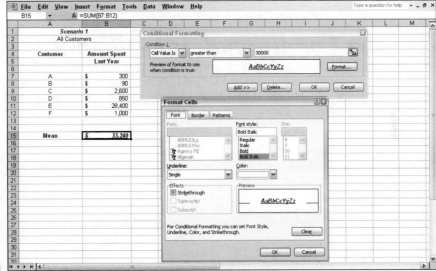

Figure 18-8:
Applying a
format
when a
condition
is met.

Conditions can be one of the following:

- ✔ A value is between two numbers.
- ✔ A value is not between two numbers.
- ✔ A value is equal to a number.

- A value is not equal to a number.
- A value is greater than a number.
- A value is less than a number.
- A value is greater than or equal to a number.
- A value is less than or equal to a number.

When the condition is true, formatting can control:

- **Font settings:** Style, color, bold, italic, and so on
- **Borders**
- **Patterns:** A cell's background color

Conditional formatting is useful to call attention to certain values in a worksheet. In accounting worksheets, for example, negative values are often displayed in red.

Use the Conditional Sum Wizard

The Conditional Sum Wizard is available as an add-in and needs to be loaded before you can use it. You do this by checking it in the Add-Ins dialog box, shown in Figure 18-9. You find the dialog box by choosing Tools ➪ Add-ins.

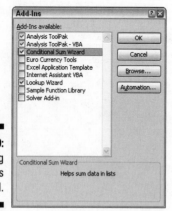

Figure 18-9:
Selecting
add-ins
to load.

After the add-in is loaded, the Tools menu has a new submenu — Conditional Sum. Selecting this starts up the Conditional Sum Wizard. This wizard walks you through setting the parameters to sum up values in a list that meet a condition. Figure 18-10 shows how the wizard starts.

Figure 18-10: Running the Conditional Sum Wizard.

The wizard steps through picking which column has the values to sum and which column has the values to test for the condition. The end result is a sum of just the values that have met the condition.

The Conditional Sum Wizard creates an array formula that uses the SUM and IF functions. The Conditional Sum Wizard doesn't provide any functionality beyond what you could do yourself — it just simplifies the task. The result is a formula such as this:

```
=SUM(IF($A$6:$A$11="San Francisco",$C$6:$C$11,0))
```

Of course though the wizard makes the entry of such a formula easier, as a good wizard should.

Use the Lookup Wizard

The Lookup Wizard comes as an add-in. Load it by selecting it in the Add-Ins dialog box, shown earlier in Figure 18-9.

The Lookup Wizard finds the value at a selected row and column intersection in a range you specify. The range must consist of at least two rows or columns. Figure 18-11 shows the wizard stepping through finding a value.

Figure 18-11:
Using the
Lookup
Wizard.

Like the Conditional Sum Wizard, the Lookup Wizard does not do anything that you could not do yourself, but it does make it easier to find a value in a table. The result of the Lookup Wizard is a formula that combines the INDEX and MATCH functions, such as this:

```
=INDEX($A$5:$C$11, MATCH(C21,$A$5:$A$11,),
           MATCH(C17,$A$5:$C$5,))
```

Both the Conditional Sum Wizard and the Lookup Wizard give an option to return not just the value that is found, but also the parameters used to get the result. This means that instead of having a result that by itself is meaningless, you can also copy out the parameters and place them next to the result.

Create Your Own Functions

Despite all the functions provided by Excel, you may need one that does something else entirely. Excel lets you create your own custom functions by using VBA programming code and then have your functions show up in the Insert Function dialog box.

Okay, we know what you're thinking — me write VBA code, no way! It's true — this is not for everyone. But nonetheless, here is a short and sweet example. If you can conquer this, then you might want to find out more about programming VBA. Who knows, maybe one day you'll be churning out add-ins of your own!

VBA is written in the Visual Basic Editor. Getting to the editor is easy, and either of the following works:

✔ Choose the Tools ➪ Macro ➪ Visual Basic Editor menu command.

✔ Or just press ALT + F11.

Now that the editor is visible, choose Insert ⇨ Module in the editor. You now have an empty code module sitting in front of you. Now it's time to create your very own function! All you have to do is type in the programming code that you see in Figure 18-12.

Just three lines of code are there, and after you type in the first and press Enter, the last one appears automatically. This example function adds two numbers together. The three lines of code are:

```
Public Function Add(number1 As Double, number2 As Double)
  Add = number1 + number2
End Function
```

Make sure you enter the word Public to start the code or you won't see the function listed in the Insert Function dialog box.

You may have to find the Excel workbook on the Windows task bar because the Visual Basic Editor runs as a separate program. Back in Excel you can now find and use the function in the Insert Function dialog box, in the User Defined Category. Figure 18-13 shows this.

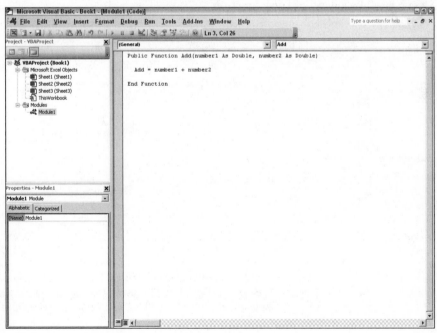

Figure 18-12:
Writing
your own
function.

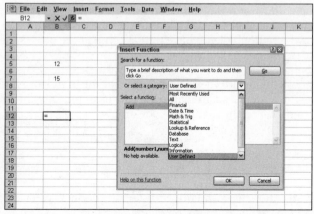

Figure 18-13:
Finding the
function in
the User
Defined
category.

Clicking OK leads to the dialog box for entering the arguments, shown in
Figure 18-14. Isn't this incredible? It's as if you are creating an extension to
Excel, and in essence you are.

You can also just enter =Add(into a cell and use the function that way — just
like any other Excel function.

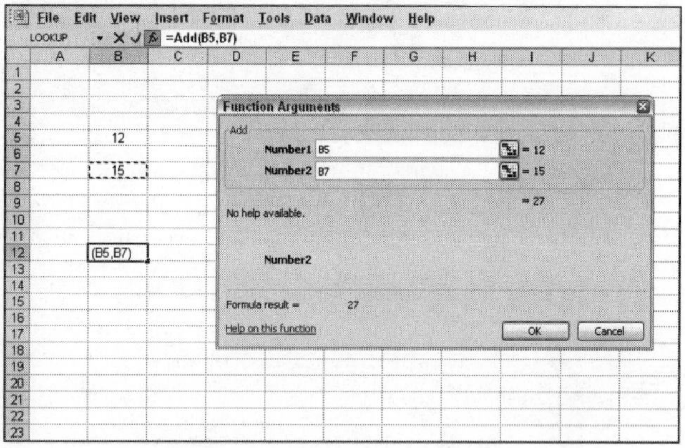

Figure 18-14:
Using the
custom Add
function.

This is a very basic example of what you can do by writing your own function. The possibilities are endless but of course you need to know how to
program VBA. We suggest reading *Excel VBA Programming For Dummies,* by
John Walkenbach (Wiley).

Chapter 19

Top Ten Functions You Must Know to Be an Excel Guru

This chapter lists the top ten Excel functions. Actually there are fifteen functions here, but in some cases two related functions are treated as a single item. To be fair, there is no absolute top ten list of functions, but over the years (don't ask how many!) we have worked on hundreds of worksheets and you start to see some of the same functions used all the time.

The functions in this list are of the type that apply to a wide array of needs. You won't see a financial function or any advanced statistical function. Just the basics. But knowing these is essential to good Excel work. You can always refer here for a quick brush-up on how to use these important functions.

SUM

Adding numbers is one of the most basic mathematical operations. And so there is the SUM function dedicated to doing just that. SUM takes up to 30 arguments. Each argument can be a number, or a range containing multiple numbers. That means SUM can add up a whole bunch of numbers! The syntax is:

```
=SUM(number 1, number 2, ...)
```

You can also use SUM with a range, as shown here:

```
=SUM(A1:A12)
```

or with more than one range, such as this:

```
=SUM(A1:A12, B1:B12)
```

AVERAGE

Although technically a statistical function, AVERAGE is so often used it deserves a place in the top ten functions. We are all interested in averages. What's the average score? What's the average salary? What's the average height? What's the average number of hours we watch TV (that's a sore spot in our households!).

AVERAGE can take up to 30 arguments. Each argument can be a number or a range that contains numbers. The syntax is:

```
=AVERAGE(number 1 ,number 2 ,...)
```

You can also use AVERAGE with a range, as shown here:

```
=AVERAGE(A1:A12)
```

or with more than one range, such as this:

```
=AVERAGE(A1:A12, B1:B12)
```

COUNT

COUNT counts the number of cells in a range that contain numbers. It does not provide any sum, just the count. So for a list with 10 numbers, COUNT returns 10, regardless of what the numbers actually are.

COUNT takes up to 30 arguments which can be cell references, range references, or numbers themselves. COUNT ignores non-numeric values. If an argument to COUNT is A1:A10, but only two cells contain a number then COUNT returns 2. The syntax is:

```
=COUNT(cell reference 1, cell reference 2,...)
```

You can also use COUNT with a range, as shown here:

```
=COUNT(A1:A12)
```

or with more than one range, such as this:

```
=COUNT(A1:A12, B1:B12)
```

INT and ROUND

The INT and ROUND functions both work by removing or reducing the decimal portion of a number. They differ in exactly *how* they remove it.

INT simply drops the decimal portion without rounding — that is, without regard to whether the number is closer to the next higher integer or the next lower integer. INT always truncates to the next lower integer. For example, INT changes 12.05 to 12, but it will also change 12.95 to 12. Also, INT changes both –5.1 and –5.9 to –6, not to –5, because –6 is the next lower integer. Be aware of this when using INT. INT takes but the single number argument. The syntax is:

```
=INT(number)
```

On the other hand, the ROUND function lets you control how the decimal portion is handled. ROUND takes two arguments — the number to be manipulated, and the number of decimal places to round to. This gives more control. A number, such as 5.6284 can become 5.628, 5.63, 5.6, or just 6. ROUND always rounds up or down to the nearest number of the next significant digit, so therefore 5.628 becomes 5.63, not 5.62.

In the case of 12.95, ROUND turns this into either 12.9 or 13, depending on the setting of the second argument. Note there are two functions — ROUNDUP and ROUNDDOWN — that round in one direction only. The syntax for ROUND is:

```
=ROUND(number, number of decimal places to round to)
```

The syntax for ROUNDUP and ROUNDDOWN is the same as ROUND:

```
=ROUNDUP(number, number of decimal places to round to)
=ROUNDDOWN(number, number of decimal places to round to)
```

IF

IF is a very handy function. It tests a condition and then returns one of two results depending on the outcome of the test. The test must return a true or false answer. For example, a test may be B25 > C30. If true, then IF returns its second argument. If false, IF returns its third argument.

IF is often used as a validation step to avoid unwanted errors. The most common use of this is to test if a denominator is 0 before doing a division operation. By testing for 0 first, you can avoid the #DIV/0! error.

One of the great things about IF is that the result can be a blank. This function is great for when you only want to return a result if the test comes out one way but not if the test comes out the other way. The syntax is:

```
=IF(logical test, value if true, value if false)
```

NOW and TODAY

The NOW function returns the current date and time according to your computer's internal clock. TODAY returns just the date. If the date or time is wrong, can't help you with that.

A common use of NOW is to return the date and time for a printed report. You know, so a message such as "Printed on 10/24/2004 10:15" can be put on the printed paper.

A common use for TODAY is to calculate the elapsed time between a past date and "today." For example you might be tracking how long a project is taking. A cell on the worksheet has the start date in it. Then in another cell is a formula that subtracts that date from TODAY. The answer is the number of days that have gone by.

NOW and TODAY take no arguments. The syntax is:

```
=NOW()
=TODAY()
```

Note: You may have to change the formatting of cells containing these functions to have the results appear correctly.

HLOOKUP and VLOOKUP

HLOOKUP and VLOOKUP are both used to find a value in a table. A table is an area of rows and columns that you define. Both of these functions work by using a search value for the first argument, that when found in the table, helps return a different value.

In particular you use HLOOKUP to return a value in a row that is in the same column as the search value. You use VLOOKUP to return a value in a column that is in the same row as the search value. The syntax for these functions are:

```
=HLOOKUP(lookup value, table area, row , match type)
=VLOOKUP(lookup value, table area, column, match type)
```

ISNUMBER

A rose is a rose and by any other name would smell as sweet, but numbers don't get off that easy. For example, 15 is a number, but fifteen is a word. The ISNUMBER function tells you flat out true or false if a value in a cell is a number (including the results of formulas). The syntax is:

```
=ISNUMBER(value)
```

MIN and MAX

MIN and MAX find the respective lowest or highest numeric value in a range of values. These functions take up to 30 arguments, and an argument can be a range. Therefore you can test a large list of numbers simply by entering the list as a range. The syntax for these functions are:

```
=MAX(number1,number2,...)
=MIN(number1,number2,...)
```

You can also use MIN and MAX with a range, as shown here:

```
=MAX(A1:A12)
```

or with more than one range, such as this:

```
=MAX(A1:A12, B1:B12)
```

SUMIF and COUNTIF

SUMIF and COUNTIF respectively sum values or count values if a supplied criterion is met. This makes for some robust calculations. With these functions it's easy to return answers for questions such as "How many shipments went out in October?" or "How many times did the DJIA go over 10,000 last year?"

SUMIF takes three arguments: a range in which to apply the criteria; the actual criteria; and the range from which to sum values. A key point here is that the first argument may or may not be the same range from which values are summed. Therefore you can use SUMIF for questions such as "How many shipments went out in October?" but also for one such as "What is the sum of the numbers in this list, of just the values in the list that are over 100?" The syntax for SUMIF is:

```
=SUMIF(range,criteria,sum_range)
```

Note too that the third argument in SUMIF can be left out. When this happens SUMIF uses the first argument as the range in which to apply the criteria, and also the range is from which to sum.

COUNTIF is used to count the number of items in a range that match criteria. This is just a count. The value of the items that match the criteria doesn't matter past the fact that it matches the criteria. But after a cell's value matches the criteria, the count of that cell is 1. COUNTIF takes just two arguments: the range from which to count the number of values, and the criteria to apply. The syntax for COUNTIF is:

```
COUNTIF(range,criteria)
```

Chapter 20

Ten Cool Things to Do with the Analysis ToolPak Add-In

*J*ust when you thought you had all of the Excel functions down pat, here we go rocking the boat. But in a good way. Excel ships with something called the Analysis ToolPak. This add-in provides several additional functions and dialog boxes that do cool things.

First start by getting that good old Analysis Toolpak loaded. Follow these steps:

1. **Choose the Tools ➪ Add-ins menu.**

2. **Check the check box for the Analysis Toolpak.**

   You can select all the add-ins you want, but for now this is all you need. The Analysis Toolpak–VBA provides a different set of functions than those from the standard Analysis Toolpak. In this chapter, we discuss the standard Analysis Toolpak.

3. **Click the OK button.**

If for any reason you do not see this add-in in the list, you need to speak to your network administrator, or call Microsoft, or call your uncle who is in the computer business.

Figure 20-1 shows the Add-ins dialog box where you select to use the Analysis ToolPak.

Figure 20-1:
Loading the
Analysis
ToolPak
add-in.

Work with Hexadecimal, Octal, Decimal, and Binary Numbers

Base 2, base 8, base 10 — remember these from school? Here's a refresher. In our daily lives, we work with numbers based on a system of 10 digits: 0, 1, 2, 3, 4, 5, 6, 7, 8, and 9. If you think about it, all numbers we put together consist of these digits. This is base 10, also called the decimal notation system, and it is based on powers of the number 10.

In certain lines of work, it is desirable or even necessary to work in another base system. Designing computer systems is a good example. The computer chips that run our PCs work with a binary system. Circuits are either on or off. This then means there are just two possible states — and they are often expressed as 0 and 1.

In base 2, or binary, all numbers are expressed with the digits 0 or 1. The number 20 as we know it in decimal, is 10100 in binary. The number 99 is 1100011. The binary system is based on powers of 2.

In other words, in base 10 you count up through 10 digits in one position before moving one position to the left for the next significant digit. And then the first position cycles back to the beginning digit. To make it simple, you count 0 to 9, and then add a 1 to the next significant digit, and start the first position over at 0, and therefore 10 comes after 9.

Binary, octal, and hexadecimal each count up to a different digit before incrementing the next significant digit. Binary only has two values — 0 and 1. That's why when any larger base number, such as a base 10 number is converted to binary, there are more actual digit places. Look above at what happens to the number 20. In base 10, 20 is represented in 2 digits. In binary, 20 is represented 5 digits.

Octal, based on powers of 8, counts up to 8 digits — 0 through 7. The digits 8 and 9 are never used in octal. Hexadecimal, based on powers of 16, counts up to 16 digits, but how? What is left after 9? The letters of the alphabet, that's what!

Hexadecimal uses these digits: 0, 1, 2, 3, 4, 5, 6, 7, 8, 9, A, B, C, D, E, and F. The letters A through F represent the decimal values 10 through 15 respectively. If anyone has ever worked on the colors for a Web site, you might know that FFFFFF is all white. The Web server recognizes colors represented in hexadecimal notation and responds appropriately.

Hexadecimal notation is used a lot with computers because the basic language of computers, which is binary, translates easily to hex (and vice versa). Each hex digit 0-F represents a 4-digit binary number, 0000 through 1111.

The number 200 in decimal notation becomes C8 in hexadecimal notation. The number 99 in decimal notation becomes 63 in hexadecimal notation.

Enough theory! The point to all this is that the Analysis ToolPak provides a group of functions to do all these conversions. These functions take into account all combinations of conversion between binary, octal, decimal, and hexadecimal. These functions are:

Function	*What it does*
BIN2DEC	Converts binary to decimal
BIN2HEX	Converts binary to hexadecimal
BIN2OCT	Converts binary to octal
DEC2BIN	Converts decimal to binary
DEC2HEX	Converts decimal to hexadecimal

DEC2OCT	Converts decimal to octal
HEX2BIN	Converts hexadecimal to binary
HEX2DEC	Converts hexadecimal to decimal
HEX2OCT	Converts hexadecimal to octal
OCT2BIN	Converts octal to binary
OCT2DEC	Converts octal to decimal
OCT2HEX	Converts octal to hexadecimal

You can find these functions in the Insert Function dialog box under the special Engineering category that appears when you load the Analysis ToolPak.

Convert Units of Measurement

CONVERT is a really great function that the Analysis ToolPak makes available. Not surprisingly it converts things, or more specifically it converts measurements. The number of measurements it converts is truly impressive. The function converts feet to inches, meters to feet, Fahrenheit to Celsius, pints to liters, horsepower to watts, and much more. In fact, there are 10 categories that contain dozens of units of measure to convert from and to. The categories are:

1. Weight and mass

2. Distance

3. Time

4. Pressure

5. Force

6. Energy

7. Power

8. Magnetism

9. Temperature

10. Liquid measure

The function takes three arguments: the value, the "from" unit of measure, and the "to" unit of measure. As an example, here is the function syntax for converting 10 gallons to liters: =CONVERT(10,"gal", "l"). By the way the answer is 37.86.

See the Help topic for CONVERT to read all it can do. I'm sure you will find a use for it. In the meantime, Figure 20-2 shows a few conversions.

TIP

Can you use CONVERT to convert currency values, such as dollars to yen or pounds to marks? No — and the reason is because the conversion rate changes from day to day in response to economic factors.

	File Edit View Insert Format Tools Data Window Help		
	B6 ▼ *fx* =CONVERT(100,"mi","km")		
	A	B	C	D
1				
2	Question	Answer		Formula Used
3				
4				
5				
6	100 miles equals how many kilometers?	160.9344		=CONVERT(100,"mi","km")
7				
8				
9	How many teaspoons are in an ounce?	6		=CONVERT(1,"oz","tsp")
10				
11				
12	How many calories are in a BTU?	251.9966171		=CONVERT(1, "BTU", "cal")
13				
14				
15	1,000,000 seconds is how many days?	11.57407407		=CONVERT(1000000,"sec","day")
16				
17				
18	1 Pascal equals how many Atmospheres?	9.86923E-06		=CONVERT(1,"Pa","atm")
19				
20				

Figure 20-2:
Converting
was never
so easy!

Find the Greatest Common Divisor and the Least Common Multiple

A greatest common divisor is the largest integer that divides each number in a set of numbers and has no remainder after each division operation. Take the numbers 5, 10 , and 100. The greatest common divisor is 5, because each of the numbers divided by 5 returns another integer (no decimal portion).

The GCD function takes up to 29 values as its arguments. Non-integer values are truncated. By its nature any returned greatest common divisor must equal or be smaller than the lowest argument value. Often there in no greatest common divisor other than 1 — which all integers share. The syntax for the GCD function is:

```
GCD(number1,number2, ...)
```

The least common multiple is an integer that is the lowest multiple common among a group of integers. For example, the least common multiple of 2, 4, and 6 is 12. The least common multiple of 9, 15, and 48 is 720.

The LCM function takes up 29 values as its arguments. Non-integer values are truncated. The syntax for the LCM multiple function is:

```
LCM(number1,number2, ...)
```

Easy Random Number Generation

The Excel RAND function returns a real number between 0 and 1. And that's it. Usually you have to massage the returned number into something useful. The typical thing to do is multiply it by some number to get it within a range of values, then add the lower limit to that, and then finally to use INT to turn the whole thing into an integer.

The days of drudgery are over. The Analysis ToolPak has a cool random number generation function that gives you the control you need.

The RANDBETWEEN function returns a random *integer* between two values. Two arguments are used — the low end of the range and the high end of the range. Just what we need! For example, =RANDBETWEEN(5, 10) returns a whole number between 5 and 10. Always.

Use Sophisticated Finance Functions

A collection of additional financial functions cover a variety of finance needs. Over 30 functions are provided that help with calculations in these broad areas:

- ✔ Accrued interest, cumulative interest, nominal interest
- ✔ Depreciation
- ✔ Coupons (the securities kind, not the ones for the supermarket!)
- ✔ Converting dollar amounts into decimals and fractions
- ✔ Price and yield for securities with an odd first period or odd last period
- ✔ Price and yield for Treasury bills
- ✔ Price and yield for other securities

If you work in the field of high finance, you will surely find some of these useful.

Generate Descriptive Statistics

You have a set of data. You need to calculate the mean, the standard deviation, and other statistical measures. Well, you can enter all the necessary functions yourself and get the answers. To be honest this may very well be preferable regardless of what we are about to show you. Perhaps you need the mean in a certain cell, the standard deviation in another dedicated place, and so on.

But if you are not that particular, then the Analysis ToolPak has just the thing for you. After the ToolPak is loaded, you find a new sub-menu item, Data Analysis, under the Tools menu.

Using the Tools ⇨ Data Analysis menu displays the Data Analysis dialog box, shown here in Figure 20-3.

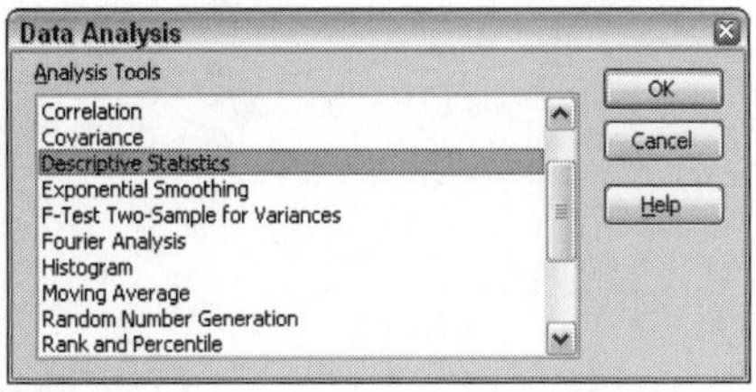

Figure 20-3:
Displaying
the Data
Analysis
dialog box.

One of the choices in the dialog box is Descriptive Statistics. Selecting that brings up the Descriptive Statistics dialog box, shown in Figure 20-4.

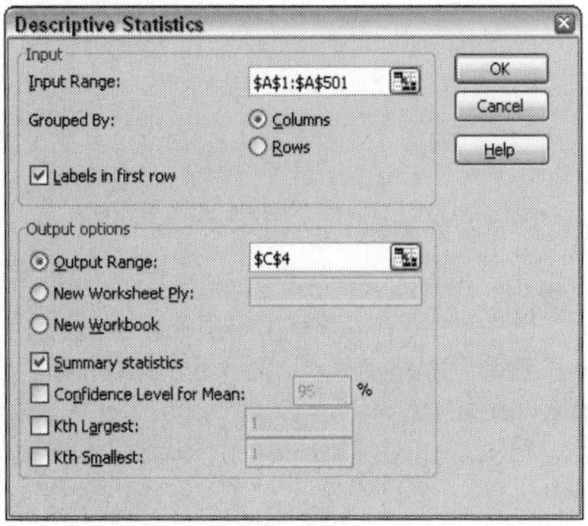

Figure 20-4:
Making
selections
about which
statistics to
return.

In this dialog box, you enter the range of the source data, the location where to display the results, and which results to display. The statistical calculations are done for you. You select how much to display. There is a basic set of statistics, but also a few extras, such as the confidence level, can be generated as well. Figure 20-5 shows the results of selecting the basic summary statistics. You could create this result with individual Excel functions but the Analysis ToolPak makes it a lot easier.

	File	Edit	View	Insert	Format	Tools	Data	Window	Help
F28				f_x					

	A	B	C	D	E
1	Observations				
2	42.83232381				
3	35.77512753				
4	46.76353776		*Observations*		
5	54.21613896				
6	53.65208858		Mean	45.31976429	
7	57.51322101		Standard Error	0.327993927	
8	29.23449724		Median	45.5564578	
9	43.30921142		Mode	41.21819973	
10	52.90606264		Standard Deviation	7.334167179	
11	37.15402131		Sample Variance	53.79000821	
12	40.01672596		Kurtosis	-0.325993642	
13	32.7950786		Skewness	-0.054568805	
14	31.66530337		Range	40.46676913	
15	37.94151503		Minimum	25.00458727	
16	39.41527907		Maximum	65.4713564	
17	29.70853661		Sum	22659.88215	
18	40.89958243		Count	500	
19	42.08277655				
20	45.97363904				
21	42.36114089				
22	42.63912765				
23	42.32686349				
24	54.69387202				
25	44.38424623				

Figure 20-5: A returned set of descriptive statistics.

Even though the Descriptive Statistics feature returns a wealth of statistical data, the results are returned as values, not formulas. Any changes to the source data are not reflected in the results. You need to regenerate the statistics.

Create a Histogram

A histogram is a set of counts within ranges — in other words, how many of your values fall into each range. The ranges are called *bins*. Making a histogram is easy with the Histogram dialog box, shown in Figure 20-6. You display this dialog box by selecting it in the Data Analysis dialog box shown earlier in Figure 20-3.

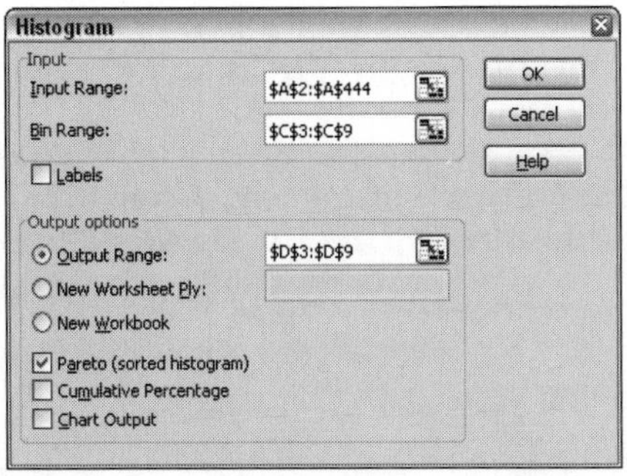

Figure 20-6: Defining a histogram.

A histogram requires the range of the source data, the range of the bin designations, and where to place the output. The returned bins and counts make it easy to show the distribution of data. Figure 20-7 shows the histogram created with the parameters seen in Figure 20-6.

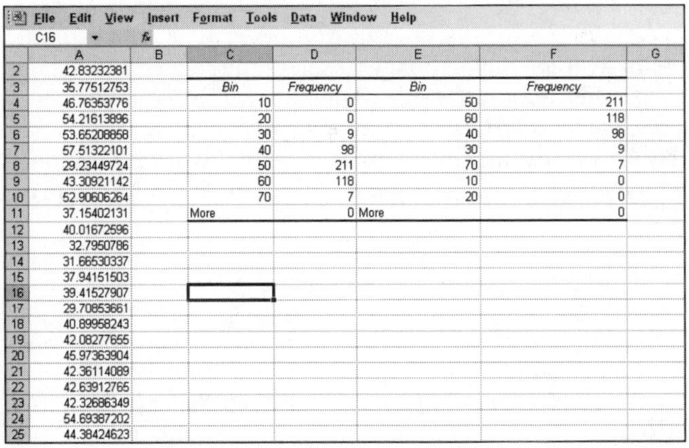

	A	B	C	D	E	F	G
2	42.83232381						
3	35.77512753		Bin	Frequency	Bin	Frequency	
4	46.76353776		10	0	50	211	
5	54.21613896		20	0	60	118	
6	53.65208858		30	9	40	98	
7	57.51322101		40	98	30	9	
8	29.23449724		50	211	70	7	
9	43.30921142		60	118	10	0	
10	52.90606264		70	7	20	0	
11	37.15402131		More	0	More	0	
12	40.01672596						
13	32.7950786						
14	31.66530337						
15	37.94151503						
16	39.41527907						
17	29.70853661						
18	40.89958243						
19	42.08277655						
20	45.97363904						
21	42.36114089						
22	42.63912765						
23	42.32686349						
24	54.69387202						
25	44.38424623						

Figure 20-7: A histogram shows the distribution of data.

Histograms often serve as the source for a chart. One of the options in the Histogram dialog box is to have a chart generated along with the data.

Generate Moving Averages

Moving averages help identify trends in sequential data. The data is period based, such as on a daily basis, and an average is calculated for a number of periods. Then the average is rolled through the data. So the first average may be for days 1 through 7, then the next average is for days 2 through 8, and so on.

One of the selections in the Data Analysis dialog box, shown in Figure 20-3, is Moving Average. Choosing this brings up the Moving Average dialog box, shown in Figure 20-8.

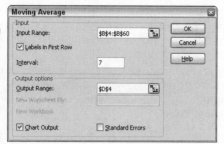

Figure 20-8:
Selecting
parameters
to create a
moving
average.

In the Moving Average dialog box, you select the range of the source data, the interval step, and the output range. The interval step is a key component. In this example, we selected 7 as the interval. Because the data is daily, this creates a 7 day, or weekly, moving average. One of the output options is to create a chart, which is selected in this example. Figure 20-9 shows the output.

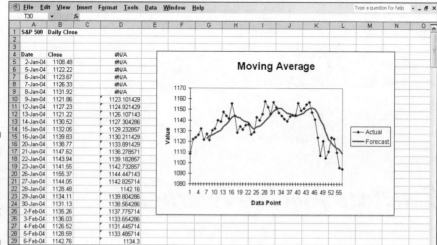

Figure 20-9:
Moving
average
values and
a chart
to boot!

Cell D4 had been selected for where the output should start. Notice that the first six cells starting from D4 do not return a useful value. This makes sense because it takes at least seven values to make an average. Therefore the first usable average is in cell D10, with this formula: =AVERAGE(B5:B11). Cell D11 has this formula: =AVERAGE(B6:B12). Cell D12 has this formula: =AVERAGE(B7:B13).

Moving averages are used to diminish the effects of spikes in data and to identify trends. Viewing a plot of raw value points can seem random and chaotic. Viewing a moving average of the data set removes some of the volatility and hopefully shows a line with a sense of direction. The chart in Figure 20-9 shows two series lines — the source data (labeled as Actual) and the moving average (labeled as Forecast). The moving average smoothes out the spikes and provides a cleaner view of movement.

Advanced Random Number Generation

One of the selections in the Data Analysis dialog box, shown in Figure 20-3, is Random Number Generation. Choosing this brings up the Random Number Generation dialog box, shown in Figure 20-10.

Excel has the plain RAND function, the Analysis ToolPak has the RANDBE-TWEEN function, and here is yet another way to make random numbers. There must be something special about them!

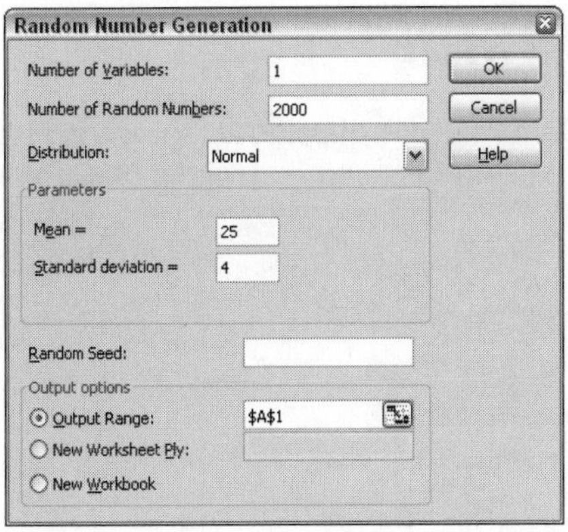

Figure 20-10:
Mucho
control over
random
numbers.

The Random Number Generation dialog box is quite advanced compared to the two random number functions. Whereas the functions just generate numbers within a range, here you have much more control:

- ✔ **Number of Variables:** The number of columns of data to return.
- ✔ **Number of Random Numbers:** How many values to return, per column.
- ✔ **Random Seed:** An optional value from which to generate numbers. Using this number in another session returns the same random values.

In the middle of the dialog box is a drop-down list from which you select the distribution type, and below it are the parameters. The type of parameters change which each type of distribution:

Distribution Type	Parameters
Uniform	low value and high value
Normal	mean and standard deviation
Bernoulli	p value
Binomial	p value and number of trials
Poisson	lambda
Patterned	low value, high value, step, number of repeats
Discrete	value and probability

Create a Random Sample

One of the selections in the Data Analysis dialog box, shown in Figure 20-3, is Sampling. Choosing this brings up the Sampling dialog box, shown in Figure 20-11.

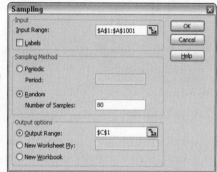

Figure 20-11: Pulling a sample from a population.

Statistical analysis is often done on a sample of data from a population, instead of the population itself. For example, you may have 20,000 observations of a periodic temperature reading and decide to use a portion of the data to run analysis.

The Sampling dialog box takes an input of where the source population data is, and where the sample data should be placed. You also select a setting for how the sample data is pulled out of the population. When the sampling method is periodic, you supply the step pattern. When the sampling method is random, you supply the number of values to return. The Sampling dialog box is a real timesaver. You can generate a sample instantly instead of hunting and pecking through the population data.

Index

• E •

• *U* •

Notes

Notes

Notes

BUSINESS, CAREERS & PERSONAL FINANCE

0-7645-5307-0

0-7645-5331-3 *†

Also available:
- Accounting For Dummies †
  0-7645-5314-3
- Business Plans Kit For Dummies †
  0-7645-5365-8
- Cover Letters For Dummies
  0-7645-5224-4
- Frugal Living For Dummies
  0-7645-5403-4
- Leadership For Dummies
  0-7645-5176-0
- Managing For Dummies
  0-7645-1771-6

- Marketing For Dummies
  0-7645-5600-2
- Personal Finance For Dummies *
  0-7645-2590-5
- Project Management For Dummies
  0-7645-5283-X
- Resumes For Dummies †
  0-7645-5471-9
- Selling For Dummies
  0-7645-5363-1
- Small Business Kit For Dummies *†
  0-7645-5093-4

HOME & BUSINESS COMPUTER BASICS

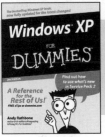

0-7645-4074-2

0-7645-3758-X

Also available:
- ACT! 6 For Dummies
  0-7645-2645-6
- iLife '04 All-in-One Desk Reference
  For Dummies
  0-7645-7347-0
- iPAQ For Dummies
  0-7645-6769-1
- Mac OS X Panther Timesaving
  Techniques For Dummies
  0-7645-5812-9
- Macs For Dummies
  0-7645-5656-8

- Microsoft Money 2004 For Dummies
  0-7645-4195-1
- Office 2003 All-in-One Desk Reference
  For Dummies
  0-7645-3883-7
- Outlook 2003 For Dummies
  0-7645-3759-8
- PCs For Dummies
  0-7645-4074-2
- TiVo For Dummies
  0-7645-6923-6
- Upgrading and Fixing PCs For Dummies
  0-7645-1665-5
- Windows XP Timesaving Techniques
  For Dummies
  0-7645-3748-2

FOOD, HOME, GARDEN, HOBBIES, MUSIC & PETS

0-7645-5295-3

0-7645-5232-5

Also available:
- Bass Guitar For Dummies
  0-7645-2487-9
- Diabetes Cookbook For Dummies
  0-7645-5230-9
- Gardening For Dummies *
  0-7645-5130-2
- Guitar For Dummies
  0-7645-5106-X
- Holiday Decorating For Dummies
  0-7645-2570-0
- Home Improvement All-in-One
  For Dummies
  0-7645-5680-0

- Knitting For Dummies
  0-7645-5395-X
- Piano For Dummies
  0-7645-5105-1
- Puppies For Dummies
  0-7645-5255-4
- Scrapbooking For Dummies
  0-7645-7208-3
- Senior Dogs For Dummies
  0-7645-5818-8
- Singing For Dummies
  0-7645-2475-5
- 30-Minute Meals For Dummies
  0-7645-2589-1

INTERNET & DIGITAL MEDIA

0-7645-1664-7

0-7645-6924-4

Also available:
- 2005 Online Shopping Directory
  For Dummies
  0-7645-7495-7
- CD & DVD Recording For Dummies
  0-7645-5956-7
- eBay For Dummies
  0-7645-5654-1
- Fighting Spam For Dummies
  0-7645-5965-6
- Genealogy Online For Dummies
  0-7645-5964-8
- Google For Dummies
  0-7645-4420-9

- Home Recording For Musicians
  For Dummies
  0-7645-1634-5
- The Internet For Dummies
  0-7645-4173-0
- iPod & iTunes For Dummies
  0-7645-7772-7
- Preventing Identity Theft For Dummies
  0-7645-7336-5
- Pro Tools All-in-One Desk Reference
  For Dummies
  0-7645-5714-9
- Roxio Easy Media Creator For Dummies
  0-7645-7131-1

* Separate Canadian edition also available

† Separate U.K. edition also available

Available wherever books are sold. For more information or to order direct: U.S. customers visit www.dummies.com or call 1-877-762-2974.
U.K. customers visit www.wileyeurope.com or call 0800 243407. Canadian customers visit www.wiley.ca or call 1-800-567-4797.

SPORTS, FITNESS, PARENTING, RELIGION & SPIRITUALITY

0-7645-5146-9

0-7645-5418-2

Also available:

- Adoption For Dummies
  0-7645-5488-3
- Basketball For Dummies
  0-7645-5248-1
- The Bible For Dummies
  0-7645-5296-1
- Buddhism For Dummies
  0-7645-5359-3
- Catholicism For Dummies
  0-7645-5391-7
- Hockey For Dummies
  0-7645-5228-7

- Judaism For Dummies
  0-7645-5299-6
- Martial Arts For Dummies
  0-7645-5358-5
- Pilates For Dummies
  0-7645-5397-6
- Religion For Dummies
  0-7645-5264-3
- Teaching Kids to Read For Dummies
  0-7645-4043-2
- Weight Training For Dummies
  0-7645-5168-X
- Yoga For Dummies
  0-7645-5117-5

TRAVEL

0-7645-5438-7

0-7645-5453-0

Also available:

- Alaska For Dummies
  0-7645-1761-9
- Arizona For Dummies
  0-7645-6938-4
- Cancún and the Yucatán For Dummies
  0-7645-2437-2
- Cruise Vacations For Dummies
  0-7645-6941-4
- Europe For Dummies
  0-7645-5456-5
- Ireland For Dummies
  0-7645-5455-7

- Las Vegas For Dummies
  0-7645-5448-4
- London For Dummies
  0-7645-4277-X
- New York City For Dummies
  0-7645-6945-7
- Paris For Dummies
  0-7645-5494-8
- RV Vacations For Dummies
  0-7645-5443-3
- Walt Disney World & Orlando For Dummies
  0-7645-6943-0

GRAPHICS, DESIGN & WEB DEVELOPMENT

0-7645-4345-8

0-7645-5589-8

Also available:

- Adobe Acrobat 6 PDF For Dummies
  0-7645-3760-1
- Building a Web Site For Dummies
  0-7645-7144-3
- Dreamweaver MX 2004 For Dummies
  0-7645-4342-3
- FrontPage 2003 For Dummies
  0-7645-3882-9
- HTML 4 For Dummies
  0-7645-1995-6
- Illustrator CS For Dummies
  0-7645-4084-X

- Macromedia Flash MX 2004 For Dummies
  0-7645-4358-X
- Photoshop 7 All-in-One Desk
  Reference For Dummies
  0-7645-1667-1
- Photoshop CS Timesaving Techniques
  For Dummies
  0-7645-6782-9
- PHP 5 For Dummies
  0-7645-4166-8
- PowerPoint 2003 For Dummies
  0-7645-3908-6
- QuarkXPress 6 For Dummies
  0-7645-2593-X

NETWORKING, SECURITY, PROGRAMMING & DATABASES

0-7645-6852-3

0-7645-5784-X

Also available:

- A+ Certification For Dummies
  0-7645-4187-0
- Access 2003 All-in-One Desk
  Reference For Dummies
  0-7645-3988-4
- Beginning Programming For Dummies
  0-7645-4997-9
- C For Dummies
  0-7645-7068-4
- Firewalls For Dummies
  0-7645-4048-3
- Home Networking For Dummies
  0-7645-42796

- Network Security For Dummies
  0-7645-1679-5
- Networking For Dummies
  0-7645-1677-9
- TCP/IP For Dummies
  0-7645-1760-0
- VBA For Dummies
  0-7645-3989-2
- Wireless All In-One Desk Reference
  For Dummies
  0-7645-7496-5
- Wireless Home Networking For Dummies
  0-7645-3910-8